T0366985

The Charismatic
CHAMELEON

This book is dedicated to all the actors I have taught
and directed and to those many more who have
so graciously allowed me to pick their brains
in the course of researching this book.

The Charismatic
CHAMELEON

The Actor as Creative Artist

LESLIE O'DELL

sussex
ACADEMIC
PRESS
Brighton • Chicago • Toronto

2 4 6 8 10 9 7 5 3 1

First published in 2010 by
SUSSEX ACADEMIC PRESS
PO Box 139
Eastbourne BN24 9BP

Distributed in North America by
SUSSEX ACADEMIC PRESS
Independent Publishers Group
814 N. Franklin Street, Chicago, IL 60610

British Library Cataloguing in Publication Data
A CIP catalogue record for this book is available from the British Library.

Library of Congress Cataloging-in-Publication Data
O'Dell, Leslie.
The charismatic chameleon : the actor as creative artist / Leslie O'Dell.
p. cm.
Includes bibliographical references and index.
ISBN 978-1-84519-412-3 (p/b : alk. paper)
1. Acting—Psychological aspects. 2. Creation (Literary, artistic, etc.) I. Title.
PN2071.P78O34 2010
792.02′8019—dc22

2009054163

Typeset and designed by Sussex Academic Press, Brighton & Eastbourne.
Printed and bound by CPI Group (UK) Ltd, Croydon, CR0 4YY

Contents

CONTENTS

CONTENTS

Preface

In reflecting upon my training as an actor, and my subsequent experiences directing and contributing to the training of actors, I am struck by several inter-related realizations:

1   That not all approaches to acting work equally well with all actors.
2   That an actor's creative instrument is a delicate and vulnerable component of the actor's psyche.
3   That an actor must take responsibility for the upkeep and protection of that instrument, because no one else can or should.
4   That an understanding of the nature of that creative instrument is necessary to keep it functioning at peak efficiency, to make modifications when the instrument falters, and to protect it from temporary or permanent damage.

These realizations have prompted the research, experimentation, workshops, and workplace applications of the content of this book. But I have also written the book I wish had been available 35 years ago.

I wanted very much to be an actor, almost as soon as I discovered acting in high school. When I went to university, I bowed to pressure to pursue a more legitimate course of studies; I determined to blend my love of drama with the study of psychology, thinking perhaps of drama therapy as a career. But late night rehearsals didn't blend well with early morning statistics classes, and I dropped my combined major in favour of my theatrical obsessions.

Our acting teacher was a brilliant, charismatic teacher and director who introduced us to the fundamentals of Strasberg's Method. Exercises in sensory awareness and emotional memory recall dominated our explorations in class, while in the rehearsal hall he emphasized complexity in interpersonal relationships. Movement and voice warm ups were introduced in order to increase flexibility, enhance concentration, and ensure a relaxed, ready state for the explorations of intense emotions drawn from our real lives. In order to explore a character's terror, he would terrorize the actress. In order to explore a character's rage, he'd abuse the actor until he broke through the social restrictions against violence.

I could see that his approach resulted in thrilling performances in others, and that all of his strategies were linked to a theatrical goal. He was not a nasty person, but I often left his classes and rehearsals feeling abused.

I graduated from that program and started auditioning for professional work. I had one or two small jobs, but they only confirmed what I felt I'd learned in his classes: that I did not, as it turned out, have the makings of a real actor. Fortunately, I had also studied directing and play writing, and I'd taken a course in experimental theatre, so when I firmly, and with some relief, shut the door to an acting career, it was in order to leap through an open window into a fulfilling career as a writer, director, teacher, scholar, and participant in all manner of non-traditional theatre projects.

Some years later, I signed up for an acting workshop in order to broaden my strategies for teaching acting. I had heard about the approach, which was based on the theories and teachings of Rudolph Laban as formulated by Yat Malmgren at the Drama Centre in London, England. Much to my surprise, I discovered that all of my long-forgotten love of acting burst forth anew, and that I had real talent as a performer of physically-engendered characters. At some point, I don't know quite when, I realized that if I had been trained by teachers using this approach to acting way, I would never have lost faith in my capacity to become a professional actor.

I subsequently sought out every opportunity I could find to explore further this approach to the making of theatre. However, I was still blinded by the ascendancy of the Method system of acting that dominated the institutions in which I worked, and so I continued to lead my students through the very exercises that I had first encountered in my own training. The only modification I made was to begin with Stanislavsky's score of physical actions, and to place a greater emphasis on the active verbs that make up objectives than on the emotional memories actors might use to bring real emotions to their rehearsals and performances.

Of course I was not the only acting teacher struggling with doubts about Strasberg's Method in any of the various guises it might be encountered. Individual voices of discontent with the emotionally abusive nature of emotional memory work, reminders of the disconnect between the American method and Stanislavsky's body of work, experimentation with radically different approaches coming out of Poland, Central America, and England – all of these combined to empower me to develop a "tool box" approach to teaching acting. I figured that my job was to offer several different approaches to the challenges of acting, and encourage the students to give each an honest, intense effort, then evaluate the benefits and pitfalls of each approach, as they slowly but surely built their own individual systems.

I was not consciously aware that I had made that modification in my teaching until I read the books of H. Wesley Balk, whose approach to teaching acting to singers was radically transformed by his encounter of theories of interpersonal communication that suggest each of us has a distinctive dominance in how we receive communication. This led Balk to modify his approach because he could no longer assume that everyone in the class shared his receptive style. This in turn shoved my teaching one giant step further in the direction of honouring diversity and monitoring the potential dangers of superimposing my predispositions on my students.

I have since come to believe that there are two types of acting teachers: those, like me, whose own training was relatively unsuccessful and who therefore blend scepticism with pragmatic diversity in their development of toolbox training, and those who had a much more creative and rewarding experience under the guidance of a master-teacher, and who therefore quite naturally seek to share the benefits of the legacy with their own students. I have come to call these two approaches the toolbox approach and the legacy approach. I see huge benefits and potential problems with either teaching strategy.

My journey of exploration into the wide variety of approaches to teaching acting that co-exist in our time continues to this day. About 15 years ago, I returned to my undergraduate interest in psychology and began to cross-reference the various techniques, and the assumptions upon which they were based, against psychological theories of emotion, memory, selfhood, creativity, and personality. I also explored theories of temperament, which further confirmed what I had come to realize: that there might well be quite different types of creative temperaments that explain why each approach to acting works for some actors and not for others.

Throughout my professional life, I have been amazed at the courage of actors. My reading in psychology confirmed what I had long suspected: that what actors do in resisting our natural inclination towards self-protection is fundamentally dangerous. I became more and more concerned with the theatre's reckless disregard for these dangers, and decided to undertake a study of the phenomenon of acting, from a psychological point of view, in order to assess the connection between those dangers and the debilitating stage fright which I have seen destroy more than one brilliant acting career.

Quite suddenly, the various threads of my concerns, fascinations, and explorations came together with the day-to-day challenges of teaching acting, and the result is the approach documented in this book. I offer it, not to overturn other approaches, but to support and enhance the experiences of every actor during training.

My theory is quite simple: I have come to believe that each of us has a distinct Creative Personal Temperament, and that when we are aware of that temperament we can truly own our creative instrument. As a direct result of this ownership, we can protect it from damage, ensure it works at peak levels at all times, and subtly adjust our acting process in order to participate with maximum creativity and minimal resistance to any and every training, rehearsal, and performance situation.

The best thing about my approach? It is simple, flexible, organic, and focussed on what you bring to your acting effortlessly, what you already know how to do, and do well.

The catch? To make use of the theory, you need to complete a private self-diagnosis and come to some conclusions about the nature of your own creative temperament. When I oversee self-diagnosis in a workshop, I can coach individuals, and set a variety of activities until, one by one, everyone reaches an epiphany followed by confirmation that their conclusions have validity for understanding and effectively manipulating their process. Reading about it is simply not the same thing. However, it's all we have, and therefore, in starting this book, I need to clarify a few things.

First, to explore my approach requires the absorption of some jargon, for which I apologize. I have tried to make the terms self-evident and to explain them vividly. During the self-diagnosis stage, when all of the options are being considered, the terms might feel like a muddled mass of words. Once you have completed self-diagnosis, you will find that things become much clearer because you'll read the book with an eye for all that pertains directly to you.

I have included some exercises in the book, but there is no way to replicate a workshop experience for a private reader. I suggest, therefore, that you test out your intuitions about your creative temperament in whatever rehearsal or training situation you find yourself. You will also be able to draw upon your memories of past experiences for assessing your probable type.

The experience of self-diagnosis is confusing until the penny drops, and there's no way around that. As you read about and "try on" the various options, you might find that all of them "fit" and therefore that choosing from among them seems difficult or even inappropriate. You might quite easily narrow the selection but be unable to determine, quickly, which of two or three suitable options describes your temperament. In addition, some people want to rebel against any attempt to box complex individuals into a limited number of categories.

When leading workshops, I repeatedly address these concerns by reminding participants that the categories are theoretical and I am not interested in coming to conclusions about an actor's overall personality. I encourage everyone to avoid rushing into a decision, to keep trying out the different types, looking for one that not only fits them but that explains their process in a way that will prove helpful. I do not think that an absolute, definitive self-diagnosis is required for an actor to benefit from my approach to acting processes. Quite often, actors leave the workshop thinking they have found their type, only to realize that another type is a better fit.

Because of my commitment to honouring diversity, and in the spirit of a toolbox approach to the teaching of acting, I do not care if my approach works for everyone, as long as it works for some. My experience has been that my ideas are of some interest to everyone, and significantly helpful to many.

There remains one final task, before what follows can make sense. And that is for me to define acting and, more importantly, clarify what, for me, makes acting good. I can do that by explaining the title of the book.

Actors need to discipline their voices, bodies, and imagination so that they can adapt themselves, like the chameleon, to the fictional character they are portraying and to the world of the play in which that character appears. We know that this aspect of our work is successful when nothing gets in the way of the audience's willingness to suspend disbelief.

Actors need *charisma*, that intensely personal energy, to fill those fictional characters with a compelling spark of individuality. As creative artists, we need our charisma to be more than a superficial attractiveness or vividness in self-expression. We need to be able to access something at the core of our being, that place beyond words or conscious manipulation. We know that this aspect of our work is successful when the audience finds our chameleon work compelling.

The *charismatic chameleon* has become, for me, the perfect description of the ideal actor.

The first part of this book contains a detailed description of my theory of creative personality types. Alternatively, if you are interested in more practical applications, I recommend skipping the Introduction and going directly to the Virtual Workshop, which begins with a brief summary of the theory and then plays with the ideas via a dialogue with an imagined group of acting students. Finally, for those interested in placing my ideas within a larger context, I offer an annotated bibliography.

PART
ONE

An Introduction to
Creative Temperament

Introduction

In 1973, in attempting to answer the question, 'Are Britain's actors better?' the American critic Robert Brustein endowed British society with a 'concern with the welfare of others' while American society was judged to be 'obsessively involved with the problems of Self.' He continued, 'Reflecting this interest in the Other, the English actor approaches his role as if it were a mask . . . varying his speech, gait and features to suit the needs of character. Reflecting his interest in the Self, the American actor usually purveys a single character from role to role, one that is recognizably close to his own personality.[1]

Brustein's comments, although easily refuted, serve to provide this discussion of acting with a theoretical framework. However, rather than suggesting that the attention to variations in speech, gait, and features as an English school of acting and the correlation of self to role as an American school, I propose a definition of excellence in acting that encompasses both approaches. What Brustein labels as the English approach, I call the chameleon side of an actor's artistry. What Brustein labels as the American style, I call the charismatic; hence the title of this book.

If we think of an actor as a charismatic chameleon, we have a ready-made standard for excellence, and one that favours performers of no particular nationality or training system. Furthermore, a seemingly infinite range of chameleon strategies are available, allowing for equally successful achievements in vastly different times and places, as changing theatrical standards and conventions place different pressures upon the techniques of the chameleon actor. Thus, performances in naturalistic plays will not be, by definition, greater achievements of the chameleon criteria than performances in plays by Ionesco or Beckett. Successful chameleon performances might include transforming a modern actor's habitual expressive capacities into those suitable for a Shakespearean king or one of David Mamet's salesmen.

The criteria for judging achievement as a chameleon is how well the choices made in voice, movement, and facial expression are seen to have served the artistic goals of the production as a whole. Clearly, a chameleon actor will demonstrate mastery of the means of expressive communication in voice, face, and body; this mastery might be more or less intuitive, based upon a sensitivity that does not always crystallize into conscious thought. In addition, the chameleon actor will demonstrate a remarkable

---

[1] *New York Times*, 15 April 1973, section 2, p. 1, quoted in Conroy, 262.

flexibility in the subtle and striking shaping of these communication systems, always seeking the perfect assimilation into the background of the artistic creation.

If the chameleon side of the actor's artistry demands technical excellence in the manipulation of expressive communication, the charismatic requires a capacity for the unleashing an intensely personal psychic energy. If this were not offered in service of an artistic creation, it might well be described as the self-indulgent obsessions of Brustein's American actor. The criteria for excellence, however, is the same as with the chameleon capacities of the actor: how well the actor's energy serves the production as a whole.

Lest it be assumed that my metaphor necessitates a dichotomy or other sort of arbitrary division in an actor's artistry, let me clarify an essential component of the chameleon and the charismatic. Although the chameleon seems to have as its focus the external manifestations of character as they function within the world created by the play, in practice the skills of the chameleon incorporate the internal psychological processes of *experiencing* the activities of the character. In other words, by *doing* the character, the actor must both present and perform. The conscious, disciplined technique is supplemented by a vast array of subliminal sensory systems that work in the context of immediate and unmediated feedback to that portion of our brain that monitors our bodies for indications of personal experience. The actor performs the actions that have been selected because they best present the feelings of the character, and in so doing, ensures that his body will inform his psychic systems that a feeling is occurring. In other words, chameleon skills are far from robotic.

In turn, although the charismatic component may seem to privilege the familiar, recognizable self of the actor, the profound energies unleashed in any charismatic creativity are such that the self is of necessity transformed. In practice, the charismatic actor is not obsessed with personal, mundane considerations, but rather transformed, transported, 'translated,' to use Shakespeare's terminology (said of Bottom wearing his ass's head).

You can get a fair way on charisma alone. But those of us looking for great acting will lose interest eventually. When we see such individuals in yet another role that is exactly like all of the others and in which, most importantly, the highly individualized charisma undercuts the effectiveness of the work in which he appears, we begin to tire of the predictability of his enacted persona and long for the creation of a fictional character. We might call such individuals, if well known, 'stars' rather than actors.

What then would we call those individuals whose technical skills as mimics allow them to disguise themselves as another character and disappear into the scenery? Do you remember the release of that 'breakthrough in animation,' *Final Fantasy: The Spirits Within*? There was something of a molehill created then by the media's attempt to suggest that living actors might be replaced by these life-like computer-generated cartoons. My response, shared by many, was that the exquisite animated drawings may very well replace *bad* actors. No computer program can generate charisma. For that reason, let us designate the non-charismatic chameleon performer an 'animator.'

In show business, the charismatic is afforded greater significance than actually serves the artistry of the acting profession. This leads to a demeaning misperception among non-actors, who readily conflate stardom with acting excellence. To balance this, many acting training programs foreground the acquisition of chameleon skills, and then wonder why so few of their graduates become successful actors. Programs that emphasize the chameleon in the classroom but advertise their program through pictures of graduates who are currently stars send an unfortunate mixed message: whether or not you expend the energy to acquire the chameleon skills we're teaching, your value to the world, and to us, rests entirely upon your charisma (and the good luck required to make it in show business).

Although many successful professional actors might be described as charismatic or, alternatively, as technically superb chameleons, our unstinting admiration must be preserved for those who are truly charismatic chameleons. Both attributes must be in evidence for excellence to be achieved. However, in selecting and promoting my metaphor of the charismatic chameleon, I am encoding the privileging of the chameleon skills. The charismatic is simply an adjective that sets great actors apart from the ordinary, good chameleons who maintain the excellence of the actor's craft.

Charisma

The challenge of an actor's job is to shape a performance. But what is being shaped is the actor herself. It is her body and her awareness, her energy and her sensitivities, her imagination and her will, that are joining forces to offer what the audience needs to encounter. Therefore, even though much of the chameleon work involves mechanical manipulations of purely external elements, there is no escaping the implications for the actor's self.

Further, we want the actor's selfhood as part of the package. Because we need a term for the very special something that such individuals bring to their work, I have chosen to use the term **charisma** as a catch-all description for that quality of inestimable value.

So now, let me talk about charisma. I'm going to use this term to replace other words that are often called upon to capture an observable fact of acting talent. In fact, I'll use it instead of 'talent' to describe good acting. I shall replace 'good' with 'charismatic' as well.

Here are some terms I would use to expand upon a description of a performance as charismatic. I might say that the performance was powerful, thrilling, dynamic. I might mention the presence of the actor, the intensity of the performance, the chemistry between performers and the sensation of direct, personal connection that the audience felt with the character or the actor. I might describe how I couldn't take my eyes off the actor, how his voice sent goose bumps up and down my spine, how his face expressed so many feelings, how I looked into his eyes and received such a strong suggestion of a real, fictional character looking back at me, seeing me, reacting to me, all the while thinking the characters thoughts and looking at the world as the character would. I would describe how strongly I responded to invitations to experience empathy, or antipathy, to think about issues or to feel striking emotions, how I felt transformed, energized, elevated, inspired, amused, and wiser than when I entered the theatre.

We associate charisma with famous people and with great manipulators, only some of whom we admire, as well as with stars. If you've ever met an actor and thought, 'But she's so ordinary, so small, so bland, so shy!' then you've experienced what happens when the charisma is turned off. And there's a very good chance that you yourself have experienced being charismatic, a state of heightened awareness, energy, mastery, and connectedness that is quite clearly a class of experience quite different from your normal state of being.

Flow

I want to add to this basic definition of the charismatic a couple of key ideas. One is that charisma is fundamentally associated with energy. A charismatic state allows the psyche to tap pockets of energy that are richer and stronger than those we normally summon. Further, this charismatic energy requires less effort to sustain. In fact, one of the indications that we've tapped charismatic energy is that we experience the absence of effort, what we might call *flow*.

Another element I will associate with charisma is *creativity*. Although actors are often used as puppets, to fulfill the creative vision of another, ours is an interpretive creative art, like musicians and dancers. Our creativity is of a different order than that of the choreographer, composer, or playwright, but it is not simple craft. I see a direct connection between the personal energy unleashed in charismatic performances and the ingenuity, inventiveness, inspiration, and leaps of creativity that actors bring to the rehearsal process.

The source of that connection is, I feel, the nature of the energy that charisma accesses. It is a personal energy, yes, but it comes from a layer of personality that rests, like a vast underground lake, beneath our individual experiences of selfhood. I like to draw a picture of an iceberg, with the surface of the ocean represented by waves. As you might remember from school, or *Titanic*, two-thirds of the mass is under water. If we think of that section above water, it might represent what we can access of our self through conscious awareness. All that's below the surface is that part that we cannot know directly, but that we sense is present and maybe even catch glimpses of in our dreams.

I'm going to suggest to you that charismatic energy comes from the two-thirds that is below the surface. Further, I'm going to suggest that down there are pockets of energy that are more profound, more fundamental, more terrifying, and more truly human than the surface of the iceberg that we are able and willing to hold in our conscious awareness. Therefore, the energy that I call charismatic is a **primal** energy, with all the potential and danger of any primal force.

As you may already have guessed, I shall argue that this charismatic energy is the birthright of any member of the species rather than some gift with which some are endowed and others are not. However, I will say that some are better equipped, by aptitude and attitude, to voluntarily access and control this type of energy. I am also going to suggest that society has a vested interest in repressing the free and unfettered releasing of primal energy in any form. Thank goodness, because otherwise we would lose what little superiority we enjoy over our animal brethren.

If we return to that picture of the iceberg, and think about the section above the water line, we discover all sorts of forces working on the ice: the warmth of the sun, the wind and rain. The jagged contours that existed when the berg first broke away from the glacier are smoothed into shapes that are individual yet which conform to the expected: no two icebergs are alike, but they all look pretty much the same.

I think that's a great metaphor for our diversity, as individuals, and our conformity within the limitations imposed by our nature as human beings and by the forces that work on us to shape our individuality. In exploring the way that charisma works for actors, I find myself talking quite often of the way we're wired, in the spirit of celebration and wonder, and also suggesting there is little to be gained from pretending we're capable of things that we're not. But I also talk a great deal about **socialization**, that process whereby we are shaped in order to conform, to a greater or lesser degree, to the norms of our particular time and place. Actors need to be particularly aware of the effects of socialization, in part to open up our access to charismatic energy, and also so that we can shed assumptions of normalcy when our chameleon work requires that we present as real a fictional culture quite different from ours.

My sense of the charismatic is that it pierces to the heart of the overlap between the genetic and the cultural. The energy unleashed is free from any of the restrictions and modifications inflicted by socialization. I also believe that it is bigger even than the limitations of our minds and bodies, that it is truly transcendent, something that connects us with God. If that word offends, replace it with 'the universal energy of nature' or any metaphor that suggests something larger than mere human genetic material.

Chameleon Work

When I think about the task of an actor, I call that the **chameleon** work. The job is to transform in whatever way is necessary so that what is presented to the audience works, in whatever way it is supposed to.

Another way of phrasing this is to say that the actor has to avoid getting in the way of the audience's experience of significant meaning. Getting in the way might be letting an American accent slip out when everyone else is speaking like they're working for the BBC, or plopping down on a couch while wearing a powdered wig. Or it might be by letting too real, too complex, too intense emotion creep into your portrait of the Wicked Witch of the West. Or it might be allowing a frequently rehearsed gesture or glance to remain mechanical when an authentic moment of human communication is what the production has led the audience to expect.

So the chameleon work takes into account genre, production style, audience expectation, the demands of the playwright and the director, in fact every element of the entire package in which you are participating as an actor. There is a great deal to consider, when attempting the full-out transformation of a chameleon, and that's why actors need to train their bodies and voices, discipline their imaginations and sensory awareness, and challenge their intellect to reflect richly on the subtle and complex patterns of human behaviour, including the way we experience relationships and how different cultures function hierarchically.

Considerations

I like to organize all those considerations into four basic categories of **consideration**, because it allows me to break down my work on a role, both in shaping my contribution to the production and also in launching different types of explorations. These considerations also shape the training experiences I seek for myself and offer actors training with me.

I divide the work into two realms for consideration, one of which addresses those aspects of the actor's work that are most directly linked to what we inherit as members of the species, what we might call the **genetic realm**, and the other of which addresses those aspects that are specific to any given culture and so which require some homework whenever we're cast in a play written or even set in another time or place. We'll call this the **cultural realm**.

The connection between the genetic requirements of the species and the development of different cultural forms is so absolute that it's impossible to separate the realms, except as arbitrary organizational tools. However, each offers us quite different strategies for starting an exploration in rehearsal, say, even if that exploration will immediately spill over to the other realm. Also, each realm suggests different approaches for training.

9

Let us have a look at the genetic realm, where our attention will be on the human endowment that the actor manipulates for chameleon transformation. These are the things that the actor brings to the work: his body, including the natural timbre of his voice, all responsive to training. Part of that body is the organ housed in the cranium, a mind that is wired to function a specific way, taking in information, processing it, and storing it for future retrieval. Although the mind and body cannot be separated, except philosophically, we can break down the genetic realm into two distinct entry points for our work as actors, and two distinct areas of focus for our training. For example, we can undertake extensive physical and vocal training, we can exercise our imaginations, we can explore our senses through intentional, heightened awareness, and we can tackle the challenges of an acting role through a physical (outside) or imaginative (inside) approach, or any combination of the two.

Now we can consider the cultural realm, and divide it in half in a similar manner, reminding ourselves that the division is to clarify different strategies for launching explorations in rehearsal and shaping chameleon transformations for performance, and for training for chameleon work. If we think of the cultural realm vertically, we can address issues of hierarchy and also considerations of how any given culture makes sense of the gap between ourselves and powers greater than humanity: God or gods, fate, nature, ka, etc. If we contrast that by thinking horizontally, we're able to focus on all of the many ways that we bind ourselves to others, and also how we sever those bonds.

Disciplined Creativity

As you can see, we are back to where we started with the actor's considerations: the genetic realm and the cultural realm. These are what we are best equipped, as actors, to manipulate with disciplined, intentional effort. We all want to be charismatic, but the day-to-day reality of our job, if we're working, and our training, if we're not, is shaped by the very real and specific demands of the chameleon's job.

Fortunately, the charismatic is so completely organic, so much a part of what you are as a human being, that it's difficult to keep it out of most human endeavours. It invades everything we do for pleasure, it permeates every activity we seek out voluntarily, and it even has a place in many jobs for which people are paid small and large sums of money.

In fact, it's more notable in its absence. We feel its loss when we are bored, alienated, apathetic, or frustrated. Some people lose touch with their charismatic energy permanently, but fortunately 'normal' in our culture is defined, in part, by a healthy blend of opportunities for energized experiences.

That's not quite enough for actors. Because of the creative nature of our work, we need to bring the process of unleashing charismatic energy into our conscious control, for rehearsals, and we need to monitor the integration of charismatic energy into our chameleon work, in order for the overall success of our performance to be finely tuned to the success of the entire production.

In thinking about the flow of creative energy in rehearsals and training activities, we are perhaps more aware when it is absent or diminished; when, for whatever reason, we feel our internal process derailed. I think we have all had experiences when we knew things weren't working, but we could not easily identify what was going wrong much less get things back on track. If we encounter too many such experiences, an overall malaise can set in, even to the point where we doubt our calling to the profession!

Courage is such an important quality, perhaps the most important quality an actor brings to her career. Over time, if this sort of malaise becomes more common than not, courage will erode, and the result can be crippling. That is why actors need to bring their charismatic energy under their conscious control, not to mess around with it when things are going well, but to intervene when the energizing, creative flow is absent.

That is what this book will teach you.

An Actor's Individuality

First, though, we need to address one more important element of each actor's creative instrument: the ways in which we fall into patterns so that, for all our individuality, there are certain recognizable types of creative experiences, and therefore distinctly different approaches to the accessing and shaping of charismatic energy.

In other words, though the energy has a set of universal attributes, our experience of it is not universal. This is the single most important difference between my approach to acting and that of almost everyone else. Experienced, successful, and self-aware actors will, quite naturally, assume that their experience of good acting to the process they use to get there. If they then write this up in a book and/or share their approach with a generation of actors, those for whom their approach works will, in turn, want to share the approach with others. The result is a legacy that can develop into an acting system or method, such as developed and recorded by Stanislavsky or Grotowski in our time, and Descartes and Delsarte for previous eons of actors.

The key to the emergence of a legacy is not that the founding individual finally landed upon THE secret, but that there was a good match between the approach described and sufficient numbers of students in each successive dissemination of the legacy. What is not so apparent is the number of actors who might have explored any of these approaches and been left untouched. Some of these would have concluded, along with their teachers, that they weren't actors. Others, however, might have continued in their explorations until they found a better match.

Chances are you've already experienced just such a mismatch at some stage in your training so far. An exercise or approach which is offered as an exciting opportunity for creative exploration, which some around you clearly respond to with enthusiasm, energy, and breakthroughs in the mastery of craft, leaves you aware of the absence of that wonderful, effortless flow that you experience with other teachers and/or in other types of exercises. There are probably areas of your training into which you expend considerable effort, and which challenge you intellectually, which you understand as being of considerable significance for actors, but which just don't push your buttons.

In fact, **effort** is one of the indicators that the strategy you are exploring is not, in fact, going to be a natural, organic means of unleashing creative energy. That is not to say effort is a bad thing. Quite the opposite. Those aspects of your craft which you acquire through disciplined effort will be, at the end of the day, the source of your greatest pride and of your most significant achievements as a creative artist. The charismatic stuff is effortless, and anyone can access it. Only a trained, disciplined, committed actor can put together the package that is the charismatic chameleon and thus achieve great acting.

Temperament and the Actor

> It is like a barber's chair that fits all buttocks, the pin-buttock, the
> quatch-buttock, the brawn buttock, or any buttock.
> *All's Well that Ends Well*, 2.2.17–20

When actors talk about their approach to acting one irrefutable fact is immediately apparent: there are as many different approaches as there are individuals. No one system could ever suit absolutely every actor's temperament, much less the various cultures and climates within which acting takes place.

The significance of this simple observation has been greatly obscured by the development of well-known and widely practised methods of acting, most of which are variations of one sort or another of the explorations made by Constantin Stanislavsky. Even those who have explored alternative approaches seldom challenge this particular assumption, shared by theorists and practitioners: that all actors approach the experience of acting almost exactly the same way.

Rather than seeking still another barber's chair, hoping to unlock the mystery of acting through the dissemination of a single system designed to be all things to all actors, let us turn our attention to the nature of the individual experiences. Can we generalize to the point of identifying some broad categories of actors, comparable to Shakespeare's pin-buttock, quatch-buttock, and brawn buttock?

We might describe various patterns in individual acting strategies as preferences, but that term suggests a relatively easy re-configuration of familiar, instinctive approaches into whatever system is on offer. Students and teachers alike report quite a different experience in the acting classroom, to which labels such as 'resistance,' 'inhibition,' 'bad habits,' or 'lack of real talent' are applied.

The earliest philosophers, when considering the patterns of individual behaviour, used the term 'temperament' to describe functions that operate at some profound and deeply entrenched level of selfhood. Psychologists talk of personality types, a phrase that summons up unfortunate implications of a limited number of square boxes into which an infinite number of odd shapes and sizes must be squeezed. Provided that we acknowledge that any generalized categories are neither absolute nor pre-determined, and further that the categories allow for a significant number of variations and permutations, then the consideration of such broad patterns might well illuminate the connection between individual actors and their personalized acting strategies.

I have developed just such a system in order to explain why different strategies work quite differently for different groups of actors. I have tried to keep the system as simple as possible, which means that it is a blunt instrument, in other words large categories into which quite a range of actors can be grouped. Even so, it goes a long way towards suggesting why actors experience what they do in the classroom, in rehearsals, at auditions, and even in performance.

Mine is a system for grouping actors by creative temperament, and it involves identifying your **Creative Personality Type**.

Categorization and Creative Flow

In order to take advantage of my approach to acting, you need to identify your creative temperament. For ease of diagnosis, I offer six types, and I predict that you will find your process described with some accuracy by one of the six types.

In this, I'm NOT attempting to come to any conclusions about your personality outside of the rehearsal hall, in what we might call civilian life. I also have no opinion on whether your type can change over time or as a result of training. Since other aspects of temperament seem to be set in the first three months of life or to be linked to genetic predispositions, I would be inclined to assume that your craft might change over time, as would your ability to channel your charismatic energy in different ways, but that your creative temperament has revealed itself in your first acting experiences and will take you through to your final curtain call.

Before we proceed with a general categorization, we need to clarify exactly what we will be using as our criteria for placement within categories. What specific aspects of an actor's experience, attitude, behaviour, and artistry are we going to observe?

This requires that we separate the essential from the surface variables. Because we are looking for some fresh insights, we will want to avoid already well-established categories such as the contrast between those who excel in different genres or media. We will also want to avoid physiologically or culturally determined characteristics such as height, weight, sex, race, native language, education, or physical attractiveness.

I am taking it as given that acting is an artistic, creative activity, even though I know that many acting jobs are about as far from art as anyone can get in our society. Therefore, we will want to understand and then observe the actor's experience of creativity.

There are many aspects of the actor's craft by which actors can be differentiated, but these have a great deal to do with the quality of training the actor has received. Therefore, we will be interested in criteria that are not so greatly affected by these differences.

The flow of creative energy from some profound level of the artist into the expressive capacities of the chosen art form is the one universal component of artistic expression that has proven to be available for categorization. The conscious, experienced form of this energy is immediately recognizable. When it occurs, there is an ease, a richness of sensation, a profundity that is easily contrasted with the more effort-filled work required in rehearsal and performance.

It would be fascinating to trace this energy flow back to its source, but pragmatically our focus will be on developing ways of accessing this creative flow. Here we discover broad, general categories of experience, within which actors can position their individual patterns of creativity.

Self-Diagnosis

In order to figure out your type, you need to differentiate between experiences of effort and experiences of flow in various aspects of your work as an actor. Effort, as we've seen, involves disciplined and intentional dedication of energy. It will call upon our intellect. When discussing any aspect of our work with those who experience flow, in contrast to our effort, we'll feel cut off from the obvious enjoyment and creativity they experience, and they will be puzzled at our struggle to understand and master the strategies.

Flow, in contrast, is effortless. Time passes quite differently during flow experiences. Even after significant amounts of activity we feel energized. Relaxation and concentration seem to come naturally. When intellectualizing about the acting strategy that resulted in flow, either in receiving instructions or applying the discoveries to a specific acting challenge, things seem obvious or we experience epiphanies. Our work feels organic, natural, and efficient. We find ourselves even more fearless than usual, or the risks seem relatively less, even though we feel that we're able to be vulnerable, open, and present.

At this point in reading the book, take a moment to draw into your conscious memory some experiences that stand out as examples of effort, and of flow. If you can jot down some details, that will help you when it comes time to conduct your self-diagnosis, particularly if you're working in isolation and have no one else with whom to discuss your process.

The Four Conduits

Let us return to the considerations of the chameleon work of the actor. You will remember the two realms: genetic and cultural. We are going to return now to those terms, but re-frame them slightly differently. In fact, we are going to identify four distinct points of access, through which the charismatic energy can be tapped. I call these points of access **conduits**.

If we consider the profound source of creative energy as a liquid mass, we might imagine something like the large pipes which move water from a central reservoir to various sectors of the actor's overall artistry. Conduits are the means by which profound psychic energy is made available to the actor; the energy flows into a trained actor's enlarged capacity for expressive behaviour.

We shall start with the cultural realm, and identify two conduits: **Relationship**, linked to the horizontal cultural norms, and **Power**, linked to the vertical cultural norms.

Moving to the genetic realm, we find two more conduits. If we zoom in on the body, specifically how we initiate through and react to physical activity, we have a conduit which we'll label **Action**. If we zoom in on the brain, specifically sensory awareness, imagination, and memory, we have our fourth conduit, which we'll label **Perception**.

You might notice that I have left out the cognitive functions of thinking and feeling, and I've said nothing about will, what psychologists call the conative function. That's because those sit at the place where conduits, the source of charismatic energy, and considerations, mastered by disciplined craft, intersect. It is also where the two realms, genetic and cultural, overlap. Thinking, feeling, and intentionality inform our experience of every conduit and every consideration.

We now have the four conduits: Action, Perception, Power and Relationship. Because we do not want to suggest any sort of real separation, we shall draw four concentric circles to represent the four considerations. Even this is not quite right, because we need a diagram that suggests an equal overlap between any two of the four circles, and this diagram does not show us what happens when we blend Power and Action, or Relationship and Perception. The diagram does, however, mark out the central, overlapping territory where all considerations meet.

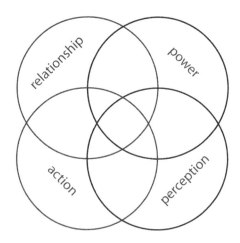

The dichotomy between the charismatic energy and the chameleon capacities of an actor is an arbitrary and dangerous one, as it implies a false separation between two distinct realms which are in fact inextricably connected. In part, the appeal of a simplistic dichotomy is the direct result of our comfortable assumptions about the nature of selfhood. We like to compartmentalize our sensations neatly into the mental and physical as well as into the authentic and the pretended.

Yin and Yang

I now want to make a general observation about how we talk about all complex human experiences. Perhaps because we have two hands, two feet, and a brain divided into two hemispheres that perform contrasting functions, we have a habit of dividing things into paired opposites. Remember *Sesame Street*? Up, down. In, out. Big, little.

Many of our adult considerations get boxed into the same binary pairings. Like male and female, for example. Or right and wrong. Part of growing up is realizing that life isn't ever going to be that simple. We learn to acknowledge that some situations are too complex for easy categorization. In fact, when we put some opposites side by side, we discover that they have more in common with each other than we'd ever have thought and a third term is needed that collapses the opposites into a unified, complex whole.

I am very fond of the symbol of yin and yang as a metaphor for a way of thinking that moves beyond simple opposites. You can see that the 'eye' of one side is the colour of the other. Also, the two halves are each necessary for the symbol. It simply is not possible to have yin without automatically summoning an equal and balancing component of yang.

We will think of each of the conduits in exactly that way. Here's how

the pairings work (Table 1 – overleaf). It is easy to see each of the eight elements on the right hand side as separate, distinct elements. If we apply those terms to a role, we can discuss the actions that the character initiates, and identify when the playwright dramatizes the character's reaction to something. We can plan for a deliberate, significant attention to one of the five senses as the touchstone of a moment, and we can chart specific ways to make use of our imaginations and memories. We can assess the relationships within which our character functions, which are warm and intimate, which are closed off, perhaps even destructive, as well as charting changes that the playwright illustrates. And we can analyse the world of the play, considering who is more and who is less prestigious than our character, and what sort of spiritual life this character is shown to have.

These are all part of the consideration of the disciplined, attentive,

TABLE 1 Conduits and Pairings

Action	initiation and reaction
Perception	sensory awareness and imagination/memory
Relationship	warm connection and cold disconnection
Power	commanding authority and submissive humility

chameleon actor. But it is only through effort that we examine these separately. When a conduit is tapped, these opposites reveal themselves as the yin and yang of the experience.

- Every action that you might initiate is also a reaction to something, and every reaction carries at its heart an initiation of action.
- Sensory awareness unlocks memory and imagination, and if you imagine or remember it will be sensory details that you summon to your mind.
- The impulse to disconnect from a relationship lurks at the core of every intimacy, and a pre-existing human connection is required in order to close off.
- No matter how powerful someone is, there are forces more powerful. And no matter how low you are in a society, you still have power over something, if only yourself.

If, as you read this last paragraph, some of the statements leave you scratching your head, puzzled, and others have you going, 'Of course,' you've already taken a major step towards self-diagnosis. That's because, if a conduit is one of yours, then you'll 'get' the yin/yang intuitively. If it's not, then you won't. However, don't worry if you 'get' them all, or 'get' none of what I've just explained. The concept reveals itself to some of us through experience, not words on a page.

Fortunately, there are many ways to diagnose your creative temperament. From here on, you'll be invited to explore each of the four conduits, and then to explore the different ways they combine. Remember, it's more important to test out all the possibilities than to rush to self-diagnosis. Keep an open mind as long as you can.

You are looking for two conduits, leaving the other two to become the focus for your disciplined development as an actor. In other words, all four are important, and by identifying two that are specifically linked with your creative temperament, you're not cutting yourself off from half the fun, and challenge, of acting.

There are six types, each linked to two conduits. At first this might be a bit confusing, but keep referring to the chart inside the front cover and soon the terms will make sense. Here's how I came up with the names of the types.

- The blending of Action and Power I call DYNAMIC to evoke the physicality of this creative personality type, and also suggest the powerful nature of that physicality.
- The blending of Action and Relationship I call PERSONAL to evoke the very physical presence of this creative personality type, and how much that registers as a relationship.
- The blending of Relationship and Perception I call PSYCHIC to evoke how much this creative personality type is attuned, through sensory awareness, to others.
- The blending of Perception and Power I call VISIONARY to evoke the power of this creative personality type, achieved through sensory awareness and imagination.
- The blending of Action and Perception I call INNOVATIVE to evoke the way this creative personality type is attuned to action, and how sensory awareness and imagination result in action.
- The blending of Relationship and Power I call MAGNETIC to evoke the way this creative personality type is attuned to the power of human relationships.

PART
TWO

The Virtual Workshop

Introduction

What follows is a composite, made up of excerpts from a number of workshops offered over a five-year period. The comments made are representative of the type of discussion that takes place as actors reflect upon their individual experiences using the vocabulary of Creative Temperaments.

In real workshops we seldom spend this much time talking. Many actors never put their discoveries into words. Fortunately for my research, many are wonderfully articulate as well as sensitive and committed to disciplined self-reflection.

The cast of characters and their Creative Personality Types:

LESLIE	Dynamic (Action and Power)
POLLY	Personal (Relationship and Action)
IRIS	Innovative (Action and Perception)
SALLY	Psychic (Perception and Relationship)
MIKE	Magnetic (Relationship and Power)
VICTOR	Visionary (Power and Perception)

The Workshop begins with a brief lecture.

The Charismatic Chameleon

Actors need to discipline their voices, bodies, and imagination so that they can adapt themselves, like the chameleon, to the fictional character they are portraying and to the world of the play in which that character appears. We know that this aspect of our work is successful when nothing gets in the way of the audience's willingness to suspend disbelief.

Actors need charisma, that intensely personal energy, to fill those fictional characters with a compelling spark of individuality. As creative artists, we need our charisma to be more than a superficial attractiveness or vividness in self-expression. We need to be able to access something at the core of our being, that place beyond words or conscious manipulation. We know that this aspect of our work is successful when we experience a sensation of FLOW.

FLOW is the effortless production of rich, complex creative energy. When people talk of being 'on' or of something 'kicking in' or any available metaphor for the euphoric thrill of acting that works, chances are they are reporting an experience of creative flow. Much of our acting training is designed to set the groundwork so that such experiences happen regularly as part of the creative process of acting.

Flow and effort are mutually exclusive sensations. That is because effort is the conscious manipulation of our physical or mental activities, and flow describes a sensation that transcends discipline and conscious manipulation. We use effort to unlock flow, to discipline the energy that flow creates, and to learn from what flow teaches us.

In search of a well-tuned engine

Specific training regimens are geared towards making the voice, body, and imagination available for conscious manipulation in service of the chameleon component of acting. Rehearsals and performances confirm that much of our work is intuitive. No matter how experienced or well-trained the actor, there is some aspect of the work that remains mysterious and irrational.

The creative engine that produces the best of our acting is a delicate instrument. When it is firing on all cylinders, sensations of flow are a regular occurrence. When conditions are perfect, there's nothing that can stop us. The director brings out the best in you, the part fits like a glove and challenges you in all the right places, the rehearsals and performances match your creative rhythms, and the entire company becomes a single, highly-charged collective.

But.

When things aren't going smoothly?

This is an engine that is very easily thrown out of sync. And there is only one person who can serve as the mechanic.

You.

The more you know about how your own individual creative engine functions, the better you will be able to fine-tune yourself for maximum flow of charismatic energy when effort is required to achieve your best acting.

The Creative Temperament

There are many attributes that we share as members of the human species. There are also attributes that are distributed differently among different groups. Some of these variations in personality are the result of socialization, some come from cultural norms, some are linked to the balance of chemicals in the body. Physicians, biologists, sociologists, and psychologists have charted these patterns of behaviour.

Actors are no different in demonstrating certain shared attributes and others that fall into broadly defined patterns.

One of those patterns is a notable difference in creative temperament.

Creative temperament is a predisposition to certain sources of flowing charismatic energy.

The six creative temperaments are: Personal, Innovative, Dynamic, Psychic, Magnetic, and Visionary.

The benefit of discovering your unique creative temperament is increased skill as a mechanic of your own acting engine.

The Four Conduits

The first step in identifying your creative temperament is the exploration of the four Conduits of creative energy: Relationship, Action, Perception, and Power.

Every actor, from the humblest amateur to an experienced and highly trained performer with undeniable talent, draws upon all four Conduits of creative energy because that is what acting is designed to do.

In rehearsal and performance it is impossible to separate relationships from actions, we cannot stop using our senses and our imagination, and political and spiritual power are part of every character's world.

But for the purpose of self-discovery, we can turn our focus to each of these Conduits in turn. You will be looking for which of the Conduits produce the richest flow of creative energy with the least effort.

Yin and Yang

These sources of creative energy that we call Conduits function through a pairing of opposites illustrated most evocatively by the symbol of yin and yang. Dark and light together make up the circle, reminding us to avoid the simplistic. Each side has a small circle, the eye, suggesting a deeper level where essence is defined. The eye is made up of the opposite shade, clarifying the paradox of opposites: at the core of each extreme resides the other.

Relationship

The yin and yang of the Relationship Conduit are the opening and closing of connections between individuals. We might experience a growing warmth of regard, increasing comfort, growing passion, strengthening trust. Or we might experience a cooling of interest, decreasing comfort and trust, the lessening of passion. At the extremes, we experience the intense longing, love, commitment, and passion of union or the violent, raging, destructive energy that can lead to pre-meditated murder.

The symbol of yin/yang reminds us that love and hate are one, that our feelings for others are always mixed, that relationships are always changing and that perfect union and complete isolation are impossible.

Action

The yin and yang of the Action Conduit are initiating and reacting. We might experience the sensations of moving forward, leading, planning, deciding, managing, and achieving, or we might respond, retreat, adjust, defend, and suffer all that is done to us. Some of our actions are under our conscious control, others are the body's more primal functioning. At the extremes, we experience mastery of our body or absence of conscious control as we jump when a door slams or we break out into a sweat.

The symbol of yin/yang reminds us that every action is a reaction, and every reaction takes the form of an action.

Perception

The yin and yang of the Perception Conduit are sensory awareness and the imagination. We can focus our awareness on the information that is flooding our consciousness from the sensing organs: eyes, ears, skin, nose, and taste buds. We can also allow our minds to roam into our treasure-house of memories, or into a future or fantasy. At the extremes, we experience the absolute tyranny of the present or the limitless possibilities of the mind's functions.

The symbol of yin/yang reminds us that the flood sensory input is channelled through our minds, and that the imagination builds its most striking effects through an evocation of sensory experience.

Power

The yin and yang of the Power Conduit are authority and humility. We might experience sensations of rising status, growing potency, greater range and scale of command. We might experience sensations of decreasing status, loss of potency, and a fall to humble status. No matter how many people are below you in the chain of command, there are others above, before whom you must bow. Even if you are at the top of the human chain, there are natural and spiritual forces to which you must submit.

The symbol of yin/yang reminds us that we experience the extremes at the same time, because of our great humility before those we most respect, admire, fear, and worship, and our superiority over, and responsibility for, the weakest and most vulnerable among us.

An Actor's Creativity

A trained, talented actor brings to every rehearsal and performance situation three immense repositories upon which to draw.

First, thanks to the training that has disciplined the body and voice, the actor is capable of enacting a wide range of activity, whether familiar or strange, and shaping the specific activity with great subtlety so that an onlooker encounters nothing that might detract from the impact the activity is intended to have upon the dramatic story telling in which the actor is engaged.

Second, the focussed concentration of the imagination and senses allows an actor to invent, to personalize, and to engage richly with dramatic text and fellow actors.

Finally, each actor brings a life-time of experiences, ranging from the most private and intuitive through to the most widely shared, both conscious and unconscious. From these, actors can assemble the raw material with which to construct complex social and interpersonal relationships that reflect the most profound concerns that infuse our culture and confound our humanity.

Creative Considerations

Action, Perception, Relationship and Power are considerations that govern the work of every disciplined, creative actor. The trained body and voice allow the actor's actions to transform, chameleon-like, as required by the style of performance and the fictional world of the character being portrayed. Focussed imagination and the heightened sensory awareness result in the charged intuition while a deliberate lowering of emotional barriers allow for enriched relationships between characters and with the audience. The subtle differences in social status are mined even as the transcendent power of the mysterious is invited and celebrated.

An actor's talent is a subtle blend of consideration and flow. The Creative Temperament of each actor determines the conduits which offer access to the most profound levels of flowing energy, and therefore which allow for the releasing of the charismatic. The disciplined effort of the actor draws upon the considerations that allow for the creation of a fictional character and thus the completion of the chameleon-like transformation required.

Temperament, Conduit, Consideration

Two Conduits are primarily associated with each of the Creative Temperaments (see Table 2, page 31). There is no hierarchy among Creative Temperaments. There is no direct correspondence between one's Creative Temperament and the range of characters one is best suited to play or the style of performance at which one will excel.

The application of consideration to action, perception, relationship and power, resulting in disciplined, skilful effort, is as likely to result in acting excellence as the releasing of charismatic energy through the tapping of Conduits. In fact, the best acting is the result of the careful blend of disciplined consideration and free-flowing charisma.

The identification of one's Creative Temperament, and hence one's conduits for accessing profound and authentic energy, is an admission of the *relative* strength of certain strategies for building charismatic performances.

Each of the Creative Temperaments offers a combination of potential pitfalls and opportunities for extraordinary creative achievement.

Diagnostics

Although the identification of one's Creative Temperament might illuminate aspects of one's life outside the theatre, that is not the intention of self-diagnosis. A well-tuned creative engine should make an actor more flexible and less temperamental, better able to serve the production and support the efforts of others, and less in need of coddling. Knowing HOW one achieves the richest flow of creative energy will help an actor GIVE more freely, and with greater courage. In other words, although self-diagnosis is, of necessity, self-reflective, the goal is not self-serving or self-indulging.

Even the most cursory reflection upon past acting experiences reveals the tell-tale pattern of contrasting effort and flow. This is the easiest means of self-diagnosis.

Test out your preliminary assessment over a period of time and in a variety of acting situations before solidifying your self-diagnosis. It is, after all, far more important to fine-tune your creative engine than to affix a label.

Subcategories of the Six Creative Personality Types

It is not possible that six distinct Creative Personality Types can describe the many different sorts of actors and their approaches to their professions. Clearly, there must be distinctive subcategories that explain some of these differences.

Crimping and Noise

One contributing factor is socialization. Whatever the individuals' unique creative temperament, their personal experiences will have had an effect, for good or ill, upon their capacity to access creative energy. In some cases an entire conduit has been crimped, severely reducing or even cutting off some aspect of the energy accessed by that conduit. For example, actors with a Perception conduit might have been chastised so regularly for day dreaming that they have to relearn or un-crimp that aspect of their creative energy. Actors with a Relationship conduit will very likely have been socialized away from using the destructive side of that source of profound energy.

Quite often socialization results in the extensive development of one component of a conduit at the expense of the other, as in the case of a Relationship conduit wherein the warmth of constructing is far more central to the individual's normative persona than the destructive or, in the case of a Power conduit, the humility of being a well-behaved child expands far sooner than the commanding energies that are required for the richest creativity emerging from this conduit.

Socialization is a pervasive, subtle means by which an individual's patterns of customary behaviour are shaped. Other cultural influences are less fundamentally damaging or short-lived. We might call these 'noise' though this shifts our metaphor of liquid energy flow to the movement of sound waves. Noise can be so familiar as to exist without our conscious awareness until someone draws our attention to it, at which point it is almost impossible to ignore. This describes very well the sort of liberating discovery that occurs when a cultural monolith is shattered and the individual artist is free to tune the creative activity more richly to the emanations from a more profound source.

Crimpings, in contrast, can be frustrating even when discovered and analysed in detail. It is all very well for someone to point out that society's indoctrinations are damaging your work as an actor. The habits of mind that have dominated your world for all of your conscious awareness are blasted out of the way only at a price, perhaps one that is too high to pay.

Slow and steady un-crimping is often safer and more productive to the creative artist.

Authenticity

Although certain styles of production require the re-enactment of recognizable ordinary situations, there is no correlation between the reality of the actor's emotions and the audience's experience of compelling human truth. The chameleon skills of the actor are equally useful in grand opera, children's fairy tales, and surrealist dreamscapes. The disciplined skill of the performer seeks to eliminate anything that might detract from the overall aesthetic unity of the production, thus limiting the possibility of an actor's work getting in the way of the audience's experiences of empathy, identification, significance, and meaningful insights.

Many performance styles are not realistic, but achieve significance by demonstrating some aspect of the human experience that the audience judges to be truthful. The actor's contribution to this experience of human truth is authenticity, which is achieved through the releasing of charismatic energy into the shape that the chameleon-like skills of the actor has crafted.

Danger, Safely

Before the workshop gets going, the group has discussed a couple of important issues. Although the group is made up of students currently training together, Leslie asks that particular attention be paid to boundary issues. The group agrees that everything discussed in the room stays in the room. Leslie asks, in turn, that students out of courtesy refrain from naming teachers, directors, or students who are not present in discussions. The students already have a clear set of guidelines about improvised fight scenes. Leslie asks that sexual as well as violent contact be out of bounds; the focus in this workshop will be on exploring the feelings that might lead to such actions rather than enactments that require careful staging.

Leslie suggests that sometimes the best learning comes from voluntarily taking certain types of risks, and so putting oneself in harms way is part of what actors do. However, she points out the difference between foolish, even self-indulgent pursuit of danger, both physical and emotional, and deliberate, thoughtful risk-taking. One of the differences is that issues of safety are never ignored; rather, the goal is what she calls 'safe danger.'

Leslie introduces the group to a warm-up that begins with physical stretching, proceeds to guided relaxation and imagination work alone and in pairs, and ends with a children's competitive game. She also introduces the concept of 'cooling down' and everyone learns a simple ritual for ending acting explorations. This involves a set of seven movements accompanied by deliberate, slow breathing, ending in a pose of energized stillness. Students are encouraged to do this with eyes open or shut, as they prefer. If shut, they can go at their own pace. If open, they should work as a team, moving as one organism with whomever they've just performed. Every workshop begins with a warm-up and every exploration ends with this simple cooling-down ritual.

TABLE 2 Conduits and Creative Temperament Types

Creative Temperament	Conduits	Considerations
Personal Action,	Relationship	Perception, Power
Innovative	Action, Perception	Power, Relationship
Dynamic	Action, Power	Relationship, Perception
Psychic Perception,	Relationship	Action, Power
Magnetic	Relationship, Power	Action, Perception
Visionary	Perception, Power	Action, Relationship

VIRTUAL WORKSHOP SESSION ONE: EXPLORING CONDUITS

The group has returned from a break after their introduction to the basic concepts of The Charismatic Chameleon. *For easy reference, each student has a copy of the chart that appears at the end of this book.*

Self Diagnosis through Reflection and Comparison

LESLIE: I'm sure, already, some of you are thinking about experiences you've had, and you have already started to spot patterns. Let's share some of these memories and reflections, and see how close we are to self-diagnosis. I'll start with myself.

My Creative Temperament is Dynamic. That means that Power and Action are my conduits, and I experience effort in connection with the

consideration of Perception — meaning imagination and sensory awareness, and Relationship — including both constructing and destroying.

In my self-diagnosis, the effort of Perception clicked for me, immediately. You remember all those warm up exercises, where you lie on your
back and the leader tells you what to imagine? I never got those. Ever.
The interesting thing is I have a vivid imagination. It just doesn't unlock
creative flow in my acting. For me, that's a consideration, something that
I train, that I develop with disciplined effort.

Perception

SALLY (Psychic): I loved those exercises. I could lie there for hours, and
when it was over, I always felt completely refreshed and filled with energy.

LESLIE: Bingo! That comment suggests to me that Perception is a
conduit for you. As a young student, were you yelled at by teachers for
day dreaming?

SALLY: Absolutely. And even now I struggle with concentration.
Someone coughs in the audience, or out of the corner of my eye I see
something move — sometimes I'm just too aware.

LESLIE: In a nut shell, you've identified both sides of the Perception
conduit — imagination and sensory awareness, and the pitfalls as well as
the potential. I bet you like delivering memory monologues, right?

SALLY: I love them. Especially when the director wants me to 'see' what
I'm remembering.

MIKE (Magnetic): I hate those. No, I mean, I love a great monologue,
but when you're supposed to be looking out a window and seeing something, my acting teacher always complains that she doesn't believe I'm
letting myself really see what's there. The harder I try, the more cut off I
am from why I chose the monologue in the first place.

LESLIE: Which was? Chances are it was one of the other conduits.
Maybe Action? Or Power?

MIKE: Maybe Power, but I don't really get what you mean by Action
yet.

LESLIE: That's a good sign that Action isn't a conduit for you. Well, the
only other one we've not mentioned is Relationship.

Relationship

MIKE: Yes, but that's universal, right? Every character is really about
relating to the other characters in the play, even if they're not on stage

with you. It's about feelings, responsibilities, who owes what to whom, who can hurt you, who you can hurt . . .

LESLIE: Sounds like a Relationship conduit, right there! Tell me, when you're working on a monologue, does it help to have another actor to play off of, up there with you?

MIKE: Of course, but that's the same for everyone, right?

LESLIE: I'll think we'll find that some of you experience a profound flow of creative energy when you can draw upon Relationship as a conduit, and for the rest it's an important consideration.

VICTOR (Visionary) But not a conduit. I have a feeling that's me, and you don't know what a relief it is to say that out loud. My main acting teacher was big on relationships, like Mike was saying, and I've worked really hard on things like analysis, biographies, all that prep work – in fact I liked imagining . . .

LESLIE: Possibly a Perception conduit?

Power

VICTOR: Maybe. I never minded those relaxation exercises. But I'll tell you what made my relationship work click, was when I took a workshop with some guy who was big on status. We played all these games, and I was totally awesome.

General laughter, and someone calls out 'King Vick!'

VICTOR: Sure. But I could do the guy at the bottom of the food chain. When you were talking about Power, that was the one that clicked for me. Specially when you described it as feeling power flow through you, and knowing that you had authority, but also humility at the same time because the power was bigger than you. The best acting I ever did, was when I did Henry V the night before Agincourt. He's a king, he's in charge, he's not afraid of the responsibility, but he's kneeling and begging God, and that's why he's so much the king, at that moment.

LESLIE: You've nailed the paradox, the yin/yang of the Power conduit. Does that make sense to anyone else?

Polly (Personal): I figure if you're in charge, that's your job. Henry was upset because of what he heard from his soldiers.

Victor and Polly immediately start arguing about the play.

LESLIE: Let's not get side-tracked into a debate about character motivation, though I will say that almost always such debates arise directly out of the contrasting Creative Temperaments of the debaters. Victor's already identified Power; my guess is that one of Polly's is Relationship, because what inspired her to leap in and comment was an insight about relationships.

POLLY: I'm with Mike on relationships. I just don't see how any actor can claim that relationships aren't central to what goes on in a scene. They're what propel you to action. Everything you do, every word you speak, arises out of the complexity of relationships. Remember, acting is reacting.

Individual or Universal

LESLIE: Okay, I have to say something at this point in our diagnostic discussion. One of the great dangers of having a Creative Temperament, which we all do, and now knowing about Creative Temperaments, is that we naturally assume that what unlocks great acting in us is universal. We're not helped in this by our teachers, directors, and publishers of books about acting that present one way as if it were the only way.

I agree 100% with Polly's comments about relationships, but only for those of you who access the Relationship conduit. For everyone else, and that would be about 50% of actors generally, I'd say that you need to give relationships careful consideration, and look to the other conduits as a source of profound authenticity in your work.

But I want to get back to Polly's other comment, 'acting is reacting.' Now, I hear that and a light goes on, because that statement is a signal of the one conduit we've not discussed much yet.

Action

IRIS (Innovative): Action, right?

LESLIE: Remember when Mike said he just didn't get Action, despite my description of the Conduit? And it's one I 'get' because I'm Dynamic so it's one of mine. In a way, it's easier for me to describe the other conduits, because for me this one is like Relationship for Polly – the obvious one. When I studied acting, thirty plus years ago, I absorbed as gospel Stanislavsky's score of physical actions, and in my teaching I place a great amount of emphasis on what actors can unlock through the body, which I consider a repository of all human experience. I'm also big on speech acts. Anyone here encountered that approach to text?

IRIS: I'm not sure if I have, but as soon as you said that, I went, 'Of course, speaking is an action. Just choosing to speak, initiating a conversation, or responding, each beat is an action. I think I 'get' Action because it's one of my conduits. You know the exercise a certain director demands we do, putting an action verb beside every beat?

Groans from some of the group.

IRIS: I know it takes forever, but it always made sense to me. I'd be there, in rehearsal, and I'd be stuck in a moment that just felt so wrong, and that verb would flash through my mind, and suddenly I'd have a place to start.

SALLY: Okay, I have one for sure – the imagination one . . .

LESLIE: Perception

Narrowing the Field

SALLY: Right. That makes perfect sense to me. But do you have to have just two? I think I use all of the others, pretty much the same.

LESLIE: It's not surprising that, just from talking, you'd only be able to

TABLE 3 Diagnosing Conduits

Diagnosed Conduit	Choices for Creative Personality Type
Relationship	Personal (with Action), Magnetic (with Power), Psychic (with Perception)
Action	Personal (with Relationship), Innovative (with Perception), Dynamic (with Power)
Perception	Innovative (with Action), Psychic (with Relationship), Visionary (with Power)
Power	Dynamic (with Action), Visionary (with Perception), Magnetic (with Relationship)

narrow your choices, not decide for sure. To do that, you'll need to try out some acting, alert to the internal sensations of flow and effort. Think of it like a test drive – you need to get that creative engine out onto the open highway and let it rip! At this point in the workshop, you're exactly where you should be – seriously considering two or three models, all set to get the keys and take one of the Creative Temperaments for a spin.

If you have one conduit, that means you're considering three temperaments, and that's a good place to be for testing out your preliminary diagnosis (see Table 3). Alternatively, you might have identified something that isn't a conduit for you. Same thing – that immediately limits your possible temperaments.

POLLY: I'm Relationship, for sure.

MIKE: Me too.

LESLIE: Well, that means you should think about Personal, Magnetic, and Psychic. Personal combines Relationship with Action. Magnetic combines Relationship with Power. And Psychic combines Relationship with Perception.

TABLE 4 Diagnosed Non-Conduits

Diagnosed Non-Conduit	Choices for Creative Personality Type
Perception	Dynamic (Action and Power), Personal (Action and Relationship), Magnetic (Relationship and Power)
Relationship	Dynamic (Action and Power), Innovative (Action and Perception), Visionary (Perception and Power)
Power	Personal (Action and Relationship), Innovative (Action and Perception), Psychic (Perception and Relationship)
Action	Psychic (Perception and Relationship), Visionary (Perception and Power), Magnetic (Relationship and Power)

MIKE: And if you just lie there waiting for those imagination warm ups to be over? And you hate emotional memory exercises?

SALLY: Mike, you write the best monologues. [to me, explaining] We do this imagination exercise, using private memory and blend it with character memory, and write a monologue. Mike's are always the best. They make us all cry.

LESLIE: Remember, just because something isn't a conduit doesn't mean you don't draw upon it for consideration. Perhaps Mike taps another conduit, maybe his Relationship one, and fills his monologue with that creative energy?

POLLY: But if Perception isn't a conduit, we're likely . . . ? (Table 4).

LESLIE: Dynamic, Personal, and Magnetic don't use the Perception conduit. Dynamic is Action and Power, Personal is Action and Relationship, and Magnetic is Power and Relationship.

Everyone examines the charts carefully. What type of actor am I?

Exploration with Improvisation

LESLIE: I suggest we do an improvisation designed to build upon whatever you've identified so far as being a source of charismatic flow. Victor, any idea of your how your creative energy works?

Victor? I've got Power, so it's Dynamic, like you, or Magnetic, or Visionary. But you guys know how I feel about relationship work, so it's probably not Magnetic. So Visionary or Dynamic.

LESLIE: Okay. Let's try out a little improv, and focus on considerations of power. But at the same time, we'll keep an open mind to other possible conduits, by shifting our vocabulary as needed. That's going to be a useful trick. We don't want to have all our eggs in one basket, as artists.

VICTOR: Sorry, lost me there.

LESLIE: You've already, yourself, described an experience of learning to grab eggs from another basket. You talked about not getting all the relationship work, except as a form of disciplined consideration, until you did the status workshop. Now, when a director or teacher or fellow actor wants to discuss process, and talks only about relationships, you can substitute one set of terms for another, a sort of translation.

Let's see how this might work. Victor and Mike, are you game to be our first guinea pigs?

They are.

LESLIE: Mike says he's a Relationship actor. Victor's a Power actor.

You guys are brothers. Let's say Victor, you're older. Mike, you've always wanted to have a better relationship with Victor, but he's seemed so closed to you.

Now, think for a moment about how I phrased those instructions. When talking to Victor, I flagged relative age. That clicks immediately for Victor. Older, higher status. Slight shift of vocabulary from Relationship to Power, and, hopefully, some creative energy is starting to flow. Guys, have I given you something to build on?

VICTOR: It would be cool if Mike were a better athlete, or going for his masters and I'm driving a truck.

LESLIE: Yes, because a Power actor is always playing with BOTH sides of the energy, commanding authority and humble submission.

MIKE: And for me, the focus is on wanting a relationship, wanting to connect.

LESLIE: Yes, and let's add the other side, and tap your capacity to destroy. Let's say you know something about Victor's girlfriend.

MIKE: Or I found out about him and my girlfriend.

LESLIE: Sure. Whatever you need to motivate a desire to destroy the relationship. To destroy him. But let that desire exist alongside your longing to open your heart to him, to connect.

SALLY: I can see how both Power and Relationship can work in this scene, but what about a Perception actor?

LESLIE: Sally, you're one, right? How about you play the girlfriend.

SALLY: Sure. Whose girlfriend am I?

LESLIE: Both, by the sound of it. Now, your eggs are in the basket of imagining – I'll leave it to you to imagine vividly past events with both the brothers.

SALLY: Lucky me!

LESLIE: But when we do the scene, I want you to focus your attention on the other side of the Perception conduit – the sensory awareness in the here and now. In other words, once the scene begins, just listen, watch, sense . . .

IRIS: Smell!

General laughter. This is an 'in' joke.

LESLIE: You bet. All the senses.

POLLY: So what are they going to do in the scene?

LESLIE: Now, that's a very interesting question. I notice that Sally is quite content with the simple instruction of sensory awareness, plus the relationship complexity. In other words, by tapping her conduit, she's unleashed a flow of creative energy that's flooding the other considerations that govern her work as an actor. Same with the guys. Victor's all set to engage Mike, based on shifting power, and Mike's all set because of the double desire in the relationship.

MIKE: I also got what you said about Power to Victor, so I'm thinking maybe I have that Power thing, also.

VICTOR: Yup. You do, man.

General laugher. Sure enough, Victor and Mike have begun circling each other like animals about to fight.

LESLIE: The fact that only Polly wanted to identify the fundamental action of the scene suggests that she 'gets' the Action conduit. Iris, from what you said earlier, I suspect you get it too. So I'm going to ask each of you to join the scenario and to suggest an activity, something that for you would unlock the creative juices if you were in the scene.

POLLY: How about we're their wives. Sally's an old girlfriend of Victor's, now she's getting it on with Mike, and it's the wedding rehearsal – Mike's getting married to Iris. I'm the matron of honour. Sally's a bridesmaid.

Someone makes a crack about soap operas. General laughter.

LESLIE: Okay. See how all of Polly's suggestions key off of relationships? One of your conduits, perhaps? The other might well be Action. So what activity will work for you, Polly?

POLLY: I'll be doing something with Iris, like her hair. That will let me do stuff that's warm and connecting, and then shift in subtle ways, when I get pissed off at her a bit. [to Iris] Don't worry, I won't really hurt you. Hey, I think I'm getting this. I like activity that allows me to express all the complexity of how I'm feeling about the other characters in the scene. And nothing pisses me off more than someone who doesn't give me anything to react to. That's Action and Relationship, right? So I'm . . . ?

LESLIE: That combination suggests you have a Personal Creative Temperament. But let's get this scene started. We need an activity for our other Action actor. Iris?

IRIS: Can you explain the relationships again?

LESLIE: Let's try another approach. If I'm right, and Action is one of your conduits, then if we simply identify an activity and you focus on REACTING, then creative things might start to happen. Let's let relationships take care of themselves, for now.

IRIS: Okay. So my activity is . . . ?

LESLIE: How about talking. Your job is to fill the silence. Because if anyone else starts to talk, you're afraid what might come out. Chatter. About anything. And react. Whatever anyone does – Polly with your hair, Victor and Mike in the room, Sally over in the corner – you can't plan anything, so just trust your reactions to be authentic.

Everyone sets up for the improvisation.

LESLIE: You all have something to focus on, and you all have a framework within which to let something happen that can surprise you. You're each using one of your conduits, consciously, and let's see if the other might reveal itself in this exploration.

The improvisation is chaotic, energetic, and filled with interesting moments between individuals as well as striking individual activity. After the improvisation.

LESLIE: That was a fun improv. Thanks, everyone. Now, let me ask you: did your 'assignment' in the improv correspond with a conduit that opened up creative energy for you? If so, then we're making real progress in self-diagnosis.

IRIS: I'm still completely confused.

LESLIE: There's nothing wrong with that. But perhaps, if you're willing, we can explore your process to see if we can identify how your creative energy flows. Can you describe your greatest strengths and challenges as an actor? That sometimes helps.

Mismatched Creative Temperaments

IRIS: I took the same status workshop as Victor, and I agree, [that teacher] was awesome in all the status games. I could tell he was getting off on it, but I came away feeling like maybe I should switch to the education major. To be honest, I feel that way after every rehearsal with a certain director, who just loves Mike and Polly and hates everything I do. I'm not exaggerating.

LESLIE: You might be surprised how often actors feel discouraged. I think we could all confess to moments of real uncertainty about our abilities and aptitude for acting. I'm going to suggest that the question of talent – do you have any or not – be avoided, and instead open to the possibility that your experience in the status workshop and also in rehearsals with a certain director are the result, in part if not entirely, of a mismatch of Creative Temperaments.

I'm going to talk about myself, here, and teachers I worked with years ago, so we don't get into specifics about anyone in this room or a teacher or director you know and I don't.

Okay, I've got a Dynamic Temperament, which means that Power and Action make sense to me. I 'get' those approaches to acting that build on one or both of those conduits. In other words, I'm more likely to experience an effortless flow of creative energy when my conscious considerations are infused with the sort of intuitions I access best through Action and Power.

My main acting teacher, thirty plus years ago, was big, big, big on imagination and sensory awareness exercises. When he directed, he'd offer suggestions that built upon the Perception conduit. Because I admired and respected him, I tried my damnedest to tap the richest possible acting, using my imagination and my sensory awareness. The result? The greater the effort, the less creative flow I experienced. The director only confirmed what I already knew, that my work was entirely lacking in authenticity, because there was almost no charismatic energy being released into the fictional roles I created. I came out of that experience absolutely sure I wasn't an actor, and I went into directing full time.

A few years later, I took a workshop with someone who was big, big, big on action. Suddenly, effortlessly, things were happening that would have made my first acting teacher so happy. I never took a status workshop, but I'm sure if I had I'd have flourished, like Victor.

The point I'm trying to make is that, by clear-eyed reflection on those acting experiences that were least successful, you might well identify your conduits, as much by the process of elimination as by selection.

Diagnosis through Self-Reflection

IRIS: The complaint I get is that my work is cold. That I'm not passionate enough. And I can feel it myself. I have such a clear vision of how it should go, but when I get up there, it comes out mechanical, disconnected.

LESLIE: I want to pick up on something you've described, what I call the 'movie in the mind' – a real pitfall for Perception actors. Your vivid imagination unlocks such exciting energy that it's tempting to invest too much in the imagined performance. You need to balance that with the other aspect of the conduit, the sensory awareness of the here and now.

But when you talk about mechanical actions, that suggests another possibility. Perhaps the Action conduit is NOT one of yours, but you've trained yourself to invest significant effort in a consideration of movement – did you train as a dancer?

Conduit or Trained Consideration

IRIS: Yes, I did.

LESLIE: That might be it, then. Alternatively, Action is indeed one of your conduits, but again you're only using half of the energy: you initiate but cut yourself off from reacting.

MIKE: Isn't reacting relationship?

LESLIE: For an actor who draws upon the Relationship conduit, any engagement with another human being unlocks creative energy. But an Action conduit unlocks creative energy when reacting to anything – music, furniture, light, memories, sensations, the texture of fabric . . .

IRIS: That is so me. I think it's part of being a dancer, but it's also in my acting. I know you guys like doing monologues to each other, but I like it much better when I'm up there alone.

POLLY: To be honest, Iris, I feel you holding back in scene work. I sense such depth of feeling, but it's like you're shy, or afraid of what might come out if you let it.

Learned Suppression

LESLIE: Polly's raised another important point in self-diagnosis. We all have to acknowledge the huge impact of socialization. Each of the conduits is designed to tap profound, immense psychic energy, which is potentially dangerous for all sorts of psychological and social reasons.

From our earliest years we've been taught to avoid or suppress that sort of energy.

For example: the Relationship conduit. We're taught to cut off the opening, connecting energy to protect ourselves from ungovernable attractions, and we're socialized to completely shut down the destructive energy.

Or Power. Women, and young people generally, are not invited to access the commanding energy in our private lives, so is it any wonder that actors who have a Power conduit need a bit of time to grow into the full riches of that particular creative energy?

We've already talked about childhood chastisement for day dreaming. What about activity? The first couple of years of school are designed to put a cap on the natural flow of Action energy.

From the outside, it's difficult to tell the difference between socialization and mismatch. Remember, this is an exercise in self-diagnosis. The bottom line for us, as actors, is that only we can possibly figure out what will result in the strongest release of flowing charismatic energy. Iris is the one who has to discover what's going on in her acting.

IRIS: Or transfer to education.

LESLIE: Don't do that just yet. Instead, why not play around with diagnosis for a bit? Because, with diagnosis comes tools for taking ownership of your talent.

IRIS: Maybe.

LESLIE: Well, every muscle in your body signals that you're discouraged and frustrated and sceptical.

IRIS: Sorry.

LESLIE: Don't be. You have a marvellous expressive instrument there.

General laughter.

LESLIE: Let's talk through the two possibilities that have emerged for Iris. One possibility: that a Relationship conduit is much favoured by creative artists she admires and with whom she's working right now, but her Creative Temperament doesn't access charismatic energy through that conduit so she is working too hard on the consideration of relationship and has cut herself off from her personal access to flowing creative energy. That's resulted in a sapping of her confidence and a downward spiral in her achievements. The other possibility: that a Relationship conduit is indeed one that she could and should be accessing, but socialization has resulted in a withholding, a cutting off of the charismatic energy.

IRIS: Either way, something's cut off, I agree.

LESLIE: The symptom may be the same, but the strategy for unleashing creative energy is quite different, and that's why you'll want to reach a viable diagnosis. The way you'll know it's viable, is that the symptom will disappear. Or, at the very least, things will get better instead of worse.

If the problem is the result of socialization, then you'll want to set yourself a training program that invites a slow and steady unlocking, supported all along by your other conduit, which is probably less restricted, and also by your disciplined consideration of other aspects of your acting. In fact, it's going to be the areas in which you expend some effort that will allow you to create a safety net for your experimentations in unlocking potent, and therefore frightening, charismatic energy.

If the problem is you've been putting your creative eggs in the wrong basket, then the solution is simple – start cracking those eggs that you do have, and let the creative energy flow into your work.

MIKE: So we'd better figure out which baskets are ours!

Avoiding Assumptions and Hierarchies

At this point in the process, not everyone is willing to proclaim a single temperament. Inevitably, classmates and colleagues offer suggestions. Sometimes, a subtle hierarchy emerges, with certain temperaments being rejected or claimed for a variety of reasons having nothing to do with valid diagnosis of individual temperament.

LESLIE: Before we move on to our test drive, I have to make two important observations. First, you must remember that it's just about impossible to tell from the outside exactly what form an actor's creative process takes. Remember that we receive charismatic energy through our own conduits. This means that if we are consciously aware of our own approach to acting, and encounter someone with whom we 'click,' then we assume that person shares our temperament. The opposite is also true. When we're not receiving charismatic energy, then it's only natural to attribute that person an absence of our conduits. As we look at socialization, we'll discover that the situation is not that simple. For that reason, I advise you to resist the temptation to label the creative temperaments of others.

The second thing I have to warn you about is privileging some temperaments over others. There is no direct link between type of temperament and type of acting success. We're going to have to look for another explanation about why, in any group of actors, some flourish and others flounder. Right now, you're working in an environment where certain conduits are particularly valued or appear more fundamental to acting excellence than others. That has more to do with the configuration of this particular theatrical and institutional culture than with talent or with the nature of acting.

Even if you never took this workshop, you will, at some future date, inevitably work with in an environment dominated by a different creative temperament. If you flourished here, you might suddenly flounder. Or if you weren't one of the stars here, you might find yourself highly valued and flourishing. Then, you'd grasp intuitively what I'm sharing with you now, even if you felt confused in the face of such ebb and flow of your creative energy.

Remember my image of test driving different models? Once you identify your Creative Personality type, well, you already know how to drive, but now you've got the owner's manual and can be your own mechanic. But because you've taken this workshop, if these ideas click for you and you put them to work, you'll be much less likely to flourish or flounder because of the creative temperament of any single director or teacher.

MIKE: And if things break down, we'll have only ourselves to blame.

LESLIE: Well, if you're the mechanic of your engine, and you don't keep the oil topped up . . .

Courage

SALLY: I understand what you're saying about the mismatch of acting styles. I can see it in rehearsals or acting class. There are some people, everything they do gets praise, and I'm not talking about nasty reasons for favouritism. It's like everything that's on offer is snatched up and the person just sails. And there are some people who can't get it, and I can see them just shrivelling up, or they start trying too hard.

LESLIE: The shrivelling up, that's the loss of courage, and the trying too hard – well, we've talked about how effort cuts off the charismatic flow.

If you think about the crazy thing we do as actors, and it's completely unnatural, this exposure of ourselves in public, isn't it? It takes tremendous courage. Psychologically, it's the equivalent of going up on point for the classical ballerina. There's real risk involved, risk to our psyches. A significant amount of our acting training, like a dancer's training, is preparation for our version of going up on point.

Anything that undercuts that courage, that chips away at the psychological preparation, can be particularly damaging to an actor's creative output. That's one of the reasons I urge actors to understand their creative temperaments. That way they can safeguard their inner processes, not by avoiding risks, but by developing the strongest possible psychological processes.

If I can continue my ballet metaphor – you know when a young dancer goes for her first pair of toe shoes? It's a wonderful moment, because she's been preparing for some time, and there's a thrilling ritual involved, that makes you feel like you're finally a real dancer. Most importantly, the shoes are fitted to your feet, and tested under the guidance of a skilled, experienced teacher. And no one ever borrows someone else's point shoes.

That's my point, too. One of the big mistakes we've made in teaching acting and talking about acting is the assumption that Stanislavsky's point shoes will fit us all. Or Meisner's, or Michael Chekhov's, or Grotowski's, or whomever's. And nothing will destroy a dancer faster than damage to her feet. Just like nothing will shrivel up the courage and creativity of an actor faster than trying to use the wrong conduits for authentic and creative energy.

VICTOR: I think we've probably all had at least one experience of mismatch, where things went wrong and there just didn't seem to be any way to get back on track. That's okay, if you've never had the other type of acting, where things just flow. But if you have a great experience, and then the next one sucks, it really does a number on you.

LESLIE: Looking back on the past, can you see how the great experiences happened in part because your charismatic energy was fuelling your chameleon work?

MIKE: I guess so, but it's more the not-so-great ones, where I can see how I could have attacked the challenge of the scene so much differently, if I'd started with the basics. Or at least, the basics for me, which I guess are my conduits.

POLLY: For me, the best and worst experiences all have to do with the person I'm cast opposite. If we click, then the work's going to be some of my best. If we don't – I'm not a happy camper.

VICTOR: Yes, we know.

General laughter.

SALLY: For me, it's the director. Sometimes, I feel like they're talking gibberish, when they give their notes. Nothing they say matches up with what I'm going for, how I'm approaching things. I realize now, from hearing you and Victor talk about power, that the worst experience I had was with a director who focussed on all that power stuff, and I never did get his point.

Labels

LESLIE: You've used a very interesting metaphor when you describe the mismatch in terms of gibberish. What we need, clearly, in situations like that, is some sort of simultaneous translation. Knowing your Creative Temperament, and also knowing something about the others, makes that sort of trick quite easy.

VICTOR: But first we have to identify which Creative Personality types we are.

SALLY: I'm Perception and Relationship. What's that? Psychic. And Mike's Power and Relationship. What's that?

MIKE: Magnetic. Cool, I like that.

LESLIE: A quick aside here, about vocabulary. We're going to fall into the habit of talking about our Creative Personality types as adjectives. For example, I describe myself as a Dynamic actor. I should really say something more like, 'I have a dynamic temperament,' meaning that my personal charismatic energy is accessed most easily within the pattern that I've labelled, arbitrarily, 'Dynamic.' But all that takes too long. So we'll end up using the labels as adjectives. That's fine, as long as we all agree that there's no such thing, really, as a Dynamic actor. That's because there's no direct relationship between one's creative personality type and the sum total of what one has to offer as a creative artist working in the theatre.

That said, I agree with Victor. The sooner you can identify the form your creative energy takes, and how best to access it, the sooner you can take ownership of your artistic journey.

POLLY: I'm pretty sure I'm Personal.

Victor and Iris are still uncertain.

Exploration with Neutral Scene

LESLIE: There's no need to rush into making a decision. We have time to explore the possibilities with another exercise.

Let's put a short, neutral scene on its feet, and use it to explore how some of these fundamental considerations are at play in exploring, rehearsing, and performing – in other words, the bread-and-butter work of the profession. That way we can test out our intuitions and insights, and also explore the trick of simultaneous translation. In our improvisation exploration, I gave different types of instructions to each of you, depending on your creative personality type. But let's imagine that I gave all my instructions and suggestions and requests and critiques using the vocabulary of my creative temperament. Your job is to take in the information I offer with TWO sets of ears.

Your first set is the most important, as it belongs to the chameleon actor. You have a responsibility to shape your performance for the sake of the audience's experience of the play. Something might be very pleasant for you, but if it derails their experience, then it has to go. For better of for worse, you have to trust the feedback you receive from your director in order to fine-tune your performance, right?

Since some of you are still exploring, let's all use this as a diagnostic tool. Try every conduit 'full out' – don't assume it's not for you just yet.

Let's use this Open Dialogue, from Robert Barton's *Acting Onstage and*

One:	Ah
Two:	So?
One:	All set?
Two:	No.
One:	Well.
Two:	Yes.

Off. The fun thing with this sort of neutral scene is that we can imagine any given circumstances we want. That means that we can use this as a work-out for our chameleon skills as actors.

It's tempting to tap the Perception conduit – drawing upon imagination to develop given circumstances. But for our purposes, let's resist the obvious for a bit, and use the scene to explore the Action, Power, and Relationship conduits first. I'll warn you in advance: it will be almost impossible, if you have a Perception conduit, for you to AVOID imagining specific given circumstances. All I ask is that you keep those to yourselves – for now.

Let's start with action. I'll play director, and choreograph the scene by supplying some specific actions to accompany the speech-acts already set.

Polly, you play ONE, and Mike will be TWO. Both begin seated side by side on these two chairs. Before Polly speaks, Mike will get up from the chair, heading for the door. Polly will then say her first line. Mike will stop, turn, and look at Polly. Polly, you will avoid eye contact. Mike will say his first line. Let's try that.

Okay, Mike, you sit down and put your head in your hands. Polly. You now stand and put your hand on his shoulder. Mike, you move your shoulder to avoid the contact. Polly you cross your arms and sit back down.

Let's try it from the beginning,

Polly and Mike run that much of the scene.

LESLIE: Great. Now Polly will say her next line. Mike, count silently to ten before you respond with your line. Then reach out and take Polly's hand. Polly, pull your hand away and say your next line. Turn yourself in your chair so that your back is to Mike, as you say it. Mike, come off your chair, onto your knees, and reach up to stroke her hair, from that position, as you say your last line.

They perform that much of the scene.

LESLIE: What we've seen here is an approach to the challenge of acting entirely through the consideration of ACTION, here defined as initiating and reacting. For some actors, that alone is enough to unlock charismatic energy from the Action conduit. The result is a flow of creative intuition, which gives the scene authenticity, even though every action is arbitrary and so potentially mechanical.

We, watching the action, can't stop ourselves from superimposing meaning onto the scene, based upon our individual conduits and our eagerness to find meaning in the presentation. The actions are like magnets, drawing meaning from everyone in the room. For some of us, the actions alone have that capacity, as they combine with other sources of authentic, flowing energy.

Let's talk about considerations of relationship, without going into any of the specifics of what that relationship might be. As I instructed Polly and Mike to move, I gave them actions that signal the yin and yang of the Relationship conduit: the opening up to relationship and the closing off, withdrawing, cooling or denying, perhaps even destroying the relationship. The actions suggested a tension between the direction the relationship was going at any given moment.

Let's have another pair explore the scene, and I'll direct through instructions about the relationship.

Iris and Victor volunteer.

LESLIE: Iris, you'll play the scene as a closing, shutting down, cooling, rejecting, denying. Victor, this will provide a good obstacle to what you'll be exploring, which is seeking a relationship, wanting to open yourself to this person, feeling vulnerable and intimate.

Just be there, on those two chairs, experiencing the relationship. Whatever happens is great, but hold back from saying the first line. Instead, explore a complexity in the relationship. Victor, hold onto that open, vulnerable, trusting warmth, but add just a touch of protecting yourself. Iris, at the same time, see what happens if you allow some warmth, a bit of vulnerability. Let your characters discover this complexity as the scene unfolds.

Iris and Victor try it, but the scene passes very quickly.

LESLIE: You didn't really give yourself much of a chance to experience the complexities in the relationship. Try again, and I'll offer three specific suggestions.

Suggestion One: combine this consideration of relationship complexity with a hyper awareness of your partner's physical presence. Really look at the person up there with you. See details you might have blocked out. Focus your hearing, picking up on breath sounds as well as the intonation of voice when there are actual words. Awaken your sense of smell and touch as well as taste so you are grounded 100% in the real here-and-now of the moment.

Suggestion Two: combine this consideration of relationship complexity with considerations of power. Endow your partner with authority and power over your physical, emotional, and spiritual well-being. At the same time, take responsibility for the happiness of your partner, who is in some ways weaker than you.

Suggestion Three: combine this consideration of relationship complexity with activity. When you're exploring closing, turn away, cross your arms, break eye contact. When you're exploring opening, make contact in any of the many ways that we signal trust and warmth.

Iris and Victor, use whatever of those suggestions works for you. To avoid mental overload, pick just one, and combine it with relationship considerations.

Iris and Victor perform the scene. Iris adds a great deal of movement to the scene. Victor moves less, but achieves a striking moment when he falls to the ground. When Iris kneels beside him, he springs to his feet and shouts out his next line.

LESLIE: You've all probably seen the pattern in the suggestions I offered Iris and Victor.

SALLY: The suggestion to really see your partner – that was Perception, right?

POLLY: And Action, that's what Iris was doing. Finding things to do to express the relationship.

LESLIE: Or finding the relationship through action.

POLLY: Either way.

LESLIE: For some actors, yes. A Personal actor, who combines Action and Relationship, would find little difference between using actions to access relationship, or using relationship considerations to discover interesting actions to express that relationship. But an actor who doesn't have a Relationship conduit but does have an Action conduit, such as the Dynamic (Action and Power) or Innovative (Action and Perception) might use action to bring creative, flowing energy to relationship considerations.

IRIS: I think that's me. When I concentrated on relationship, that felt a little mechanical. But the minute Leslie said I could move around, and do things, I just went with whatever happened, and it was much easier to explore what might be going on in the scene. To be honest, I think I sort of forgot to think about relationships opening and closing, and just kept an eye on whatever Victor was doing.

VICTOR: For me it was the power. But I think I was also getting a lot from whatever Iris was doing. I felt really connected. I guess I felt her watching me.

MIKE: I totally saw the power. I'd picked up on that already, and when you suggested thinking about vulnerability, it made so much sense to me. Because that's what happens in a relationship, right? You love someone, you automatically give them power over you, and if you know they love you, you also know you have the power to hurt them.

LESLIE: Power and Relationship go together in a very interesting way, which Magnetic actors get intuitively. Think about how the combinations work. Commanding power plus warm, open relationships – that's like the loving parent. But commanding power can also co-exist with the cold, closing Relationship energy – like having the power to hurt someone who loves you, and using it. Then, if we think about the humble side of the Power conduit, we can imagine someone being vulnerable and giving power, voluntarily, to someone as the relationship warms and trust increases. That's easy. But what about the other type, when from a position of humility, you close off the relationship.

MIKE: It's like you're saying, I know you are more powerful than I am, but that can't make me love you.

SALLY: I want to pick up on what Victor and Iris were saying, about knowing someone's watching you. I mean, really watching. That was what I got. In fact, for me, that was what made the scene work. It felt real to me because I could see them picking up on each other. That's what made if feel like a real relationship to me.

Test Driving Discoveries

LESLIE: Just listening to you talk about what you experienced watching the scenes, and what suggestions aroused the quickest, richest response – that's going to be an important clue for self-diagnosis of Creative Personality Type. But I want to let Sally have a go at the exercise. For fun, let's put a third person up there, who won't have any lines but might affect how the scene plays out.

Sally, Mike and Victor settle who will say which lines.

LESLIE: Let's return to the suggestion of hyper-awareness of the other two actors up there with you. That's one half of the Perception conduit. Since you three know each other quite well from your shared training experiences, feel free to draw upon memories. Just stand there for a moment, take in each of the other two, and allow your mind to roam freely, like a shopping expedition through the store house of your memory banks.

Immediately, it's apparent that there are lots of shared memories.

LESLIE: For this exploration, don't let anything show. It's important that you not signal where your imagination is taking you, until the exercise begins.

Now, I want each of you to imagine a fictional situation involving three characters. You can include whatever you want from reality, but the pretend situation must be different from reality in a very important way. You're free to blend fiction and reality whatever way you want, but the fictional elements need to be the most important elements for the particular given circumstances of the moment we're exploring.

Keep the details to yourself, for now.

I'm going to give three suggestions, and I want you to add something to your imaginary scenario for each of these suggestions.

Suggestion One: Add something specific about your relationships, if you haven't already. I want these to be complex relationships, so if there's something that binds you, then add something that is pushing you apart. If you've decided on an antagonistic relationship, be sure to add something that is positive. Remember that these are FICTIONAL elements you're adding.

Suggestion Two: Add something specific about the relative power you have in the fictional reality of the scene. Give yourself something that establishes your authority, prestige, status. Also, give yourself something that results in humility, vulnerability, loss of control. Add something to the fictional story, the given circumstances, for this little trio of imaginary characters.

Suggestion Three: Imagine a situation that requires activity. You have something to do, and some time pressure working on you. Things are happening around you, and you'll be reacting to these imaginary events throughout the scene.

Now, as neutrally as possible, still just standing there, not signalling your imaginary scenario but taking in the real, here-and-now presence of the other two, let's run the lines of the scene, to remind ourselves of who says what, when.

Sally, Victor, and Mike say the lines, but are unable to remain entirely neutral.

LESLIE: Okay, let's share the scenarios. Sally, you go first. Don't tell us everything, just the most important elements: how you imagined the complexity of relationships, the relative power, and the activity you'd be doing.

SALLY: I imagined these two were my brothers, and I had this whole complete story about their relationship with each other, and all the ways they bugged me and how much I loved them, ways we got along, ways we fought, how our parents treated us differently, tons of stuff. For power, I had Victor as the older brother, running things now that our Dad was gone, and Mike the youngest, and for activity I had a war, and Mike had been drafted so I was going to help him pack.

LESLIE: Let's try the scene, using that scenario. Mike and Victor, it means putting your stories aside, and going 100% with Sally's. And let's have Iris help direct, by blocking the scene.

We play around with the scene, with suggestions from Iris for staging.

MIKE: I went with love triangle, with Victor and me best friends, from when we were kids, closer than brothers, until this tore us apart. And my feelings for Sally – she dumped me for the other guy, so I had tons of possibilities for mixed feelings. For power, I went back and forth a bit. I thought maybe she went with the more successful guy, then I decided it would be more interesting if I was the powerful one, and she chose the loser. Sorry Vic.

LESLIE: What about activity.

MIKE: I was thinking an office, and she's the secretary, I'm the boss, something like that.

Again, they act out the scene, with Polly offering ideas for blocking.

VICTOR: Okay, mine is really weird. I was this priest, who fell in love with a woman, and Mike was someone I trusted enough to tell, but he had to report me to the Bishop. And the scene was in the waiting room, and Mike's just come out, from talking to the Bishop, and Sally and I are there, knowing we'll have to go in there, one by one, and betray each other.

Iris and Polly both have interesting suggestions for staging the final version of the scene.

LESLIE: Some very interesting things came out in that experiment. It's interesting to see how the change in the given circumstances, the imaginary scenario, completely changes the delivery of the lines, the blocking, the emotional connections. But for me, considering you individually, from the perspective of Creative Personality Types, it was fascinating to see your different creative strategies emerge.

All of you have imaginations and can use your sense to take in all sorts of information. You all have the capacity to reflect with great insight upon the complexities of relationships and how power functions in our culture. And you all have expressive faces, voices, and bodies, so that you can adapt yourselves to just about any enactment.

But when I observe you at work, I can see that you are quite different creative artists. There are subtle but distinct differences in the way you enter into the authenticity of a scenario, and the way you seek creative solutions to the challenges any given acting situation place upon your craft.

Since you've been working on this scene with intentional self-reflection on process, my guess is that you, too, are aware of a natural predisposition towards one of our six types.

A show of hands. Some are sure, some are not, because they're still deciding between two possibilities.

LESLIE: The point of this last exercise was in part to test drive your creative engines for self-diagnosis and also to explore simultaneous translation, which you all accomplished without thinking about it too much. And that's the fundamental point about the charismatic. It doesn't matter what releases it. All that matters is that it is released and shaped so the audience can sense authentic personal energy filling the fictional artifice that we call character.

POLLY: So when a director wants you to look out an imaginary window and really see the swans on a lake?

External Shape, Internal Energy

LESLIE: What is the director saying? First, there's a description of the external, visible activity that has been requested for the audience to absorb. But there's also a request for the gift of a certain type of energy. Those with a Perception conduit, which might include the director and playwright, and about half the audience, want to see the charismatic energy that their Perception conduit unlocks. But if you're not a Perception actor, you need to know that, and then say to yourself, I will give them the shape of the moment that they desire, but the charismatic energy that I will use to fill the moment will come from another conduit.

MIKE: Such as?

LESLIE: Well, think about Relationship. If there's someone else in the room, the action of turning away might be a closing off. If you speak of the view, that might be a reaching out, for connection. When you rehearse, you are in relationship with your fellow actors and director, and can fill the moment with all that they feed you. When the audience arrives, you can absorb their energy like a sponge and position your creative work within that relationship.

POLLY: Is there a way of connecting simply with the actions themselves?

LESLIE: That's the way I approach such moments. I find that careful attention to and awareness of the exact movement, the exact intake of breath, the exact way the eyes move when gazing into the distance – all of which I absorb from living in this body, 24/7 – is available for me when enacting such a moment.

IRIS: Say the director asks you to both love and hate someone in a scene? And you're not a Relationship actor?

VICTOR: You could translate that to Power, and play around with shifts in authority and humility. That would give you the complexity.

POLLY: And actions – you could really tune your reaction, specially if they were a Relationship actor and fed you constantly.

SALLY: And awareness. Really looking at your partner, things that repulse you and turn you on, coming out of the details of their clothing, how they hold themselves, facial expressions . . .

Someone calls out 'Smells!' General laughter.

SALLY: And memories. You could invent vivid memories of terrible things, for the hatred, and wonderful things, for the love.

Creative Problem Solving

LESLIE: I think you've got the idea of simultaneous translation. And I have to comment on the sort of suggestion that came from each of you. The problem-solving devices you already have in place are most likely tuned to one of your conduits. Victor suggested Power, which we've talked about already as a rich alternative to a Relationship conduit. Polly, who is strongly tuned to her Relationship Conduit, also uses the react side of the Action conduit. Sally already knows how to use the awareness side of her Perception conduit as well as the potency of her imagination.

You've offered these in part to please me, I think. You're demonstrating that you're good students, and that you've been paying attention to the vocabulary I've been using and the way I've been talking about your creative processes. But I think you wouldn't have grasped things so quickly if you didn't experience a simple flash of recognition. Perhaps relief, or a renewed surge of confidence. Or maybe something quieter – just, 'of course!'

Many actors report to me, after participating in this sort of workshop, that I didn't tell them anything they didn't already know. Maybe they'd never discussed it in quite this way, using these terms, but that's about it. The real benefit of self-diagnosis, for everyone, is on those occasions when the work isn't going as well as hoped, and this vocabulary, this way of reflecting upon your acting, might allow for another 'Of course!' moment as you fine-tune your engine and get on with your job.

MIKE: So you're saying we need to pick one of the types.

LESLIE: There's no need to box yourself into one category too soon, before the system I'm describing matches up with your individual experience as a creative artist. In other words, don't worry if you haven't selected the label that suits you best. Even if you've selected one, keep an open mind as we proceed. We need to get to know the six Creative Temperaments a bit more, before you'll experience that 'of course' epiphany that confirms a match up between the terminology I'm using and your internal process.

Also, our community of actors would be a boring group if there were only six variations available for all the roles and all the performance styles. There are many, many additional variables at work in the psyches of each of us. Let's take that as given, and fight any temptation to reduce complexity to simplistic types.

MIKE: I'm glad you said that. I've never liked personality typing, for that reason. It really bugs me when some guidance counsellor sticks a label on me, after I've answered a bunch of stupid questions, and tells me that's who I am – extroverted, sensing, judging, whatever.

LESLIE: I agree with your distrust of those who use personality typing, which is ironic if you consider the point of this workshop. Here's how I see the relationship between fine-tuning your engine and discovering your creative temperament. In order to be your own mechanic, you need to understand yourself, and discovering your temperament opens up one type of self-knowledge that will help you to tune your psyche to your work. You don't have to pick a label in order to explore, but the explorations will result in concrete tools for self-adjustment if you make use of a system to give shape to your sensations. In other words, you don't select a label as a means of self-knowledge. With self-reflection comes the knowledge that verifies the accuracy of the label.

There are lots of different systems for personality typing. Since my only interest is in unlocking charismatic energy for actors, I'm less interested in the validity of the typing than I am in the usefulness of the specific tools for tuning engines.

Bottom line: if this approach works for you, use it. If it doesn't, toss it out the window. All I ask is that you give it a thorough test, and to do that we need to move on to the next level of exploration, for which you need to select a Creative Personality Type for exploration. You've shopped round the used-car lot long enough. Time to pick an engine and take it on the road for a test drive!

SALLY: I'm dying of curiosity. What types do you guys see yourself as?

VICTOR: Can you remind us of the names and what conduits go with each?

LESLIE: Here's the pattern:

- Three Creative Personality Types an Action Conduit: Dynamic, Personal, and Innovative
- Three Creative Personality Types a Perception Conduit: Innovative, Visionary, and Magnetic
- Three Creative Personality Types a Relationship Conduit: Magnetic, Psychic, and Personal
- Three Creative Personality Types a Power Conduit: Dynamic, Magnetic, and Visionary

At the conclusion of the first workshop, the group commits to exploring one creative personality type. We put the chart up on the wall for reference – in pencil, to allow discoveries and changes throughout the workshop process. Some categories have more than one name as a few participants continue to explore three conduits.

In a workshop setting, I fight my predilection towards monologues, but inevitably I get going on something about which I feel strongly, and speak at length about one of the issues touched on during the group's exploration of Creative Personality Types. I've restricted such digressions to the spaces between the Virtual Workshop sessions, each offered in order to place my approach to creative temperament within a larger context. Here, then, is the first of those digressions.

Digression: How do you know you are you?

This is not as ridiculous a question as it seems. Psychology, and long before that Philosophy, have dedicated immense resources to an examination of those aspects of our physiological and cognitive experiences that are linked to the sensation of selfhood. The various theories that have resulted are of interest to actors only insofar as they might be used to shed light on the intuitive creative process whereby an actor presents a fictional character which strikes us as having as valid a self as any and all of us watching. Is this a *trompe d'oeil*? Do the conventions of the theatre allow us to see what we want to see? Or is a great naturalistic actor's accomplishment the creation of a series of distinct self-hoods, each made-to-order for the production in which it appears?

We have such a profound sense of self that it becomes an amusing intellectual pastime to speculate on what aspects of our experience go into providing us with that sensation. We have a sense of self because we have a self that makes its presence constantly felt. It little matters if that self is an essential element of our being or a collection of sensations that govern all of our existence. We know we have a self because it is our self that does the knowing. However, this sort of circular reasoning denies us an opportunity to dissect how selfhood is created in order, as actors, to manipulate that creation of selfhood in service of a fictional story requiring the enactment by personalities we call characters and, in naturalism, choose to present as being as much like ourselves as possible.

The collection of sensations that provide us with selfhood might be divided into the cognitive and the physiological, for the purposes of acting. In the cognitive category, we can begin with point of view. We have a sense of 'I' because we have the sensation provided by our eyes (and ears and all other sensory organs and the areas of the brain that organize these sensations into coherent patterns). Actors are familiar with the challenge of manipulating those aspects of point of view that are most accessible to manipulation. For example, attitudes to social issues. Whatever your views on racial equality, it is possible to portray a bigot by understanding such an individual's point of view. Actors quickly discover that the world looks different when you are playing a slave or a king.

Memories serve as a potent talisman of selfhood, even though we learn fairly early on in life to question whether we do in fact remember everything, or anything with complete accuracy. Actors learn to endow the fictional memories of their characters, as supplied by the playwright, with the same cognitive weight of their own memories.

We occupy a series of roles within a complex web of relationships, and these also maintain our sense of self. Over time, in retrospect we might be quite struck at how completely we've changed, so much so that someone who knew us then might be justified in not recognizing us today. But we still recognize ourselves, and therefore something more profound must provide us with this sensation of selfhood. A sudden change in role (job loss, for example) or relationship might rock us psychologically, but we retain the sense of having a self who is undergoing this trauma and which is being forced to endure these changes.

Physiologically, despite all of the changes at the cellular level, we are unequivocally a single continuous organism. The blood sample taken and frozen at birth contains the same genetic material as that collected in an autopsy. But only modern technology offers us proof of this; our actual experience is of such transformation that not one of use would ever be prepared to identify unknown adults from their baby pictures.

The physiological provides us with a subtle, never-ending, and immensely complex sensation of selfhood that runs parallel to the cognitive markers with which we are more familiar. An actor intuitively uses the physiological in the creation of alternative 'self-sensations' for the creation of a fictional character. In theory, a systematic exploration of the physiological self-sensations would greatly expand an actor's capacity to create and portray a wide range of fictional personalities, each of which would have as profound a sense of selfh as the actor's. In practice, the actor manipulates the physiological without danger to the self-sensations that provide the foundation of a singular personality. We can be thankful for this practice, and set aside the theory which suggests that an actor should ever attempt to create an entirely new sense of self.

VIRTUAL WORKSHOP SESSION TWO: EXERCISES FOR SELF-DIAGNOSIS

As the group gathers the next day, some reveal that they have changed their mind about the diagnosis they conducted yesterday. Others have not changed their minds. We adjust the wall chart accordingly.

LESLIE: Everyone's had a chance to let the ideas from our first encounter of conduits and creative temperament gestate. Some of you are now quite sure that you've identified your Creative Personality Type. Others are less sure than they were at the end of the first session. That's only natural, I think, as we're reflecting on a very complex process, and there's lots to consider.

Let's explore the possibilities further, because there's no rush to complete self-diagnosis. In fact, it's better to take your time and explore all of the possibilities as fully as possible.

Similar but Significantly Different

LESLIE: What we haven't talked about much is how the pairing of conduits affects the experience of conduits. In creative flow, there's no way to pinpoint, exclusively, a source of energy. And we don't really want that, do we? When the engine is running well, we don't want to muck around with exactly what component is contributing what to the smooth functioning. Whenever we need to tinker with the engine, we can use our intellect to launch a specific vector of our creativity, but every other element will function at the same time. It's an engine, a collective, an integrated system.

For the purposes of this exploration, we can manipulate our engines a little, and we can also learn by exploring the subtle differences between the types, which comes in part from the pairing of conduits, which greatly affects the experience of creativity.

We'll start with something purely physical because it's first thing in the morning and a good work-out will prepare us for the rest of the day's explorations.

Dance of the Yin/Yang

I call this 'dance of the yin/yang' which I can explain best by a demonstration, with Iris and Polly. How many of you have done the mirror exercise with a partner?

Not every hand is raised, so Iris and Polly demonstrate. They stand facing each other, an arm's length apart. Polly begins moving her arms slowly and Iris mirrors her movement. As I call out 'switch' Iris takes over leading the movement.

THE YIN/YANG DANCE OF ACTION

LESLIE: You can see, in this exercise, how Iris leads slowly enough so that Polly's movements match hers perfectly. When they switch leaders, it's so smooth that an observer can't tell who is leading. This is the exercise that we're going to build on.

At the heart of the mirror exercise is simple action, and the trading off of the tasks of initiating movement. Remember that initiating is one side of the yin/yang of the Action conduit. The other side is Reacting.

With Polly beginning as the initiator, let's see if we can get a true Action yin/yang going. Polly will initiate an activity, and Iris will react with another activity. Iris, trust your intuition, and simply react in whatever way seems to come out of whatever Polly does. When I ring the bell, Iris will initiate, and Polly will react. Then, when the bell rings, switch back, and so on. Ideally, the flow of movement should never stop, and the passing of initiating should be invisible to anyone watching.

The two women move around each other, connecting through movement and passing leadership back and forth. After a few miscues, their dance becomes one fluid duet.

IRIS: I have to say that it was impossible to separate reacting from initiating, even when I was supposed to be leading. Polly would give me something in a reaction that would spark the next movement I initiated.

LESLIE: That's the experience of the Action conduit, and why the yin/yang symbol is such a good metaphor. There's really no separating the two components, not when they're linked to the free flow of creative energy. Someone without an Action Conduit would find it easier to separate the two sides, to do one at a time.

Chain of Sharing in 12 pairs

Dynamic & Magnet share Power
Magnet & Psychic share Relationship
Psychic & Innovative share Perception
Innovative & Personal share Action
Personal & Psychic share Relationship
Psychic & Visionary share Perception
Visionary & Dynamic share Power
Dynamic & Personal share Action
Personal & Magnetic share Relationship
Magnetic & Visionary share Power
Visionary & Innovative share Perception
Innovative & Dynamic share Action

POLLY: That was fun. I could see using something like that as a warm up for scene work. It builds trust and a great connection with your partner.

THE YIN/YANG DANCE OF RELATIONSHIP
LESLIE: Spoken like a true Relationship actor! And that's where we'll go next. I'm going to build on the initiate/react dance by adding another component, a movement metaphor for relationships. Now, this is going to make best sense to Polly, but we're going to build a chain of sharing that allows for interesting combinations. By 'chair of sharing' (Figure 5) I mean a pairing of actors who have one shared conduit, for that 'click' of flowing creative energy, but who also bring contrasting conduits; we could work our way through the group with such a chain.

First, here's the basic movement pattern for Relationship. Let's get everyone on their feet to explore together. To get into the emotional energy of this movement you have to tap your human fight/flight instinct. Think of all the vulnerable organs contained in our torsos. If we're under threat, we're not only going to tighten all our muscles in preparation for fight or flight, we're also going to close ourselves off, through some sort of crossing motion. We find a modern residue of that movement in the crossed arms or twisted presentation that signals closure to Relationship connection.

Everyone has fun creating the posture of disapproving snobs.
LESLIE: In contrast, we have the open stance of the invitation to embrace, also familiar − think a big, wide-armed, smiling greeting . So now Iris and Polly can demonstrate the yin/yang dance of the

Relationship dance. Two 'rules' to this movement pattern. First, the movement must never stop. Don't open your arms, lock them in that position, and move around the space. Remember that relationships are always in an active state of change. You're always opening, or closing.

Second rule: whatever emotional shift your partner is exploring, you're going in the opposite direction. So, if Iris opens, Polly reacts by closing, and vice versa. I've set up here something more dramatic than two people who hate each other or two people in perfect accord. This yin/yang dance is going to be about needing something that is being denied you. Because when you, Polly, want to initiate a connection, Iris will be shutting herself off from you. And when you decide you've had enough and close down, that will be the moment she changes and starts to open to you.

Now, you two are Action actors, and I know you can take even the simplest movement pattern and use it as a key to creative energy. So although the exercise might start with the simple mechanical movement of opening and closing, feel free to follow your intuitions and trust your Action conduit to take you wherever the dance leads in terms of emotional connections, subtle or overt conflicts, etc.

Take advantage of the chair of sharing: Polly, since yours is the Relationship conduit, you're the one to push the envelope in terms of authentic connecting and destroying. Iris will be using her Perception conduit, and you'll share the Action conduit.

After a brief trial that allows the women to try out the exercise and test how it might work for them, they launch themselves into an extended dance during which Polly takes primary initiating responsibilities at key moments as they explore the emerging relationship, but otherwise initiating and reacting blend into a seamless whole. They explore the range of subtle opening and withdrawing as well as aggressive, almost violent rejection and longing. As an added benefit, it is clear that these two, who have demonstrated personal animosity, connect in an intense and satisfying way as creative artists. They embrace to the applause of the group as the improvisation ends.

LESLIE: After that brilliant demonstration, such a hard act to follow, let's see how this movement dance might work for the rest of you. Let's keep using our chain of sharing. Polly, pair up with Mike, who shares your Relationship conduit. Mike, the movement could easily become mechanical, but it's your job to infuse it with all the energy of Power, your other conduit's creativity, and taking advantage of Polly's action. In other words, look for a 'click' of connection via Relationship even as you each bring your own insights. Sally, you pair up with Iris. Same thing. She's bringing this to you infused with her Action conduit's energy, and you'll experience it with a special focus on your Relationship conduit. But you two share a Perception conduit, so open yourselves to feed off each other using your heightened sensory awareness. Victor, you'll get to try it a bit later.

The pairs explore the yin/yang dance of Relationship. Each pair takes the movement exercise in quite different directions.

VICTOR: Amazing to watch how actors who share the same conduit approached each other completely differently.

LESLIE: Yes. A reminder that we need to honour diversity even as we take advantage of shared connections. What we're seeing is that the Relationship conduit, which fuels the work of Magnetic, Personal, and Psychic actors, *feels* quite different to each of those. It's the same with all of the conduits. Power, for example, which I experience as a Dynamic actor, is going to be a different type of energy when combined with Perception, in the Visionary, or with Relationship, in the Magnetic.

Our mental capacities and our physical capabilities are a different order of consideration than relationships and power, which are given shape by the social constructions with which our species surrounds itself. We all have bodies, and we all have senses and mental abilities. That's a heritage that pre-dates our entry into consciousness. We can think of the four conduits as divided between the genetic realm, what we might call the biological areas – activity, imagination, senses – as opposed to the socially constructed areas – relationship and power, which I call the cultural. In other words, an Innovative and a Magnetic actor are on opposite ends of the spectrum, the Innovative as the purest representative of humanity, and Magnetic as the purest representative of culture, society, and human history. The other four are a blend of the two realms.

Some of the difference in the experience of feeling is the result of the specific make-up of our bodies and senses, our cognitive abilities, etc. Some of it is the result of slightly different socialization, the specific variation of the cultural soup in which we swim.

THE YIN/YANG DANCE OF POWER

LESLIE: Let's combine Action and Power, now, so Victor gets a chance to explore something.

SALLY: Can you talk a bit about Power? That's the one I just don't get.

LESLIE: I'll need Victor and Mike to back me up on this. They both have Power conduits, and the thing with Power in the state of yin/yang flow is that submission and empowerment co-exist, always. Here's a spiritual way of saying it: 'Even the most powerful is humble before the divine, and even the most humble is the divine in human form.'

MIKE: I like that, a lot.

VICTOR: Do you think there's a correlation between the Power conduit and personal faith?

LESLIE: Now that's going to sidetrack us for sure. I'll offer what insight I can.

I think that we're a species that is inclined towards the transcendent, like a plant inclines towards sunlight. It can take so many different forms, whether it's a named divine being or an intuition of forces at work, like Fate, or a celebration of the marvels of the universe and the perfection of the atom. I suspect that the conduits affect how we experience inspiration in that realm of our lives. And that's about as far as I would go, until break. Back to work!

The basic movement pattern we're going to use for Power is rising and falling. Let's get everyone on their feet. One of the givens of movement, for our species, is our constant fight with gravity. I'm going to assume you've explored falling in your acting training?

General response: fight training, trust exercises, imagination work.

LESLIE: Let's tap into the primal human experience of gravity by crouching down, and slowly rising. As your muscles work, feel the tug of gravity, and feel the power of your capacity to fight it. Keep going, letting the sensation of lifting extend even when you're standing, arms up, up on your toes, eyes up, imagination taking you up to the ceiling, through the ceiling, flying up through the clouds, up through the atmosphere, breaking out into space.

Now, let's start from an imagined and enacted height, stretching up as far as we can, and slowly come down, letting gravity pull you back, giving in to gravity, slowly dropping down, closer and closer to the ground, kneeling, drop your head, and let your imagination take you down in scale so that you feel the full force of the entire gravitational field of the planet locking you forever to this place. Feel the weight of the atmosphere on your skin, pressing into your bones, dragging on your muscles.

We do this a few times — a great workout for the thighs!

LESLIE: I bet Victor and Mike have already spotted how this fits with Power.

MIKE: Rising is growing in power and authority, and kneeling is humility.

VICTOR: Which we still have today, kneeling in prayer or before a king.

LESLIE: That's very much the association our cultural institutions have made, in the long history of human religious systems and social customs. Think about the bow, with head dropped and hands away from the sides. Your body is saying, 'I humble myself before you. If you wish to cut off my head, I leave myself vulnerable to you for that purpose.'

Let's explore the yin/yang dance of Power. Like the Relationship yin/yang dance, we're going to be more interested in constant change than in fixed states. So we'll seek an experience of rising, and an experience of sinking, rather than movement down low or movement up high. Let's have everyone experiment a little. You might start upright, and explore the emotions connected to sinking to the ground, or you might start on your knees or crouching, to explore the sensation of rising up to greater power and authority.

Those of you with an Action conduit – well, just doing the movement will arouse emotions. They don't have to be humility and power exactly. Don't get hung up on anything that limits or rejects what your creative conduit offers you. Those of you with Perception conduits can use sensory awareness of movement, but memories or imagination might kick in as well. Relationship people – hang in, we'll get to you in a moment.

Everyone explores rising and sinking movement.

LESLIE: Now let's add something for the Relationship people, that also builds on Power. This will make most sense to Mike, with his Magnetic Creative Temperament, combining Power and Relationship. This is the shape the yin/yang dance will take. I'll be in the center, and when I'm standing, you all are down low. As I sink, you rise. As I rise, you sink. Let's try it once, mechanically.

We do. Everyone stands in a circle around me and we move in opposite directions.

LESLIE: This is easy for me, because as a Dynamic, with Action and Power, for me action IS power and humility, and power comes from doing and reacting. But Mike's experience of power is through people. Relationships are experienced in the context of the constantly shifting connections between people. People who theorize about power suggest that it comes from below, that people give power to their leaders. I don't know about you, but that's what I feel when you are all down, looking at me. I'm filled with power, but you're giving it to me, and you could just as easily take it back. So let's try that. The first time through, I initiated the change in direction. Now you, working as a group, initiate the rising and falling, and I'll react by falling in humility before your growing power, or rising up because you ask it of me by sinking down.

We try this. The group works easily together in the simply yin/yang paring of opposite movement.

LESLIE: Let's give Mike a chance in the middle of the circle, and then Victor. Mike will combine Power and Relationship, and Victor will blend Power with Perception.

The group tries both explorations.

LESLIE: I found it interesting the subtle differences between the two versions, Mike's and Victor's. Magnetic versus Visionary. What did you on the outside of the circle experience.

IRIS: Mike's contained lots of striking connection with individuals, and he really seemed like a father when he was standing over us. I got the feeling that Victor was praying when he was on his knees and dropped his head, almost as if we were disembodied spirits tormenting him, and then he looked up, almost like he was receiving his power from heaven, and then we knelt in awe of him.

SALLY: I felt that too. Victor was way scarier.

POLLY: Except there was one time, Mike looked at me, and I felt – this guy could cut off people's heads.

VICTOR: I got that from Mike.

The Magnetic Yin/Yang Dance

LESLIE: Because Mike has both Relationship and Power, he's going to help us take the yin/yang dance to the next level. We're going to have two movement patterns working at once. We'll have the opening and closing of Relationship plus the rising and falling of Power. Mike can demonstrate. We have two conduits, two movements each, four combinations: rising plus closing, rising plus opening, falling plus opening, falling plus closing. Let's look at them one by one.

Rising and closing, which is a movement metaphor for the growing sensations of power and authority combined with the severing of connections and possibly even moving towards destruction. That would be the 'off with your head' type of energy.

Then you could sink while opening. This would be the sensation of humility, giving power over to someone else, while opening yourself to the most vulnerable sort of connection.

POLLY: The king falls in love. Arthur and Guinevere.

LESLIE: Third possibility: start the humble position and closed in order to explore rising while opening. This might be an angry, oppressed person who becomes more prestigious and at the same time opens himself to connections with people.

VICTOR: It's like the power of love opens him up to being a better person.

MIKE: That's actually the story of my life, by the way.

A momentary pause as we silently acknowledge the simple honesty of this shared insight.

LESLIE: For the fourth combination, we have sinking and closing.

Someone takes power from you, or you give it up, and at the same time you close yourself off from them and maybe even figure out a way to destroy from below.

POLLY: Wouldn't it be easier to destroy when you have power?

SALLY: Oh, no, humble and destruction – that's your typical passive aggressive.

Mike does the four movements, then all mimic the pattern.

Magnetic Pairs

LESLIE: Mike's demonstrated the basic movement variables in the dance. This is the yin/yang of Relationship in the context of Power. Just a reminder of the only 'rules' – don't lock in any one position. Keep working in opposite directions so one is always closing when the other is opening, and one is always rising while the other is sinking. Other than that, stay connected, and trust your creative energy to take you somewhere interesting, maybe dangerous. However, rather than doing exactly what Mike does, you're all going to access creativity in slightly different ways. Let's watch pairs of people explore the dance, and see how the combinations play out.

We'll start with Mike and Polly. Trust each other and let something happen. Start with the dance, stick to the rules, but open yourself to your unique experience and draw on what your partner brings.

Mike and Polly try the movement exploration. The group shares their reactions.

LESLIE: Let me put your responses into the framework of the temperaments. The movement pattern of the dance is Mike's type – Magnetic, Power & Relationship – but remember that this exploration through movement is geared towards those who share the Action conduit, which Mike does not. So the exercise really benefited from Polly, who is Personal, Action and Relationship. Just by doing the actions, Polly can access creative energy through her Action conduit, which fills the movement with authenticity. There are also subtle shifts in leading and following at work in their dance.

Their shared Relationship conduit infused the movement with rich possibilities, particularly in their use of proximity – getting closer and pulling apart, a movement they used as another way of suggesting the opening to connection and intimacy and the separateness of closing.

Finally, Mike's Power conduit allowed for authentic energy to flow into the rising and falling action, which Polly reacted to, which they both experienced as relationship complexity.

SALLY: It was like a whole relationship, loving, abusive, breaking up, getting back together.

POLLY: I understand Power, and definitely the times when one of us was standing and the other was kneeling – those felt right. But for me it was a vibe Mike puts out that pushes my buttons, which is why my acting is so much better with some partners than others.

IRIS: Only if you keep falling back on the same old relationship stuff. But I saw a freedom of movement, without the typical Polly mannerisms. You played a striking character opposite Mike's forceful king. I really saw Arthur and Guinevere.

LESLIE: Polly, you say your best acting comes with certain partners. Is that something you'd like to change?

POLLY: Well . . . I guess. Because I don't always get to choose who I work with.

LESLIE: My hope is that these explorations will set the groundwork for greater creative flexibility in any of a variety of match ups, as you learn how to draw upon the insights offered by people with different conduits. Let's keep the issue of easy versus challenging partnerships in mind. Victor, why don't you give this exercise a try, working with Mike.

Laughter – these two have a complex relationship.

LESLIE: The two guys share Power, as we've already seen. But Mike brings the Relationship conduit, while Victor brings Perception, because Mike is Magnetic, and Victor is Visionary. Remember that this is the Magnetic yin/yang dance to explore the power of relationships. Victor, use your awareness and whatever imagination or memory impulses that

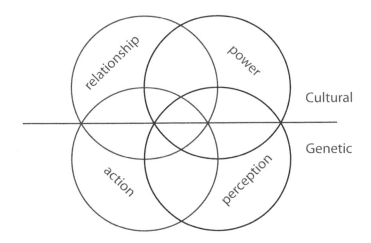

FIGURE 6 The World of Considerations

67

arise, while Mike taps his Relationship conduit, and build on the natural connection you share through the power.

For us watching, remember that neither of these two has an Action conduit, so we'll be interested to see how they blend their conduit work with this simple activity, which is, for them, a consideration, not a conduit.

MIKE: Can you talk about considerations? I'm not sure I'm clear on that term.

LESLIE: Whenever I talk about considerations (see Figure 6), I'm switching my focus back to the chameleon side of your work as an actor. There's a great deal that you're responsible for, when you contribute to the success of the production by transforming yourself to blend into the world of the play. When you survey the list of things to work on, I call that list your considerations. Some of these considerations link directly to your conduits, and some are not.

Think about those aspects of the actor's craft that are based upon the genetic predispositions of our species. So, we have the flexibility of our communication systems that allow us to alter our voices, our facial expressions, and the way we move. We also have that remarkable instrument of the mind, and all the uses we can put it to. We also have those aspects of our work that are connected to the vertical and horizontal connections that form the larger cultural context for everything we explore.

POLLY: In other words, the considerations match up with the conduits.

LESLIE: Yes.

VICTOR: And when you talk about educating our Considerations, you're telling us to pay some attention to the two areas in which we don't have conduits.

LESLIE: Even more than that, I'm saying that all four areas need special attention, as you blend the charismatic with the chameleon in your acting training. In all four areas of consideration: your work on your body, your work on your mind, your consideration of inter-personal relationships, and your analysis of systems of power, you'll be aiming for a blend of inspiration and perspiration.

SALLY: A blend of flow and effort?

LESLIE: Yes.

After a quick refresher on the rules, Victor and Mike treat us to a very physical, competitive dance.

LESLIE: Okay, I can see you two are battling for control, in the Power yin/yang, being forced into humility and fighting your way up into power. But that means that only the closed, destroying side of the Relationship conduit is in play. You open yourself as a ploy, or reluctantly, usually combined with another movement like pulling back or half turning away.

Consider your butts firmly kicked, and try again. You're going to have to take a giant risk in your relationship exploration. You're going to have to give up control, and allow something to happen, coming from the construction side of the Relationship conduit.

SALLY: I felt like you were in a battle to the death.

LESLIE: Exactly. But why don't you try a slightly different image, that of enemies who respect and admire each other, who, in a different situation would be best friends.

SALLY: Or lovers. Who are also competitors.

VICTOR: David and Jonathon. Fighting to the death.

The second dance is much richer, with greater variety in movement and more interesting blending of complex feeling. General congratulations as Mike and Victor celebrate a productive exploration.

LESLIE: Mike, you and I'll watch as two different pairs explore the yin/yang dance of Power and Relationship. Let's put Victor with Iris and Sally with Polly.

Victor and Iris share the Perception conduit, so their heightened awareness of each plus the imagination and memory energy they bring will open up some interesting creativity. Iris brings the Action conduit, so for her the movement alone should offer some interesting creative juice. Victor brings the Power side of the dance. Neither of them has a Relationship conduit, but that's okay. They can bring their disciplined consideration to the relationship component of the dance, and use the simple movement pattern of the dance to guide them.

Polly and Sally share the Relationship conduit, so they're going to have fun with the opening and closing movement. But neither of them has a Power conduit. Instead, Polly brings the Action conduit, so trust those movements of rising and sinking to open you to feeling. Sally, you have awareness plus memory and imagination to draw upon.

Okay, let's see two pairs exploring the yin/yang dance of Relationship and Power.

Various insights result from this exploration. Everyone is struck by the diversity in the group's experience of conduits.

LESLIE: We've accessed Relationship and Power energy. The fact that these two are both found in the cultural realm means that these are going to be particularly suited for explorations of socialization. We've used movement for our exploration, which of course invites Action energy.

SALLY: What about the Perception people?

LESLIE: Good point. The three Creative Personality types with access to the Perception Conduit are Visionary, Psychic, and Innovative. They share that wonderful creative energy you can access so effortlessly, from imagination and memory as well as from sensory awareness in the here and now. We can expect Visionary actors to be particularly aware of the POWER of that mental capacity, and to use it to empower them as an actor. We expect the creative Perception of Innovative actors to be linked to Action, both initiating and reacting. Sally, as a Psychic your perception is experienced within the context of relationship; we'd expect your capacities to be particularly attuned to other human beings, right?

SALLY: That's so me!

Certainty and Uncertainty

General discussion of who is sure of their type and who is still considering options.

POLLY: The thing that most clicked for me, so far, was when you made some crack about me wanting to stage the improv.

LESLIE: Was that what I said?

POLLY: It was when Victor and Mike were brothers, and Sally was watching them, and I suggested the scenario and what Iris and I would be doing.

LESLIE: My apologies. I didn't mean that as a criticism. It's a function of your Action conduit, isn't it, that you'd want to shape the scene with activity? And your Relationship conduit naturally led you to suggest interesting relationships.

POLLY: Whatever. The point is that I've always thought of myself as a Relationship actor – it was the conduit that I recognized first, though I went back and forth on Perception and Power. I have a vivid imagination, and I'm very alert when I'm acting with someone, totally keyed on whatever they're feeding me. I also like to be in control, in the sense of organized and disciplined, well-prepared. But I don't mind being directed, I like a strong director.

LESLIE: But you decided finally on the Personal? Which is Relationship and Action

POLLY: Well, I still have an open mind, but I can see that my awareness is really my reaction to what the other person does, and that my preparation and taking direction are more part of my professionalism. It was when Iris and I did our movement that I realized how completely creative action and reaction is for me, just that focus alone, and how much my relationship work is really about doing things, and reacting to what my partner does. When I'm not getting stuff, it's because I'm not getting things to respond to. It's my Action conduit that's unhappy, as much or more than my Relationship conduit.

Part of why I'm figuring this out has to do with socialization, like you said. I realized that there have been some experiences in my life that have taught me to avoid reacting. I won't go into the details, but I'll just say there was a time when my impulsive actions got me in real trouble.

What I loved about the dance improv with Iris was that it was just movement, and I sort of turned off the Relationship side, and so in a funny way there was more trust, more comfort, than if we'd been playing a big emotional scene. And there was a freedom to react, and the emotions that came were calmer, if that makes sense.

IRIS: I felt it too. I trusted you, completely, which is amazing if you consider it.

SALLY: Maybe because you trusted yourself? More than if you had to initiate and react in a relationship scene?

POLLY: You are psychic! That's it, exactly. Also, we're two women, so I didn't bring that automatic association with the dangers of impulsive action.

SALLY: I'm not the only one with Perception, am I?

LESLIE: Let's explore that conduit in the next exercise.

Perception Pairs

LESLIE: Some of you are quite sure you've found a good match; others remain sceptical. I encourage everyone to view the label as temporary until we've explored the individual types.

We'll test your intuitions against another fun acting challenge.

I'm very fond of Anita Jesse's 'I want you to' scenes, as tools for exploring Creative Personality types. I've borrowed these from her book, *The Playing is the Thing* – where she provides 50 of these.

We'll use a few of my favourites.

First the rules: you'll work in pairs, and each will be given one line. I will say the line, and you'll repeat it after me, several times if necessary, because it's important that you use exactly what you're given, those words and no others, in that exact order. I'm going to add a few more restrictions. You are required to say your assigned line, over and over. You can explore intonation, pauses, volume, speed, inflection, in fact any and every strategy for shifting the way you say your line. You can also explore movement, including physical contact within the boundaries of safety: no violent or sexual contact although those emotional qualities can of course be suggested in other ways.

You won't be able to discuss given circumstances in advance. Be prepared for the scenario to float free; as with any improv, just go with whatever happens even if it seems to shift.

There are a couple of traps you'll want to avoid. The first is that you become mechanical in your delivery, simply repeating yourself, hoping that alone will gain what you want and need. It won't. Another trap is for one person to always initiate, and the other always to respond, so that the two lines, in that order, are always a unit.

Don't establish one way of relating and hold onto it. If the relationship is adversarial, be sure to explore the possibilities for intimacy, tenderness, caring, and be sure to explore a shift in power several times in the scene.

Above all, you'll want to be hyper-aware of whatever your partner is doing. Use all of your senses, prepare yourself to react to whatever comes at you, open yourself to the scene as it plays out, without pre-planning the outcome.

Without going any further, let's have a pair give it a try, to see how it works.

Victor and Mike leap to their feet, eager to try. Their lines: Victor: 'I want you to admit you let me down.' Mike: 'I don't owe you anything.' They toss these back and forth in a variety of intonations for a few minutes.

LESLIE: A bit of coaching, before we use these as a tool for exploration of Creative Personality types. First, you guys got right away the simple perfection of these two-line scenes. The 'I want' character has a clear-cut need, as set by the text. The other character cannot, because of the text he's been given, be anything but an obstacle to that need. This is the perfect recipe for conflict and connection – the perfect recipe for dramatic action.

You noticed, also, that I forced you to push through the first, most obvious approaches, there came a time when you locked a bit, and it got a bit mechanical and repetitious. Then, because I didn't stop the exercise, you really got ingenious, and began exploring alternatives.

MIKE: I felt the given circumstances changed. Is that allowed?

LESLIE: Since you didn't consult on the fictional context of the scene, you were already in no man's land with regard to details. So, yes, that sort of change is fine.

VICTOR: For me, it was more that I finally started to change my strategies. Which I do in real life. If shouting won't get what I want, I try some smooth talking.

POLLY: I liked when you shifted gears, like Leslie suggested, and it wasn't always Victor starting and Mike responding. It changed, so that Mike shifted things and Victor responded.

SALLY: I saw real complexity, particularly after they got past the obvious, like you said.

IRIS: Yes, and their movement was much more varied. They tried all sorts of different approaches, trying to get a resolution to the conflict.

LESLIE: Did you have an imaginary situation in mind? I'm asking those watching, not Mike and Victor.

SALLY: Absolutely. Completely. From the second they started.

LESLIE: Another example of how the audience is willing to meet us far more than half way, if we let them. They'll create their own meaning if we give them something, anything, to engage with.

MIKE: After the boring bit, when I wondered when you were going to let us stop, and then we pushed past and got the point – I felt the scene could go on almost indefinitely. I had no idea how it would end, when you stopped us. Earlier, I had a scenario going that pretty much ended one way.

LESLIE: That's a good point. You know how, when we play a role in a scripted play, we know how it ends for the character, but the character can't know? These little two-line scenes have no ending. That's another reason why they help you get into the moment. You can't play an ending that hasn't been written yet.

Sally and Polly have a chance. Their lines: Sally: 'I want you to admit you brought this on yourself.' Polly: 'You never see my side of it.'

LESLIE: Okay, before you begin, let's recap. Sally, you're exploring the possibility that you're one of the Perception types: Psychic, Visionary, and Innovative. That means that you can count on using your heightened sensory awareness to connect with whatever Polly offers you in the scene. You'll also be able to let your imagination invent whatever scenario works for you, and also draw upon memory. That's such a rich and intuitive source of creative energy for you, you can almost let it function on its own. If, however, you ever feel the scene grind into a mechanical, dead end, you can kick-start the scene with some specific attention to your Perception conduit. When the flow dries up, remember to TRULY listen, watch, smell, touch, and taste, and you'll reconnect with Polly.

Polly, you're exploring either Personal (Action and Relationship) or Magnetic (Power and Relationship). That means that you're going to be able to count on the Relationship conduit with some confidence. Same as with Sally, you can pretty much just let it take care of itself. Whenever you feel the flow slipping away, you can consciously kick-start your charismatic, creative energy again by opening up to Sally or, if you're open, by closing off. But my guess is that you'll be fuelled richly by that conduit, given the nature of the two-line scene.

Sally and Polly both have Power as a possible second conduit. Sally might be Visionary, which is Power and Perception. Polly might be Magnetic, which is Relationship and Power. To test just how this conduit might work for them, let's pre-set one aspect of the given circumstances – their relative power. Victor, since that's a conduit of yours, any suggestions?

VICTOR: Mother and daughter?

MIKE: Or professor and student. Then they can play they're closer in age.

POLLY: I'm in her office, complaining.

LESLIE: But the power can't all be in one direction.

VICTOR: Polly's got some hold over Sally, and Sally knows it.

LESLIE: Let's not go too far in specifics. We have two important ideas, one of which gives Sally power over Polly, and the other gives Polly power over Sally. Remember, both of you, that the power is linked to a greater power, larger than both of you – in this scenario that's the university system, which gives power to professors, but also controls professors and can punish them severely if they step out of line. So Polly has transgressed, and Sally is somehow connected with the punishment. At the same time, Sally is vulnerable to that greater power, and Polly is somehow connected to that possibility.

MIKE: And they both know it, right?

LESLIE: Yes, that's necessary because the two-line scene gives no text for the exchange of such information. One final instruction. Shape the scene to be a little demonstration of the complexities of power. But when you feel yourself running dry, fall back on your known conduits: Perception for Sally and Relationship for Polly.

They try the scene. It's a moderate success.

LESLIE: I didn't let that run on too long, because I want to give you a chance to explore some of the other options for second conduits. For both of you, the power element makes sense, and some interesting things come out. But you're also drawn to the possibility of another conduit, and there has to be a reason for that. It might be that you're still exploring the ideas, or that your Power conduit is muted, as a result of social pressures. Or it might be that you're not, in fact, Visionary and Magnetic, but something else.

Polly, let's explore Personal, which is Relationship and Action. Sally, we'll shift you to Perception and Action, to see what happens. This time through, same thing with regard to using your known conduit. But toss out the scenario of the university professor and the student. Instead, let's find a scenario that is built on activity, one in which sometimes one, then the other, initiates. Suggestions? Iris, you're pretty sure you have an Action conduit? Let's take advantage of your creativity.

IRIS: How about one of them's sorting a bunch of stuff and the other's trying to tidy up the place.

POLLY: Like room mates? And my parents are coming for a visit?

LESLIE: Sounds good. Sally, would you like some real objects to play with?

The class gathers all sorts of junk from back packs, and they start the scene. After a moment, it runs aground.

LESLIE: Sally, it's important that you play with Action, not just Perception. You need to connect with Polly, through the shared exploration of Action. Remember that you need to initiate activity sometimes, and also you need to react, spontaneously, to whatever Polly does. And Polly, don't lose track of the complexity of the relationship. Watch out for the trap of being entirely closed, through anger. Blend in the other side, the vulnerability, the warmth.

They try again. The scene is more successful.

Rethinking First Impressions

SALLY: I don't think Action is one of my conduits. I loved everything that Polly did, but I realized that I was really responding to relationship stuff. I was playing with opening and closing, and to be honest I didn't think about reacting or initiating very much at all.

IRIS: But what you did was great!

LESLIE: What that suggests, though, is that the activation of a conduit produced creative energy that flowed into her actions, rather than actions themselves generating the creative flow.

SALLY: I'm pretty sure now I'm Perception and Relationship.

LESLIE: Polly?

POLLY: If I have to choose, it would be Action rather than Power. I really like just doing things, and reacting to what she's doing. That gave me a sense of control, though. Is that still Power?

LESLIE: Control is one side of the Power conduit. You'll know it's one of your conduits if the opposite, the voluntary giving up of control, the humility or submission, is equally inspirational.

POLLY: I'm leaning towards Relationship and Action.

LESLIE: Great. Let's shift things a little, and pair people up for interesting blends of similar and different conduits. Iris, you're Innovative, correct?

IRIS: Action and Perception.

LESLIE: Let's put you with one of the guys. Mike, you're Magnetic?

MIKE: Relationship and Power.

LESLIE: That makes you and Iris exact opposites, which can be a rich and fulfilling acting partnership, but presents a real challenge for finding the 'click' of effortless connection, so let's wait on that one. Victor?

VICTOR: I'm Power and Perception, so Iris and I would have Perception in common.

LESLIE: Perfect. Let's agree on one or two aspects of the given circumstances – and add something interesting for you two to imagine. Let's put this in a specific setting.

SALLY: At the beach.

LESLIE: A few more details? Not the scenario, but sensory reality?

SALLY: Hot. Perfect sand. Warm water.

MIKE: But sharks out there.

POLLY: And a storm brewing on the horizon.

SALLY: Deserted. No shade, and it's the ocean – very salty.

LESLIE: Excellent. We can tell, just by the way the two of you received each of those suggestions, that your imagination is fired up by those details. Here are your lines. For IRIS: 'I want you to tell me why you are doing this to me.' For VICTOR: 'This isn't about you.'

As partners, sustain each other's creativity through your shared Perception conduit. You've got your imaginations, which will go off in different directions but feed creative energy into the scene. To bind you in the here-and-now connection, you've got your sensory awareness of each other. Really see, really listen, really smell and touch and taste.

In addition, Victor, you can play all sorts of variations with regard to power. Explore vulnerability, humility, submission, giving up of control. Also explore command, authority, empowerment, responsibility. Remember, also, that power isn't just between you two. It's also the power of the sea. The infinity of sand, the vastness of the ocean. It's about fate, God, whatever higher power you want to invoke. It's about your power over the fragile elements of nature you could freely destroy, the sensation of mastery over your body, anything like that.

And for Iris, fill the scene with activity. Initiate some things, react to others. Don't forget that you can react to things that you imagine happening on the beach, or real things in this room. In other words, it's not just Victor who offers you things to react to, and all your initiations of activity do not have to be connected with him.

Just as your shared conduit sustains your partnership, build on your differences to expand your exploration. Iris, suck up all you can from Victor's insights into power. Victor, build on the blocking that Iris discovers through her creative, intuitive explorations.

Neither of you has a Relationship conduit. However, you understand relationships, and everything that you explore using the other three conduits can, will, and should flow into the complexities of the relationship between these two, and between you as actors in the scene.

This is a strong improvisation, with lots of inventive interaction using just two lines.

Acting Habits

POLLY: Everyone got to do the type of acting they do best – Sally's very emotional memory work, Iris as a dancer, and Victor doing his King act.

LESLIE: I'm not sure if 'getting to do the type of acting you do best' is a cop out or a good alignment of creative temperament. Obviously, you'd want to expand your range as an actor through careful attention to the flow of your creative energies into a wide variety of characters and performance styles. And you don't want to fall back on the familiar, what you know you already can do, especially when exploring new possibilities in a relatively risk-free environment like a workshop. But I'd be interested in hearing from the others in response to Polly's comment.

SALLY: I know what she means. It was like all the energy flowed into a familiar shape, whatever was handy. But that was mostly because I was trying to pay attention to exploring conduits, and didn't take any time –

LESLIE: I didn't allow you any time!

SALLY: True. But I think Polly's right. I could have taken a bigger risk. Because I was getting into some new things during the preparation.

IRIS: I felt like I was taking real risks.

POLLY: I'm not criticizing.

IRIS: I think you are.

LESLIE: Let me jump in here. Clearly, in order to learn and grow we need a blend of butt-kicking to keep us moving forward as creative artists – and there's nothing more tempting than the 'if it ain't broke, don't fix it' school of acting – and sensitivity to difference in process. Polly's challenge was valid, but having heard your assessment, now we can all applaud and support your achievement. Victor, we haven't heard from you.

VICTOR: I'm like Sally, I think. Some of what happened was 'same old, same old.' I love performing, and I let that get in the way. Sorry.

LESLIE: It was enjoyable for the group as an audience. Did you risk anything new?

VICTOR: Sort of. What I got from this was how connected power and imagination are for me. And awareness. If I'd been really, really brave, I'd have given Mike a lot more power over me.

LESLIE: This has been a good demonstration of how, by exploring and taking ownership of your creative temperament, you can set challenges for yourself as actors. Remember that the conduits have the potential to access the most profound levels of our humanity. Together, the two conduits are bigger than the sum of their individual components. The energy they unleash can fuel any character, any dramatic situation, any performance style, provided you've worked on the basic skills required of the truly charismatic actor.

Reality Check

MIKE: You have to find the real for the audience to believe in your reality.

LESLIE: I'm not sure that's true. I think that audiences want to have an experience, and your job is to get out of the way so that they can. I place greater emphasis on the disciplined flexibility of an actor's transformative power than on the psychological manipulations of sensations of reality.

What you call 'finding the real' I call authentication. If it had to feel real to the actors in order for the audience to believe, I'm not sure how opera or Snow White and the Seven Dwarfs could work, and they do. So do anti-realist plays and outrageous farces.

Authentication is, for me, the releasing of an actor's unique, individual energy into the artificial framework of the character. The character is not a real person, even in the most naturalistic of plays, but the actor's charismatic energy is real. I'd also argue that the conduits allow an actor to reach a profound level of human experience, something beyond the conscious experience of social norms that we call 'reality.' If Victor doing Henry V gives me goose bumps, it's not because I believe he's channelling Henry Plantagenet, but because he's accessing something strikingly true, and bigger than Victor or Shakespeare combined. If Victor tells me he believes he's Henry when he does the speech, I'm going to book an appointment for him with a mental health worker, cause it's time for the loony bin when someone's hold on reality is that shaky.

IRIS: So you don't believe that we have to become the character to find the emotional complexity and depth of the scene?

LESLIE: It's a different metaphor I'm using. 'Become the character' means, I think, releasing real, authentic, personal energy into the fictional framework of the character. So, yes, metaphorically rather than literally, that's becoming the character, because it's your energy that infuses the actions of your body and the concentration of your awareness and imagination.

SALLY: I like to think that each character is a part of me, that I bring out and polish up so it matches what the production needs.

LESLIE: That's another metaphor for what I'm describing. I'd put it this way: you use your conduits to draw upon energy from your psyche, and your disciplined consideration of character offers the shape that is then visible as the character to others.

Stanislavsky and Conduits

POLLY: So does that mean you don't use Stanislavsky?

LESLIE: Because I consider an actor's expression of emotions part of the chameleon craft, I'm very concerned that actors develop the capacity to express a wide range of emotions with subtlety and in a variety of ways. And for that, I find Stanislavsky very useful.

VICTOR: Now that's a surprise. I got the impression you're anti-Method.

LESLIE: Not really. Stanislavsky was a man of his times, limited in the same way Freud was limited, but Stanislavsky's writings document such a wide range of explorations, that there's something there for every Creative Personality type. Also, Stanislavsky is my model for a toolbox teacher. He encouraged his students and also his disciples to make use of whatever worked and to keep experimenting so that new approaches could emerge that suited different countries, different companies of actors, different production styles.

POLLY: That's ironic, because now he's used to prove that there's only one way to good acting.

LESLIE: By some teachers, yes. And the benefits of legacy teaching cannot be denied. If you studied under someone who helped you to develop a process that works reliably, you want to pass it on. If you can study with someone who offers a clear and coherent articulation of that process, even if it doesn't match your temperament, then your craft will be greatly enriched by their insights.

MIKE: You just have to tune them out whenever they say, 'This is the only way.'

IRIS: Or, 'If you don't use this approach, your acting will never be any good.'

LESLIE: I agree that some teachers can be tyrannical, but think for a moment what the best of them are really saying. It's quite simply, 'This way works.' And that's true. I challenge each of you, to think for a moment. Haven't you, at some point in this workshop, had a similar thought? All you Perception people, when I say that I simply don't experience images the way you do, wasn't there a moment when you blinked a few times and said to yourself, 'You don't?' Or the Relationship people. When I said that I simply don't experience my acting in terms of relationship, the way you do. I think one of you even said, 'How could you not?'

> **Emotion Words**
>
> embarrassed
> frantic
> nervous
> terrified
> ruthless
> spiteful
> awkward
> jealous

We have to accept that our creative experiences are so vivid, so natural, so completely true and integrated into every other aspect of our humanity, that it's not a bizarre conclusion to arrive at – that everyone else functions the same way. And when we add our experiences watching good acting – when we're receiving through our conduits as well – is it any wonder that the whole idea of Creative Personality types is counter-intuitive?

SALLY: Meaning?

LESLIE: Our intuitions tell us the opposite of what I've been teaching you. But once you've realized the diversity all around you, you can see what previously you'd never have imagined.

There's a saying, you've probably heard it, often at art galleries. 'I'm not an expert, but I know what I like.' Artists respond, 'You like what you know.' Another variation on that: 'Seeing is believing.' True enough. But it's also true that we only see what we believe to be there.

Emotion Words via Stanislavsky

You've succeeded in side-tracking me from our explorations, but enough talking. Let's get to work.

I want to start with a list of emotion words (Figure 7). I've taken these from an exercise in the very first, Stanislavsky-based acting textbook, I used 30 plus years ago, Charles McGaw's *Acting is Believing*. The title says it all.

I know this will be old hat to you, but I want to go back to the basics. So imagine this is an introductory class, and we're going to learn about objectives, obstacles, given circumstances, and emotional memory. Let's pick a word to work on together.

IRIS: Ruthless.

LESLIE: Everyone drop in on that word.

Puzzled looks.

LESLIE: That's my term for when you isolate yourself, physically and aurally – by spreading out in the space and creating a bubble of awareness so that you can zoom in on your own voice. Then you say the word, over and over. Not mechanically, but with awareness of how your muscles and breath creates the sound. Between each sounding, you let the word work on your imagination, your memory, your intellect. What does it mean? How is it used? Make up sentences in which it might appear, then say the word aloud. Dropping in is a way of taking ownership of the sense of the word – two meanings of 'sense' – as in its meaning, and its sensuality when spoken aloud. You're blending your explorations to unify making sense and sensing.

They drop in on 'ruthless.'

LESLIE: Now, without any prompting, even beginning actors would bring conduit energy to their preliminary explorations of an emotion word. It's almost impossible to avoid, given what is encoded in that sequence of sounds through the instrument of language. How about you each contribute, according to your conduits, what a beginning actor might experience. Shall we start with the Relationship people?

MIKE: Absolutely, because the use of a word like ruthless within a relationship – that's powerful.

POLLY: Like slamming a door in someone's face, someone who needs you and who's reaching out for you.

SALLY: The second Iris said the word, I remembered something that happened to me.

LESLIE: Memory is part of Perception.

SALLY: I know, but it's Relationship as well. Because it was how I felt I had to be, to break off the relationship.

LESLIE: Other Perception things? Iris? Victor?

IRIS: Not so much a memory, but a set of images. Mostly of people, but also a massive storm – that came out of an image of a massive army sweeping across a group of defenders.

VICTOR: I had memories, like Sally, but also some images, specially when I was making up sentences that would use the word. I liked doing that. It reminded me of vocabulary lessons in Grade 6. We'd learn the definition and then use it in a sentence. Mine were always totally bizarre. Drove my teacher crazy.

LESLIE: How about power? That's how I access a word like ruthless.

VICTOR: For me, power's in there with the images. Someone or something hugely domineering, crushing someone. Or someone going up against a ruthless force, voluntarily.

MIKE: Risking everything and maybe even defeating the ruthless dictator, who's blinded almost because he's so powerful. That's really like an idea that came to me.

LESLIE: That leaves us Action. Polly? Iris?

POLLY: I kept thinking of people doing things, or having things done to them, by other people. I didn't think of forces of nature at all. When I hear ruthless, I think people.

IRIS: My images were very active. But another thing I noticed. I was reacting to my images. My body was getting tense and the way I'd say the word changed.

LESLIE: That's the other side of Perception, and no one's commented on that yet. How the word felt when you said it. Awareness of your tongue, lips, mouth, breath . . .

SALLY: I have to keep reminding myself not to go off into my imagination. It's hard, because the minute I come back to here and now, all I can focus on is the sound of everyone else saying the word over and over.

LESLIE: Did you find that interesting, in any way?

SALLY: Distracting. Yes, interesting and that's why it was distracting. I'd have liked to just listen.

LESLIE: The awareness side of your Perception conduit feeds into your aural receptors. That's good to know. You can put into your toolkit a simple reminder – really listen to HOW your partner is saying the words, and you'll always be in the here and now.

Okay, let's continue with our imaginary introductory acting class. Let's have some quick definitions. Objectives?

IRIS: Isn't objectives another way of finding the action? We were taught to replace the emotion word, which will result in indicating, with 'I want to DO something' – and the something had to be an active verb.

SALLY: With a target. Actions are always towards someone.

VICTOR: Or against an obstacle. The larger the obstacle, the stronger the fight.

LESLIE: And to identify the target or obstacle, don't you create given circumstances?

MIKE: Yes, and it's also a technique for reading plays. What did the playwright set out as the 'rules' of the world of the play.

POLLY: And for your character. The facts that you have to start with.

LESLIE: And where does emotional memory fit in?

SALLY: That's what you use to bring it all alive.

LESLIE: What about power and relationships?

MIKE: Relationship is in the target. And you get power stuff through the obstacles.

LESLIE: Do you need a play to access that energy, or does a single word do it?

MIKE: I don't know about anyone else, but for me the word's enough.

VICTOR: Emotion words pack that sort of a punch.

LESLIE: I agree. Fascinating, isn't it, how language works. With an emotion word like 'ruthless' comes situations, contexts, within which the word makes sense to us. Effortlessly. If the task is to replace 'ruthless' with an active verb, Action actors are all set. But actors who don't access creative energy through the conduit of Action can tap insights through sensitivities to the complexities of human relationships, and to the subtleties of power.

POLLY: Okay, we have power, we have relationships, we have action; all we need is something for the Perception actors.

SALLY: Like I said before, if a personal memory doesn't pop into my head, then I'll imagine something so vividly it might as well have happened.

LESLIE: Be sure to balance all the imagination and memory with a complete sensory awareness of the here and now, taking in whatever your partner's doing.

VICTOR: I don't know about anyone else, but I find systems like this too mechanical. Too programmed.

MIKE: I have to agree. It's important for me that I don't plan too much. I just try to hold onto my sense of the target, the imagined relationship, plus maybe an obstacle, and the given circumstances, sure, but my main focus is my relationship and how it needs to change. Then I try to take in whatever I'm given, and then trust my impulses.

POLLY: But you channel all that into specific action, don't you?

SALLY: I can find things to do, but if I have to find a single verb – I hate that.

IRIS: Maybe it's mechanical if you're imagining what it should be and trying to keep control instead of letting things happen?

VICTOR: I have to tell you, I wish we could stop using the jargon. It drives me crazy when a director asks me what my motivation is.

LESLIE: I'm going to argue that there's something to be gained from learning a technique developed by and geared towards actors who don't share your conduits. In your case, Action. Here's why. Although you live in your body, and it is responsive to the impulses towards movement that emerge from your conduits, your creative insights aren't coming from Action and so anything you can grab hold of to sharpen your sense of the body as an encyclopaedia of human experience, the better. Working with someone who keeps asking you to pull action verbs out of your brain is going to help you build a connection between what comes organically, thanks to the conduits, and what is equally available as an acting resource, through effort and careful consideration.

POLLY: I think that's what our training does.

LESLIE: It can, but you need to work with a variety of teachers, with a range of creative temperaments. But you can find these insights in all sorts of places. I trained with someone who I think, in hindsight, was Psychic. My other influential teacher was Magnetic or Visionary. But there was

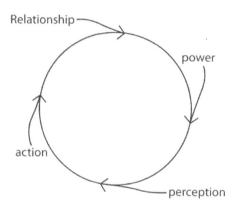

FIGURE 8 Introduction to Acting

nothing stopping me from encountering Personal and Innovative teachers, or Dynamic ones, who would be a perfect match with me. There are always workshops, and courses in history, psychology, literature − my

TABLE 5 Stanislavsky and Creative Personality Types

objectives	actions to initiate
obstacles	reactions; also power (who has more) and relationship (target)
given circumstances	relationship complexity; status and faith (power); also memories
emotional memory	imagination and sensory awareness

Greek tragedy prof was brilliant on power and relationship complexities in those plays. As soon as you have a conscious awareness of what you bring to your work, through your conduits, then you can start looking for ways to inspire your disciplined efforts, as well as for interactions that will recharge your creative batteries, so to speak. I recommend a balance of shared and contrasting conduits.

Okay, what we're learning is that the combination of objectives, obstacles, given circumstances, and emotional memory is going to work for everyone, because it invites involvement from all four conduits. There's plenty of Action, there's Relationship, there's Power, and there's Perception. In an introductory acting class, you might be introduced to these in a specific sequence, but that's arbitrary, right? Some entry-ways will appear closed until you enter through another access point, and then the energy flows around the complete circle. You've just demonstrated that it doesn't matter what order you start in; your conduits are going to respond to any invitation to get involved. It's more like a circle than a sequence (Figure 8). And figuring out what strategies truly work for you is a good way to confirm your diagnosis.

IRIS: Can you take us through the types (see Table 5) and how they use objectives?

LESLIE: Sure, and then we'll move on to the other words on our list.

One:	Ah
Two:	So?
One:	All set?
Two:	No.
One:	Well.
Two:	Yes.

Playing Emotions

LESLIE: Let's go through our list, repeating each word several times as a quick dropping in, to warm you up, then we'll get started.

The group drops in on embarrassed, frantic, nervous, terrified, spiteful, awkward, jealous, distracted, and bewildered.

LESLIE: Your skill level and your aptitude for this sort of work means that your conduits have already released energy into these words. If this were a beginning class, we'd prime the pump with a deliberate, systematic work-through but your pumps are primed.

Now we need to sharpen our ownership of this process, of releasing charismatic energy into the word, by drawing on the familiar system we've all learned. Objectives, obstacles, given circumstances, and emotional memory. By this time, you know your own engine well enough to consciously monitor the sequence.

Here's what you need to do. We'll use the same open dialogue scene we played with in the first session. And we'll pair you up in combinations we haven't tried yet. Let's start with Iris and Sally. You two share a conduit.

IRIS: Perception, right?

SALLY: But I'm Relationship, and Iris is Action?

LESLIE: Yes, we have an Innovative actor and a Psychic actor. Why don't you run the lines to refresh your memory (see page 85).

The girls prepare.

LESLIE: Now, pick TWO of the words you've just dropped in on. Go for an interesting contrast. The challenge I set you is to transform your descriptive words into something that can be acted. In other words, building on Stanislavsky's system, enter into the circle of objective, obstacle and target, given circumstances, and emotional memory, wherever you wish, and work your way around all four strategies.

They try the scene.

LESLIE: Can you share your process with us?

IRIS: I start with objectives, that's easy. My words were embarrassed and jealous, so I had the objective of 'I want to avoid' and 'I want to hurt' with Sally as my target. The obstacles, well, I was counting on Sally to stop me from leaving, and I figured she'd not let me hurt her either.

LESLIE: Did you have a scenario in mind? For given circumstances?

IRIS: Absolutely. In fact, now that you mention it, I maybe had the scenario before the objectives. Or pretty much the same time. As soon as I said those words.

SALLY: Me too. To be honest, I didn't consciously do action verbs, because I'm not very good at them. But I had an elaborate relationship all worked out. My words were distracted and embarrassed.

LESLIE: How about Mike and Polly, next. You two share a Relationship conduit, right?

POLLY: I'm Personal, so that's Action and Relationship.

MIKE: Relationship and Power. I'm Magnetic.

LESLIE: Got your words? How about this time, you collaborate on given circumstances, and then privately work through your objectives, obstacles, and emotional memory?

Polly and Mike have a brief conference, then run the scene.

MIKE: I think I'm like Sally. I didn't really use objectives, but I had a complete scenario in mind, and a very strong memory I was tapping into.

POLLY: I've never liked emotional memory work, but objectives work for me. Mostly, though, it was playing off of what Mike was doing.

LESLIE: We won't attempt this today, but for a moment I want you to imagine what would happen if we paired two actors who did not share a conduit, say Victor and Polly.

VICTOR: I'm Visionary, so that's Perception and Power.

POLLY: Yes, we're opposites. I'm Relationship and Action – Personal.

SALLY: It explains a lot, you know. Thinking about the hundreds of scenes we've done in pairs. Why some click, and others are like pulling teeth.

LESLIE: So, back to Polly's comment about seeking partners unlike ourselves. I think I'd have to counsel actors to challenge themselves to achieve the greatest range and flexibility in their acting, but I'd not want anyone to pretend that they could ever be all things to all people. So I see nothing wrong with Polly knowing that her acting is richest when it's firmly grounded in relationship work. She might need to say, at an audition, 'Oh, I can work with anyone.' As long as she doesn't lie to herself!

VICTOR: No chance she'll do that.

Polly slugs Victor, who pretends to be mortally wounded.

MIKE: I don't know about anyone else, but I want to be able to work equally well with everyone. Anyone.

LESLIE: I'm going to suggest that, in order to accomplish that goal, you need a good balance of charismatic energy from your conduits and disciplined effort in the areas that don't come as easily. In other words, you can work your way through the entire circle offered by objectives, obstacles, given circumstances, and emotional memory, blending conduit insights with strategies acquired through deliberate practice.

I've some specific suggestions, in connection with each of the conduits, whether you have that one or not. First, Action.

The audience don't care what goes on inside. All that matters is what is expressed, and how it is expressed. Another way of putting this: whatever impulses you tap, they must result in, if they don't arise from, action. That said, remember that it can range from subtlety, invisible to anyone but those who are looking for the manifestation, to activity that would cause a passer-by to stop and stare. If Action is your conduit, rehearsals are an opportunity to plan and practice some movements that work for you, knowing that they'll always unleash authentic creative energy. When it comes time to perform, beware of initiating pre-planned actions separate from any input of authentic energy. In a way, you need to let the action take care of itself, and be sure to let yourself REACT to whatever is really happening in that particular performance. If you don't have an Action conduit, you're going to have to work a bit harder to build a connection between whatever does unleash an uninhibited flow and effective actions.

And you'll have to work extra hard to train your body for maximum flexibility and awareness. I recommend doing whatever relaxing, centering warm up will best allow your impulses to manifest themselves in natural movement.

For Iris and Polly, this is obvious; for Victor, Mike, and Sally this is something to work at.

LESLIE: Now, Perception: Whatever the playtext, you must use your imagination to flesh it out. In particular, you'll want to endow your partner with appropriate invented attributes. You can choose to add elements to the given circumstances that take the scene in any of a variety of directions, blending fantasy with personal memory. When it comes time to perform, be sure to take in, with all your senses, the sights, sounds, smells, tastes, and touch sensations that are present in this room, today, rather than dwelling entirely on the 'movie in the mind.' Be sure to include yourself in your sensory awareness. Open yourself to absorb what you experience, rather than what you think you should experience.

As with the action component, even if Perception is not your conduit you still need to tap your imagination and use your senses when you rehearse and perform. You'll need to focus your deliberate practice on strengthening your capacities in this regard. In particular, pay close attention to a relaxing, awareness warm up which will allow you to be fully aware in the here and now.

For Iris, Sally, and Victor, this is obvious; for Polly and Mike this is something to work at.

LESLIE: Next, Relationship: We've seen how relationship complexity is encoded in the very words we speak. You need to avoid simplistic generalizations in favour of subtlety, nuance, specifics, and a blend of conflicting emotions. As with the first two considerations, you can choose to shape the complexities in a variety of ways. If Relationship is your conduit, you'll make use of the real relationship you have with the other actors in your scene, as well as your life-long sensitivity to the way people relate to each other. If Relationship is not a conduit, then simply think through the implications of the scenario and instigate whatever warm ups help you to establish trust and ease inhibitions in preparation for an intense engagement with a fellow actor. When it comes time to perform, be sure to explore the warm, connecting aspects of the relationship in equal measure to the closing, destructive aspects. Fight any temptation to enact the relationship as it should be. Instead, work within a relationship that is constantly changing, open to whatever happens as the rehearsal or performance unfolds each time.

For Sally, Mike, and Polly, this is obvious; for Victor and Iris this is something to work at.

LESLIE: Finally, Power: We've seen how the emotion words as well as the scenario strongly suggest experiences of shifting power and humility, command and submission. You need to bring a sensitivity to the relative power of men and women, of small town and university campus, of different levels of formal education, plus sensations of loss of autonomy and control in one's private life. Don't forget that there are also powers beyond the human scale. Play around with these ideas in whatever way you wish. If Power is one of your conduits, make choices that will allow you to explore the greatest shifts from command to submission, from authority to humility. Beware of planning in order to keep control! If Power is not a conduit, simply think through the implications for the relative power of the characters, and instigate whatever warm ups help you to feel confident and willing to risk allowing something to happen that surprises you. When it comes time to perform, be sure to give up control over the improv, and open yourself to the potency of whatever occurs.

For Victor and Mike, this is obvious; for Sally, Iris, and Polly this is something to work at.

Regardless of your Creative Personality Type, acting will require a commitment to deliberate practice. Luckily, your conduits are always available to energize hard work with the flow of creative engagement.

If this was a beginning class, we'd have worked our way through that list of emotion words, slowly and methodically, doing all the work associated with Stanislavsky's system for each emotion word. We'd do this, not only to practice the technique, but also to explore how shifting the verb, the obstacle, the target, details of the given circumstances, the emotional memory, any of those elements shifts the emotional state being expressed. All of this I consider vital for the chameleon actor. We have a vast number of emotion words in our language, all suggesting subtle variations of emotional experiences. Just like a painter learns to mix colours in preparing his palette for each painting, so too an actor needs to mix and match shadings of emotion when shaping the performance of a character.

POLLY: Chameleon work? I thought emotions were what the conduits released?

LESLIE: Not exactly, though I know it feels like that. In fact, this exploration invited you to open up your conduits, and see how much creative and charismatic energy you could pour into the shape suggested by emotion words. That doesn't mean that I discount the interiority of experience that we associate with those emotion words. What I'm suggesting is that the expression of specific emotions, and subtle shades of emotions, is part of the work an actor does for the audience. It's part of the external presentation of the character within the world of the play.

Our virtual workshop continues the next day. Time for another digression.

Digression: Love/Hate Chameleons

Fantasy role playing is a component of childhood play that most developmental psychologists, educators, and parents appreciate as an important aspect of normal psycho-social maturation. We are less likely to view the fantasies of adolescents as benign, and our experience of the discomfort of enforced role play, when the demands of the workplace or social setting are at odds with our sense of a natural, familiar selfhood, inclines us to distrust and fear pretence. We are particularly disturbed to discover our inability to discern skilled liars and some of our favourite horror stories revolve around the capacity of the terrifying Other to disguise itself within a circle of the familiar and trustworthy.

This is the source of our love–hate relationship with our capacity for a chameleon's transformation. On the one hand, we are attracted to the freedom offered by fantasy role playing, most particularly during those times when our habitual patterns of normal behaviour are dissatisfying, complicated, undergoing change, or no longer effective. The ready-made and vibrantly constructed roles of the actor's world are particularly appealing because they provide opportunities for the striking presentation of a self in the public eye. The fantasy self is invited, by the fiction of the play, to affect significant change, to experience extremes of feeling, to establish intense and fulfilling relationships, or to demonstrate moral strength in a manner quite outside any offered by life outside the rehearsal hall.

At the same time, an awareness of the duplicity of habitual role playing, the potential for shame and guilt colouring the experience of activities that are not easily integrated into patterns of behaviour offered as normative, and the pervasive uncertainty associated with an ongoing search of self-actualization can all contribute to a profound repulsion at any indication of pretence. Paradoxically, the theatre offers the equally potent seductive goal of authenticity, the holy grail of psychological realism. Intense self-scrutiny is as likely to reinforce neurotic behaviour as to encourage self-knowledge when the goal is the compelling expression of strikingly articulated emotional states. And when only the intense and strikingly articulated is held to be authentic, non-theatrical interactions, which are so pale in comparison, can lose their capacity to be experienced as real and meaningful.

Here we have the great irony of acting: that the very capacities which make great acting possible are those which fuel the seductive neurosis that so damages the reputation and artistic discipline of the art form. Certain individuals are attracted to the theatre because it provides opportunities of escapism and self-exhibition. The chameleon skills are acquired in order to avoid finding or being oneself, and the unleashing of charismatic energy is sought through authentic experiences of selfhood in order to avoid having to function authentically within one's private non-theatrical situations.

In large part, this unfortunate situation exists because of the artificial dichotomy we allow between the chameleon and the charismatic. Escapism flies in the face of the profound connection between what we do and who we are. Self-exhibition for the purpose of authenticity flies in the face of the essential inauthenticity of public displays of private events, and the fundamental difference between theatrical expressions of feeling and non-theatrical experiences of emotion. Our capacity for dishonesty in non-theatrical settings is confirmed by the actor's chameleon skills. There is no use disguising this fact by pretending that the actor is actually in pursuit of something authentic and true, nor by claiming that the fantasy role playing is benign exploration or escapism.

In addition, far more attention must be paid to the persuasive social forces that mediate between our experiences and our sense of normal, credible, authentic behaviour. How often, in pursuit of the authentic, do we reinforce our culture's prejudices? How often, in placing authenticity as the ultimate goal, do we reinforce the unfortunate belief that our culture's norms are humanity's norms, thus opening the door to cultural imperialism? Far too little attention is paid to the important moral dangers of the actor's craft. I urge every member of the acting profession to wrestle with such issues, for which there is no easy answer; avoidance represents a great danger.

VIRTUAL WORKSHOP *SESSION THREE*: CONDUITS AND CONSIDERATIONS

As the group gathers, they discuss the discoveries they're making, in connection with a current project in which they are all involved.

LESLIE: What I'm hearing from your discussion is that the vocabulary of conduits and personality types is useful in assessing your creative experiences, and you're learning about your own charismatic energy in part by comparing it with that of those who are similar but not identical. I can hear from your comments that we need to consider carefully the positives and negatives associated with each of the temperaments.

Gifts and Pitfalls

LESLIE: Let's talk about the 'gifts' that come with each type. This is a good general terms for the benefits you'll discover in the intuitive, effortless charismatic energy. As you articulate the gifts inherent in your type, you'll perhaps arouse envy in those who do not share your conduits.

Not to worry. Because each type also comes with a collection of negatives, which we'll call 'pitfalls' – which overlap to a limited extent with the individual blind spots and acting habits that result from each actor's life experiences. These gifts and pitfalls are general, rather than personal, and linked to the temperament, not to an individual's talent or training.

IRIS: Can we come back to the issue of mismatches? I'm thinking of those situations when nothing you do seems what your teachers want, and whatever they offer just makes you say, 'I guess I'm not an actor.' I feel like I still need a concrete, specific thing to do in those situations.

MIKE: 'Something to do.' There's that Action conduit!

LESLIE: Yes, and I share your eagerness to find something to do, so let's plan some strategies. First, though, we have to address head on the actor's equivalent of penis envy, to borrow from Freud. I'm talking of course about envying the conduits that others enjoy and you don't have. If every Creative Personality type were treated equally, then there'd be no need to envy other types. But when you feel that you're not an actor, it's very likely that you're working in a creative context that privileges some types over others.

Nods of agreement from the group.

LESLIE: So let's get it out there. There are four conduits. You have two. Thinking about the other two, and the actors in our group who have them, what do you envy? What can they do effortlessly, that directors and teachers want?

POWER ACTORS

SALLY: People with the Power thing, they terrify me. In a good way. Remember when we did those Greek myths? I was cast as Medusa, and that whole god thing was a disaster for me.

IRIS: Whenever the director wants you to fill the space with your presence? Those Power actors, you can really see them commanding the stage.

POLLY: This is going to sound strange, but for me it's the way they do their power, that's so interesting. I mean, there are lots of people who are bossy. Or they're in a position of authority, and their job is to order other people around. But from them, the power feels hard. Forced. With Power actors, you feel their power, but you also feel that you have a relationship with them, and they're on your level, or even below, at the same time as they're filled with something powerful. Like the power flows through them, but the second it leaves, they're going to need you to help pick them up off the floor.

LESLIE: Since I have a Power conduit, I have a strong response to what you've just said, as I'm sure Mike and Victor do as well. So let's hear now from the Power conduit actors. Those are your gifts. What are the pitfalls that come with the gifts?

MIKE: Polly hit one of them. And by the way, I really heard Polly's conduits while she was talking. Power is something that's done to her, that she reacts to, but within a relationship. Even so, she nailed it with that business about picking us up off the floor. That's what's scary about the Power conduit. It isn't all about commanding and authority. The humility is always there.

VICTOR: It's fun being commanding, and any chance to fill the theatre – I'm there! But there's a price you pay. Because people don't like being around that sort of power. I know Sally said that she was terrified in a good way, but it can get in the way in class, say, when you're releasing that sort of energy and people are pulling back.

LESLIE: I'll add that the socialization that crimps the command side of the Power conduit can cut the heart out of your acting. I realize now that's part of what I was experiencing, way back when, at the time I decided I probably wasn't an actor. First of all, no one was talking about power issues, in any of the plays we were doing, so any intuitions I might have contributed were automatically discounted. Secondly, whenever glimmers of that type of energy emerged, they were rejected on interpretive grounds, with comments like, 'I don't think your character would do that, would she? Isn't she afraid at this moment? Isn't she eager to please everyone around her?' Because there were such narrow ideas about the characters I was cast as. Ideas that today we'd label sexist.

MIKE: I've got to share something with you, because it's the same but opposite. I was once cast as a slave, and the director kept wanting me to enact what she wanted to imagine it would have been like to be a slave. I wanted to explore the combination of abject submission, terror, the sort of gutlessness that happens after years of abuse, combined with flashes of a power that would eventually rise up, even if not in my character's lifetime. I think she hated the submissive character on political grounds, but she really hated when I defied her, personally.

LESLIE: A very good assessment of the gifts and pitfalls of the Power conduit. Let's do the same thing with the other conduits. Because I think we can all see the pattern. Keep thinking of the gifts and the pitfalls. Each conduit has both.

RELATIONSHIP ACTORS

VICTOR: Can we do Relationship next? I think it's ironic that you guys started with Power, because in our program, I think we all agree, the Relationship actors are the flavour of the month. So I envy them that.

LESLIE: In the long years of your career, I'm sure each of you will work with a variety of directors. What we need to discover is a way for you to thrive even when you're not the flavour of the month. Can you be more specific, what you envy?

VICTOR: It just happens. Over and over, we're put into scenes with these complex, multi-faceted relationships, and for them it's just there. If they need to work quickly, like a cold reading, they've got something. If they're supposed to explore all the possibilities, they never seem to run out of interesting variations.

IRIS: I envy the chemistry that they have together on stage. It's electric. I feel so emotionally closed, in comparison.

LESLIE: Yes, that's what I envy, as well. There's a type of engagement, actor to actor, that allows them access to a communion, a connectedness, that I always feel left out of. Also, they have that with audiences.

VICTOR: And directors. And teachers. And techies. They can turn on the charm, and everyone's eating out of their hands.

LESLIE: I wonder if we could say the same thing about Relationship actors as Polly said about Power actors. Everyone has relationships. And many, many actors are warm, approachable, friendly, collaborative, easy going – all those positive things, that make you want to build and maintain a friendship, even after the show's over. But the Relationship actors bring something more. It feels different, to be on the receiving end of their warmth. Perhaps because you know that they are also capable of the other extreme.

VICTOR: And if you're on the receiving end of the cold side – look out, frostbite!

LESLIE: You can hear our envy, can't you? And also our conduits, revealing themselves in the way we receive your charismatic energy? What can you Relationship actors share with us about the pitfalls?

SALLY: It's dangerous. Because relationships are dangerous. And what you were saying about socialization? That's so much what gets in the way, at least for me.

MIKE: I feel that if I open up to the full power of my Relationship conduit, there's going to be a misunderstanding. By that I mean something messy, inter-personally. And there's no way that I can explore the combination of full power and full destruction. So both of my conduits are crimped by socialization.

POLLY: I think it's me that Victor's talking about, and I know lots of people think I'm just faking it, when I 'turn on the charm' one minute and then the next it's frostbite. But there's a difference between fake and temporary. When I'm working with someone, I have a relationship with them, and it's easier if it's a respectful, affirming relationship. What you give, you receive. So I'm respectful and warm, and everything works more smoothly. And when the work's done, it's done. Professionals understand that.

SALLY: It's not pleasant, you know, being so aware of everyone else. I can tell when someone's just being polite, but they really didn't like the show. And getting notes? It's torture. I wish I didn't care so much what other people think of me.

IRIS: I still envy you Relationship guys.

ACTION ACTORS

SALLY: Well I envy you Action actors. I never know what to do, up there.

MIKE: And when a director says, 'Just do whatever feels right?' I want to say, 'Sitting on a chair for the entire scene feels right to me!'

VICTOR: Or the other extreme: a week of blocking rehearsals. I'm feeling more and more like a robot, moving wherever I'm put and writing it down in my script.

SALLY: And you know those shows where you have to get the timing down perfectly? I'm so bad at that stuff. I'm always looking the wrong way.

MIKE: And life study work. Remember, where we followed someone around at the mall, and then adopted a completely different way of walking, sitting, all that? Whenever we talk about the chameleon skills, I always think that the Action actors have it easiest, just changing themselves physically to fit whatever role they're playing.

LESLIE: That might well be a bias in my approach to acting, even though I've tried to honour all six temperaments. I've very, very fond of my Action conduit. I love that the body is a repository of human experience. I love the flexibility it allows in characterization, and I particularly admire actors who can do those extreme transformations. But there are pitfalls. Maybe Iris and Polly can help me out.

IRIS: I've been doing a lot of thinking about my time as a dancer, since we started talking about the Action conduit. I started off saying, 'Oh, of course, and that's why I love dance.' But then, I realized there's a reason why I left dance to study acting. The sort of movement that we do in dance is easier if you don't have an Action conduit. Because the flow of energy gets in the way of the precision and clarity we need, at least in a certain type of dancing. And there's the react side. All the years I danced, I used the initiate side, but I could only react if my reaction was precisely what the choreography required.

LESLIE: That's a very interesting insight. I've always found it relatively easy to repeat movement patterns exactly as expected, which is a very useful skill, for example, when acting for the camera. But perhaps that's as much from my Power conduit as my Action conduit. It's a form of control.

IRIS: I also think that I was a good dancer because of my Perception conduit, rather than my Action conduit, if that makes any sense.

SALLY: But I have one of those, and I'm terrible at those pre-planned, perfectly timed things.

POLLY: Maybe it's the combination of Action and Perception? For me, because it's Action and Relationship, I'm always reacting to what other people do. If I like blocking rehearsals, it's not because I like getting the moves sorted out. It's because the director makes it so clear, through the blocking, what he wants us to do.

SALLY: So you can figure out how to please him.

MIKE: Or resist, if you have to.

POLLY: It really bugs me when directors spot minute changes in the blocking, and then get on my case about why I changed things. I'm only going to change what I do when what I'm receiving changes. And I don't muck around with the big stuff. But that's how the scene stays alive, with those little shifts in exactly how I react to whatever my partner's doing.

LESLIE: I wonder if that sort of a director has a Perception conduit, and therefore is hyper aware of what you're doing, but doesn't have an Action conduit, and so doesn't get how important reacting is to keeping the conduit fully flowing.

PERCEPTION ACTORS

SALLY: Perception is the conduit we haven't done yet – for gifts and pitfalls. Can we do it now? I'm dying of curiosity.

POLLY: That's easy. All that emotional memory work? That's when you guys are the flavour of the month.

MIKE: And all those monologues where a character stands there remembering something, and the director keeps saying, 'You have to really see what you're describing. That's the only way the audience will see it too.'

LESLIE: And that wonderful eye for detail. When I'm acting opposite someone like Sally, who combines Perception and Relationship, I'm almost terrified of her capacity to see into my heart.

MIKE: And anything requiring physical contact. You just know they're super sensitive, and free, at the same time, to experience you that way, as an acting partner. They're alive in their skin.

POLLY: I think our voice teachers are Perception people, because they hear everything. They see everything. And they just put their hands on the one place where the tension's holding. How do they do that?

LESLIE: What I so admire about the emotional memory work, is that for them it truly does work. For me, it was always something I did. I concentrated on my senses. Great. I imagined whatever. Great. For them, it's like a key to a door that is locked for me. I have memories. I have an imagination. I use them all the time, particularly when I'm writing. But when I'm acting? I can do the work but I sure do envy the flood of feeling that they access.

IRIS: I worry that I'm too inhibited to access that sort of emotional flood, and that's why I can't make it work.

SALLY: Believe me, it's not that pleasant. I know that part of the reason I've done so well as an actor is I can turn on the emotions: fear, grief, passion, anything where I get to emote full volume. Some directors really like that. I had to learn not to use my private life, quite so much, to use imagination instead. Or it got too messy.

VICTOR: Do any of you struggle with concentration?

IRIS: Absolutely. It's impossible to shut off my ears, and if the room's too hot or cold, it really affects what I'm working on.

VICTOR: Or how about your imagination? I can't not remember stuff, and I have to really fight not to get dragged into an emotion that's coming from a memory that the character wouldn't have, that doesn't fit what I'm trying to explore.

SALLY: With me, it's imagining. Not so much in acting, but in real life. I'm always bursting out laughing at the wrong time, because I've just thought of the most ridiculous situation involving someone who's all serious.

IRIS: For me, it's the 'movie in the mind'. When you said that, it made so much sense to me. I'm always imagining the perfect performance and then I try to do exactly that, and everyone hates it. Even me. That's what I did as a dancer, by the way. I'd envision the perfect ballerina, and then do that for the mirror. When the image matched my imagination, I'd memorize how it felt, so I could reproduce it without the mirror.

VICTOR: 'Movie in the mind' isn't just because you're a dancer. I have it too.

SALLY: I guess I do, too, but my movies are always changing, so it's easy to toss one out and dream up a new one.

Character Shape and Chameleon Energy

LESLIE: How do we all feel now, about each other's conduits? Still some envy, I'm sure. That's only natural. The grass is always greener over the septic tank. I hope that everyone's also learning to value your own conduits, because now it's time to move to the next step, in response to Iris, who asked for a specific strategy to cope with mismatches.

Just a few reminders. First, charismatic energy is neutral. The conduits

FIGURE 10 Character via Playwright

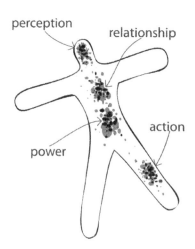

FIGURE 11 Conduits Release Flow of Charismatic Energy

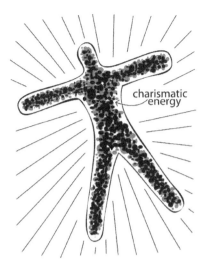

FIGURE 12 Performed Character

access it differently, and we experience it differently depending upon our creative temperament, but the actual energy is NOT aligned with any one type. Therefore, if I release energy through a Power conduit, there is nothing to stop it from flowing into relationship work.

Next, the chameleon craft can shape any type of acting work. Action, Power, Relationship, and Perception considerations can be brought to bear on scenes that explore characters engaged in activity within a relationship in a fictional world where larger issues of relative power are on the table, using language that signals what the characters are remembering and imagining.

Here's a diagram to illustrate. Here's the 'shape' of the character, that you're going to transform yourself into as far as the audience is concerned (Figure 10). Now, the fictional character has been shaped through specific dramaturgical strategies: through the actions he must perform and react to, the memories and dreams that he describes, the relationships he's engaged in during the play, and the society evoked by the world of the play (Figure 11). Down here, we have you, which is a much, much more complexly shaped persona, and we have your conduits, which allow for direct access between your psychic energy and the container that is the fictional character. You can plug in anywhere, and – bingo! – the shape inflates with authentic human energy, and the audience perceives a living human being (Figure 12). Best of all, you only need one point of contact, one opening, for the creative flow to bring any character to life.

And that's my final point, perhaps the most important one. Remember that audiences receive via their conduits, and therefore whatever charisma you bring to your acting, they will experience as Dynamic, or Innovative, or Personal, or Visionary, or Psychic, or Magnetic, regardless of your Creative Personality Type. Among the receivers of your charisma, we need to include your theatre colleagues, as well. Victor's list: the director, the actors, the audience, the techies, the theatre manager, the critics, the janitor, the cat that keeps the rodent population under control.

Don't forget that, ever. You don't need to be like your acting partner, to fuel their creativity. You need to release your own creativity, and they will receive in a way that best suits the way they need to work. Sure, you'll still irritate the hell out of each other, but that's all surface stuff, when you get right down to what's important, your work as creative artists.

Okay, now let's see how each of the conduits might function for simultaneous translation.

IRIS: Can you explain that term, again?

How Translation Works

LESLIE: The pragmatic reason we're addressing this issue isn't for the audience. They'll be thrilled with what you offer, regardless how you got there. It's those colleagues who have enough insight, and authority, to undercut our courage by suggesting that our process is not what is needed to make the moment work. They might even go so far as to announce that the ONLY way to solve the moment is strategy X, because that works for them and therefore they assume it works for all good actors. Why? Because when they observe charisma, they receive it that way!

But it can also come indirectly. Say the director never comments on process, but you keep getting notes that make no sense. They're gibberish. Now that you can recognize conduits that you don't share, you can spot their vocabulary.

Here's how the translation works. Let's assume the feedback is coming from someone you trust and respect. We'll imagine that you're not delivering charismatically, for whatever reason. You know it. They know it. Absence of flow, right? And this person, who you trust, keeps giving you feedback on a conduit that is not one of yours. Whatever the specifics of the comment, you need to translate it into a tune-up to your creative engine, but in a way that the energy flows where it is most needed, and right away.

Let's address relationship feedback, since that's so important to the creative culture here. The notes focus on the way you're failing to enact the character's relationship as richly and fully as required.

Perception people, you need to open your heightened sensory aware-ness and direct it entirely towards your partner. Really see, and hear, and smell, right now, in the present. That will result in a very similar sort of attuning to another that Relationship actors achieve effortless. Also, awaken your imagination to endow your partner with attributes that are character-specific, and that arouse in you the sensations that are called for.

Power people, you need to be sensitive to the subtle shifts in power relative to your partner. Keep shifting, from commanding to submitting, from authority to humility, always keyed to the other. This is your version of the natural engagement of Relationship actors.

Action people, you also can attune yourself to your partner, through the reaction side of your conduit. Yes, you can plan actions to initiate that will read as relationship, but what will make it come alive is integrating whatever impulses emerge in the moment, in direct response to your partner.

If you can find a way, through your conduits, to offer your charismatic energy to your Relationship colleagues in a way that is strongly connected to relationship considerations, then you'll be giving them what they require, and they will experience it as Relationship energy.

I 'do' relationships quite well on stage. Some people are surprised when I say that's not one of my conduits. That's a sign that I've mastered simul-taneous translation.

I've worked extensively with directors whose entire rehearsal process consists of 'We need to dig into the heart of this relationship.' I've found a way to unleash my natural charismatic energy into that working envi-ronment, by playing with Power and Action. I've also delivered image-filled memory speeches, and performed in strange imaginary worlds, the same way.

My guess is that you're all well on your way to similar intuitive trans-lation. I'm probably just saying aloud what you already know, right?

VICTOR: I figured out, early on, that I had to find my own way into some of what directors felt was super important but that just didn't push my buttons. If I tried to fight them, it was a waste of effort. So I just adapted. I do a lot of my work on my own, for that reason.

LESLIE: My guess is that those of you for whom relationship work requires careful consideration and effort have picked up some translation strategies from those Relationship actors who share your conduits. It's the Psychic actors who can help non-Relationship people develop strategies for using Perception in a way that keys to relationship work. It's the

Magnetic actors who can help non-Relationship people develop strategies for using Power so that it reads as Relationship. It's the Personal actors
who demonstrate how energy from an Action conduit might flow into
the shape that is a relationship on stage.

POLLY: Another reason why it's ideal to work with people not your
type.

IRIS: How about Power? We were all in a Shakespeare class where all
the teacher talked about was power – the great chain of being and all that.
I never did figure out how it all worked.

LESLIE: There are many plays in which power isn't part of the fictional
world shaped by the writer, though Power actors and directors are going
to bring those issues to the table regardless. But the demand for power
consideration is even greater in those plays in which power is very much
part of what the playwright explores.

Perception actors, you can use your imagination to locate the various
markers of relative power that are available, and bring to them a richness
of connection through strategies of endowment and substitution. You can
also use your heightened awareness to locate subtle signals of power in the
here-and-now. To do that, you might need help expanding your awareness of power – and for that the Visionary actors are going to be
particularly helpful, because they combine Perception with Power.

Relationship actors, you'll need to put yourself at the mercy of those
who have higher status, and realize how much you can hurt people below
you in status. To do this, you'll have to subject all of your relationship work
to a consideration of power. Just who is more powerful at this moment?
And for that, Magnetic actors are going to be particularly helpful, because
they combine Relationship with Power.

Action actors, you'll need to figure out how power is enacted in the
fictional world of the play. How do people 'do' submission and command?
You'll also need to react richly to any manifestation of these activities
around you. And guess who can help?

POLLY: Dynamic actors, who have Power and Action.

LESLIE: Yes. Like me. Being directed by someone who knows how to
stage the rituals of power can help Personal and Innovative actors acquire
all sorts of strategies for doing authority and humility.

MIKE: We've done my two conduits, so I'm really curious about the
other two.

LESLIE: Yes. And we'll discover that the strategies shift in an interesting
way as we move from cultural considerations to genetic ones.

For example, action. You all have bodies. These are in simple fact the
instruments that you learn to play like musicians. The physiological

makeup of the body is such that it is the location where charismatic energy manifests itself. The flow of energy results in the sensation of impulses in the body. For Action actors, the connection between initiating activity and energy flow, as well as between reacting to activity and an impulse to the body, is a neatly closed circle of impulse and energy. For everyone else, your conduits result in energy that must, by definition, be experienced physically.

The process for simultaneous translation is therefore relatively straight-forward. You simply need to let whatever impulses emerge from your sensitivity to power or relationships, or your memory, imagination, and sensory awareness, flow into the body so that they can manifest themselves in activity. The activity might be pre-planned or spontaneous, depending on the performance or rehearsal context.

Dynamic actors, with their Action and Power, can help the rest of the Power gang find activities. Similarly, Personal actors can help their Relationship colleagues, and Innovative actors can help the Perception group to fine-tune ways of letting impulses from one conduit flow into activity.

The same thing happens with Perception. You all have cognitive capac-ities. You all process data from the sensing organs via the massive cognitive mechanism that draws upon memory, and that can shape an infinite number of possibilities as yet only imagined. Just as you cannot act outside your body, you cannot turn off your mind.

When you're thinking about simultaneous translation, remember your goal. It isn't to become a Perception actor. It's to offer Perception colleagues what they need, which is your natural charismatic energy flowing into something they can RECEIVE as Perception. So, we're talking about playing a character who is shown to be hyper aware, or who has speeches that evoke strong memories or a vivid imagination.

Once again, it's our colleagues who can help us the most. I look to Victor, as a Visionary, because he combines my Power with his Perception. I look to Iris, as an Innovative, because she combines my Action with her Perception. What suggestions would you guys offer me, if I have to deliver a big memory, sensory awareness speech?

VICTOR: Feel the power of the images.

IRIS: Remember that sensing is something that you do. So is speaking about what you sense or remember.

VICTOR: Also, focus on how the images signal power. Specially the verbs. Eagles soaring. Leaves trembling in the wind. That gives you command, and submission.

IRIS: And look for images of activity. If it's people, what are they doing?

If it's nature, what's happening? If it's you, what are you doing? You can be very specific in that, even if the playwright doesn't give you the words.

LESLIE: See how helpful they are? Mike, you're in the same boat I am, without a Perception conduit.

MIKE: I'd ask for help from Victor, who shares Power with me, and what he's said really helps. I'd add, imagine people who are authoritative. Imagine or remember relationships where I've felt humility or authority.

SALLY: I'm the one to help with that, because I have a Relationship conduit, like you, with Perception. And that's the secret. Imagining relationships. Like Iris said. Look for it in the words of the speech. If there's a person's name, that's huge. Or a word like mother, child, friend – those are like hooks you can use for all sorts of relationship stuff. And physical objects. One trick that someone told me ages ago was to take every prop I have to use on stage and attach it to another character – like my father gave me that umbrella, and my necklace I inherited when my grandmother died, and my bitchy sister was with me when I bought that vase. It's corny, I know, but it's a great way to blend the two.

MIKE: So if I had a speech in which I talked about, say, a beautiful painting? And I've spent hours doing my homework, going to galleries and looking at paintings in books?

SALLY: Why don't you think about the relationship? Maybe you first saw the painting with an old lover? And that's the type of relationship you long for with the person you're talking to?

VICTOR: Or the power of the painting. How humble it made you feel. Or how knowing all about it makes you more powerful than the person you're talking to.

POLLY: My turn, my turn. These are all such great suggestions. I had to do one of those memory speeches, so naturally I made it all about the other person on stage with me, which was fine, except the director wasn't convinced I was seeing the memory. So I tried sort of what Sally suggested, focusing on the relationship in the memory. But the speech, the sharing of the memory, was always something I just did, to get the reaction I needed from the other character. Does that make sense?

IRIS: It does to me. The doing part, anyway. It's like your character chooses to remember. Like you turn it on, in order to do what you have to do in the scene.

LESLIE: These insights into memory monologues are excellent, but what about sensory awareness? Say you're playing Sherlock Holmes? Hyper-aware. Perception folks – help us non-perception guys out!

IRIS: Be aware of what people are doing. That would be for Action people. Also what else is happening, that you might react to. If you truly react, not just do the planned action, it will be identical to Perception people letting the impulse flow into action.

SALLY: Be aware of people, I'd say. If you're really tuned to others on stage, then it will seem as if you're reading them with total awareness.

VICTOR: Pick up on all the shifts in power, instantly. If you link those sensations with something happening around you, it's impossible to say whether you sensed it externally and then sensed it with your Power side, or the other way around.

LESLIE: This is all excellent, and I'm going to add one more element. You know when we were talking about the genetic endowment: how we all have a mind, and part of that mind is our sensory awareness? Even if Perception is not one of our conduits, we all have receptors that work all the time. When Relationship actors talk about being attuned to another person, or Power actors talk about being sensitive to subtle nuances in relative power – these are very specific types of 'reading' the world around us, of taking in data through our sense and making sense of what's coming in.

True, Perception actors experience a profound connection between sensing and charismatic flow. But every conduit is linked to the mind, as much as to the body.

Iris mentioned reacting, for the Action people. Think of how you absorb in order to react. It might be a human agent, or it might be something in the environment, or it might be something so subtle you attribute it to a sixth sense. Anything we call intuition, insight, inspiration – those are all the result of our minds taking in and processing – something.

So part of simultaneous translation for non-Perception actors is to sharpen their awareness of how they do, indeed, absorb, intuit, 'read' people and situations, including those that are what we would call spiritual or transcendent.

Receptive Mode Dominance

MIKE: Does this have anything to do with learning styles?

LESLIE: I think that's very likely somewhere in the mix. Theories about neuro-linguistic programming (that's the fancy name for what I think you're talking about) are now being applied to the performing arts, in some very interesting ways.

Acting, along with quite a few other careers, requires that we become professional communicators. Whatever personal habits we have, in the way we interact in our private lives, have to be expanded so that we can meet any communication challenge. That's the output side. We've now realized that there's a very interesting connection between output and input. In other words, how we RECEIVE affects everything we experience. And patterns of reception are set in the first three months of life.

We have sight, sound, touch, taste, and smell. Babies are already experiencing these before birth. They're born able to recognize their mother's voice. Sensations of touch, taste, and smell are what dominate their awareness. And their eyes focus at exactly the distance from a woman's nipple to her face, ideal for a baby gazing up at a mother while nursing.

Now, as a result of how the brain programs itself to process information, individuals develop a dominance in one of three receptive systems. It might be aural. Remember that this occurs before babies acquire language, so they're responding to the non-linguistic patterns in speech. Pitch, rhythm, tone, timbre, all that stuff.

Or, it might be facial, including all that passes via eye contact. Remember that nursing baby gazing up into its mother's face.

Or, it might be kinesthetic, which is the catch-all term for movement, gesture, how the body holds and releases energy. Babies are sensitive to that because they experience the world through moving, long before they're consciously aware that those toes they're sucking are their own.

What scientists have observed is that aural babies babble, facial babies move muscles in their faces, and kinesthetic babies move their entire bodies. In each case, these exploratory movements program the brain in connection with the survival instinct. What do I need to learn to survive? In other words, it's profound, fundamental connections between receiving through the senses and making sense of what is received.

When these patterns are well established, language is added. That's why it's called neural-linguistic programming. With language comes an entire set of thinking possibilities, and in our language systems we see the intersection of the mind and body, as well as the genetic and cultural. As language becomes imprinted on the brain, an entire set of predispositions are in place. That's the raw material we draw upon as actors.

The better we understand the imprinted predispositions, the better we'll be able to transform bad habits into flexible communication systems, and the more creatively we'll be able to bring our unique individuality to our explorations and performances.

SALLY: How do we know what our program is?

LESLIE: You should assume you use all three equally well, as integrated adults. Because the dominant receptive mode is keyed to the survival instinct, you might be able to spot one of the three moving into the predominant position at times of greatest stress, when you're in danger, or something is going very wrong in your most cherished relationships.

Dynamic actors need to explore receptive mode dominance in connection with reacting. That's where it will manifest itself most directly. I happen to be aural mode dominant as a receiver, so I'm very reactive to sounds. Also to the para-linguistic markers in someone's speaking. I find actors whose voices are unattractive, inflexible, or mannered extremely irritating. I suspect that I also sense subtle indicators of power aurally. Perhaps that's why I love music so much.

Magnetic actors need to discover mode dominance in order to sharpen their reading of other people, within relationships, and also their sensitivity to power. Mike, any thoughts on that?

MIKE: I'm really keyed to faces. If I can't have eye contact in a scene, it's death for me. Voices, well of course I hear what they're saying, and body language I get as well, but if they have their back to me, I feel cut off. Also, actors who have sort of a rigid mask, like a fake, frozen smile – that's something I pick up on right away.

LESLIE: Excellent analysis. What about Power.

MIKE: I was thinking about that. Obviously, for me power is – do I dare to look in that person's face, if they're awesome. But I was also thinking about the face of God. I realize that spiritual things for me are personal, and it's not the touch of God's hand, or the sound of his voice, but gazing upon his face. That's what I long for.

LESLIE: Anyone else have a sense of their receptive mode dominance?

POLLY: It's not faces, for me. Even though I'm a Relationship actor. Maybe because I'm Action, it's kinesthetic?

LESLIE: I don't think there's a direct link, because I'm also an Action actor and mine is aural.

POLLY: I'm just thinking about what I react to, and how I read people. I get a huge amount from how they move, how they sit, their posture. Even when they have their backs to me. It's like I can read the tension in their shoulders. Also, little gestures. The ones they don't even know they're making.

IRIS: I think I'm the same.

LESLIE: Let's see how that similarity in receptive mode dominance plays out with these two Creative Personality types. The Personal has reacting, the 'yin' of the Action conduit, and receives within relationships. So you're reading kinesthetically, that's what you absorb as you experience the react side of your Action conduit.

In contrast, the Innovative has sensory awareness from the Perception conduit, and front and center in the awareness is receiving signals from bodies. Plus, as you absorb for reaction, you're reading kinesthetically.

IRIS: It sounds like a double dose.

LESLIE: Yes, and I think that's true for all of the Perception actors. Victor?

VICTOR: I think I'm also aural. Voices really matter to me. I can tell something's wrong, at home, just by the way my mom says hello on the phone.

LESLIE: As a Visionary, you're getting a double dose: through your Perception you're picking up on all the senses but your hearing is heightened still further, plus you're using that mode dominance to 'read' subtle indicators of power.

What about you, Sally?

SALLY: I think I'm facial, like Mike. I just love acting opposite him, because he's got such an expressive face, and eyes. To be honest, I had to learn how to make eye contact, because I get such intense stuff, it's almost overwhelming.

LESLIE: In some ways, your Creative Personality type experiences receptive mode dominance more purely.

SALLY: Sorry, you lost me there.

LESLIE: My apologies. Let me try again. Because you're a Psychic actor, your conduits are Perception, with awareness in the here and now through all the senses, and Relationship, which links your awareness to other people. Now, when it comes to mode dominance, that's all about HOW the senses receive from other people. Why? Because survival, for our species, is accomplished collectively. We're born too soon. Other mammals can stand and seek food within hours of birth. They might still need the protection of the herd, but compared to human babies? We've years of complete vulnerability, and we need to form bonds with our primary care givers. There are lots of studies about how, as adults, we're encoded with instincts to protect infants. But this programming of receptive sensitivity is the other side, what babies do to figure out the adults. So. Relationship and Perception.

All Relationship actors can tap into the survival instinct, when working in a relationship, when you open yourself to another to the point where their rejection of you would destroy you, emotionally.

All Perception actors can tap into the survival instinct, when imagining situations in which the stakes are life and death.

That leaves only the Dynamic actors, like me, experiencing the intersection of conduit energy and reception mode dominance as separate experiences, awaiting integration.

SALLY: Maybe that's why you can explain it.

TABLE 6 Mode Dominance, Conduits and Considerations

	Vocal Mode	Kinesthetic Mode	Facial Mode
Action • initiating	speaking, vocalizing	activity	smiling, frowning, etc.
• responding	vocalizing in response to tone of voice	moving in response to body language	facial expression in response to same
Relationship • constructing	gentle, soft, warm sounds	opening, caressing, contacting actions	contact, warmth of expression
• destroying	loud, harsh, cold sounds	closing, hurting, removing actions	removal, coldness of expression
Perception • observing	listening	reading body language	reading faces
• envisioning	imagining sounds	imagining movement	imagining faces
Power • commanding	hearing power in self/ humility in others	rising and seeing others fall	staring down
• submitting	hearing power in others/ humility in self	falling and seeing others rise	looking up in awe

LESLIE: Here's why I've spent some time on this issue. You remember simultaneous translation? Well, think of your audience. About one third will be aural, one third will be facial, and one third will be kinesthetic. You need to express richly for all three groups.

That means, if you're a Psychic actor with facial mode dominance, like Sally, and you're trying to please a Dynamic actor with aural or kinesthetic mode dominance, like me, you've got quite a challenge. You need to make sure that, no matter how much you receive through the facial mode, you express in all three modes. Also, you need to channel impulses into activity, and expand your sensitivity of relationships to include power.

MIKE: No wonder acting's so difficult.

LESLIE: Yes, presented like that it seems a daunting challenge. But in many ways it's more organic than it sounds when I describe it. Because we do in fact receive and express in all the modes, and the connection between mind and body is genetically encoded. So your 'mind work,' via the Perception conduit, can easily and richly prompt body experiences. Similarly, our culture has vertical as well as horizontal patterns of relating, for you to reflect upon and imagine.

Here's a chart that shows how we can play with mode dominance in the different conduits and considerations (Table 6).

Personalized Warm Ups

LESLIE: This discussion has got very theoretical For a practical application of knowing your Creative Personality type is in the development of a personal warm up. What's the custom, here, for pre-show, pre-rehearsal, pre-class warm ups?

VICTOR: We have an hour of movement and an hour of voice first thing every day, so we come to all our classes warmed up from that. For rehearsals, it depends on the director. Same with shows.

MIKE: Sometimes the actors request group warm ups, and take turns leading them. That's if the director doesn't require them.

LESLIE: Warm ups that come to you from another creative artist are invaluable. If that person shares even one of your conduits, you're going to benefit from the stimulation of that natural energy flow. But in a way they're even better in the areas where your conduits don't match, because then your craft benefits from the insights of their conduits.

I recommend that you think about how best to warm up your creative instrument, now that you're aware of CP typage. Let me give you a couple of specific suggestions.

First, consider the different types of situations for which you might want or need to warm up. There are classes, a time of exploration and mastery of craft. There are rehearsals, a time of exploration and practice of craft in service of the production. There are performances, when you're preparing to offer the package that is your unique charismatic energy, plus your craft, in a performance event for which people have invested their time and money. Also, what about auditions, when the package you might offer is being judged?

The other thing to keep in mind is that the way you warm up areas of consideration, in which your craft is engaged, is different from the way you access conduits. That's because conduits don't need to be warmed up. Just about the opposite. If you access a conduit, warming up the system is the immediate and natural result. Sometimes, though, we might need to prime our conduits, like you prime a pump. Like a kick-start, first thing in the morning, something to clear out whatever's built up over time.

One final comment: let's not forget cooling down. If we think of our instrument the way athletes thinks of their bodies, then we're going to want to take some care that we don't leave ourselves vulnerable to damage after the intensity of some of our work.

We're far enough along in our exploration for you guys to do the talking. Why don't you share with me what works for you, as a warm up, and your sense of why.

MIKE: I like group warm ups, though I know there's a lot of grumbling backstage when they're called. I'm probably one of the worst grumblers. But that's because I hate warming up physically. If there's no group warm up, I never quite get around to it. If we're all doing it together, then I do it and enjoy it.

LESLIE: And how do you make sense of that, given your Creative Personality type?

MIKE: Relationship – all the way. That energy makes even the most mechanical stretching and articulation drills less of an effort. So, I'd say my conduit energy is flowing into my work on craft.

LESLIE: The perfect combination, I'd say. And your type?

MIKE: Magnetic. Relationship and Power.

IRIS: I'm probably your opposite, Mike. I need to do a very private, very physical work out, which I usually do at home unless I can come early and know I'll have the space to myself. I've always known about the physical, that's my Action conduit. But I'm Innovative, which is Action and Perception. I realize I need silence so I can open my awareness to the messages from my body, and so my imagination can flow without interruption.

POLLY: I've never liked group warm ups, and I'm a Relationship actor like Mike.

LESLIE: Relationship and Action, right?

POLLY: That's right. Personal.

LESLIE: Maybe because the actions aren't linked to relationships? Mike's other conduit is Power, so the sensations of submitting to the leader of the exercise, and feeling the power of growing mastery over his craft are going to be naturally creative and energizing.

POLLY: I'm trying to put this together with my own natural process. I'm thinking that, if rehearsals have gone well, and I'm going into performance with a solid sense of the relationship, and the actions, and I know I can trust my partners, then it's as if the rehearsal was the warm up.

IRIS: What about the non-conduit areas? Perception and Power?

POLLY: I don't think I really get Power, except as something that you work out in rehearsal, when you're thinking through the world of the play. I understand that. But it's not part of the warm up, for me. Perception? I guess I just count on my sensory awareness being pretty much constant, and my imagination's already had a good work out in rehearsals.

IRIS: So you're saying you don't need to warm up?

POLLY: To be honest, I've always thought that people who do an elaborate warm up in the middle of the rehearsal hall are just showing off. 'Look at me, I'm a serious actor!'

SALLY: Is that just because of your type? Rehearsals give you what you need?

LESLIE: I'd be very surprised if there's a direct correlation between Creative Personality type and the need for warming up. But I think you've made an interesting observation, Sally. We may find that our needs are quite different depending on the entire context surrounding any given situation. I can see, for example, how some types of rehearsals and performances would require quite a different type of warming up than others, depending not only on the requirements of the role, but also on the rehearsal process to that point, and the person's situation at that moment in her life, and personal creative habits which would include rituals of psychological preparation.

I think one of the benefits of training is the acquisition of a considerable range of possible activities that might be useful in warming up, that are available when an actor discovers that he's in a situation requiring a warm up of some special sort.

What I'd recommend is that you develop an awareness, based on your understanding of Creative Personality types, and in particular the difference between charismatic energy from a conduit as compared to the disciplined mastery of craft, so that whenever you encounter an exercise, perhaps in a class, perhaps in a group warm up led by someone else, perhaps in your reading, that might be particularly useful to you, you add it to your repertoire, so it's available to put into use when the situation requires.

VICTOR: So, if we're like Polly, and we don't have a personal warm up, what should we be looking for?

LESLIE: As you try out different warm up activities, be aware whether the sensation is one of energizing, unlocking of creative flow, or attention to craft. Challenges to craft will require a warm up that assists in advancing your mastery of a specific consideration.

Examples? You may be cast in a role that requires you to research a time quite different from our own, and then imagine yourself in that situation. That's a type of warm up for rehearsals, for example, that non-Perception actors might deliberately assign themselves.

POLLY: I do that, all the time. But I don't do it as a warm up half an hour before curtain.

LESLIE: Good point. But you might explore a personal version of the imagination/sensory awareness consideration, which is part of your craft as an actor, by a conscious, intentional effort to be hyper-aware of the costume and props you use in the performance, linking them to your research, to ground yourself in the alternative reality which is the world of the play.

POLLY: Would that be like walking the set, sitting on the sofa and chairs, after I'm dressed? Because I do that, if I can, particularly if I'm a bit nervous, like opening night.

LESLIE: Yes. I would consider that an excellent warm up, because you're blending your Action conduit, source of charismatic energy, with a consideration: imagination and sensory awareness.

IRIS: How about for non-Relationship people?

LESLIE: An excellent question. Your warm up, Iris, draws richly upon your conduits. But really, it's the areas that aren't your conduits that need the special consideration, right? So the traditional vocal and physical drills, which work best for Action actors, aren't going to help you at all in preparing those aspects of your craft that are the real demonstration of your abilities as an actor. Anyone have any suggestions? Here's where you can learn from people who have access to the other conduits. What we need is something that builds on either Perception or Action, but that addresses Relationship or Power.

SALLY: Okay, for Perception and Relationship – in the crowded dressing room, soak up the buzz of back stage energy. Don't block it out with your imagination and narrowly focussed awareness.

POLLY: That is so what Iris does, in the dressing room. It's spooky, like we're not there.

SALLY: I don't mean this as a criticism. Maybe, once you're warmed up, then you can slowly, carefully, open your awareness to the people around you, preparing for the relationships of the characters?

LESLIE: An excellent suggestion. Once the conduits have filled you with charismatic energy, then you'll be much more relaxed, confident, and creative – so you'll be ready to make use of what you receive from others, in a way that enhances rather than destroys your preparation.

IRIS: I can see how that works, and in fact there was one very difficult performance, in which the other actress and I sat quietly in the wings after we'd got into costume, and I started relating to her as her character while we were waiting. I'd study her dress, her hair, her hands. It was calming and also passed the time. We had a long wait for our scene.

LESLIE: How about Power?

VICTOR: I think anything you can do to feel the power of the play, the theatre, all those people buzzing out in the lobby – you know when they turn on program sound? If you use your awareness and imagination, and feel the power they're giving you, and also the huge and awesome power that makes you humble?

MIKE: If you can attach that to the play, to the other characters – who your character is in awe of, and who you look down on.

VICTOR: Plus the social systems, that make you powerful, and the ones that you have to submit to. Plus God. Or fate or whatever.

LESLIE: Since Action is the other conduit for Iris, there might be a ritualized action of submission and command that could be part of her physical warm up, that would link to the considerations of power that are part of her craft.

POLLY: I think that's what I'm doing when I walk the set. I'm thinking of the period piece, where the set was my home, and I had power over others there, because they came to visit me, or wanted something from me that I could refuse to give them. But there was a big portrait of my father, which I used for my relationship with that character – he never appeared – so I guess that's me working on the consideration of power. Warming up to that.

LESLIE: So far our discussion seems mostly about warming up for performance. What about for rehearsals?

VICTOR: Depends on the director. Some start with a group warm-up, or play games that lead into the work of the rehearsal. Some just tell us to warm up before we arrive.

LESLIE: Since you're immersed in a training program, you're not as much in need of warming up the creative instrument by the time you get to rehearsal, but can you identify what happens when you don't warm up sufficiently?

IRIS: If the director jumps right into the work, and it's a rehearsal day so it's the first thing we're going that day, I always feel like the first twenty minutes or so are the warm up. If I've gotten to rehearsal early, to warm up like we're supposed to, it pisses me off that everyone else takes so long to get truly present and energized.

LESLIE: Is the preparation for good rehearsing different than the preparation for a good performance?

VICTOR: Depends on the director and the stage of rehearsal. If it's supposed to be a free-flowing, creative time, then I'd guess you need to prime your conduits. If it's technical, or addressing something that you need to master, then you'd better warm up your craft, right?

POLLY: But can you separate them? Don't you need both, all the time?

MIKE: Maybe it's the other way around? If the director's really into playing games and experimenting, then maybe you need to come in with all your craft considerations operating on full energy. And vice versa – if it's a technical director, then you need conduit stuff to solve the problems?

SALLY: If there's a mismatch, that'd make a big difference. If the director's games and explorations match your conduits, then maybe you don't need a warm up as much as if his approach is something you have to work at.

IRIS: And there's a difference between warming up the body and voice, and awakening your imagination, right?

VICTOR: And remember the line across the circle? (see page 67). When we were talking about considerations? There's a difference between the upper two, Action and Perception, and the lower two, Relationship and Power. From the consideration side, at any rate.

SALLY: You've lost me.

VICTOR: Okay, I might not have this right, but I was thinking about the difference in my approach to the two that are not my conduits. I'm Visionary, so Power and Perception just happen for me. My considerations, where I have to develop craft, and where I need a different kind of warm up, are action and relationship. I can warm up my voice and body, and I've learned lots of strategies from people with an Action conduit how to relax my body, and get it more responsive, more natural, flexible, all that. But my relationship work, the craft part of it, that's homework about the text, about the society, what sort of relationship the playwright has given me to play. So I might come to rehearsal having done some work on the text, or some research. That's completely different than doing some stretches and tongue twisters.

LESLIE: Very nicely explained. What we're seeing here is that there are so many different conditions under which you're called upon to offer your creative instrument, which consists of you mind and your body, disciplined in execution of the considerations of your craft, plus that mysterious and unique something we've called the charismatic.

Some of your preparation for rehearsal involves intellectual activities, during which you consciously challenge the cognitive endowment of our species to contribute to your work. You think about relationships and power, in the world of the play. You imagine all sorts of things, including possible actions. Your disciplined mastery of craft includes education in how to use the brain effectively, how to read plays and analyze them, how to research and make use of what you discover, how to serve the dramatic structure of the play, how to make astute interpretive choices to serve the themes of the play.

Some of your preparation for rehearsal involves the preparation of the physical instrument, in which I would include not only the muscles that control movement and speech, but also disciplined concentration and focussed awareness, and emotional expressiveness. Your disciplined mastery of craft includes the mastery of heightened levels of flexibility, awareness, duration of sustained concentration and activity, range of experience, familiarity, and thus expression.

I think our discussion of warming up for rehearsals and classes is skewed by the fact that you're in a training program. Let's imagine, for a moment, that you've graduated and moved to a busy theatre city, where you're working as many hours as you can at a rent-paying job while racing to auditions. To keep yourself at the peak of your craft, you've signed up for some classes. You've paid hard-earned money for these classes, and you know you need them. You don't want to waste the first twenty minutes getting warmed up, right?

So here's my question. What classes would you want to take, to keep your creative instrument in top-notch shape, and how would you want to warm up for those classes? See if you can link your intuitions to your Creative Personality type.

Ideal Learning Environments

IRIS: Sorry to be so naïve, but can you give us examples? All I can think of is dance class, but that's different.

LESLIE: Dance class might be one option, or singing lessons – practical considerations for expanding the type of role you might audition for. Acting for the camera, if that's not part of your training. Scene study. Monologues. Shakespeare. Voice work. Creative movement.

VICTOR: How about things like academic courses, say in history, art, psychology?

LESLIE: Why not, if that would accomplish what you figure you'd need. We're imagining that there's quite a gap between acting jobs, during which you're working hard, waiting tables or driving a cab, something completely removed from acting, and you want to protect you creative instrument from atrophy.

POLLY: Can we assume the class would be a good one?

LESLIE: If you can define what would be good for you, then I think you're well on your way to understanding your Creative Personality type and how to protect your instrument.

POLLY: A good class for me would be led by a teacher who pushed me to take risks, but created an environment in which I felt safe and supported. That means honesty, but also courtesy.

LESLIE: Absolutely. That's the ideal. What else?

POLLY: Also, people taking the class who are equally dedicated and serious.

MIKE: And equally talented?

POLLY: Not necessarily. Well, maybe. If we say that talent is that they're charismatic. I don't care if they're as well trained as me. I just don't want them to suck me dry and give nothing back. Sometimes people who've never trained formally can knock your socks off.

SALLY: I'd like to be in a class with people who are better than me. More talented. Better trained, or braver. They take me with them.

LESLIE: I think what you're saying would go for everyone – it's the dream class. But can you be more specific? Think about your personal conduits?

SALLY: I'd like to be doing relationship work in the class, for the flow, but I'd like to be challenged in the areas I don't do so well, or so easily.

LESLIE: Would the challenge come from the other actors, or from the instructor?

VICTOR: If I think about my dream class, it's like what we were talking about earlier, one conduit in common and the other different. So, someone who's really into imagination and Perception, but combines it with relationships, and gives me concrete strategies for relationship work. Or a status workshop, so I can play around with power, but the person's also really physical, maybe clowning.

IRIS: That fits with what I was thinking of. I'd like someone who was very movement oriented, but used movement to explore relationships. And power. I like that idea, a clowning workshop.

SALLY: So I'd do something like scene study, for the relationships, but with a teacher who was really into the physical stuff. Clowning in pairs!

POLLY: I like the idea of the status workshop, because I'm still trying to get a grasp of power. Maybe movement based, because of my Action conduit, or scene study. Another suggestion for me: I once took an English class with someone who was really into the imagery in Shakespeare. I'd love to do a Shakespeare text class with someone who did image work in scene studies.

LESLIE: Your descriptions mirror my experiences, as well. I endured a complete mismatch during my university training, and so it was workshops that offered first the opportunity to cash in on my conduits. The most important was the purely physical approach, which was explored by the instructor very much in terms of relationships and Perception conduit impulses, both sensory awareness and imagination work. The other was my introduction to considerations of power, which began entirely physically but quickly became about relationships, because the majority of the actors participating were, I suspect, Relationship actors. In the first, the shared Action conduit fuelled my hard work on Relationship and Perception. In the second, it was the kick from the Power that opened me to new strategies for relationships.

Okay, so we've identified the perfect class for each Creative Personality type – a blend of one of your conduits and one non-conduit. Now. How would you warm up for your ideal class? Imagine you're arriving at the class, which you've paid good money for, with a little time to spare but in a physical, mental, emotional, and energy state that is NOT what you'd want to be in to get the most out of the class. How would you warm up?

SALLY: As I was traveling to class, say by bus, I'd let my imagination take over to transport me from the tedium of my job to the excitement of the scene I'm working on.

LESLIE: Would you imagine the upcoming class, or the world of the play?

SALLY: Both, but mostly the world of the play. I love doing that, and it gets me energized. Enthusiastic. Eager to start. That's my Perception conduit. I guess, for my Relationship side, I'd be thinking about the other people in the class, the teacher – anyone but the people at work.

LESLIE: And if it was the clowning in pairs?

SALLY: Right. Well, I'd need a good physical warm up. And I'd use my sensory awareness to keep it energized and not just mechanical, because if it's just stretching, I'll avoid it or rush it. Hey, I think I'm getting the hang of this!

LESLIE: I think you are, indeed. A blend of conduit energy and the demands of a craft-based consideration. Anyone else?

POLLY: For the Shakespeare scene study, I'd read the scene the night before, circle the images, and do my homework for each one.

LESLIE: Good discipline. And the creative spark would come from . . . ?

POLLY: That's a very good point. It would all be deadly, head stuff , so . . . I need something from Relationship or Action or both.

IRIS: How about developing an interesting movement for each image. Something really intuitive, not just a mime. I do that when I'm memorizing lines.

SALLY: Or each image could become a little story, and you always include another character in the story, so that the image becomes about the relationship.

LESLIE: Anything you'd do to warm up, say in the few minutes between when you arrived and when class started?

POLLY: Well, I'd probably do something physical and vocal, specially if I was tense from work and rushing to class.

IRIS: If you developed some movement for the images, you could make those moves part of your warm up, so it wasn't just mechanical stretching.

LESLIE: What do you think of these suggestions, Polly?

POLLY: I like them a lot. I specially like anything that avoids mechanical stretching.

VICTOR: Okay, I'm probably in the same clowning class as Sally, so my preparation is physical – but I'm going to combine it with Perception. I really liked what Iris said about her warm up, physical movement with heightened sensory awareness.

SALLY: You could combine that with imagining absurd situations, right? For your clowning?

VICTOR: I'm also imagining that part of the homework for the class is life study, where we're assigned to go out and watch real people, then build our clown skits on what we've observed. I figure I'd be on the alert for power issues, in my skits, and I'd be using my Perception to find good ideas, then challenging my physical flexibility to create interesting clown action.

MIKE: What about Relationship?

VICTOR: Maybe I'd go to another class for that.

LESLIE: That's one of the benefits of post-graduate studies. If you've relocated to a theatre center, where there are a variety of classes and teachers, you can pick and choose as part of an on-going strategy to enhance your craft through a variety of combinations. I recommend one clear, exciting, energizing match, so your charismatic energy is regularly unleashed, plus one area of clear challenge in an area that requires effort and so special consideration via deliberate practice.

Conduits and Considerations

POLLY: So you'd say studying with someone who is exactly your type would be wrong?

LESLIE: Not wrong, and maybe very necessary, particularly if your confidence and courage has taken a beating due to the tough reality of getting work as an actor. But you'd do that knowing that your craft isn't as likely to expand and might even slip if you didn't also seek some challenges. You'd want to warm up for such a class carefully, making sure that your conduits are fully engaged. And you'd want to cool down from such a class equally carefully.

Remember that the four conduits match up with the four general areas of consideration. If you and your teacher or partner match up exactly the same, then two considerations will require effort, and two will flow freely. How much more creative your rehearsal process would be if you could draw on creativity more broadly!

MIKE: So the best would be opposites, so each of the conduits is covered?

IRIS: But working with someone who's a complete mismatch would be damaging, right?

LESLIE: Again, it might be just the challenge you need when preparing for a particularly risky opportunity or if you felt your craft slipping and wanted to give yourself a tough workout. Artistic collaborations benefit from collisions between participants, because true artistry comes from energized effort, our own and others', so you might actively seek such collaborations when you select scene partners for private work, or for a collective theatre project. While technique is still being built, and while the conduits are being explored and the engine tuned, my recommendation would be one shared conduit, for the flowing, effortless creativity in that area of consideration, and two more areas to which each of you contributes, to divide the work of planning and shaping the scene.

VICTOR: What about the one area that no one has a conduit for?

LESLIE: That will be an area for disciplined effort from both partners.

POLLY: I know this is going to sound like a complete contradiction, but the only thing I hate more than someone who can't connect is someone who does just one type of acting brilliantly, so that's all you get every time you're partnered with them. I'm starting to realize that it might be because they're really good at using their conduits, and so that's all they're doing. They're not working on the other things, their non-conduit areas. And that means they're not really disciplining their charisma, either.

LESLIE: That's a very important insight you've offered us all. Sometimes your weakest areas as an actor are going to be your conduit-related areas, because it's always come easily so you've never had to use discipline consideration.

It's like a singer who has always had a lovely, natural talent but has never learned to read music. This person can go a long, long way picking up melodies by ear, and sensing harmonies based on the accustomed patterns of the popular music with which she is familiar. But do you think she could master an operatic role?

I find the same thing with actors whose conduits have allowed them to flourish in certain types of roles, and then quite suddenly they're cast in a part that requires a blend of chameleon-like effort and charisma.

POLLY: So you're saying we should seek out opportunities to work with someone who doesn't have a Relationship conduit, so we can learn from their relationship work, which is going to be an effort for them?

LESLIE: Effort makes it sound like failure. Consideration is the word I prefer. It's the disciplined, trained side of your work, that balances creative intuition. My recommendation always would be to confront acting challenges by drawing upon all four areas of consideration, because it is a combination of charisma and the disciplined chameleon that makes for the best acting.

VICTOR: So that's why you want us to work with a variety of types.

LESLIE: I think you'll learn the most from other actors who do NOT share your type. Even if the pairing results in some misunderstandings. The blend of contrasting conduits allows for creative problem solving from a variety of perspectives, which is going to be required when it comes time to address the impact of socialization.

Let's clarify some vocabulary. I use the general descriptive term 'social-ization' to refer to all of the habits that are part of your adult personalities. Under that general category, we have the restrictions, or crimpings like someone has compressed or clogged the conduit so the energy flow is restricted, often in one particular component of the yin/yang flow. We also have encrustations, another specific type of residue, which is specifi-cally all of the acting habits that we have developed over time. These are like pre-planned outlets for the creative energy, the 'same old, same old' that you have spotted in each other's work and diagnose in your own self-reflection. We can think of these as the barnacles and plant growth at the mouth of the conduit, where the creative energy breaks into the surface level of our acting choices. By definition, creative energy will lead us to discoveries, some of which would involve risk or brand new explorations. So if the energy is being channelled into familiar, restricted packages, we're losing a great deal of the benefit of the charismatic. The energy will give our work the key identifying markers of authenticity, so our audiences will be pleased, which makes this sort of restriction particularly dangerous if it reinforces damaging cultural stereotypes. Complacency, resistance to invention and risk taking, is a serious occupational hazard for actors.

Time for another digression.

Digression: Socialization

Just what is the noise that interferes so profoundly with our use of the conduits, even to the point where we might not be able to identify our personal performance personality type?

Without a doubt, socialization plays the greatest role in creating and maintaining noise. If we return to our definition of terms for our experience of selfhood, we see that the persona, which is the primary means by which we know ourselves to be an individual, is in fact a constantly evolving negotiation about the range of behaviours, roles, and styles of expression that will be used in self-creation.

If we extend this convenient metaphor of negotiation, we need to consider who are party to the negotiation and how does negotiation take place. We might imagine a scene between a parent and a child, where society in its wisdom sets restrictions upon the relatively irrational, self-indulgent child; some of those restrictions are oppressive but many are welcomed. In such a scene, the brilliant creative artist would be like an adolescent: parent's rules are old-fashioned, self-serving, counterproductive, and far less weighty than the artist/adolescent's drive towards self-expression. We might also imagine a three-party negotiation, perhaps comparable to family counselling, where the self is divided into two components, perhaps the rational and the irrational. Society might serve as the counsellor, helping our mind and soul contain and yet live with our own irrational and potentially destructive emotions and capacity for evil. Alternatively, if we imagine society and the species' collective unconsciousness as warring opponents seeking an uneasy truce, we might envision a rational, mediating self seeking to reconcile the two in hopes of avoiding mutual destruction.

All of these metaphors cast an individual's experience of self as a character, in other words a noun. What happens if we consider our sense of self as a process, a verb? Suddenly the metaphor of negotiation serves quite a different theory. Our experience of self-creation is the experience of constant, unending negotiation, or communication. We experience the communication systems of our psyche through all aspects of our psychophysical being, and we experience the communication systems of our society in the form of cultural hegemony.

All societies have a myriad of strategies for shaping the development of individual personalities. Even the most superficial examination of an education system reveals how children are shaped through socialization. But there is another layer of shaping that is less obvious and therefore more difficult to resist. Certain behaviours are deemed 'normal,' while others are labelled deviant. Everything contributes to creation of this cultural hegemony: advertising, popular entertainment, social pressure, traditions encoded in families and community organizations, the very language we use to make sense of our experiences. This creates a pervasive 'noise' that interferes with our perception of everything around us and within us.

It is tempting to attribute to brilliant creative artists a capacity to rise above the forces of cultural hegemony, somehow achieving a clarity of perception and a capacity for communication that is truly universal so that they are, like Shakespeare, 'not for this time, but for all ages.' But scholars have determined that creativity occurs when the individual's inspirations, combined with a significant will and disciplined productivity, intersect with a specific field with limited and defined range of expectations, within a social context set by a particular time and place. Therefore, rather than suggesting that creativity demands a resistance to the pressures of socialization, we might consider an artist's special capacity to reduce the noise that such socialization causes. The nature of the individual's sense of self and experience of being will of necessity be mediated through an interaction with her culture; therefore, what might differentiate an artist from others living at that time and in that place might be an increase in the sensitivity to the mediation itself.

By becoming more aware of how we negotiate our sense of self, and how society communicates its approval and disapproval of various choices within that constant negotiation, will not lessen the need to negotiate, but rather improve our capacity to negotiate without the noise of confusion, illusion, misperception, and wilful naïvety.

VIRTUAL WORKSHOP *SESSION FOUR*: SAFELY DANGEROUS

The group gathers, discussing their Creative Personality Types, connecting them with things that come easily and things that they've struggled within their professional and personal lives.

123

Perfectionism

IRIS: There's something you said earlier that's stuck with me, and I've realized is really getting in the way of my acting. I'm not inhibited so much because I'm afraid of strong emotions, but because I have such a clear idea of how I want it to be and anything less is so disappointing.

SALLY: That sort of imagining gives me real trouble in my private life. I'm always envisioning how conversations will go, and then it's never what I expect.

IRIS: With me, it's a type of perfectionism, which is part of the reason I switched from dance to acting – so I could be freer. It started out okay, but recently it's gotten much worse. I've tried to grow a thicker skin, I've psyched myself up to take risks, I've sweated buckets on preparation —

VICTOR: Maybe that's the problem. I know I had a big breakthrough when I learned to stop working so hard and just go with the moment.

LESLIE: That would make sense for your Power conduit, half of which is submitting, but I'm wondering if we can help Iris explore her creative engine using her conduits, which are . . . ?

IRIS: Action and Perception. I'm Innovative. Something you said before has really stuck with me. You talked about the 'movie in the mind' – and I've been thinking about that non stop ever since. I remember a dance teacher saying to me that I needed to discipline myself to be in the present as I danced, not in the future, thinking about the complex sequence coming up, or in the past, thinking about the mis-step I made in the opening.

Present Tense

LESLIE: You've made a very important observation about the experience of time. This is a mental capacity that we all share, how we experience the passing of time, marked by the rhythm of our heart beat and our billowing breath: in and out, in and out. Actors with an Action conduit are very aware of the relative tempo of movement. The point I'm making about time relative to the here and now is that it is very much a part of the Action conduit. The other human experience of time, when we are freed to roam forward and backward in time as well as space, is triggered by our capacity to imagine and remember, from the Perception Conduit.

SALLY: But doesn't the awareness of the Perception conduit bring us into the here and now?

LESLIE: Yes, but when you give yourself to complete sensory awareness, isn't there a certain timeless quality about that as well? I'm thinking here of a zen exercise of meditation on a smooth stone.

VICTOR: I don't have the discipline for that sort of awareness, but I can see how it might happen. I'm always flipping back into memory and imagination.

Disciplining the Flow

LESLIE: Yes, and that's another important point about the conduits – just because they unlock free-flowing creative energy doesn't mean that there's no need to work hard to discipline the riches they offer you. The mastery of a zen-like total here-and-now awareness might be a discipline that comes more easily to someone without the Perception Conduit.

POLLY: How could that be?

LESLIE: You tell me. I'll give you a clue. Remember when we were in the early stages of self-diagnosis? You spotted one of your conduits because you experience BOTH sides of the yin/yang, the blending of opposites. In fact, you couldn't separate them, they flowed into each other so completely. Connecting and disconnecting for Relationship, initiating and reacting for Action, commanding and submitting for Power —

SALLY: Imagination and Awareness for Perception. I remember that. I know I can't do sensory awareness exercises without a flood of memories.

LESLIE: Pure command, without a touch of humility, is something non-Power actors access easily. Same goes for just engaging in warm relationships. Or initiating all the time, without even a touch of reaction to anything else. Actors without the conduit can bring a simplicity, a lack of opposites, to any one side of a conduit's area of consideration.

POLLY: Because charismatic energy is a flood of blended, flowing – whatever – and it takes the consideration work, in the non-conduit area, to create a specific, limited shape like we've been talking about. Just awareness. Just imagination. Separated.

LESLIE: Exactly.

Craft and Creativity

POLLY: I've just had a huge epiphany. I'm pretty sure that Personal is the correct label for me, it matches everything, but I never liked the implication that I didn't have a vivid imagination or that I wasn't able to make good use of sensory input. But now I realize that I do both those things, but they're always considerations, and the free-flowing creative energy is coming from my conduits. In fact, it's my considerations that allow me to be a good actor. A trained actor.

VICTOR: For me, it was relationships. See, I have really strong and important relationships, in my private life and also with my acting colleagues. I'd be pissed off if someone said I was unreliable as a friend or weren't there for the rest of the cast. And I do a lot of prep about relationships – character histories, stuff like that. So I agree 100% – in a way I'm most proud of my work in what you call our considerations, our non-conduit areas.

LESLIE: What we're discovering is that every one of the Creative Personality Types comes with positive and negative possibilities from the conduits. Yes, they unlock creative energy, which we need for authenticity and charismatic star power. But they also encompass potential danger zones and blind spots.

At the same time, the areas of consideration, which at first sight seem weaknesses, turn out to be sources not only of our safety nets, but also our achievements in the disciplined side of acting, without which our charisma floats free and fails to fuel effective acting.

But back to Iris and her 'movie in the mind' – which I'm suggesting is a particular pitfall for Perception actors.

Directing from Within

POLLY: One of our teachers calls it directing from within.

MIKE: If I direct myself, I indicate like crazy – I make the cheesiest acting choices.

VICTOR: Maybe if you gave up control? I know I have to avoid planning too much, for that reason. I like control, but I need to take risks.

IRIS: Believe me, I've tried not planning anything, and my work's not any better.

MIKE: The trouble is that my imagination is so powerful, I feel like I've given control over already.

LESLIE: Because we've defined creative as flexible and fluid, taking flow as the sensation that confirms creativity is present, then the sort of self-direction that you've been warned about is cannot be a creative contribution from the actor, but a rigidity, more like what Iris has described. Not being able to let go of the movie, and trying to recreate it somehow, resulting in disappointment all round. That's what we want to avoid.

MIKE: I think it's better if I replace the movie of the performance with a movie about the character and the world of the play.

IRIS: I wish I could just shut down that part of me.

LESLIE: Any thoughts on an alternative to avoidance? I ask that because I'd hate to see you cut yourself off from the imaginative creativity of your Perception conduit.

We have to separate preparation, which is a creative 'priming the pump' so that the flow can happen in rehearsal, right? We have to separate imaginative preparation from trying to enact the 'movie in the mind'.

If you attempt to shut down the creative flow from your imagination, that can't be a good thing, right? But if you rely on it too much, and hook your Action conduit exclusively to the demands of one half of the other conduit, that's a recipe for disaster.

This is a test, to see if anyone has spotted the pattern in what I'm recommending to all of you. Has anyone spotted a common thread in all our discussions?

SALLY: Problems come when you don't use both sides of a conduit.

LESLIE: Sally, you get a gold star! Remember the yin and yang of each conduit? Action is initiate and react. Perception is imagine/remember and sensory awareness. Relationship is connecting and disconnecting, and Power is commanding and submitting. Every conduit can become a serious problem if you use just the yin, without the yang.

VICTOR: Iris is using imagination to prepare, but in rehearsal she's not using here-and-now awareness, which would take over from the movie.

POLLY: And even with the Action conduit – the movie plus initiation is when she comes with something planned, but if there's no reaction, then she's too rigid and can't pick up on what other actors are offering.

LESLIE: And remembering that reaction impulses can be in response things other than people, there would be possible reactions to her own body, to the room, to whatever is happening in her life that day, to colours and textures and smells. If the awareness energy is feeding her creative engine, along with reaction, that could balance the careful planning of the imagination, and she could blend the initiation of planned activity with the reaction energy for something much more fluid and flexible.

IRIS: Can I try this out?

LESLIE: Sure. First, just take a moment to use your powerful creative imagination to plan a series of actions that you know will unlock some forceful feeling for yourself as an actor. That will play to your strengths as an Innovative Creative Personality Type and also put you in harm's way, with regard to your old, bad habits. Why don't you go out into the hallway and plan a short movement piece.

Iris leaves the room.

LESLIE: Okay, our job is to offer Iris a rich set of actions and sensory input to which she can react. We'll need sounds, textures, colours, and movement. It doesn't matter what you offer, because she'll be able to use everything in the room. Let's watch her offering in order to plan something interesting. Polly and I will look for things to do. Mike, Sally, and Polly will look for ways to engage Iris in a relationship. Mike, Victor, and I will think about how to take control away from Iris, and we'll be counting on Victor and Sally to use their hyper-awareness to give us all good ideas. Above all, let's open ourselves to receive, as richly as possible, through our conduits.

SALLY: You're making us use our conduits, aren't you?

Iris returns and presents her movement piece. We simply watch, like the usual polite audience.

LESLIE: I assume that went pretty much as you envisioned it?

IRIS: Yes.

LESLIE: So why would you want to change that? I'm playing Devil's Advocate here.

IRIS: It's dance, not acting. My focus was on the aesthetic perfection of the movement, which matched what I'd choreographed for myself out in the hallway.

LESLIE: It was very beautiful, and an audience will get a strong emotional and thematic message from what you offered. We bring meaning with us, remember. We receive the gift of your charismatic energy, simply from the activity. We sense its presence and therefore experience authenticity, and that arouses a response in us that comes, in part, from our individual conduits. In fact, we read into the event as a result of creative energy we bring to the event, even as audience members.

SALLY: I so get that. You say it was just dance, but I saw such a clear character, such strong feelings.

VICTOR: It was powerful. The beauty of the movement gave it power.

MIKE: I couldn't take my eyes off of you. I agree with Victor.

IRIS: Thanks, guys, but there's a reason why I'm pursuing acting, not dance. I love dance, but I can already dance. I also love acting, and I want to be as good an actor as I am a dancer, maybe better.

LESLIE: Okay, let's shift to the awareness side of your Perception conduit and the react side of your Action conduit, as Victor and Polly suggested. I'm going to ask you to present the movement piece again, recreating the movie in your mind with as much accuracy and feeling as you can.

Iris does the piece again.

LESLIE: Here we see one of the gifts to the actor from Iris's Creative Temperament, the Innovative, which accesses Action and Perception conduits. When you need precision in blocking, an Action conduit is very useful, particularly when coupled with the heightened awareness of the Perception conduit, which allows you to monitor exactly what your body is doing and remember it for repetition.

But we want to challenge the awareness side by linking it with REACT instead of initiation of actions. Iris, we've planned something for you to react to. Your job is to open yourself to the creative awareness of what is going on around you, and allow your Action energy free-flowing reaction to what others offer. You might react to their activity. You might also react to sensory details quite separate from the rest of us. Also, things have changed since you created the dance. It's only been a few minutes, but life goes on. So you have a new set of memories to draw upon, fresh imagination, and slightly different input from your own body.

Iris bravely attempts the exploration, surrounded by a flurry of interventions from the rest of the group. It's a tug of war between her desire to maintain the dance and her willingness to react.

LESLIE: The real challenge here is letting go of old habits – encrustations – and freeing your own conduits from the discipline of your training. I could see the fight, moments when you'd respond to something, but it would come out as a sort of stumble, and you'd almost automatically recover and proceed with the next movement. The trouble is, the movement was one you had planned to initiate, so at that moment you lost the full potential of your action conduit's yin and yang. When it worked, it was because you were able to feed the reaction energy into the next initiation of action, and that action subtly changed as a result. Once a brand new action emerged, but only once.

IRIS: If felt that, as I performed. There were moments when a new movement impulse was right there, and I resisted it. Can I try again?

LESLIE: Of course, but the rest of us have to promise to avoid duplicating anything of what we did last time. Give us a moment to plan something.

Iris goes out in the hallway and the group plans something that works even better to challenge and enrich her initial presentation. Iris returns and goes much farther, this second time, in fluid, flexible reaction. Almost nothing remains of the original movement.

IRIS: That was fun, but I can improvise movement, which is what that felt like. I just threw out all of my earlier ideas. I guess that's what I have to learn to do. Start fresh every time.

LESLIE: Perhaps. But it seems a shame to sacrifice either part of your conduit. In fact, I think I'll go a bit further. It would be a deeply destructive to set out to cripple a conduit. You'd be cut off, forever, from one quarter of your charismatic energy. If you build your acting technique on that sort of dishonesty, I can't imagine the price you'd pay as a creative artist. I feel strongly that you need to honour the artist you are, which includes honouring the gifts and learning to live with the pitfalls.

SALLY: Surely we can use the gifts to overcome the pitfalls?

POLLY: I really believe you can blend the planned choreography with free-flowing reaction, if you have a few more chances to experiment. Isn't that what [one of our teachers] always says? If you get it the first time, the challenge wasn't hard enough?

LESLIE: I agree. We have to give Iris, and us too, the time we need to explore new ways of releasing creative energy. I think this exercise deserves one more attempt. Let's just clarify our goals. The rest of us now have some idea of what might happen, but as there's no director, we're all going to have to allow our impulsive creativity some freedom. Iris is our leader, as it's her job to integrate what we offer, and her reaction to it, into her original piece. That means she has to make use of her planning to provide our exploration with an aesthetic shape, but the best results will come from the greatest creative flow, meaning flexibility in reaction plus here and now awareness.

On this third try, Iris blends some planned moments from the first presentation with the more chaotic and improvised activity of her interactions with the group. The exploration lasts longer and has an interesting dramatic shape. It's not great dance or drama, but Iris is pleased with the emotional richness she tapped in the work. I notice that there is a marked change in her presentation and in the group's attitude towards her work.

Cooling Down

LESLIE: We had an excellent discussion yesterday about warm ups. But we didn't talk about cooling down. Have you explored such activities in your training?

MIKE: Only after movement class. And I guess what you have us do, after we present something – that's a type of cool down, right?

IRIS: I think lots of our teachers do a cool down without calling it that. I'm thinking of how one teacher ends class with a type of discussion or quiet reflection after pushing us to do very exposed and emotionally intense work.

LESLIE: Let's talk about just such a class, or rehearsal. We'll imagine that some very challenging but successful work has taken place, and you've unleashed some strong and therefore potentially upsetting charismatic energies. We've talked already about the potential dangers of this sort on deep-reaching unleashing. Can anyone who's had such a class or rehearsal experience share what the cool down felt like?

POLLY: It was a putting back together of the me, separate from the character. The teacher Iris mentioned, her strategy is to have us quietly recover, then talk a bit. When we talk, it's rationally, objectively, about the play or the language or the props or whatever.

VICTOR: Sometimes it's the other way around. We talk for a bit, about what happened, how we feel about it, and then we sit quietly, maybe writing in a journal or just thinking.

LESLIE: What do you think is going on, for each of you in that situation?

POLLY: If I think about it in terms of conduits, I can see that I'm pulling back from my relationship and action work. I'm pulling back on the socializations we were talking about. Shutting the conduits back down.

VICTOR: I'd say the same. But I'm still using them, in a way. If I've been totally in the imaginary situation, I'm thinking about the incredible power of being swept away, maybe sort of laughing at myself a little.

POLLY: Yes, I use my Action also, because I do little shaking out sort of things, to release emotions and let them go.

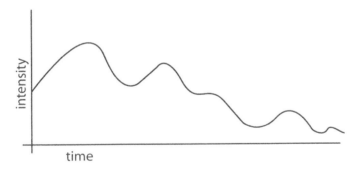

FIGURE 13 Emotional Explosion and Residue

LESLIE: This is very good self-analysis. I'm going to make a few general comments and then offer some specific suggestions for each Creative Personality type.

Perhaps you've heard of the term 'de-briefing?' If we consider our most challenging explorations, the one where we take real risks, as dangerous operations, then we should give careful consideration not only to warming up, but also to disengaging intense emotions, restoring emotional equilibrium, reapplying the healthy, normative socialization that keeps us out of jail, right?

I feel very strongly about cooling down, or debriefing. I feel that we can all go much further, in our acting, in terms of taking risks and allowing the fullest, riches opening of conduits, if we know we can return to a normal, healthy level of socialization. I think we need to practice such restoration, cooling down, what I call de-briefing. I'm opposed to acting challenges that invite students to leap into very deep waters without first ensuring a tried and tested method of de-briefing. I much prefer a short plunge, followed by an exploration of a variety of debriefing strategies until everyone finds something that works, followed by a further leap, followed by a test of the debriefing strategies, followed by a further leap, and so on.

Because conduits are the source of the truly transformative, truly creative, and truly terrifying energies, they are also going to be part of the debriefing as well as the reason why de-briefing is needed.

Each of the conduits can be used slightly differently in debriefing, depending on whether it was the primary or secondary source of potentially damaging energy. Option one – the experience is primarily connected with that conduit; therefore the selected disengaging actions CONTRAST. Option two – the experience is primarily from your other conduit; therefore the selected disengaging actions MIRROR in diluted form.

You need, in fact, a brake and a spin of the steering wheel. That's because the energies don't switch off like a tap. The residue permeates your psyche, which we could draw as a series of bumps, of decreasing height, as you move further away in time from the greatest release of dangerous energy (Figure 13).

An added consideration: the body-based conduits, Action and Perception, are slightly different than the cultural ones: Relationship and Power. There's no difference in the danger or the amount of charismatic energy that each releases, but there is a significant difference in how we experience the conscious, disciplined manipulation of the body-based versus the cultural-based conduits.

Action: you can summon very potent energies by initiating and reacting. Therefore, you can step away from the residue of such sensations by performing actions that arouse contrasting, safe and relaxing sensations. In addition, if the scene has aroused strong and dangerous energies from another conduit, you can use the Action conduit for purposeful release of the energy. In this case, the pattern of release is slightly different, as you need to offer the energy from the other conduit a similar shape for a mirroring expression.

IRIS: Sorry, I'm lost. What do you mean by mirroring?

LESLIE: If you think of a mirror, reflecting back what your other conduit has released, then can you envision how you could use your Action conduit to find an activity that is similar to, but not nearly as intense, and so an activity that could be part of a de-briefing?

IRIS: Like if my Perception drew on memories of pain, I could do a little dance that's like that pain but not so intense?

LESLIE: That's exactly what I had in mind.

Perception: you can summon very compelling energies by imagination and sensing. Therefore, you can step away from the reside of such energies by turning your disciplined awareness and imagination to a contrasting focus. In addition, if the scene has aroused strong and dangerous energies from another conduit, you can use the Perception conduit for the purposeful release of the energy through images and sensory awareness that are similar but less intense.

IRIS: Mirroring, but this time with your imagination?

LESLIE: Yes. De-briefing around Action and Perception, what I call the 'genetic' conduits work really well using these two simple strategies: contrasting and mirroring.

The experience of braking and spinning the wheel is different with regard to Relationship and Power conduits. There is no equivalent to the abrupt change offered by contrasting actions and contrasting images; nor the defusing via mirroring to catch lingering residues.

Relationship: The releasing of conduit-based energies in the relationship realm will colour the actual relationships that exist between participants. If the primary shift has been towards intimacy, then the other side of the conduit can be used to pull back, establish appropriate boundaries, etc. If the primary shift has been towards destructive relationships, then some conscious attention to warming, opening contact will reverse the trend. It will simply not be as simple and malleable as the body-based conduits.

Power: Like relationships, the experience of commanding authority and humble submission will permeate every aspect of the rehearsal and performance experience. If the primary shift has been towards command, then the other side of the conduit can be used to re-establish a more socially acceptable blend of authority and humility. If the primary shift has been towards humility, then the other side of the conduit can be used to re-establish a more healthy self-confidence. But there is no way to arrest or re-direct these sensations, as one can with the body-based conduits.

MIKE: So what you're saying is that I'm screwed?

LESLIE: It's true that Polly, Sally, Victor and I, who have at least one of Perception or Action, can develop de-briefing strategies using the contrast or mirror method. But do you find the idea of de-briefing beyond the scope of your conduits?

MIKE: I've never thought about it much, but I can see, when you describe de-briefing, that it's something I already do. Most of the time. I like the image of slamming on the brakes and spinning the wheel at the same time.

LESLIE: Can you describe your process, using the language of conduits?

MIKE: It's something to do with what we were talking about with the two sides of every conduit. If I've gotten out of touch with humility, which I need to keep my power in check, then the braking comes from reminding myself not to be so full of myself. If I've gotten carried away with the rage of the character, I just remind myself how much I actually like the actor playing opposite me. Mostly, that's all it takes to shut down the excess feelings.

SALLY: That idea of a residue, lasting for a while? That's something I have. Bad, sometimes.

LESLIE: As we've just heard, from Mike, our conduits are the source, and intuitively part of the solution. If you leave de-briefing to the conduits alone, you're battling fire with fire. That works, as we know, but only if applied very carefully, as when a controlled burn is used against a forest fire. The best control is going to come from your considerations. In other words, from your non-conduits. That's because they, by definition, are the focus of your effort, which, as we know, automatically cuts off flow. Remember, considerations are where you demonstrate your disciplined, controlled, and artistically sophisticated work ethic. I think you'll find that it's as easy to develop a personal de-briefing as a personal warm up. Until now, you've done it intuitively, but to go the distance you'll need to do it consciously and carefully. In other words, it needs to be a component of your craft and mature discipline as a performer.

De-briefing with Considerations

LESLIE: Let's turn our attention to the function of each of the four considerations.

Action: If Action is NOT a conduit, then you will be able to use a simple, ritualized or learned activity to disconnect your conduits. For Magnetic, Visionary, and Psychic actors, simply performing a series of mechanical movements associated with anything but the rehearsal just completed, will serve as a natural disconnect, like stepping on the clutch in a standard transmission. Putting on your street clothes. Looking up a telephone number. Washing out your coffee mug. Tidying your space at the makeup mirror. The more normal, familiar, and mechanical, the better. The stronger association with ordinary, boring, daily life, the better. The farther the actions are from those you are required to perform while acting, the better.

Keep in mind that this sort of action serves the same function when performed during a short break, and plan accordingly. Sometimes, it will be a bad idea to interrupt your creative flow by taking care of a normalizing activity. Other times, it may be exactly the best way to construct a safety net.

Perception: If Perception is NOT a conduit, then you will be able to use any of a variety of concentration and focus exercises to dissolve any lingering, inappropriate effect of your deepest charismatic energy. Again, make these as mechanical, as uninspired as you can. Summon into your head ten memory snapshots of people in your family. Sit quietly listening to some music, staring at an interesting pattern, or taking in the rush of activity on a busy street. Use your discipline to engage yourself in a bit of effort, the opposite of flow. It won't take much, provided you select the focus of your imagination and/or awareness wisely. Look for things that take you firmly and far from the fictional world you've just been exploring. Remember that a return to normal levels of socialization is the goal, so avoid anything that is in any way connected with the work you're just completing. Because Perception is an area for effort, for craft, and not a conduit, your intellect and disciplined awareness of process will assist you in locating the perfect exercise.

Dynamic, Personal, and Magnetic actors need to remember that imagination and sensory activity, if linked to things outside the world of the play, serve as disconnects, and monitor carefully what they spend their time doing during the breaks in rehearsal. You don't want to get distracted with making up the shopping list while waiting to enter into a highly-charged scene.

VICTOR: What you're saying reminds me of the tricks they teach you in the military. How to keep from losing it during battle.

LESLIE: Fascinating. I can see the similarities. Disconnection from an intensity that is overwhelming the body and the mind. You notice we started with the two considerations from the genetic realm. Now for the cultural realm.

Relationship and Power: For actors who do NOT have these conduits, these are intellectual concerns. Your conduit energy flows into these considerations, and you are perfectly able to enact characters within relationships and/or experiencing authority or humility. But for you, a conscious consideration of one or the other, depending on your type, will be like putting your foot down on the clutch of a standard transmission car. The engine might still be firing, but it's not churning the wheels. You can use this break to shift to a lower gear, defuse some of the excess energy, and launch your cool down procedure, bringing the racing, roaring, over-heated engine to a safe and fully controlled stop. Dynamic, Visionary, and Innovative actors can squeeze off conduit flow by shifting their attention to the challenge of enacting a complex relationship. Personal, Psychic, and Innovative actors can do the same by shifting their attention to the challenge of exploring issues of power in the world of the play.

A conscious shift from conduit to considerations, as we will discover in our explorations, can serve as fast and efficient ways of moving an actor out of the dangerous territory of excessive conduit energy.

MIKE: And you're saying we should plan our de-briefing strategies?

LESLIE: Yes. Explore them, test them, and practice them often enough so that they're ready and waiting when needed. Just as a driver might encounter black ice or an oil slick on an otherwise clear road, so too we actors sometimes find ourselves unexpected in emotional melt-down territory.

IRIS: I guess it's like everything else – one strategy won't suit everyone.

LESLIE: Very good point. Let's move closer to individualized de-briefing strategies by applying my suggestions about conduits and considerations to each of the six Creative Personality types.

I'll start, representing Dynamic, which is Action and Power. De-briefing is something I need to take care of when my commitment to authentic action has taken me into risky territory, summoning an intensity of energy that needs to be shut off, redirected, and which entails a lingering residue which could affect my physical and mental well-being. I also need to be sensitive to the sensations of authority and humility that I might experience authentically while engaged in a chameleon enactment of a fictional world, as these will not dissolve automatically. I need to restore a socially acceptable balance between the yin and the yang of the conduit.

Because my considerations are perception and relationship, I'll be using them, plus some simple actions, for contrasting and mirroring. So, to de-brief, I might sit quietly and summon up some images that anchor me to my private, non-actor life. I might intellectualize about my character, placing her out there as someone to consider, perhaps even discuss, with particular focus on her relationships. I'd shift from speaking 'in character,' using 'I,' to speaking of character, using 'she' or 'her.' The challenge of a concentration exercise will remind me of all of the aspects of my disciplined craft. The intellectual discussion of relationship will remind me of the responsibility I have to be the best chameleon I can be.

But I'll also take advantage of my Action conduit and make sure that I give myself some time for a physical work-out as part of a cool-down. If the actions have been the main route I've used to explore the conduit's darkest energies, I'll consciously set myself to use actions to summon alternative, contrasting energies, equally authentic, equally physical. If my other conduit, Power, has been the primary source of the frightening energies, I'll set myself to use my Action conduit to summon similar, but less intense energies, in a pattern that invites the gradually decreasing waves of sensation that are part of the residue of the experience.

Let's apply this to a specific role and rehearsal situation. Let's imagine I have to play someone facing death for her religious beliefs. I want to put myself in harm's way, to create a situation for danger, but safely. In one rehearsal, I voluntarily push the envelope as far as I can, knowing I have a good de-briefing technique in place. I leap into the most dynamic, terrifying, authentic movements, not caring just now how anything looks, but seeing where the actions and reactions will take me, seeing what intensity of primitive, wrenching energy might be released. You'll notice here, there's nothing about personal experience. There's nothing comparable that I can draw upon, consciously, but my body is an encyclopedia of species-specific memory, and I'm courageously going to see where it takes me. Well, let's say there's some interesting stuff to work with, but it's time to pull back into the safety zone. To begin my return journey, all I need to do is stop the action. But the intense emotions linger. That's what's dangerous, but only if I pretend my explorations have been without personal risk.

So I launch my debriefing. I do a few movements, intentionally summoning quite a different type of energy. Perhaps movements of freedom, if I've been exploring bondage. Movements of control, if I've been exploring hysteria. At the same time, I can use some considerations to get me grounded in a disciplined manner, so I might start intellectualizing about my character's relationship with others on stage. Who does she trust? Who likes her, who is she frightened of? Finally, I need to acknowledge, at the core of my being, that the sensation of complete humility and submission, that I've been exploring, is with me still. I can use my mastery of disciplined technique of imagination and memory to restore just enough of my sense of command to ensure that my healthy self-image is back in place.

Now, let's imagine it's the next rehearsal, and for whatever reason it's my other conduit that is the primary source of the energies. This time, I leaped into an intense, soul-destroying submission and opened myself to an extreme sensation of power, something far bigger than anything I could draw out of my puny personality. My way back to a healthy self-image is the same, using the considerations of relationship and perception to balance power's yin/yang within societal limits. My use of actions, however, is different. Rather than directly enacting contrasting emotions, my intentional cooling down actions work best to soak up and disperse, gradually, the residue from the Power conduit energies. So if I found myself grovelling on the ground, as an expression of extreme and terrifying humility, I might sit with head bowed, then gaze up into the fly gallery, awed by the scale of the building, relative to my size. I might roll my shoulders in, inviting sensations of shyness, uncertainty. Each action would mirror the overwhelming energy, but in a smaller, more manageable scale. I would also want to make use of a disciplined imagination or sensory exercise, simply to disconnect myself from the free flow of conduits and put myself firmly back into the effort-filled, craft-oriented state of disciplined mastery.

Is this starting to make sense? The idea is to get to know yourself, get to know what is potentially the most dangerous for you, thinking it through with an awareness of how the conduits work, and how we process the sort of energies the conduits unleash. Then, you need to develop your personal cool down rituals so that they're there to be used when needed.

Who'd like to go next? Perhaps you have a role in mind, which you'd have liked to debrief from in a more controlled and reliable manner? Or something coming up that you'd like to prepare for?

POLLY: I have to confess I'm worried about super-bitch roles, which I'm cast in a lot. And it's not so much that I can't debrief, as that I'm afraid that others won't realize that I'm not available the way the character is.

LESLIE: That's a tough one, isn't it. The better we do our work, the more successful the chameleon, the more likely people in the audience will assume that we're playing someone very much like ourselves. And the truth is, when we release our charismatic energy into the chameleon construction, the authenticity is indeed coming from us. I know that naïve fans can be a problem, loving and hating the characters we play and confusing them with us. But how much of your worry is that you'll not be sufficiently different when they meet you backstage, to know instantly that you're not the character you play?

SALLY: I don't think I'm following you.

POLLY: She's saying I don't like those roles because they're the real me I'm trying to keep hidden.

LESLIE: Not quite. I'm asking if that's what you're experiencing. Are you afraid of what people think or of being who you truly are? Either way, it's a valid concern, but please remember that what some might call 'super-bitch' I'd call a powerful, confident, self-actualized woman.

So let's approach your question from the perspective of debriefing following good conduit work that has released strong, profound, authentic energy. You're Relationship and Action, correct? The Personal Creative Personality Type?

POLLY: Yes.

LESLIE: Let's play around with the so-called super-bitch role. We'll imagine two rehearsals, one in which you'd primarily use Relationship and the other in which you'd use Action, in both cases to take you into such powerful emotions that you do indeed need to de-brief.

POLLY: Sure. The rehearsal using the Relationship conduit, well, I once had to humiliate another actor, and I think I did it a little too well. What I mean is, my character had to humiliate his character, but I got the impression that it was personal for him, so it was personal for me too. We'd sort of been going out, before that.

SALLY: I have that problem, too. But the other way. Like when I'm cast as a sex kitten? Some guys have a problem realizing it's acting.

LESLIE: Because relationships, like power, are socially constructed, we have to acknowledge that the real relationship between actors has been affected by the rehearsal, both of which take place as part of a larger social construct. From your side, as well as your partner's. Also, some plays are about relationships that challenge cultural norms. First, let's focus on your psychic health. Once that's back on track, you'll be more likely to find a natural way of restoring a healthy relationship, at least with those actors mature enough to realize that it was a rehearsal, not life.

So, imagine a rehearsal in which your relationship conduits have tapped an intense amount of charismatic flow. Thinking of your considerations, you might start with perception, and set yourself some awareness or memory exercises to turn off the potentially destructive energy. Because perception is consideration, not a conduit, you don't have to worry about these exercises arousing inappropriate feelings. Instead, they'll reconnect you with the discipline of the craft.

The other consideration is power. Any sort of intellectualizing about the relative power between the two characters, or issues like spiritual faith, fate, forces of nature – not to connect with the violent feelings or sensations of the scene, but to position you back into your function as a skilled and trained actor.

Remember, also, that you can use Action to help in the cool down. Remember that your strategy is to use the second conduit to catch the residue from the conduit that's the source of your discomfort, so you're looking for similar but far less intense actions as a means of releasing the left-over energies.

POLLY: That's not going to help me rebuild a relationship, though. When I've destroyed the other actor.

LESLIE: I think you have to accept that, if your conduit was engaged, the destructive emotions were real, in that an authentic energy was released. If you try to reconnect with the actor before you've debriefed from those feelings, he'll pick up the bad vibe. And if his are still pulsing, you'll pick up his dangerous energy.

POLLY: What if it was my Action conduit that I was using? I had to slap him, and we rehearsed it over and over. He tried to make a joke about it, but I could tell he knew I always felt something nasty when I hit him.

LESLIE: Because you are Personal, activity unleashes authentic energy. Every time. So what you explored in the rehearsal is potentially unhealthy if you don't debrief. You can use activity to put on the breaks and spin the wheel in an entirely new direction. Shift to gentle, quiet movements, whatever works to redirect you sharply away from intense and violent interpersonal engagement. You can also keep using your considerations for the disengaging effect of disciplined effort, and the other conduit, in this case Relationship, for that combination of mirroring and diminishing – for example a gentler version of rage, perhaps irritation, that you can start to laugh about. Any one of these strategies, or all of them, can be blended into a package – whatever works to defuse the inappropriate and unhealthy sensations.

SALLY: I can see how de-briefing might give you the courage to go further the next time, but that's no help if only one of you has the skill to work on intense scenes like a professional.

POLLY: I agree, but I figure we can only take responsibility for ourselves, in situations like that. If he doesn't know it's acting, and gets his little ego squashed, that's his problem.

LESLIE: True, but I also think a relationship actor will find it easier to establish routines for de-briefing with partners once personal debriefing is addressed.

VICTOR: Okay, I think I'm getting this de-briefing thing. I'll share with you guys about a role that I played in high school, when I didn't turn off the imagination energies like I'd know to do today. What happened was, I kept dwelling on the images I'd used to get into the scene. Bad idea, for lots of reasons. Now, using my conduits – well, okay, I'd do a quick sensory awareness exercise, focusing on my jean jacket which had this elaborate embroidered eagle. Complete change of mood. Or develop some happier images to focus on. And real, not the play. I'd also have to restore a better balance in the Power thing, which was way out of wack and got me in a lot of trouble outside of theatre. I could develop some physical stuff, or discuss relationships, my non-conduits – all that was harder for me so I avoided them like the plague, when I should have been using them to give myself more disciplined control over my own talent, such as it was at that time.

MIKE: I'm also going to talk about high school. The relationship thing, like with Sally and Polly, I can see how restoring balance, adding warmth back to extreme anger, and cooling down the hot stuff – that makes perfect sense. I can see how I could use Perception, like Victor said. I always hated those imagination exercises, and those 'stare at this interesting object' – but I can see how doing one of them would instantly get things back into the safety zone. Action's my other non-conduit, and starting an intellectual discussion about the blocking – that makes me feel like I'm back at work, not at the mercy of too much reality. That makes it a consideration, right? I also think that I could put what I discovered, by going that far, to work in the actual performance, if I blended whatever happened from my conduits, right away with my considerations, so that's an added benefit of this sort of de-briefing.

LESLIE: What about your other conduit? Power?

MIKE: I'm like Victor, I guess. If the power was what got me cranked up, then I guess I have a bunch of things to put it back in balance. Quiet stuff. I've never tried the other approach you suggested, trying to echo the over-powering sensation, but in quieter and quieter versions.

IRIS: The minute you said that strong emotions leave a residue, that approach made sense to me. I guess it's because, for me, action not only summons authentic feelings – if I'm swimming in a sea of murky feelings, not really sure what's going on, if I start moving, a gesture will become like a bucket, and it scoops up the feeling and gives it shape, so I figure out what's really going on. Does that make sense?

LESLIE: It does to me. Iris, because you're Perception and Action, being Innovative; both of your conduits are body-based, and therefore both of your de-briefing strategies are going to be that first type, what I call brake and spin the wheel. That doesn't mean that you can't use your considerations as well.

IRIS: I can see that, from listening to the others. If I'm pushing my personal limits, then without really knowing I was doing it, I'd use movement and imagination. The problem was, it usually took me a few hours or days to work through the residue. I can see how developing a more conscious, controlled de-briefing could shorten that time, and be a lot healthier. Also, I think I'd be much braver, be willing to go much further, knowing it wouldn't take days to come back.

LESLIE: And how might you use your considerations, in your debriefing?

IRIS: I like what you said, that anything that puts us in the space of using effort, being the disciplined and trained actor, grounds us in a good way, which would speed up the processing of the residue. See, I think the conduit would keep firing. The rehearsal would be over, but the images would still be there, like Victor said, or I'd find my body echoing the movements, but not in the decreasing way you described. For example, I'd by lying there, falling asleep, and suddenly the movement or the image would come, and trigger a wave of that feeling, very strong. It wasn't fun. And there's no way I'd be willing to risk going further, if that was the price I'd have to pay. I never thought of lying there intellectualizing about relationships and power, as a way of shutting down the creative flow, or redirecting it into useful acting ideas, like Polly suggested.

MIKE: I guess I'm the other extreme. I'm Magnetic, which means that both of my conduits are on the culture side. So I guess I have to accept that all of my acting is going to affect my relationships and my experiences of power.

LESLIE: You're going to have to take care to restore a healthy balance in both those areas. But think how you can use Action and Perception exercises. Non-conduits, as you call them – what I call considerations that are the focus of effort.

MIKE: I remember one show I did, also in high school. We used to have incredibly intense rehearsals, and then I'd head to basketball practice. The next year, it wasn't nearly as difficult a part, but I got tied up in knots. I've just realized, one of the big differences was that it was a different time of year. No basketball. You've given me lots to think about. I particularly like the idea of getting the debriefing in place and then venturing into some dangerous territory to test it and build confidence. I can tell right now, I'll go further, knowing I can get back. But maybe that's because I've had a bad experience.

LESLIE: Perhaps. But I think we've all peeked over the edge of the abyss, even if we haven't lost our balance. The conduits take us to a level of authenticity, a depth of feeling, an intensity of emotion, that we should be frightened of. We'd be fools not to be. Not every role requires hugely intense feelings, but even a light comedy or gentle drama can draw upon authentic sensations that need to be carefully processed.

I'm going to pick up on something that was said earlier, when we talked about Polly's experience of Iris as a partner in an emotional relationship scene. Polly talked about the sensation of Iris holding back, and I said we had to leave it to Iris to figure out if Polly was sensing a mismatch of conduits or a resistance to the somewhat frightening energies a conduit could release.

Negotiating Socialization

IRIS: I'm 100% sure that it's a result of my not trusting my real conduits, and trying to be something I'm not as an actor.

LESLIE: I think you're right. And I'm glad, because that means we can talk generally about socialization without talking about you specifically. And we have to come to terms with socialization in order to fine-tune our personal safety net.

I'm going to draw on my own acting experiences here, to let you guys off the hook, because some of this can get pretty personal and you should only talk about it if you're comfortable. You might remember me talking about power, and how women specifically and young people generally are socialized away from the command side of a Power conduit. That was very much my experience as a young actor. I was, in fact, terrified of my own power. I had vivid memories of being called 'bossy' as a child, and I'd internalized the very clear message that to be powerful was to be a bitch, a word that seemed to be said with a particular disgust by people I admired and wanted to like me.

Add to that the fact that as a student and as an actor working with authoritative directors (often male and usually much older) a sense of humility was only natural, plus being cast as sweet young things – well, I'm sure my Power conduit was decimated by socialization.

In other words, I was trying to draw creative energy through an access that was down to about half its natural capacity. There are a variety of metaphors that work here. You could think of small pipes from childhood never replaced by conduits of the size needed to handle adult concerns. Or you could think of crimping, like when an external force squeezes a pipe and it buckles in on itself.

You could also use the metaphor of a blocked drain, and start to think about the backup in the energy system. 'Look out, Fred, she's gonna blow!'

Now, socialization is a good thing, for the survival of our species. The last thing we want is to create people who unlock all of society's crimping, encrusting, blocking, etc. and let their personal energies out all over the place. Even in rehearsal. Specially in rehearsal.

We're not talking about mental health here. We're talking about accessing creative energy in service of an artistic activity. Unblocking for other reasons – call the plumber, or a therapist!

Various jokes here about ads for plumbing supplies and Draino.

Seriously, folks, if you abruptly unplug a blocked drain in your psyche, the result can be damaging. I'm often horrified at the reckless disregard for psychological health that we not only accept but even encourage in the theatre. I once taught in a program where the acting students figured it was a bad class if two or three people didn't leave the room in tears. Uncontrolled weeping and nervous collapse were the hallmark of acting excellence. Yes, tons of psychic energy was unleashed, but the cost was too high and the payoff, in terms of performance excellence, too low.

I'm a great believer in psychological safety nets, and that's what we're going to explore right now, provided you're willing to get up and try another type of improvisation.

General enthusiasm. Too much talking – time for some acting!!

LESLIE: I'm glad you're so enthusiastic, but I have to warn you, this will require you taking personal risks. Okay, now we have to be honest, and consider what our instincts are warning us about our individual social-ization, our individual danger zones.

Now, I don't know you, except for this workshop, so you'll be able to fool me very easily. You'll be able to present a bit of acting as a real personal challenge, when it's something you already do quite easily, and I won't know the difference. You might find it a bit more difficult to fool your classmates, but even they can't see into your private internal processes and could mistake a new type of external manifestation for a dangerous opening of a conduit.

So only you can plan how to meet this challenge, which is, quite simply, to dissect your process in connection with an acting experience that you KNOW is dangerous, so we can all learn more about how to negotiate this sort of challenge safely.

Emotional Blow Out

MIKE: I don't mind going first, because it's not really a secret. I completely lost it last year, while rehearsing a role that I identified too much with. I should have said something when they announced the play, as soon as I read it. Parts of the play matched up just about exactly with some unpleasant memories I have. When I saw the cast list posted, walking up to read it, part of me knew that if they gave me that role, it was going to be a problem, but then I saw my name, and no way I was turning it down, much less explaining why it was going to be too much to handle.

144

SALLY: It was something you had to work through.

POLLY: I agree, but not in rehearsal. I say that even though I was completely supportive of Mike all during rehearsals, and after.

LESLIE: Okay, this is a good example of how profoundly the sudden onslaught of charismatic energy can flood your acting with negative results, for the show, for the company, for the actor.

At this point it's tempting to indulge in a little amateur psychology, but I'd rather not. All I would say is that sometimes conduits open up for reasons of their own. It might be something in your private life, a trauma that shakes loose some of that socializing. Or it might be a unique match of character and persona, when the playwright offers a character digging deep, and you are suddenly flooded with pre-socialization energy, something you haven't experienced since your youth, but now in full force.

You don't want to face this sort of geyser unprepared. You don't want it happening in front of an audience, and you don't even want it happening in rehearsal, because pre-socialized energy is HUGE.

Without going into any more private detail, can we explore how an actor needs to access conduit energy as completely as possible and as safely as possible?

VICTOR: Would it be better to let it all out, early in the process, then get back in control so by performance you're able to make use of what works for the show?

MIKE: I think my big mistake was suppressing what was really going on. Tons of stuff was happening and I was so busy pretending everything was same old, same old. Like you said, a blocked drain, and then an explosion.

SALLY: We've already talked about this, so I know Mike knows what I feel about the show. Some of what he did was the best acting I've ever seen from him, but the actual performance wasn't that good. It was pretty embarrassing. Things like not loud enough, lines forgotten, stuff like that.

LESLIE: Would it be better to avoid roles that might overload your system and blast socialization's restrictions out of the way?

MIKE: I'm going to say no. I'm thinking of how hard we all work to get rid of inhibitions that get in the way of our work. Also habits, and they're very much socialization, or protection from unfamiliar intensity. Do any of us want to be able to play only characters that are like who we were when we came to acting school?

General response. The answer is clearly 'No!'

MIKE: I can say this because I was just a total jerk, totally trapped in

145

my jock persona from high school, and completely unprepared to play anything other than a commercial for breakfast cereal.

IRIS: Thinking in terms of conduits, how would you recommend opening up?

In Harm's Way

LESLIE: That's what we're going to try right now, if we can stop talking and start exploring. Okay. Here's the challenge. You know your conduits. You know your socialization. You think of an acting challenge that risks going further, deeper, into more dangerous, pre-socialized energy than you've had to cope with so far.

For those of you with a Relationship conduit, it might be in the area of truly opening to complete vulnerability, in a manner of relationship that is personally unfamiliar and so you can't count on well-established habits of control, of channelling and restricting the experience. Or it might be in the area of truly destroying the connection with another person. Or a combination of the two.

For those of you with a Power conduit, it might be a level of commanding or submitting that has the same sort of unfamiliarity or extremity or is combined in some way that you've been socialized to avoid. Look for something that is building up like a pressure cooker, or filled with signposts screaming: taboo! Don't go there! Danger!

Socialization work is most necessary with these two conduits, given their connection to the cultural realm. A lifetime of relationships within hierarchical cultural institutions – well, that's what socialization is! It's no wonder that Relationship and Power are the focus of so much of our concern. If we think about what actors bring from the genetic realm, the capacities of the body, which have the strongest connection to the Action conduit, and the capacities of the senses and imagination, which is the territory of the Perception conduit – the interplay of socialization and training function differently in those areas of consideration. There are activities that are deemed inappropriate, and things we're not supposed to dwell upon, but theatre gives us permission to rebel against those 'norms,' even as we train ourselves to put aside mental and physical habits that get in the way of the versatility required in our chameleon work.

Now, this means that Iris, who has an Innovative Creative Temperament, and therefore an action and perception conduit, will experience this socialization work differently. Everyone else should have some raw material to work with simply by addressing, with some honesty, the sort of acting challenge that is marked with the tell-tale warning signals of socialization – something connected to Relationship or Power.

SALLY: I'm having a bit of trouble figuring out the difference between socialization and misuse of emotional memory. We've been trained to make use of personal memory only if they're not so fresh and raw that we can't channel the feelings into an appropriate substitution.

LESLIE: Good point. There are specific risks from intense feelings sparked by both Action and Perception that, as adults, we learn to monitor and control in order to fit in with socially acceptable expressions of feeling, and for personal mental health. 'Safely dangerous' is the goal, always.

Okay, as we're preparing for the exploration, you're job is to plan a little scenario that would put you directly in harms way, so to speak, with that danger zone.

MIKE: And if we have both Relationship and Power?

LESLIE: My guess is that one of the two conduits has been socialized in a more extreme manner. Or, another way of putting it, that you're at a different stage in unlocking and using the conduits, and you could explore the more dangerous, least unlocked conduit for this exercise.

So here's the next challenge: is anyone willing to (a) identify one conduit where you intuit a build-up of untapped energy due to socialization, and (b) imagine an acting situation like what Mike described, one that would take you into direct contact with a potentially messy explosion. Any volunteers?

Victor bravely agrees to try.

Power Pitfall

LESLIE: Victor, remind us of your Creative Temperament.

VICTOR: I'm Visionary, which means Power and Perception. I've been thinking about Power, and I totally see your point about teachers and parents not wanting me to access my commanding side. Specially my dad. But I've been playing powerful roles as far back as high school, and I get off on the rush of unleashing that energy. It's the other, the humility, that scares me. I can see how, if I push it as far as it can go, that it's like losing your entire self. Like erasing your soul. I had a good friend kill himself a couple of years ago, and that's what I think of, when I imagine going that far into humility. So that's going to be my scenario.

LESLIE: Brave choice. You'll be able to use your Perception conduit for additional creative energy, in building the moment, right?

VICTOR: It's going to be hard not to. Though Sally's right, I'm not sure this would be good for an emotional memory exercise, because it's still too raw.

LESLIE: Safely dangerous – that's the key, right? Only you can judge the best balance between risk taking and safety. Use what works, and maybe draw more on your sensory awareness rather than the memories that are too loaded.

VICTOR: Okay. You want a monologue? I have one that really fits – it's so scary how close it fits.

Safety Net

LESLIE: Hold on, one more stage before you jump into an exploration. This is really the crucial ingredient – the NON-conduit work that will be the safety net for whatever happens.

In Victor's case, he's working with Power and Perception conduits, leaving him relationships and action for consideration. This means that he can coolly, rationally, in a disciplined manner, plan an activity and set up relationship work that will allow him to make his way back from wherever his conduit takes him.

So, it's a very simple exploration, like bungee jumping. You make the leap, and the activity and relationship are the cord that bounce you back into the safety zone. Ideally, you'll bring something invaluable back with you, something that you can use safely and effectively with the help of you considerations.

The leap is internal, private, with whatever external manifestations emerge – maybe nothing, maybe something. It's your conduit, you're the only one who can use it to fuel your internal process. Also, you have the most direct access to the symptoms of socialization that are part of who you are, that you don't want to erase, but that are currently restricting your conduits.

Stage one. Muck around, let something happen, unleash some energy. Push at those encrustations. Un-crimp the pipe. Shake up your familiar, safe habits. Keep it small, private even, at first – to test your debriefing strategy. When you know you can get back safely, push harder, see if more encrustations can shake free. That's all in the preparation.

Stage two. Start the pre-planned activity within a relationship. For that, you need advanced planning. Suggestions, building on your scenario?

VICTOR: If Polly could be my sister? And she comes in, and sees me, getting ready to kill myself, and comes over and hugs me, big sister-like.

POLLY: Sure. When?

LESLIE: You need an activity, Victor. And a clear cue for Polly would be ideal.

VICTOR: The activity will be taking off my shoes and socks. And Polly can come in when I'm down to one sock.

LESLIE: Great. I like the specifics of that plan. When you're ready.

Victor's improvisation. In the 'leaping' stage, he simply sits, bowed with the weight of his submission to what he's remembering and imagining. Then he begins the activity, Polly makes her entrance, they embrace. A discussion follows about what people observed and what Victor experienced.

LESLIE: Okay, to summarize: Victor thinks he could go even further, now he's experimented with using the cooler, more rational considerations, in other words NOT his conduits, as a type of safety net for the effective use of dangerous explorations. Also, his unique capacities and talent as an actor is very much a product not only of his Creative Temperament, but the specific form his socialization takes. In other words, socialization isn't a negative thing, because the unlocking results in a type of acting that only Victor could do.

MIKE: Victor chose that speech because he couldn't do it easily. So that made his work special. What I'm getting from this is that there's something in our best work, when we touch on really deep human truths, that comes from what we might think of as problem areas, like our inhibitions.

LESLIE: Excellent point. I'd add, that it's the blend of socialization's pressure on the energy flow PLUS your areas of consideration – your NON-conduit areas – that results in the strongest types of shaped dramatic event, what we call great drama. In other words, artistic sensitivity, the capacity to tap into the most disturbing mysteries we face as a species, is directly linked with an artist's personal struggle.

VICTOR: So we should stop calling our challenges 'weaknesses.'

LESLIE: Yes! Anyone else feel they could share something about private process, about challenges that might turn out to be unique capacities for artistry?

POLLY: I've been trying to think of what I could offer, and who I'd ask to work with me. It would have to be a man-woman scene, and – no offence, Victor – I'd pick Mike for that sort of thing.

VICTOR: Sure. Cause I'm not one of those Relationship actors you like so much.

POLLY: But that's the point. I realized, if Mike and I work together, it will definitely fall into some old habits. And it's not because of the scenes we've done in the past, because I've done as many, or more, with Victor. It's something about trusting the impulses, which, to be honest, I don't. Specially in love scenes. Specially when there's some real activity, you know what I mean? And for me, to do that activity is to feel those feelings. So, in a way, I'd trust Victor more, if I were going to explore the scary stuff. Sorry, Mike. I've changed my mind – I'd like to do this with Victor.

LESLIE: In fact, Victor's a very interesting choice. He's the opposite: Visionary to your Personal. He has Power and Perception, you have Action and Relationship. That means that you can explore blending Action and Relationship, with the safety net that his conduits are your considerations, and vice versa.

VICTOR: Can you repeat that for me?

LESLIE: Conduits allow access of the potentially dangerous, because too intense and pre-socialized, energy, and considerations are where the disciplined training is going to kick in automatically. Safety is always going to be easy to integrate with effort. When partnering, the one who has the conduit brings a free-floating, inventive and intuitive creativity, and so can push explorations into messy risk-taking. The one who the consideration offers just that – the disciplined, thoughtful shaping of the energy for safety and the disciplined control that results in a successful performance.

In other words, your job will be to discipline and shape Polly's Relationship and Action energy. In turn, Polly will shape your Power and Perception creativity. Since you're assisting her exploration, we'll focus on her process to set up the scenario. Polly, can you share a bit more of what you're interested in exploring?

POLLY: You guys are going to laugh, but I'm actually very shy.

She's right. The group is amused at this self-image.

POLLY: No, it's true. I was painfully shy, all the years growing up, until I discovered I could hide behind a character, in the theatre. Maybe shy's the wrong word. Private. And I was raised in a very strict environment. Anything sexual was, like – shhhhh! So, I find love scenes very, very difficult. Specially when the director says, you two just work something out between you.

LESLIE: Polly, we need to set up your safety net, which is going to come from considerations of Power and Perception. Let's link Power to control, and Perception to memory. Victor is going to help you access control by approaching the action of the love scene entirely from the perspective of blocking, controlled movement. Just like staging a fight scene. Not something to be improvised, which forces you into a level of engagement that embarrasses you. Also, Victor is going to access the memory side of Perception by providing the given circumstances, the past history of these two characters. That will help you to separate Polly from the woman in the scene.

What I'm going to suggest is that you two go off and plan something.

Now, Polly, I know that's the very thing you talked about disliking so much. My hope is, that by undertaking the challenge you'll develop concrete strategies for dangerous safety when staging a love scene. Keep it very short, and simple. Block it, together, blending Action and Power, Relationship and Perception.

They don't take long and return with a beautifully touching enactment of a tender embrace that evolves into a passionate kiss.

VICTOR: Well, I enjoyed that.

POLLY: It's still not easy for me, but I can see how I could use what you're suggesting, considerations of power and memory, to manage that sort of scene. And I want to say something else, about working with Victor. I realized, when we were preparing, that I've been keeping myself closed to him, and I also realized why. It's because I think I've always known, subconsciously, that I could choose to trust him, and choose to open to him, but that's dangerous. Does that make any sense?

SALLY: It does to me.

IRIS: It sounds like you're discovering that what you assumed was your strength is also linked to what you fear.

VICTOR: And vice versa.

IRIS: What?

VICTOR: Your weaknesses are to be trusted. That's what I meant.

Sally offers to go next.

Relationship Pitfall

SALLY: I'm a Psychic actor, which means Perception, my favourite, and Relationship, which scares me. When Polly talked about holding back, for fear of what might come out, that's me. I've had some really unpleasant experiences where I've got way too involved with someone because of the chemistry that goes on in rehearsals, and to be honest I'm really struggling with a moral issue here. I don't want to embarrass anyone, but we all know that sometimes real stuff starts happening, when you're working on a sex scene.

MIKE: You weren't supposed to notice.

General laughter.

LESLIE: How about the other side of the Relationship conduit: the destruction of a relationship?

SALLY: Oh, I'm very good at that! Bitch and Slut. That's what they call me.

LESLIE: Those are cruel words. Our profession doesn't have a great reputation with regard to relationships, does it? Let's consider the issue of creative energy. If you have this incredible resource for deep, rich, complex energy, and you're afraid to use it, then it's like you're cut off from what could make you a brilliant actor. But you don't want to live up to those nasty words, because then you'd be paying a price on the private level that you can't and shouldn't have to pay.

If we can't find a way to use that energy safely, then it's not much use to us, right?

SALLY: Not if you want a happy and lasting relationship, which I do.

LESLIE: Here's my question. Is there any difference between this and Victor's exploration? He pushed himself into some dangerous territory, towards suicide, but within the safety of a fictional scenario, and when he was done, the socialization against suicide was restored. It was actually easy to get back to stability, because the spring cleaning we performed on his conduit allows him to draw on both the yin and the yang of Power. Humility is balanced with commanding power. The character he played, deeply flawed and troubled, had no authority, no opportunities for power. But Victor, by achieving some strong acting, re-established the blend of authority and humility which is needed for his acting and even, I'd suggest, for the scene.

Where am I going with this? I'm heading towards the 'destroy' side of your Relationship conduit. You said that you do 'destroy' well, but my guess is that you don't actually do it well enough to balance the connecting side. If you did, you'd find it as easy to shut off the strong connection with a fellow actor, when the rehearsal is over, as to turn on the strong connection during a love scene.

SALLY: I can end a relationship, like that [finger snap] but I feel like a total Bitch when I do.

LESLIE: Ah ha. That's socialization. What you need is a firm command of that finger snap OFF, with no regret, no guilt, no shame, no self-judgement.

Remember, we're talking about creative energy, not relationships in your private life, which will, and should, remain complex and inevitably influenced by the social norms of our society.

SALLY: But this is a real relation. With the actor, I mean.

LESLIE: Sally, you make a very good point. The relationships that we form when working together are, indeed, real relationships. When you work with someone over time, given the emotional intensity of our work, are we surprised when those relationships become significant in our lives outside the rehearsal hall? So the problem isn't just as simple as separating the fictional from the real, because both are involved. It's easier to develop an on-off switch for fictional relationships. It's a larger question of personal boundaries when you're thinking about work-place relationships.

POLLY: But everyone who works together has that – like office romances, you know.

LESLIE: I think we have to leave personal choices for discussion at break. Our focus needs to be on that on-off switch for enacted relationships. So let's try an exploration. We'll set up the safety net first. Remember, we use non-conduit areas for that. For you, these will be Action and Power. I'm going to give you a very specific bit of blocking that blends these, for the experiment. And we'll do it a couple of times, as it's going to be simple and short.

SALLY: It's like practising your recovery before you take the leap.

MIKE: Like Victor said, knowing how the safety net works, makes it easier to go further.

LESLIE: There are benefits to non-conduit work. The absence of charismatic energy locks you firmly in the realm of disciplined chameleon work, where you should feel safest.

SALLY: But mechanical.

LESLIE: A little, yes. But remember, this is for the purpose of exploration. In performance, your safety net would remain out of sight.

VICTOR: The safety harness is under your costume.

Bungee Jumping

LESLIE: Nice metaphor. So, Sally, are you ready to be safely dangerous? Like with Victor, we need to develop a scenario that puts you in harm's way, so to speak. You need to send yourself out on a dangerous acting mission.

I'm going to volunteer Mike, whose Relationship and Power conduit will be particular useful for this exercise.

A strong reaction from Sally and Mike clues me into some shared history. Leslie seeks confirmation that they are both comfortable with the pairing before proceeding.

LESLIE: Sally, don't bring your Perception conduit into play by drawing on memory. Instead, see if you can discipline that creative force by a strong focus on the other side, sensory awareness. It's going to be powerful enough, when combined with relationships.

SALLY: Oh, it's powerful, all right.

Mike and Sally are already manifesting sexual chemistry.

LESLIE: Wow! Slow down a sec. Let's get the Action and Power set. Sally, your blocking is simple. You'll kneel at Mike's feet, looking up at him. He'll stroke your cheek.

SALLY: Thanks. And I'm supposed to control myself? Like how, exactly?

153

LESLIE: You're right. I want you to throw yourself directly into the most dangerous sort of emotional engagement, to begin with. But the point is where you're going next, which is the Action and the shift in Power – from that position, you'll close up. Cool off. Then, rise up from the floor. Mike, become humble, using your Power conduit as she rises. You might even sit down. Sally, the power in the relationship is now all yours. And destroy him. Just stand over him, looking at him, and cut him to the heart. Kill him with all the power of your Relationship conduit.

Sally tries the exercise, and quite enjoys it. It's clear she is presenting something familiar, a performed moment with minimal personal risk.

LESLIE: Yes, it's fun. But now I want you to go further. You know the move – it's something that you've considered and undertaken with the cooler, rational part of your trained acting self. And you understand the concept of the shift in power. That's what will sustain you in the scene. As you tap your Relationship conduit, accessing the destroy energy, push gently past the restriction that society places on that energy. See if you can access something even more dangerous, without shame.

Sally tries again, and the exercise shifts to something slightly darker, but not much.

LESLIE: That's the balance to the opening side of the conduit. You're still holding back from anything dangerous, right? It's safe, it's in your control, it's clearly acting because Mike isn't really being hurt.

SALLY: I think I'm holding back from it being real. It's not authentic yet.

LESLIE: It might not reach a level of authenticity until you can release the other side of the conduit, which is where we'll go next.

Same action. Same attention to a shift in power, which Mike is helping with because it's one of his conduits. But now, you're going to sit a bit longer in the open relationship position, and I'm going to ask that you bring all of your memories and sensory awareness into full force, and allow the most dangerous type of inter-personal feelings to emerge.

Then, see if you can shut those feelings down through an authentic, real shift from opening and connecting to closing and destroying. Because there will now be a real emotional connection, between you and Mike as well as between your characters, to shut down.

Sally tries again, with little difference.

Resistance

SALLY: I'm not taking the big risks, I'll tell you that right now.
LESLIE: Any idea why?

MIKE: I can feel the resistance. Like you come to the point and then turn away. Maybe because it's an improv? If it was in a play, you'd go for it?

SALLY: That's part of it. A play would be the safety net. But the point is, I need my own safety net. Or bungee harness, to pull out of the relationship. I think the real problem is I don't trust the safety net.

LESLIE: Perhaps I didn't suggest the best one for you. Maybe only you can guide the experimentation, find what works, and then venture into risky territory, testing the safety net a little further each time.

IRIS: I can see how that could work, but it would take some practice.

SALLY: But it's worth doing, in my case, anyway. I know you said earlier about it not being therapy, but I think some of what I need to work through is connected with some non-acting baggage. So I need to deal with that too, sooner rather than later.

LESLIE: Yes. In fact, I highly recommend that you assess your own individual potential for bursting dams or other sorts of collisions between healthy socialization and acting challenges. If this needs to be explored in the context of private therapy, then I urge you in that direction, like Sally has said. Please, be careful about pushing yourself too far, too fast. Also, I urge you to expend some of your training time developing your debriefing or safety net strategies, including testing them out so they will be there when you're under stress.

I'll say it again, because it bears repeating. We can't lie to ourselves. Our work requires that we muck around with some heavy stuff. Just like a mountain climber wouldn't set out to conquer Everest with a sprained ankle, you guys should think carefully about bungee jumping into Everest-like depths of your psyches carrying a shit-load of personal baggage and out of kilter as a result of old, untreated emotional scars.

Thanks, Sally, for your honesty and courage.

SALLY: Even though I didn't get anywhere.

LESLIE: I think you got somewhere, and I think the results will show up in your acting, even if that didn't happen today.

It's the end of the session. Time for another digression.

Digression: Temperament and Aptitude

Creativity research suggests that there are certain personality traits that creative people share, though there is no agreement as to what a list of these traits might include and, as soon as a list is proposed someone can offer a case study proving that a spectacularly creative individual demonstrates only a very few of these traits. This is comforting, because I suspect that there are as many variations of human personality within the acting community as within the general population. I would hate to contribute in any way to the 'diva syndrome,' that unfortunate error made by many young performers who, thinking that an actor must demonstrate a certain temperament, adopt an stereotypical artist's persona in a desperate effort to bluff, to mask uncertainty or to outshine competitors. These sorts of impersonations require a great deal of focus and energy to sustain, energy diverted from the charismatic potential of the young actor and unavailable for the demanding work of the chameleon.

What has proven much more appealing to me are the theories that have replaced the question 'Who is creative' with the question 'Where does creativity take place?' It is refreshing to take the focus off of the single genius or artist and place it upon the context within which that individual rose to prominence. It reminds us that even the greatest stars could not be successful if conditions were not right. If this understanding fails to make a diva more humble, surely it will offer encouragement to those thousands who toil out of the spotlight to create the conditions for great events of artistic creativity.

Psychologists use the term 'domain' to describe the relatively self-contained craft of discipline within which the creativity occurs, and 'field' to describe the cultural environment within which the activity is perceived, both of which must be supportive of the individual for creativity not only to occur but to be known to have occurred. Actors work within a tri-part system of field and domain due to the unique event of rehearsal, which combines creativity and presentation undertaken by participants in the domain and field. To restate this idea in ordinary words: actors during rehearsal are involved in creative activities within the discipline of acting, side by side with other actors engaged in the same function, and in addition each of the actors present is representative of the forces that assess and acknowledge the achievements of creativity in the field. You might be working away on a scene, giving yourself over to some sort of transformational imperative, supported by your partner, who is spurred on by your creativity even as s/he inspires you. Then, as you break and receive notes, you might be moved to say to or about your partner, 'That was great acting,' meaning that you acknowledge the essential creativity of what just took place. When the play moves into public performance, the critics and audiences weigh in to challenge or confirm the assessment of members of the field. Over time, when your assessment of your fellow actors and that of your audience correspond regularly, your function as the voice of both domain and field is affirmed. That is why a young actor can be so encouraged by the praise of an experienced colleague.

Because almost all theatre companies must be equally successful in both field and domain to survive financially and artistically, theatre professionals place great importance upon developing capacities to judge the work of colleagues in a viable blend of domain and field considerations. Acting that demonstrates a mastery of all of the techniques of acting but fails to appeal to an audience is not 'great' acting. Acting that arouses a huge response in the general public but which leaves other actors cold is not 'great acting.' We all know actors who are much admired by only other actors or only by the public, and therefore those who are admired by all hold a special place in our regard.

Most theatre schools and companies are, to a greater or lesser degree, meritocracies. Those who are the most talented have the most prestige and, more often than not, play the largest roles and collect the biggest salaries. If this is not the case in fact, it represents the ideal towards which we aspire. The identification of that elusive thing called talent, by teachers and directors, and the nurturing of that commodity by all who care about the excellence of the profession, is a central component of the majority of theatre institutions.

But what exactly is talent, in this context? Is it a natural capacity for mimicry linked to a strikingly charismatic personality? Or is it in truth simply the predisposition of certain individuals that happens to match the current fashion in physique and personal style? Although I would love to argue that talent is another word for the charismatic chameleon, I fear that what is deemed talent has as much to do with conformity to expectation as it does with any inherent artistic capacity.

The reasons for my conclusion are two-fold: (1) the techniques of mimicry can be acquired by anyone and, (2) everyone has access to profound creative energies. Why then is not everyone excelling at this particular artistic activity and, furthermore, why do some individuals with a desperate desire to be actors demonstrate little or no aptitude for the work?

Although everyone is physiologically capable of chameleon-like mimicry, a limited number of individuals have a natural aptitude for the rigorous training and dedication required, even by those who make it look easy. There is, after all, an element of intentional and hyper-aware self-manipulation that does not really appeal to most people. Often, an individual who aspires to a career as an actor discovers not so much a lack of ability as an abundance of resistance to this aspect of the craft.

Similarly, although everyone has the capacity to access profound creative energy, a far more limited number of individuals have the courage to address the noise and crimping that are the inevitable side-effect of socialization. Once again, it is less a question of limited ability as of maximum resistance to a very special kind of self-diagnosis and remedial re-configuration.

Even with these not unexpected limitations on the pool of potential actors, it is quite clear that far more aspire to the work than are accepted into professional training programs, and not all of those enjoy professional employment, even occasionally. Here is where the effects of conformity are most felt. With regard to the chameleon component, our cultural definitions of character types sets very specific ranges of physique, vocal habits, and personal expressiveness. Actors who naturally fall within the range are free to concentrate their chameleon techniques upon the more subtle and achievable nuances of characterization. Those at the margins might, by dint of extraordinary effort and will, force a slight expansion of the accepted range, but that is the best that might occur, and rarely.

The situation with regard to the charismatic is even more problematical, being more subtle and less often overtly articulated. Influential artists in positions of authority quite naturally respond to actors whose creative energy matches, either in part or entirely, their own. I'm going to use myself as an example, thinking about the many years I was the Artistic Director of a university theatre and its principal director. I'm a vocal mode dominant, Dynamic temperament director and I'm going to be drawn to vocally expressive actors who respond intuitively and strikingly to my notes addressing issues of status and the actions and reactions that will shape the audience's experience of the play. As a Dynamic Creative Personality type, I make use of the conduits of Power and Action, and appreciates actors who can pick up on my intuitions and creative insights and run with them. A Psychic actor at my university, having the only Creative Personality type that does not have at least one conduit in common with me, and surrounded as s/he inevitably would be by artists enjoying a richly creative experience with the A.D., quite naturally will come to believe that what the others are experiencing is real acting and that s/he is, sadly, lacking in talent. Sadly, I look back on some conversations I had with unhappy students and realize that my artistry, or rather my ignorance about my Creative Personality type and mode dominance, was very much at the root of the problem.

Almost every actor I have talked with during the writing of this book has shared at least one overwhelmingly negative and one stunningly positive interaction with a teacher or director. The negative experiences most often involve a creative artist endeavouring to share the secret of good acting and the recipient being forced to conclude that, given that the secret simply doesn't work for her, all the effort in the world will result only in shameful failure. Perhaps the memory is further darkened by actual as well as perceived failure: being shamed in front of classmates or rehearsing and performing a role that never really worked.

The positive memories turn out to be founded on the same conundrum, only in this case the recipient enjoyed a natural accord with the teacher, director or school of acting. Sometimes the individual reports something like, 'Not everyone liked [this director or teacher] but those of us who did loved it and I did some of my best work with [that person].' More often, the surge of unleashed creativity drowned out all other considerations and sometimes resulted in the individual declaring, with complete confidence, that the approach that was so successful for her is not only the best but the only legitimate approach to good acting.

It is this pattern of shared epiphany which results in certain creative temperaments being in fashion at certain times, in certain institutions, and even in certain industries. The reports and records of influential directors and master teachers reveal quite readily the creative temperament not only of the artist but also of the observer and those who write the testimonials that accompany such works. In institutions with a single or dominant acting teacher and/or director of productions, the result can be a systemic predisposition towards an approach to acting that simply will not work for approximately one sixth of the potential actors and works only partially for all but another, favoured, sixth. The successful graduates or stars will be drawn disproportionately from those temperaments which have the greatest natural accord with the 'house style' and everyone else will be left to assume that, no matter how hard they work and how much they long for the opportunity, they simply lack the aptitude to undertake a career in acting.

Charismatic teachers working within a legacy such as the Method pose a particular threat to impressionable student actors. Is the teacher truly inspiring, or are the students in awe of the names being dropped? A mismatch in this context can be particularly damaging to a young actor's courage. Often such teachers claim theirs is not only the best, but the only way of achieving acting that embodies the values the teacher claims are entirely and universally admired. Further support for the ascendancy of a single approach is often found in the advertising for the program that proclaims famous graduates, even though the students who go on to enjoy successful acting careers will have adapted even the most rigidly and religiously presented system into something uniquely suited to each individual's personality and the requirements of the various roles they undertake. Teachers who have themselves flourished within a well-estab-lished approach will enjoy notable success with students for whom there is an inherently pronounced correlation between the system and the student; in other words, the teacher's temperament and that of the successful students will tend to match perfectly. Those students who expe-rience a partial correlation will experience alternating exhilaration, as some techniques unlock the profound creative flow of their tempera-ments, interspersed with barren despair, when the suggestions from the teacher who only yesterday inspired such excellence now result only in strained effort and frustratingly imprecise criticism. And those for whom there is clearly no correlation between techniques offered and personal temperament? Despair, crippling loss of confidence and, if they are fortu-nate, dismissal from the program.

Fortunate? Yes. Because, like the young dancer in *A Chorus Line*, they will be more likely to find a teacher who is a better match.

VIRTUAL WORKSHOP *SESSION FIVE*: MISMATCHES AND SIMULTANEOUS TRANSLATION

As the group gathers, it's clear that Mike has arrived with a question.

Type Casting

MIKE: Okay, I have a question that's been bugging me. What if the char-acter is written to be one type, and you're not that type?

LESLIE: Can we differentiate between type casting and Creative Temperament? Type casting has mostly to do with societal norms, right? Certain physical characteristics are associated with certain attributes, and casting directors sometimes want to reinforce those associations and sometimes challenge them. More reinforcing goes on than challenging, and that's a reality of the business about which we need to be pragmatic.

But Creative Temperament is different. We're talking about releasing charismatic energy, which floats free from assumptions about character type. The 'ditsy bimbo' is just as likely to have a perception conduit as Hamlet.

MIKE: But that's my point. Hamlet is written to have a certain tempera-ment, and if you don't share that, you're always going to be off-balance. You'll be doing so much translating, you'll barely have time to memorize your lines!

LESLIE: Yes, you'll need the simultaneous translation for the creative colleagues who assist you in preparing the role. But when it comes to your interaction with Hamlet, or I guess to Shakespeare who created the role, that's another matter. If we acknowledge that the character of 'Hamlet' is an artificial construction, and set our disciplined actors' considerations to work in shaping a viable enactment of that fiction, via chameleon skills, then I'd argue that charismatic energy from any source will make that enactment authentic.

Shakespeare and Hamlet are perhaps not the best examples, because of the complexity of characterization. You'd probably find lots of Relationship, Perception, Action, and Power in that role. A better example would be a character who is more narrowly defined.

I'll share an example from my own experiences, not to put anyone on the spot. I was cast as the young woman in a play by Tennessee Williams called *Suddenly Last Summer*, way back when I worked with that teacher who was so big on emotional memory work. I don't know if you know this play, but near the end the character I played had a long speech that was a vivid, highly emotional recollection of a traumatic event. The rest of the play shows her reflecting on her past relationships and being batted about by two other characters as she opens herself to their attention or closes herself off for protection. I'd say, from the outside, that she has been given the attributes of a Psychic temperament – and that Relationship and Perception are the keys to her personality and emotional truth.

Now, I felt horribly mismatched to this role, with my Dynamic creative temperament. This poor girl had no power, no authority, and she didn't do humility much either. She was not one of the prime movers in the play, being more of a pawn for two other active characters. Because of her mental turmoil, she didn't react naturally to them either. So Power and Action conduits would seem dead ends for finding her reality. I didn't use those terms then, but that's what I experienced.

The assistance I received from my teacher-director reinforced my assumptions about the character's temperament. It was pretty obvious that he wasn't getting what he wanted from me, so he offered all sorts of suggestions for internal process, all of which fit nicely with the external attributes of the character and left me sweating with effort and completely uninspired. The result was a dull, un-charismatic performance. I think this director-teacher was particularly drawn to plays with characters like this, because in the next course he cast me as the wife in Harold Pinter's *Old Times*, and she had a similar long memory monologue, was similar in her lack of activity to initiate and reaction to anything around her. That entire play was about relationships.

I reflect back on those acting experiences, and the apparent mismatch of my temperament and the characters' attributes, and I come to quite a different conclusion today. Here's how things might have worked for me, if I'd known then what I know now.

The visible manifestations of character, as offered by the playwright, the aspects that I was required to present to the audience, are all actions. As that is one of my conduits, I could have unlocked charismatic energy at any moment, if I'd trusted myself to 'find' the character's emotions and experiences simply through movement, gesture, eye contact, tension, release, breath, sound, proximity, and if I'd played freely with the twin components of initiating and reacting, not in a macro sense, given the script, but microscopically, in my own acting.

Although there were minimal overt manifestations of authority or humility, those that were there could have been used as keys to unlock my charismatic energy. Remember our squiggly shape? All you need is one point of contact, between the shape of the character and your conduits, and they kick into high gear, if you let them. Then, once creativity flows into your work, in transforms the effort of any consideration into flexible, fluid, energized material for shaping. And I could have used my experiences of humility or control within the acting moment to access flowing creativity.

MIKE: But won't actors who share the character's temperament have more opportunities for releasing their charismatic energy, because of the spin Shakespeare or Pinter or Williams has put on the scenes?

Avoiding Mismatch

LESLIE: Possibly, and most definitely if the director sees the character a very specific way and casts accordingly.

Here's something that I've witnessed many times. An actor comes in and releases huge charismatic energy into a well-shaped fictional character. A true charismatic chameleon. The director, who has a specific creative temperament, assumes that the actor shares that temperament, because that is what the director experiences as he responds to the charismatic energy.

So the director casts the actor and proceeds to offer feedback. But the actor doesn't respond to that feedback. The actor's charismatic energy dries up; the director's faith in his actor dissipates. The director tries to shape the character to match the internal processes he is sure must be in place for a brilliant performance, and the actor, confused, follows those instructions to the best of his ability. Although disciplined consideration might win through in the end, the journey will not be pleasant.

But if the actor knows his own temperament, he will not be as easily derailed by the director's feedback and assumptions. The disciplined chameleon can offer the character shaped to suit the director's fancy, plus the charismatic energy that is so compelling and attractive.

IRIS: Shouldn't the director be the one to adapt?

LESLIE: When it comes time for you to direct I'd hope you'd be sensitive to creative diversity, because you've taken this workshop. Then you can be the one to adapt. It's easy to do. Just change your metaphors!

MIKE: Sorry, lost me there.

LESLIE: Say I'm giving notes to a fairly large cast. I have to assume that I have some of each type in the group. And I want them to give me a more energized, aggressive performance. They're letting the play get too slow, too languid, too safe. I might say something like: 'Folks, I need you to pick up your cues. I need you to sprint instead of walk, and punch instead of dab away at your speeches and blocking.' That's for the Action people. Change the behaviour, change the feeling. But I don't stop there, just because that direction would make perfect sense to me as an actor. I continue, 'You're playing it safe, particularly in your relationships. We trust each other, don't we? Lovers, I need some real chemistry. And the fight scenes – dig down and find your inner pit bull!' That's for the Relationship people. Then, something for the Perception gang: 'You can't sleep-walk through this show. You've got to wake up, and rip off the top layer of your skin, so that everything you see is a blow. Every word is a slap. And it's got to be what's being said and done in that moment. The only way this show works is if you have the courage to open yourself to it, every night, as if for the first time.' Finally, the Power actors. 'This is a terrifying play. There's a reason why primitive people used the theatre for religious ceremonies. We can't dumb this down. We can't make it just entertainment. We have to let it sweep us off our feet, lift us to the sky, drop us down an abyss, toss us around like little rag dolls.'

SALLY: I could so feel the difference. When you hit my conduits, I got your message loud and clear. I understood the other comments, but what you said about ripping off a layer of skin, that gave me goose bumps.

IRIS: I think your ideas are as much for directors and teachers as for actors.

LESLIE: I do too, but we're actors here, and it's our job to offer directors the raw material they need. So let's focus on training for that. The last thing I want to do is encourage actors who feel they can only be directed one way. But to be honest, I don't think that's what happens when someone learns about Creative Personality types. It's been my experience that the least flexible actors, the ones who are hardest to direct, are the ones most disconnected from their own charismatic energy. Let me rephrase that. They've no way to manipulate their natural charisma, and when confronted with situations that sap creative flow, they fall back on complaints about superficial, external factors such as the temperature of the rehearsal hall, or they cling to some element of interpretation in desperation. Once the conduits are tapped, and effortless creative flow infuses your work, it's much, much easier to throw out your preliminary thoughts on character in order to suit the requirements of the director.

SALLY: What if the director says that there's only one way to play the scene, and you know it won't work for you that way? Can we talk about a specific case?

LESLIE: I don't want to know names, but sure, let's talk about your concerns. Is the director telling you something about the external presentation, what the audience will see, or your internal processes?

SALLY: Both. But connected.

LESLIE: If you can offer the external, then how you got there doesn't matter, does it?

SALLY: But the director says it does.

LESLIE: That sounds to me like a teacher–director, someone who is as interested in training as in shaping a production for an audience. That sort of commentary on an actor's internal process is much less common in non-academic theatre work. Can you give share more details from this specific example?

SALLY: Okay, I'm a character who's about to commit suicide, and he wants me to set things up mechanically, in a deliberate, slow, manner. And he says the only way to play the scene is to be totally numb, totally cut off from all the emotional trauma of the earlier scene. But when I do it that way, he says it's like a robot. He wants every action to be significant, controlled, but disconnected.

LESLIE: That direction makes perfect sense to me, because I'm one of those actors with an Action conduit. Just doing action that way would open, for me, a effective source of creative energy. Perhaps he shares that conduit? Any clues about his other conduit?

POLLY: I thought you said we weren't supposed to guess at other people's types?

LESLIE: The point isn't to label the director, but to figure out how best to translate his feedback and suggestions. In listening to his vocabulary, you can identify certain words that suggest one creative type, and reposition the comment by changing the vocabulary to your own creative type.

SALLY: Perhaps he's using the Power conduit, with the reference to control?

IRIS: Is it Perception? Does he suggest you focus your attention on each sensory detail?

SALLY: No, in fact he specifically says not to. He keeps saying I should be barely aware of what I'm touching, what I'm seeing. He talked about being swept away, giving myself over to a tidal wave of despair.

LESLIE: Sounds like Power. This sounds like exactly the sort of temperament mismatch Mike identified: a character that manifests a different temperament, in a production directed by someone who pays particular attention to attributes that line up with that different temperament. And if you're Psychic, and the character (and possibly director) are shaped as Dynamic, then we're talking about exact opposites. Just like I was cast as a Psychic character, and had to find my way into the role from my Dynamic conduits. Hey, we should switch parts!

SALLY: I'd love to, because the roles you described, with the memory speeches and tons of relationship stuff, that's the type of role I just love.

LESLIE: Okay, so we know the problem. Polly's correct to remind us that we don't know the director's Creative Personality Type, but we know the fundamental collision in interpretive vocabulary. That's what we need to do the simultaneous translation.

Let's assume he's on to something effective in his staging of the scene. I want to make that point again. My entire theory about individual temperament was developed so that actors can serve the needs of the play more effectively. Actors who resist a director's staging because it doesn't match their temperamental needs are just that – temperamental. A finely-tuned acting engine can contribute to the success of another's interpretation of the character and play with complete freedom, because of the flow of creative energy that is always available through the conduits.

In Sally's case, let's agree that knowing her conduits don't match the director's is not an invitation to demand that the scene be staged a different way.

VICTOR: But if the director was open to exploration?

LESLIE: All of the same considerations apply. If the acting choices serve the production, great, but nothing justifies make acting choices that are self-indulgent, selected simply to serve the actor.

VICTOR: Can't they serve both? Choices for the actor's best creativity and the production?

LESLIE: Of course. But my point is that an actor with a well-tuned engine doesn't need to make choices to serve himself. That sort of self-serving is necessary when your engine is NOT well tuned. Creativity is, after all, the greatest resource available for ensuring that the needs of the production and the needs of the actor are met. If you unlock your creativity, you'll find a way to ensure rich and fulfilling inner processes without effort, so all your attention can go to the considerations of your disciplined, chameleon-like acting skills.

IRIS: Fine, but then what? We still can't deliver the goods when we're cast in a role that doesn't fit, or with a director who wants us to work in a different way.

LESLIE: My guess is that it isn't the role that doesn't fit, and it isn't the director's guidance that's the problem, but your own self-confidence. The director doesn't care how you get there. Nor does anyone in the audience. However, if your work is based solely on effort, then the audience will sense, and the director or acting teacher will probably know, that it's not authentic, that it's the result of consideration without charisma.

SALLY: Can we get back to me, please?

Channel the Energy

LESLIE: Yes, let's! Without knowing the play or the scene, I'm going to assume that the director is correct: the mechanical movement, the appearance of disconnection, are going to work. I'm also going to assume that your disciplined attention to the considerations of the character, and your trained body and voice and focussed concentration, can give him the chameleon-like enactment. But neither you nor he is going to be satisfied till you fill that external, visible character-signalling activity filled with your unique charismatic energy.

SALLY: I know you say that directors doesn't care how we get there, but this director does. And when I do what he asks, it feels empty.

LESLIE: I'm sure it would, if you approached it using his conduits, which are not yours. But all you need to do is switch the vocabulary, and then get out of the way so charismatic energy fills the moment, effortlessly. If you think of the character as a vessel, and the conduit as a pipe, all you need is the tap. Once you turn on the spigot, even a quiet, gentle flow is enough to get you to where you can make the moment authentic for yourself, and so for him and the audience.

What about allowing your sensory awareness to function?

SALLY: But he said not to.

LESLIE: He doesn't want to see the external manifestations of awareness, but remember what I said about charismatic energy being neutral.

If you unleash through your senses and memory, but channel the energy into the enactment, that will be quite a different use of the conduit than if you let your unique charisma flow into your habitual manifestation of the charisma's effect. Do you understand the difference?

SALLY: Not really.

Encrustation

LESLIE: That's what I mean about you getting out of the way of the creative flow. Attached to our conduits are a life-long set of habits, the familiar baskets into which we pour the creative energy. That's what has to be removed, so that the energy can flow into the CHARACTER's habits, which are different from yours.

Let's try an exercise. Here's my scarf. Let's imagine it belongs to your lover, who just left you, and you're summoning memories of your happiest moments by touching and looking at and smelling.

Laughter at this 'in joke.' Sally does the improvisation.

LESLIE: That looked effortless, and I felt you could have sustained the moment for even longer.

SALLY: That's just about the opposite of what he wants.

LESLIE: On the outside, yes. In that improv, your entire body was engaged. Your face and eyes, your hands, your breathing, even the sounds you made – the conduit opened up into every aspect of you, and you held nothing back. In fact, you went out of your way to share with us, dropping social inhibitions, right?

SALLY: That was the point of the improv, wasn't it?

LESLIE: Absolutely. But now we have to challenge your chameleon skills. We'll do the same improv, imagining this is the scarf of your lover, but I want you to play a character quite unlike you, a woman who shows nothing in her face, her voice, her hands. Or, if you like, a woman who fights herself so that nothing will show, because she's killed those feelings. Use your disciplined physical control to enact the mechanical movements – and make that the vessel into which the charismatic energy pours. It will feel unfamiliar at first, but don't mistake that for unnatural, unauthentic.

Sally tries again. There's still too much movement.

LESLIE: What we're seeing here is a demand being made on your chameleon skills, to set aside your own habitual activities in favour of what the character's external shape needs to be at this moment. You have to allow for her to be a person who holds herself back voluntarily, not because the movements are empty of sensation and memory, but because the memories and sensations are too strong to bear.

Sally tries again. Others in the class find her work more mechanical in a haunting, disturbing manner. Someone comments that they could believe such a woman might commit suicide, or murder. Sally is pleased.

POLLY: I was going to disagree when you said habits, because I don't think of my acting technique as a bad habit, but if we said 'comfort zone' instead, then that's a legitimate concern I have. I've been very happy here, and also in high school. I've had good luck, I've had great parts, I've had teachers that have been excellent for my type of actor. Before this workshop, I'd have said that I was one of the most talented of our year, but I realize now that I can't say that, because what's happened is that there's been a near perfect match between what I most need as an actor and what our teachers and directors have wanted us to explore.

Now I'm starting to audition outside school, and it's been brutal. I really want to leave the small pond and jump into the big lake. I want to prepare myself for working with directors who aren't perfect for me, and with actors who don't give me what I need but they're the star, and I have to give them what they need. That's what I learned from the few minor professional credits I've earned so far.

What I'm realizing is that my talent is no good to me if I only get that feeling of flow when conditions are ideal. As soon as it starts being work, everything I like best about my acting fades away.

Flow versus Effort

LESLIE: Since we're most aware of flow when it's absent, either the moment it eases and we reflect backward to the sensation, or when we seek and cannot find it, we should take a moment to talk about its opposite: effort.

There's nothing wrong with effort. In fact, it's the key ingredient of deliberate practice.

IRIS: You've used that term before. Can you explain what you mean by that?

LESLIE: That question could derail the workshop into a digression of several hours! But quickly, I'll just say that, if you compare an average athlete or musician, say, with someone world-class like Tiger Woods or Jascha Heifetz, you'll quickly discover that what sets them apart isn't so much talent – lots of people have an aptitude for sports or music. What makes them so extraordinary is their capacity for specific, ongoing, painstaking practice. I recommend *Talent is Overrated* by Geoff Colvin if you're interested in this topic. He doesn't talk much about actors, but he identifies a real problem for us. Sometimes, we theatre people buy into stories about instant stardom, apparently effortless excellence, or 'you can't teach talent,' which might be true but misses the point. What we can teach, and learn, is how to practice our craft so that our abilities are polished to the blinding sheen the world calls talent.

So, for me, effort is part of deliberate practice, and highly valued for that reason. You'll need a great deal of it, to master the chameleon skills of the profession. You'll use effort to learn a specific accent or dance steps. You'll use effort to educate yourself about different times and places, in preparation for playing roles in plays that do not reflect the culture you know. That's not to say that flow can't occur, even in the midst of physical and intellectual training of the most disciplined sort. Thank goodness it does, but we know we have to be sufficiently goal-oriented so if all that happens is effort, we don't stop.

But when we get into a situation when we're expected to tap into our creative capacities, the absence of flow is problematical. As a result, our efforts change, right?

MIKE: We start to push. Or at least I do.

IRIS: I know I manufacture things, when I feel under pressure and nothings coming in that flowing way.

SALLY: I panic. I can't seem to concentrate, and I start to feel completely stupid, to the point where I can't understand simple instructions.

LESLIE: Physiologically, we over-expend energy. Our physical and cognitive activities are no longer as efficient. That's what gives us the sense of loss of control. In addition, held tension lingers in the muscle groups that are outside the range of our conscious awareness at that moment. That's part of what gives the sensation of pushing, and of mechanization. I'm particularly interested in Sally's word: 'stupid.' I think we can assume that your I.Q. doesn't drop fifty points, so what's going on, do you think?

POLLY: You're getting in your own way. You know perfectly well what to do, and you're blocking yourself.

LESLIE: Any idea why?

POLLY: My guess is inhibitions.

VICTOR: I'm not sure that's always the case. Sometimes we don't know what to do. It's not coming naturally, and when we apply a learned technique, all we get is effort. So we keep applying the technique, but with a little more effort. But we don't have a clue how to solve the moment, so all we can do is keep trying until something breaks through and gets us there.

POLLY: That's because we're still learning.

LESLIE: I'm not sure it ever gets any easier. I'd hope that you'll continue to be cast in roles that take you into the unknown, because I believe that that is what it means to be a creative artist. If your experience of effort remains at the same level as dance class or accent work, then I don't think there's anything wrong with disciplined, effort-filled exploration. Deliberate practice, right? Skill acquisition can be its own reward. Also, you can learn how to invite flow into even the most boring repetition, by linking your conduits to the task at hand.

IRIS: Like imagining something vivid and entrancing during *barre* exercises.

MIKE: Or trying to get a group vibe going during the yoga warm ups [a teacher] inflicts on us every morning.

LESLIE: Great suggestions! I guess what I'm saying is that creative problem solving is a skill that you can study, deliberately, so it's there for you when you venture into the unknown. And since flow unlocks creativity, your conduits are going to be useful when you need to be particularly ingenious.

SALLY: What about when you used to have flow, and suddenly don't. Or the approach worked like a charm in class but suddenly doesn't in rehearsal and you start pushing too hard?

VICTOR: That's when I fall off the wagon. Bad habits are like booze to me. Put me in that situation, it's like that moment when Jack Nicholson walks into the bar in *The Shining*.

LESLIE: Okay, I'm going to ask, how do you know the habits are bad?

VICTOR: They're fake. It becomes all about entertaining the audience – getting the laugh, or impressing them with my big booming voice. It's bullshit acting.

LESLIE: Let me play devil's advocate here for a moment. Can you guess what I'm going to say?

VICTOR: You're going to say that some types of acting call for just that, and that maybe I'm at my most charismatic when I go for the big effect.

Fake versus Authentic

LESLIE: Yes, with a slight shift. I'd say that you could be equally charismatic doing your full-scale, heightened delivery type, and I'd be curious if the judgement of 'fake' is external, from someone whose preference is for subtle, complex naturalism, or an internal assessment.

VICTOR: It's both. When I'm doing outrageous comedy, and someone tells me that sort of acting is fake, I agree, but it pisses me off. Part of me wants to put the box office numbers for Jim Carrey's latest beside all the 'real' dramatic actors, and say to that person, 'If that's what fake gets, let me be fake.'

SALLY: Maybe fake's the wrong word. It sure is charismatic.

VICTOR: No kidding. But the reason I'm still here, and the reason I agree with the label 'fake' – is when I'm supposed to be digging into something serious, and dangerous, and I just do the big voice and moves, I know it's crap. Sorry for the language.

LESLIE: I think you've helped us to separate two quite different uses of the term 'fake.' The first, as you've suggested, comes from someone whose personal taste in performance genres is in collision with another style, coupled with a fundamental misunderstanding about what makes a performance authentic from the audience's point of view. And that is the presence of charismatic energy. No one cares when Jim Carrey's actions are exaggerated, because the level of personal energy he pours into his work is exactly what the doctor ordered for that style of entertainment. So when you receive an external judgement of your work, be careful about automatically internalizing that standard of values. As Victor said, you may want to seek the very thing that is being rejected, and that's your right as an artist.

Victor's also offered us another definition of 'fake,' one that comes from his monitoring of his own internal processes. That's the sort of effort experience I want to explore.

IRIS: Victor, how much of your doing the big moves is your Action conduit? I mean, something that works for me, and now I know why, is learning my lines with big bold moves. I used to think is was to help me remember, and that's still the case, but now I also realize it's because the movement itself releases flow, which gives me the insight and ownership I love.

VICTOR: I don't have an Action conduit. I'm Perception and Power: Visionary.

LESLIE: Using your understanding of your conduits, like Iris just did, can you describe what you experience, and speculate why?

VICTOR: I'll try. It's like I know what the moment needs to be. I can see it in my mind. I know my acting has to be powerful, because I know how powerful the feelings are that have to be conveyed. I'm thinking Greek tragedy, here. Or Shakespeare. King Lear with the dead Cordelia in his arms, howling. Then, rehearsal comes. I don't want it to be fake, that's the point. I know the scene would be 100% better if I let something real happen. But I go for the effect instead. Then I get trashed.

LESLIE: Any sense of what's happening when you go after big effects, in terms of your conduits?

VICTOR: I've been thinking about that. I think Polly nailed it. Inhibitions. I'm scared shitless of going to that place, where I need to be to play Lear.

LESLIE: A legitimate fear, I think, and one that you'll want to work through carefully, sooner rather than later. But can I say something? You're still talking about the challenge in terms of psycho-realism. It's an approach to acting that works very well for some actors, and for some types of theatre, but by no means is it the only approach to good acting, nor is it necessarily the best approach to every acting challenge. In a nutshell, the assumption that an actor needs to feel, for real, what the character is feeling, has been challenged by psychologists and theatre practitioners. Some actors and acting teachers still swear by it, but many, myself included, refer to that as the myth, or fallacy, of method acting.

We don't need to debate that now. In the long run, it doesn't matter. If that system works for you, then use it. If it doesn't, then why risk your mental health and creative confidence beating a dead horse?

Victor, I still need you to talk about what happened in the Lear scene, from the perspective of your conduits, if you can.

VICTOR: Okay, here's what I think. I used my Perception to plan the scene, and all the ideas were good ones, but since Action's not my conduit, when it came time to do the moves, they were empty, they were just effort. In fact, I pretty much closed off my Perception conduit, because I hated how they felt, I didn't want to take in anyone else because I didn't want to pick up on what they thought of my work, and I definitely didn't want to start imagining what it would be like for Lear, because when I do that my throat tightens up, I can't breathe, and no way can I deliver those lines.

LESLIE: And power?

VICTOR: I'm doing control, all the way. No submission. No humility to the power of the words. No awe in the face of death. And it's all about controlling my acting, trying to be tragic, instead of accessing any sort of flow.

LESLIE: I think we have now a working definition of 'fake' from the perspective of conduits, thanks to Victor. This is exactly the sort of self-awareness and self-tuning that I spoke about when we began. Out there in the real world, if your creative engine develops a knock or bogs out when you step on the gas, or plain won't start on a cold morning – well, you've got to be your own mechanic. You've got to go in there and tease apart your process, to see how to tune back up the engine.

In the case of Victor and King Lear, we can see what a good match this role is to his talents. His big voice and capacity for heightened gestures are well suited to the tragic scale of the role. His powerful Perception allows him to imagine the horror and pain, vividly. His intuitions about power and humility will allow him to explore creatively the theme that Lear embodies: tragic hubris. You're far too young for the role, of course, but in school it's a good workout for your particular acting engine.

Big problem, though. There are dangers in playing the role, and intuitively Victor avoided the dangers by blocking his conduits and switching to an effort-based approach to the scene, using the consideration of initiated actions. Since he's not an Action actor, this was safe. However, since his conduits had already been engaged with the role, in preparation, and were eager to continue contributing, it felt blocked. The contrast between the sensations of creative exploration, fuelled by conduits, and the rehearsals based on effort only increased the sensation of absence of flow.

SALLY: Sorry, I don't quite get that last point.

LESLIE: If Victor's first work on the scene had been with a director who blocked it, Victor would have expended effort to learn the moves. That would be more like the disciplined effort of mastery of craft. But remember when you were talking about how to make relatively tedious work more fun? The door to flow is easy to open – all you have to do is put the invitation out there. Any time flow wants to join in, it's welcome. Inexperienced actors – not you guys, who now know the secret – have to hope it visits often, because it helps the time to pass more pleasantly, and effort suddenly feels like fun.

Okay, so when you start with effort, and add flow, that's one sensation. But Victor developed the idea for the moves with creative flow. Then he slammed the door shut. So it's effort with the door closed, and flow pounding on the door wanting back in, so additional effort is needed to keep the door shut. That's what you might call 'inhibitions.'

IRIS: Can we talk more about inhibitions? You've talked about taking care of our psyches, as much as a dancer takes care of her body. But we've been taught that inhibitions are bad for actors, that we have to get rid of any we have.

LESLIE: Victor, do you mind if we continue using the King Lear example?

VICTOR: Go ahead. I'll tell you, there are some emotions I don't mind feeling, if the time is right. I guess I fall into the school that says you don't have to feel the real emotion in performance, specially the ones that are messy, but you need to feel it for real, at least once in the rehearsal process.

LESLIE: Let's build on that point, and explore your experience as we address Iris's concern. First, I'm going to observe that it sounds to me like you did experience the emotions, for real, while preparing the role at home. You spoke of the tight throat, the inability to breathe?

VICTOR: But not in rehearsal.

LESLIE: The work you do at home isn't rehearsal?

VICTOR: As soon as the real emotions came, I did everything I could to stop them.

LESLIE: And you stopped that private rehearsal?

VICTOR: You bet.

LESLIE: Okay, so that addresses my concern about inhibitions. You were all alone. There's no need to be inhibited, if we associate that with protection from embarrassment.

VICTOR: I didn't want to feel those feelings.

LESLIE: But you're willing to act them.

VICTOR: It's like you said, it's for the audience, and for them, it's not real pain, it's awe. Even if it's some junky made-for-TV disease of the week movie, they're having a good time crying.

POLLY: If we're not willing to feel what our character feels, for real, then maybe we don't have the right to play the character.

MIKE: Sorry, I'm not interested in really feeling what it's like to murder someone.

POLLY: But you have to discover that you COULD murder someone, don't you?

SALLY: We all could murder, if we had to. We don't have to do it to act it. But we have to shake off the crust, that society has asked us to create, and get into the dark stuff that's down there.

LESLIE: Victor, you described tightened throat and shortness of breathe. If you suddenly had those symptoms, say while walking down the street, what would you do?

VICTOR: I'd sit down.

LESLIE: If they didn't pass, but got worse?

IRIS: You'd get yourself to emergency.

LESLIE: I think so. Let's say we were doing an emotion memory exercise, and Victor, Sally, and Iris started to recall intensely emotional experiences. Psychologists have demonstrated how emotional memory works, and it's quite something, in terms of the activity in the brain. So, let's imagine that Sally starts weeping uncontrollably.

SALLY: That's me!

LESLIE: Iris gets up and starts moving around the room, clearly agitated. Victor reports that he's having trouble breathing. What's happening in acting class? To be blunt, it's practicing psychotherapy without a license. What good are those emotions to your acting?

POLLY: Iris might find some interesting movements to use in the scene. I agree with Victor, that she'd never want to go that far in performance, but she could use the discovery.

LESLIE: But if she could find those movements without experiencing something emotionally traumatic? Wouldn't that be safer? I guess my point is that those inhibitions are there for a reason – our mental health – and you blast them out of the way at your peril. If you'd go to a mechanic to remove a cancerous tumour in your brain, then by all means let someone with no training muck around in your psyche.

POLLY: But you said we needed to remove encrustations. And why spend so long on de-briefing if we're not going after huge emotions?

LESLIE: Good point. Let's see if I can clarify, because it is a bit of a paradox. Yes, I agree, intense experiences are often the goal, and conduits unleash a type of energy that can be particularly frightening because it comes from a place that exists outside the reach of socialization. But that energy is also emotionally neutral. It's just energy, pure and simple. It's what fuels the chameleon quality we so love in actors. It's what brings authenticity to the pretending we do when we act. Enacting emotions is just that – enactment. Part of the chameleon skill of the trained actor. Making emotions the focus of our work is, in my opinion, misguided.

SALLY: So you don't approve of emotion memory exercises?

Conduits and Teaching Acting

LESLIE: Here's what I think of that particular strategy. In fact, it's what I think of all strategies. It depends. On the goals of the instructor. On the conduits of the students.

First, the students. Let's assume 50% of them share the conduit that the exercise addresses. They 'get' it and flow results. But they don't need it. They draw on memories intuitively, all the time, and it only takes a minimal effort to shape their conscious awareness of the conduit. The other 50%, however, will always approach the exercise through effort. They will benefit the most from it, because it will help them to develop specific strategies for chameleon work.

Now, the instructors. If the instructors are satisfied with these goals, then all's well. They will set up the exercise and get out of the way, then assist the students in making use of whatever emerges. However, most instructors who use a great deal of emotional memory work do so because they're part of a legacy. That means that emotional memory works for them, and they learned it from someone for whom it works. Now they're

passing it along, not as one tool among many, but as THE tool, the requirement.

MIKE: No kidding.

LESLIE: That's the sort of situation in which Perception actors might
be pushed too far. They're already attuned to the exercise, and when the
teacher pushes the class in an effort to get the non-conduit actors to share
the experience of flow, all that happens is that the non-conduit students
expend more effort, and the conduit students go further and further, and
the next thing you know, the poor teacher is in the middle of emotional
fallout that is unhealthy for everyone.

MIKE: I get the feeling, sometimes, that people like the emotional fire-
works. The teachers and directors, I mean.

IRIS: And some actors.

LESLIE: There may be some truth in that. It might be from a mistaken
belief that the capacity to feel extreme emotion is a requirement for acting.

MIKE: It might also be that they like manipulating people, and then
cleaning up the mess.

LESLIE: Perhaps. My guess is that they don't realize that there's a difference between the expression of strong emotion accompanied by
authentic energy from the psyche, and the experience of situations that
arouse strong emotions. We have to be careful about throwing around
terms like 'real' and 'true.' Would any of you know the real feelings of losing
a child? I hope not.

SALLY: But we could imagine.

LESLIE: Could you? If you talk to parents, one of the things you'll hear
us say is that we never knew it would feel like this, having a child. If you
do an exercise in which you summon up intense feelings, playing the role
of a grieving mother, then the real emotions are those of an actress identifying strongly with what she imagines a grieving mother might feel.
You're experiencing emotions, yes, but who's to say whether they're the
feelings a real mother would have? You can't even know if they're what
you'd feel if it were to happen to you.

VICTOR: All we should care about is whether the audience believes
you're grieving.

LESLIE: I'd question even that. If you began to do the scene, and
suddenly I started to feel that you were expressing something from your
real life, that you'd lost a baby, then I'd be very uncomfortable. I'd stop
being interested in the dramatic scene, and I'd want to respond as I would
to a grieving mother, which is not how I respond to good acting, or good
theatre.

IRIS: So that brings us to where we started: faking it. Audiences can tell that. And they don't like it, in a naturalistic drama.

LESLIE: What is it that they're seeing, when they label it 'fake'?

POLLY: I think they see the effort. Effort is what makes it mechanical, or rigid. You can see when someone's trying too hard. Even just walking across the room. They're not completely relaxed.

IRIS: The way the body is held, when someone is self-conscious, which is different from the energized stillness that is relaxed and alive. We practice that in dance all the time.

VICTOR: I think also audiences get upset when the actor breaks character, which is what happens when someone's so caught up in real emotion that they stop playing the role. The chameleon is sacrificed.

LESLIE: Yes, I'd say that one aspect of the chameleon is sacrificed in order to achieve a false goal of interior reality. As I've said before, I feel that the expression of emotions is part of the chameleon work, and that the form the expression takes must serve the audience's needs. If the expression includes inappropriate tension or rigidity, if it's mechanical, and that shatters the chameleon transformation that creates character, then we've got a problem. If it overflows the shape offered by the play, then we've also got a problem.

The solution is quite simple. Apply all of your effort to creating the best possible shape, to serve the requirements of the play. That includes stylistic things like the scale of movement, and interpretive things like inviting audiences to laugh or gasp in horror. It also includes selecting specifics for how best to express the emotion, some of which you may acquire through life study or through rehearsals in which you invite an emotional experience in order to explore how you might express that emotion.

However, what makes it all work isn't real feelings, but the flow of charismatic energy. And that brings us back to where we started: defining flow through defining what it is not: effort.

So, to summarize: we want flow. We also want effort, if it's what we might call the 'open door' effort, which invites flow in but doesn't fret if flow comes and goes. We don't want the closed door effort, which shuts flow out. Instead, we want to learn how to deal with what the flow brings, safely. Finally, on those occasions when we want flow, and it doesn't come right away, using effort makes things worse instead of better. We need a name for that type of effort.

POLLY: How about door building effort.

LESLIE: That might be a good term for using your conscious awareness of your Creative Personality type to invite flow when confronted with specific acting challenges.

MIKE: How about wall-building effort? You think you're building a door, you want to build a door, and all that you're building is a wall blocking you from what otherwise would come naturally, if you stopped building.

LESLIE: I like that. Let's use the image of wall-building instead of words like fake. That means we're able to sharpen our analysis and awareness as we explore processes of good acting.

VICTOR: But we still need a word for what I was doing. We could just call it bullshit acting.

Credibility and Dishonesty

LESLIE: Can we go one step further, and exploring the possible meanings of fake? It might mean that the actor doesn't understand, and so has to fake it. It might mean the actor doesn't want to understand, and so decides to fake it. In which case, there might be two factors at work: an instinct for self-protection, which we'd want to honour and incorporate, and an avoidance of public failure: also legitimate, but one that a disciplined actor has to put aside, because risk of failure is a pre-requisite of artistry. You guys know this, right? Out of failure comes discovery, especially in rehearsals and classroom exercises. I think we can agree that 'do not lie' is a good dictum for actors, with regard to their own work. So, for me, the best word to describe the dishonest work of the third option is 'bluffing' – it's a very special type of dishonesty, not quite as despicable as a con like 'the dog ate my homework.' You want so very much for it to be true, and you're faking, not to avoid the work, but in desperation to get where you need to be. Sure, ego stuff is on the line, but the fears, the embarrassment, the competition, the eagerness to please – we can all understand how bluffing might happen. And sometimes you bluff in public while desperately doing the work to catch up. I know someone who was asked in an audition if he could ride a unicycle. 'Sure!' And then frantically, when he got the part, out there every day on a unicycle, so on the first day of rehearsal he could say, 'Damn, haven't done this for a while, guess I'm a bit rusty. I'll work on it between rehearsals.' Sure enough, he worked every second he could, and by opening night he could unicycle, brilliantly.

We need a different word for limited life experiences, when someone wants to understand, and probably believes that sympathetic imagination will result in understanding, though they'd be wrong. I call that myopic dishonesty. Imagine, if you will, someone coming up to Nelson Mandela and saying, 'I know just how you must have felt when you accepted the Nobel Peace Prize after all those years of oppression, imprisonment, and struggle for freedom, because I once played you in a movie, and I summoned real tears of joy and affirmation when we shot the Stockholm scene.' That's an extreme example but it reminds us how easy it is to assume that the emotions we've felt, when we've had an emotional experience in rehearsal, is the 'real' emotion someone would feel in that situation – I mean in real life. The emotion is real, but the situation is not. It reminds me of old-fashioned sensitivity training, when they'd get people who were being trained to work with the disabled to spend a day in a wheel chair or a couple of hours blindfolded. I remember a friend who was paralyzed after a car accident sneering, 'Sure, but they know the whole time that at the end of the exercise they're going to get up out of that chair.'

I remember when I played Stephanie in *Duet for One*, and my first rehearsal in a wheel chair. The actor playing the psychiatrist, a very nice man, kept on trying to help me by moving me around the furniture. I wanted to learn how to move the chair myself. This was a real emotion. Very real. We discovered several effective moments which were later used in the performance, based on that rehearsal. I'd be myopic, however, to assume that what I felt was any comparable to what someone suffering from M.S. might feel.

POLLY: But you wouldn't call that anger 'faking it,' would you?

LESLIE: No, it was real anger. I wouldn't say I was feeling what the character was feeling, or that my feelings were true to the character's. In that sense, I was faking it, because I can only guess what she might feel. But my job it to imagine richly, and then do my best to let the play work for the audience, so they gain whatever insights the playwright can offer, with my help.

SALLY: Did you do any research?

LESLIE: Yes. In fact, I have a relative who died of M.S. not long before I did that role. She used to speak of her illness with great honesty and courage, but I couldn't use her much as a life study, because the character in the play responded to her illness quite differently.

MIKE: What did you use? In terms of your conduits?

LESLIE: Well, I'm Dynamic, which is Action and Power. So, yes, I worked hard to recreate the actual observable symptoms, and I found that if I moved my body that way, and opened myself to what my body might teach me, certain moments always worked. They always flowed and appeared authentic to those watching. The text of the play also gave me opportunities to tap into my power conduit. She had a long speech about the awesome power of music, which she was cut off from due to her disease. There was also a marvellous power struggle with the psychiatrist, so I was able to work through a rich, complex, fluid on-stage relationship by exploring control and submission, humility.

There were things I struggled with, as well. I'm not a Relationship actor, but I think the other actor was, and so was the director. And the scenes were all about discussing her relationships with her husband and others. For a while, I got very much off track, trying to access her and summon up authentic emotions through relationship work. I didn't know about conduits then, at least not consciously, so that effort left me feeling that I simply couldn't play a role that required deep feeling. The other aspect of the text that challenged me was the description of past events. She would tell the doctor about things that had happened. The director kept on experimenting with exactly how much my character should relive those memories, forgetting all about the psychiatrist, and how much the stories should be told to get a reaction from the psychiatrist, which is clearly suggested in the script of the play. I could understand, intellectually, what she was after, and I could do whatever version she asked for, but I suspect I didn't offer any truly creative insights, in large part because I didn't have a Perception conduit.

Whenever she'd suggest trying a section and really seeing the memory, really reliving it, I'd fake it. I know the actions I had to do to make her think I was transported out of the here and now, and the actions that signalled a return to the here-and-now, and I could do those actions exactly when she wanted them. Eventually, they became authentic for me, not because I ever really 'saw' what I described, but because I filled in a lot more of the physical, and that unleashed some flow, which made it feel authentic for me. And then I could relax, stop working so hard, get out of the way of the action of remembering, moment by moment.

VICTOR: Can you explain that a little more? I think I understand, but I'm not sure.

LESLIE: The play is made up of several different sessions, and she's at a different stage, with regard to her illness, for each session. That really played to my strengths as an Action actor, because I did my homework, both research and working on the movements at home. So, for any given memory speech, I also had a physical pattern that was the illness. In one rehearsal, or maybe it was between rehearsals, I realized that I should switch my focus from deliberately enacting those movements to fighting to suppress them, as she was fighting to deny her illness. That was a giant leap forward, for me. Also, when I was memorizing her long, long speeches, I'd move freely around my living room, almost dancing her memories of freedom and music, and romance – whatever. Then one rehearsal I had the sort of epiphany that feels like luck but that's also the result of hard work: I realized that, if I were transported by the memory, I'd stop fighting to hide the symptoms. I'd tried letting little glimpses of the free movement show through, but that wasn't nearly as effective as when little bits of the disease-movement snuck out. It was a sure sign that the character was caught up in the memory, and I also had a forceful sensation, of loss of control, which was useful in building the moment, specially when I 'returned' to realize that the psychiatrist had learned more than I'd wanted him to. From the freedom of the memory, I snapped to the humiliation and grief – and I just hated him and that disease. It was a good discovery. So the final package that I was able to offer was a mixture. I had to lie about what I could never understand, and I had to bluff about really seeing those memories, but I was able to pour a great deal of authenticating energy into the performance through the discoveries I'd made thanks to help of my Power and Action conduits. Not my best work, but I was proud of my effort.

SALLY: What do you think would have allowed you to do your best work?

LESLIE: I wish I'd known then what I know now about debriefing. It was an intense role, and the emotions it summoned were not pleasant to experience, even in my myopic version. I had very strong feelings, you might imagine, about the disease itself and the horror of the story hit very close to home. I'm sure my natural instincts for self-protection kicked in, and so it was almost impossible to tell the difference between bluffing because I couldn't do it and bluffing because I didn't want to. If I'd known about debriefing, and if I'd developed some good strategies for working my way back out of the wrenching emotions, then I'd probably have been able to go further, to allow my conduits to take me deeper into – whatever might be down there.

SALLY: What about your fellow actors? Couldn't they help?

LESLIE: Yes, and he did. It's a two-hander.

SALLY: It sounds like a great play.

LESLIE: Yes. Have a look. Great scenes, great monologues for women. My fellow actor was wonderful to work with. He had an interesting challenge, because the psychiatrist in the play was presented as a good doctor, caring and effective, but the actor, who'd been in therapy himself, had a very negative response to the doctor's game playing, which he had to master in order to play the role. For most of the rehearsal, we both hated his character – which isn't what the playwright wrote!

In thinking back on his work, I'd guess he was a Relationship actor, and maybe Action, which would make him Personal, or perhaps Perception, which would make him Psychic. I know that I received his gaze as an intense, forceful invasion or lifeline, depending on whether my character was fighting him or grabbing the support he offered. But he could also do some marvellous, simple actions that gave me a strong sense of the warmth of the relationship, within the very special limits of psychiatry, and when he slammed the door shut, it was absolute.

In other words, we may have shared one conduit: Action, or we may have been opposites in terms of conduits but able to be there for each other, and in fact assist each other by being creative in each other's blind spots, so to speak.

POLLY: Wouldn't a better match up have helped you more? Specially the director?

LESLIE: Perhaps. But I value the blend of effort and flow, particularly when I've set myself a challenge that I know is going to make me grow as an actor, even if I fight it every step of the way! As soon as you've mastered the simple trick of simultaneous translation, you'll want to seek out opportunities to work with creative artists who do not share your creative temperament. Why? Because their Conduits will educate your Considerations.

Artistic Living

LESLIE: As intelligent adults, we absorb and process a great deal of information. Our senses and our intellect process sensations, activities, and complex information to create the context within which we experience our daily lives and our nightly dreams. It's more than just data; it's why we enjoy flashes of insight as well as empathy for others. It's why we can imagine things that have not yet occurred, or could never occur in the world as we know it. This is where we all begin, as actors. It's what we have in the bank.

This immense resource can be tapped through simple, linear processes, for which language is uniquely suited. It can also be tapped through chaotic, web-like leaps of connection, too many, too multi-faceted, and too swift for the slow and clumsy formulations of sentences. However, such rich stream of consciousness are, by definition, undisciplined, without focus, excessive in form and content. It is only when they are blended with the boring, linear mental activity that they become that human endeavour we label artistic creativity.

Each of the conduits offers direct access to chaotic leaping. However, if that is the sum total of your use of this energy, you are not acting. You need to find the perfect blend of flow and effort, like Sally said.

MIKE: I bet you're going to tell us that we'll find this perfect blend by working with people who don't share our type.

LESLIE: Yes, I would say that, again and again.

Let's take, for example, Relationship and Power, which are your conduits, Mike. These conduits tap into the complex web of experiences that informs each of us of the subtlety of vertical and horizontal connections. The web is made up of everything we've ever felt, observed, experienced, or learned about. While in the unprocessed, unfocussed form, we experience it as a vague sensation, a set of intuitions, a barely conscious level of awareness of patterns. If invited to focus on these patterns, say by a playwright, we experience that flash of epiphany: 'Ah, yes, that is so true!'

Someone who does not have those conduits processes the data in a relatively straightforward manner, efficiently but without the spark of creativity. However, as a result of training for the creative profession of acting, such people learn to look beyond the obvious to the complexity, the mysterious, the paradoxical. They actively seek more information about the world of the play and the characters in it, looking for subtle indicators of relative power and tangled relationships, so that they draw as richly as possible from whatever they have on account in the bank.

This is where the artistic application of effort and the disciplined application of flow intersect. The work is equally creative whether the intellectual effort, though linear, is inspired by the actor's creative intent, or whether the overwhelming chaos is disciplined for the same reason.

Let's consider, now, the very special flood of data that fills our banks, thanks to our physical being, specifically our sensory awareness of the world around us and the way we experience the world through the body we inhabit.

Here, the experience of the balance between chaotic flood and disciplined focus rests upon the combination of intention with sensation. We see, hear, smell, taste, or touch and our muscles move, intentionally or spontaneously. We experience sensations and at the same time position those sensations within the vast data bank of other sensations previously processed.

By the time we reach adulthood, we are all relatively skilled at existing in a constant soup of processed sensations. Here again acting training has a huge impact. We learn to focus our attention on these sensations, and to experiment with intentional and spontaneous awareness and processing. Actors with Action and Perception conduits need disciplined explorations as much, if not more, than those without these conduits. It's relatively easy to learn to be more aware of specific sensory input. It's much more complicated to disentangle sensations from the tangled web of associated sensations within which they are experienced via the Perception conduit.

IRIS: I'm getting confused. Can you give us an example of what you're describing?

LESLIE: Good idea. Let's think about all the disciplined work was needed to create the very specific character as created by the playwright. I'll use *Duet for One*, since we were just talking about my work on Stephanie in that production.

For some of the work I had a special sensitivity or richer intuitions, thanks to my Power and Action conduits, but I couldn't let my conduits do all the work and ignore the considerations. Yes, I'm particularly tuned to power, but I still had to read the play very carefully, and do some home-work, to catch all of the indications of power in the play. I knew intuitively that simply doing the activity that Stephanie initiates, and reacting the ways the script demands she reacts would put me in touch with authentic, living energy, but there was a great deal of work ahead figuring out exactly what moves to select and how to shape her lines into speech acts. I also needed to work through exactly what it is that I'm reacting to every second I'm on stage. Yes, I used whatever my fellow actor gave me, but I had to experiment in all sorts of ways to discover which reactions would serve the play well.

SALLY: You make it sound like so much work. But almost everything you talk about comes clear just from rehearsing the play.

LESLIE: I agree, because in rehearsals we blend effort and flow. The conduit energy makes it creative and alive, but the craft is what turns it into artistry. It's the considerations that make it acting. The point I'm making is that a conduit simply isn't enough. I'd argue you need hard work on considerations for every play, even the most naturalistic, when you're playing a character almost exactly like yourself.

MIKE: Maybe specially when you're playing a character like yourself.

POLLY: Good point.

IRIS: If all you offer is conduit energy, unshaped, then you're not really acting, are you?

LESLIE: I guess we'd call that living. And what we need, in our work as actors, is artistic living.

VICTOR: So the danger of working only on roles that you can perform almost entirely through conduits is that you won't be developing strategies for non-conduit work.

SALLY: Also that you won't learn how to enhance your conduit work.

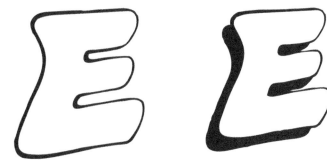

POLLY: Okay – take me. I'm a Personal actor, so my intuitions about relationships, from my conduit, still need some work, some effort. And for that I could borrow strategies from you guys who don't have that conduit.

LESLIE: For whom relationship is an area for disciplined craft.

VICTOR: Like me.

POLLY: I think I'm getting this. I can learn to shape my conduits from people who don't have them, and learn about my non-conduits from people who do have them. So – Sally for tricks about those memory speeches she loves.

SALLY: Any time, girl. I have a question about that. Is it better to draw on something equivalent from my own life? A substitution? Since the magic if could be a lie?

LESLIE: It's magic, right? Not real. That's why it works. Either imagined or a substituted real-life memory, both would tap flow because of your Perception conduit. So is one better than the other? It's better if it works, right? If it blends flow and effort, it's ideal. You put yourself in an invented situation and it comes alive for you, without knowing exactly what the equivalents are, and without effort. But you need to work with the details offered by the playwright, make them come alive. That's what might require some effort.

SALLY: Like research. I love hunting for pictures to put in my journal.

LESLIE: We need a balance between complexity and clarity. We need to draw on the authentic creative energy each of you brings to your acting, but we also need disciplined effort so that you enact the characters as shaped by the text.

Let's consider a less complex, more obvious type of relationship scene, say Romeo and Juliet – the balcony scene. Or any other love scene. (The bubble letters above are explained overleaf.) From a relationship point of view, it's all opening, right? But if that's all it is, you've missed an opportunity to benefit from the yin/yang of the conduit. But if you go too far

185

into closing, destructive energy, you damage the delicate mood of the love scene.

Here's a hint on how to solve the problem. You only need a moment or two in which to express the withdrawing, closing side, to validate the rich, full insight of your Relationship conduit. Love scenes are written to evoke a very special moment in a relationship. As an actor, you can let the dominant colour of the scene take care of itself. In your text analysis, you need to look for contrasting colours. It's that shading that brings the dominant colour into relief, creating three dimensions.

Did you ever draw bubble letters as a kid? And did you ever do the shading, like this? (page 185). The love in the scene is the bubble figure. The playwright's done that for you. Your job, as an actor, is to add the shadings. With Shakespeare, because his text is so rich, you'll be able to draw the contrasting colours out of the text. In other plays, you'd add them through what we call subtext: gestures, facial expressions, tone of voice, activity.

I'll tell you what I see in the scene, in addition to Juliet's concerns about Romeo's character. It's a competition. Who loves more completely, more purely, more recklessly? Also, whose definition of love is the true one? I'm not saying that's what the scene is about. But that's there, in the text. The audience doesn't need you to prove they're in love – Shakespeare's giving them all the proof they need. But they need you to help them hear the great subtlety and complexity of the love relationship between these two, as he's shaped it by the words they speak.

That's the complex relationship that's right there in the scene. Now, your job is to find the contrasting shadings. The rivalry, the old hurts, the familiar irritations, even at the moments of greatest warmth. And you need to find the love, the tenderness, the trust even when you're hurting each other.

Or, in the case of Stephanie and her psychiatrist, in *Duet for One*, we had to find the love in the heart of all that antagonism.

SALLY: So in the end, did you pull it off? Was your performance believable?

LESLIE: How are we defining that word?

POLLY: Did you really get into the part. Was it real for you, when you performed it?

Real Emotions

LESLIE: Does it matter if the actor really feels the emotions his character is supposed to be feeling at that moment? To be honest, I don't know.

MIKE: I wasn't sure how to bring this up, but I gotta say – we talked about this a couple of times since we started working with you – whenever you talk about emotions being just on the surface, not real – that goes directly against everything we're being taught here.

IRIS: Not everything.

POLLY: But the main focus of our acting training, which is pretty much pure Stanislavsky, I guess you'd say.

LESLIE: I'm glad you said something, Mike. Your reactions gave me that feeling, and thanks for your respectful willingness to try out my exercises regardless. But it's time for me to talk about this a bit more.

Stanislavsky's observation, that emotions are not subject to the control of the actor's will, and therefore have to be tricked into emerging by various strategies, was the conundrum which sparked his explorations of emotional memory recall, which became the central strategy for Strasberg and the American Method, as well as his action-based system of objectives and obstacles and later his score of physical actions which developed into what a method of physical actions.

Now that we've learned about conduits, we can see how these techniques appeal to two: Perception and Action, and suggest that Constantin's Creative Personality type was Innovative. Elsewhere in his writings he speaks of communion, the intense engagement with fellow actors, which became a central strategy for the controlled, intentional summoning of emotions for some of his students, presumably those who access a Relationship conduit along with one of Action or Perception, in other words Personal, or Psychic students who later became influential actor-teachers. Power doesn't seem to have interested him as much, which was hard on some of his protégés. But that's not why I'm casting aspersions on his methods.

I'm going to assume that you, like me, can remember back to early encounters with amateur acting, perhaps in high school, where classes, rehearsals, and sometimes even performances had a quality of emotional masturbation, where part of the appeal was an excuse to vent emotions, the more intense the better. Another type of self-indulgence is a therapeutic working out of private issues through role playing – a viable form of psychological counselling if that's the point, but not particularly appropriate for theatre. The result of both of these emotional pitfalls was, in my experience, shows that were much more fun to be in than to watch.

Since the whole point of training for a professional career is preparing to work in a context where the pleasure of those who pay is far more important than those who are paid (we hope!) the question of the actor's feelings is re-framed as, 'Does it matter to the audience if the actor is really feeling the emotions the character is supposed to be feeling?'

Don't jump to the conclusion that your answer is going to be yes.

I agree, in some types of plays, in some theatrical conventions, that's part of the pleasure of the audience. 'Oh, my,' they say, 'Isn't it amazing how the actor really cries?'

IRIS: But if they're saying that during your big sobbing scene, haven't you reminded them that this is just a play, and they're so busy admiring your work as an actor they've stopped experiencing the character's grief?

LESLIE: Momentarily, yes, but that might be part of the pleasure they seek in attending live theatre. I'm going to suggest that they don't want it to be too real. The framing device, the 'as if' of the theatre conventions we all share, protects them from the far more intense responses they'd experience if they felt a real person was really sobbing just a few feet away. The fact that they 'pop out' of the fiction for a moment and consciously register the excellence of the actor's craft is a device to keep the emotions carefully framed for maximum entertainment.

SALLY: But people know when you're faking emotions.

LESLIE: They know when you're expressing them unconvincingly. But that's part of your job as a chameleon, to have the disciplined craft to express emotions in a manner that the audience finds entirely suitable for the story being told. Notice I say suitable, not credible. Emotions that are carefully expressed to replicate the expression that would occur in real life are appropriate for only certain types of play writing and production styles.

MIKE: I'm not disagreeing, but I know that if I'm truly present and connected with the character, and something real happens inside me, then all sorts of problems disappear, like self-consciousness, inhibitions, indicating –

LESLIE: How would you define indicating?

MIKE: Knowing what the emotion's supposed to be, and doing something to suggest that emotion, rather than letting something real happen. Forcing the moment, rather than allowing something spontaneous and true to come out.

LESLIE: How did you know it wasn't real, that you were just suggesting, that you were forcing?

MIKE: It was mechanical. Rigid. Wrong, in that it didn't feel right.

LESLIE: Quite rightly, you assumed that, if the expression of the emotion felt mechanical, rigid, wrong to you, then it probably would appear wrong and thus represent a failure of your chameleon craft, right?

MIKE: Absolutely.

LESLIE: Mike, have you ever played a role in period costume?

MIKE: Sure.

LESLIE: Were you instructed to sit in a specific manner, in according with the customs of the time? Or use a snuff box or handkerchief a certain way? Something as simple as flicking the tails of a morning coat out of the way before sitting? Or as elaborate as sitting to show the shape of your calf?

Leslie demonstrates, and the group laughs.

LESLIE: Yes, you laugh, but if I were dressed properly, and performed these actions with grace and style, I'd be inviting you, through my chameleon skills, to believe I really was a Restoration fop. When I first learn those moves, they feel unfamiliar, mechanical, wrong. But over time, with repeated usage, and as they become connected to other elements of the fictional world, they start to feel normal, natural, effective ways of presenting the emotional reality of my character.

POLLY: But that style of theatre is always artificial.

LESLIE: Is it? Isn't there something real at the heart of the Restoration fop? It might be exaggerated so the audience can laugh, but the longings, fears, needs, and sense of self are also as true as that experienced by the protagonist of the most naturalistic, modern drama, or we'd view it with indifference and boredom.

VICTOR: One of our teachers says that we should feel every emotion our character does, for real, at least once in the rehearsal process. That's the way we find the way to express each feeling truthfully.

LESLIE: That sounds to me like a very successful strategy for the chameleon side of the actor's job, because 'truthful' means, in practical terms, what the audience needs in order to find meaning in the play. So, if it's bursting into song, or speaking directly to the audience in a poetic monologue, or screaming and weeping – each of those has a validity, a credibility, a 'truthfulness' in the context of the production style.

VICTOR: I think she meant it differently. Truthful means like in real life. And the point is to find the real life emotion at the core of unrealistic things like bursting into song and poetic monologues.

LESLIE: And so, if I say that those 'real' emotions are no more or less an enactment than the singing of the song or the heightened rhetoric of elaborate poetry, you'll disagree?

VICTOR: I'd assume, from what we've discovered about the charismatic energy, that enactments of emotions are part of the chameleon craft, but the real emotional sensations we need to find are part of the charismatic, and the best way to access them is to use our conduits.

SALLY: That matches up with what I've experienced in the workshop.

Whenever I use my conduits, I feel something. It's easy, it flows, and it's true feelings, not faking, like in indicating or forcing the moment.

LESLIE: I'm glad that's been your experience, but now I'm going to say something that will perhaps strike you as truly radical. I'm going to suggest that all your work on emotions, your own and those of the character, are considerations for your chameleon craft, and that the conduits do not, in fact, allow you access to emotions.

POLLY: Even though that's what we experience?

LESLIE: Yes, because the experiences that you label as real emotions are, themselves, constructed events. Although they seem spontaneous, natural, and therefore true in some way manifestly different than the fakery we associate with indicating, they are in fact a complex set of behaviours and perceptions, packaged according to the time and place in which we developed into adulthood. What allows us to experience one package as 'real' and another package as 'fake' has to do with the construction of the package. Fake means that the package is badly put together and therefore doesn't match up with anything we've used, up until that moment, in our ongoing experience of selfhood. However, as we've seen with the examples from period plays, what feels fake and mechanical and artificial might just be unfamiliar. If you moved to another country, say India, the first 500 times you performed 'namaste' you'd feel stupid. But if you lived there long enough, when you returned to North America you'd feel just as stupid shaking hands.

I want to return to Mike's description of 'real' feelings. He talked about them being spontaneous, but mostly he described sensations of 'real' feeling being absent, and he talked about being forced. In that description, I hear effort, which suggests to me that 'flow' is one of the sensations at work in what he describes as 'real' feelings while acting.

What you experienced, I believe, is the flowing energy that is also present in a variety of real-life experiences of feeling. The nature of flow, its effortlessness and fluidity, duplicate another attribute present in a variety of real-life experiences of feeling.

The combination of those sensations, plus your ability to package emotions, which you acquire as part of your development of self-awareness, allow you to experience a successful completion of what you perceive of as the assigned task: the enactment of situations and relationships that are credible and authentic, complete with what our society would label as a correct (i.e. 'real') package under an emotion-word label.

If, however, we were working in a different type of theatre, where the validity of an actor's work isn't linked to the presence or absence of real emotions, you'd be reporting the sensations of gracefulness, fluidity, ener-gized sensitivity, or whatever. You'd be fascinated by the range of movement that can be performed without effort, the expressiveness of your gestures, the mobility of your facial muscles. Or you might speak of the calm, the spiritual connection, the transcendence, as is the experience in other theatrical cultures.

Yes, the charismatic energy is awesome. But it is not linked to any specific type of human experience, until it flows into the form that we give it. And that form is set not only by the task at hand, but also by the theatrical expectations we've set, and the packages that we've absorbed from our culture.

The session ends, but the topic of real emotions carries over into a heated discus-sion, including a lengthy digression from yours truly.

Digression: The Authentic Chameleon

Many theories of acting hold that it is the actor's excellence that compels or, at the very least, facilitates the audience's capacity to experience the character as a real person rather than an actor. While it is undeniable that an actor can shatter the audience's willing suspension of disbelief, inad-vertently or intentionally, some credit must be given to the audience's participation in the experience of belief. There is an overwhelming body of evidence that suggests there is no clear-cut correlation between the actor's achievements and an audience's emotional connection with the fictional character.

No actor ever becomes the character. The character is fiction. The audi-ence and the actors know this; in fact, the audience needs to know this in order to give themselves freely to an emotional engagement with the performance. At the same time as the audience remains constantly aware of being in a theatre and watching a show, they are seeking opportunities to be enticed or compelled or even surprised into an experience of belief. Each audience member takes from the many, many aspects of the perform-ance a pattern onto which a belief in the truth of the character can be placed. In other words, the audience member creates the truthfulness. Each audience member believes just as much as is appropriate for a indi-vidual optimum experience of that event.

With this in mind, we realize that the actor's responsibility is to avoid anything that will get in the way of the belief-creating experiences of the audience. Some people out there in the dark are predisposed to believe almost anything. Others are disinclined to allow any experience of belief and so are profoundly moved when any such experience occurs. All of these, and every variation in between, will attribute to the production the responsibility for their belief-creation experiences. They will praise some shows and condemn others and they will also be quite sure that they know what they like, which is an optimum individual belief experience though they are unlikely to describe it in those terms.

The greatest fallacy proposed by the Method theory of acting is the idea that an authentic experience on the part of the actor guarantees an audience's experience of belief, and therefore that the pursuit of a natural, authentic character is the primary goal of all acting. The duties and responsibilities of the method-trained actor form a paradox: she is expected to transform in any of a variety of ways to suit the fictional character she is portraying in the production of the moment, but she is expected to do this authentically, or 'naturally.' The chameleon duties require an actor who can appear to be a credible doctor, lawyer, or Indian Chief. As an added challenge, the actor knows more than the character he is playing, for he has read the end of the script, and can see the camera and the audience while the character sees only the operating room, the office, or a prairie vista. The responsibilities to the natural lead actors to attempt the impossible, to not know or see what is known and seen, to trick the self into feeling what is not felt, and even to induce a temporary psychosis whereby the actor believes she actually is the fictional character.

The double-helix tension between the chameleon's mimicry and the honesty-within-artifice necessitates careful attention to both the external manifestations and internal sensations of Playing a Character. Externally, a sufficient number of details must be amassed for the chameleon to transform successfully and blend into the background. These might include costume pieces and mannerisms as well as the movement patterns set in rehearsal and the lines of dialogue offered by the playwright. Because the transmission of character-building material is so complex, technical skills such as clarity, expressiveness, boldness, and deep resources of energy are required to sustain a performance. All of this falls into the category of technique, in sharp contrast with the intuitive, introspective, and emotionally charged process whereby the actor pursues authenticity, honesty, and all manner of self-induced illusion.

If we re-examine the connection between chameleon transformations and believability in light of our consideration of the charismatic, quite a different analysis of an actor's contribution to an audience's suspension of disbelief is possible.

The first change is in the structuring of the paradoxical nature of the actor's challenge. Instead of viewing her mimicry as the technical outside of the performance, in contrast with her intuitive, private, emotional transformation in service of the authentic interior of an honest portrayal, we reposition both of these considerations within the chameleon category of the actor's artistry. Any effort made to undergo a transformation, whether manifested in externals such as accent, clothing, or posture or suggested by subtle manifestations of a shift in attitudes, aspirations, or emotional predispositions, is part of an actor's responsibility to evoke a credible fictional personality in keeping with the fictional creation that is the play.

The other side of the paradox rests in quite a different element of acting, the infusion of the self into the fiction. This is nothing as simplistic as revealing those aspects of oneself that correspond to the character, which we might describe as playing oneself through the character, although casting practices suggest that such correspondences are highly desirable. The capacity of a relative young and very pretty actress to play a young and attractive character is an example of the chameleon actor resting upon a familiar background. If that same actress delves into her soul and discovers a capacity to hurt others and indulge in cruelty for personal pleasure, our respect for her capacity to break away from the type into which she is usually cast will mark a conscious awareness of the triumph of a chameleon's technique. In either performance, whether the chameleon is making a huge or minor transformation, the paradoxical contrasting element is the charismatic infusion of unique, individual creative energy into the performance of a fictional character.

This energy is not the same thing as an individual actor's personality, the conscious experience of selfhood. It is something much less specific and much more profound. Rather than being based upon personal experience combined with imagination, this creative energy is a species-specific phenomenon that is true cause of the audience's willingness to suspend disbelief. Given an audience's eagerness to meet the creative artists more than half way, combined with all of the conventions within which both actors and audience share the event of performance, any charismatic energy offered in service of the production will be received by the audience as proof positive of the authenticity of the chameleon's true, honest, natural existence.

This reconfiguring of the correspondence between authenticity of personal feeling and good acting immediately releases many aspiring actors from the burden of an unfortunate misperception: that unless they can actually feel what the character is supposed to feel then they will not be able to convince an audience that the character is real. In extreme cases of misinformation, which can result in the bizarre notion that actors actually believe they are the fictional character they are playing, we can see how the striking capacity for mimicry which our species enjoys has been perverted into a dangerous brush with psychosis. This is not to suggest that an actor has no responsibility for the subtle, most interior aspects of characterization. In certain types of acting experiences such attention to detail is the only means by which the blending with background in service of the fictional creation can be achieved.

The releasing of charismatic creative energy during, through, and because of the chameleon transformation is what infuses the actor's craft with that which the audience recognizes as authentic human experience. Such a release of energy can occur when the actor is consciously or intuitively making use of familiar elements of his own personality, so that the chameleon transformation is minimal, or when the actor has constructed an elaborate fiction demanding the greatest possible technical excellence. It can also occur when the actor is participating in the most artificial of performance styles, where no effort is being made to convince the audience that the performance is anything other than what it is, a shameless bid for applause, laughter, and a paycheck.

VIRTUAL WORKSHOP *SESSION SIX*: QUESTIONS AND CONCERNS

The group gathers for a final workshop session.

LESLIE: Last chance to ask questions. For clarification, or to explore challenges that you're facing, to see if your conduits can help.

Monologues and Impulses

MIKE: Do you have any suggestions for picking monologues?

LESLIE: Given the high-stress, high-stakes situation at an audition, I'd recommend going with a monologue that effortlessly opens up to your conduits. That's not to say that effort – filled consideration couldn't help you with any character. But as you're going to want the richest flow of personal charismatic energy under conditions of high stress, that's what I'd do.

For example, as a Dynamic, I'd be looking for something that would allow me to tap into my sensitivity to power at both extremes, commanding and submitting. And I'd want something active, but in the special way that suits my conduits. Since I don't have either a Relationship or a Perception conduits, I'd have to stay away from anything where I'm supposed to imagine someone doing something and reacting to it.

POLLY: Can you give us examples?

LESLIE: Sure. Looking for a monologue that suits me as a Dynamic Creative Personality type, I might go with something like Bonnie in *Homeward Bound* by Elliott Hayes. Bonnie is my age, and although her situation is not one I've ever experienced, thank goodness, her way of dealing with things makes sense enough to me that I enjoy that comforting sensation of recognition when I read her lines. It's not quite 'I would do that, in that situation,' but more, 'If I'd been raised the way she was, and had her life experiences, I might well feel that way.' And I like the way she deals with the situation. She's not all weepy. She's got guts and a sense of humour. That's important, I think. That level of connection. It's reasonable that I would be cast in that role, and if I were, I could do a good job of it. That's part of what I'm demonstrating at the audition.

The given circumstances: her husband of many years has terminal cancer, and her dysfunctional family has gathered. She's gearing up to tell them that Glenn has decided to end his life before the cancer is too advanced, and she is going to assist him.

Leslie performs the speech. The group applauds politely.

LESLIE: Thanks, I appreciated that! Now, let me talk about what how this speech matches up with my acting processes. For me, as a Dynamic actor, this speech allows me to explore the way that different actions reveal authority and humility, and how powerful actions are, as well as humbling. Bonnie asks some questions about God – those allow me to draw upon a sense of humility. But the speech also makes me feel powerful, because every one of the speech acts in this monologue is an act of power. Bonnie says things that no one else is ready to say, and by saying those things, she overturns their assumptions of superiority over her. That's what leapt out of the speech when I read it the first time, always a good sign. Right away, I could see moments when I could trust my Power conduit to take me somewhere.

Because I'm an Action actor, I need to work through the actions of a speech like this,. To shock is one, for sure. Since I'm not a Relationship actor, I don't need other actors up there with me to provide a target. Just initiating the action will, if I let it, tap into some flowing creative energy. The react side is more difficult, but I like this speech for a couple of possibilities it opens up for me.

Like many such monologues, it's like she's thinking aloud. For me, that becomes reacting to myself. Each phrase is an action, and as it happens I'm already reacting to what I've just said, and linking that reaction with what comes next. Just hearing those words come out of my mouth, I react to that with what comes next, almost as if I realize that my words are doing something, to me, and to everyone else in the room – and I'm taking in what I've just done, and what I could do. The power of words. But then I back off, defuse the power, in reaction to myself again.

POLLY: How would you recommend approaching a speech like that if you were a Relationship actor?

LESLIE: Well, Relationship actors are in a bit of a pickle, in auditions. There's no one else up there, and you're not supposed to engage the auditors directly, out of courtesy for the demands of their job. Usually there's a set of fictional relationships that give the scene its kick. If I also had a Perception conduit, then I'd be able to imagine all of that, in preparation and during delivery. If possible, though, I'd try to get a few actors to rehearse it with, who'd be there for me, to help me explore the monologue as creatively as possible, so I could take ownership of it.

SALLY: Besides imagining the other characters, would you research specific images, and spend time preparing memories for all that she talks about?

LESLIE: I don't have a Perception conduit, and yet I find my imagination engaged. The images are so specific, and so vivid, that I couldn't NOT imagine it. I think I picked the monologue because the writer did that Perception work for me! But when it comes time to perform it, to summon the image is effort work. It's my Action conduit – just saying the words aloud has an effect on me and on everyone around me - and my sensitivity to power – how humble and yet powerful each image makes me feel – that's what I count on.

I'll share with you a trick I use when performing a monologue. I allow myself to react to whatever really happens in the room. I don't know if you noticed, but when I did this for you, there was a definite reaction from you guys. I didn't look at you, because you're not present for my character, but I trusted my impulse to react, and channelled that impulse into what followed.

IRIS: I so felt that. It was like, 'How dare you be embarrassed. How dare you squirm.'

LESLIE: Yes, you were most obliging and gave me a couple of good laughs, which I was hoping for. I had to redirect my reaction to that, though. Leslie, the actor, was thinking, 'Yes!' For Bonnie, the character, I had to allow a reaction of victory, but only in her last line. Because I'd taken the line before as a humbler moment, I had a real sense of rising up above the other characters in the play before whom I usually feel quite inferior.

VICTOR: What sort of speech would you recommend for me? Visionary, so Power and Perception.

LESLIE: You'd want to look for something that lets you tap into your sensitivity to power, but also that allows you to visualize. Perception actors are so lucky that way, because many, many good monologues are memory pieces, filled with sensory details.

When you page through monologue books, look for something that gives you an immediate connection on your first encounter. You should read the first sentence or two and say, 'I like it already!' That's a sign of connection, between your conduits and the writer's, which is almost as important as a strong connection between your sensibilities and those of the character the writer has created. With your conduits strongly engaged, you'll have a firm foundation for your work on the monologue and later your use of it in auditions.

Right away, you want to dive into the monologue, put it on its feet, follow whatever impulses emerge and see where they take you. Don't make your selection based on your intellect. You need to pop it up into the performance zone, in terms of engaged personal energy, to see if the connection between conduit and text is going to unlock useful impulses.

At this stage in the work, it's important not to edit yourself. Perception actors, like Victor, and also Sally and Iris – don't rush! Stop regularly to drop in on images. Take your time. There should be lots of sensory stuff, without having to work at it. Don't squelch it, during that first encounter, even if you end up taking an hour to get through the speech.

Relationship people, enlist someone to deliver it to. Don't be shy. Pair up with another Relationship actor and offer this quid pro quo: if I be there for you to read a new monologue to, then will you be there for me?

MIKE: Doesn't the book get in the way, if you've not memorized it yet?

POLLY: You can still make eye contact. Just break away regularly.

SALLY: Or touch. Just having another actor close by helps me. If I know that person's listening carefully, with feeling.

LESLIE: And that's something you Relationship actors can do for each other. Be there, receiving, within the relationship. Power actors, well, you need to open yourself to the power of speaking, the power of language, of images. Just like the Action actors need to discover that speaking is an action.

IRIS: I find that the book gets in the way of exploring movement.

LESLIE: Even a small movement will mark the impulse for further exploration later. Above all, it's important that you trust your impulses, in that first encounter. Whatever you do, don't start marking out the tricks you'll use, to make it an exciting event for those watching. Too soon for that, and you want those choices to come out of creative impulses from your conduits.

SALLY: Don't you want that in all your acting?

LESLIE: During a rehearsal process, when you're preparing for a production, the blend of disciplined effort and creative flow can range widely. You can build a strong performance even if rehearsal conditions are filled with effort. But for an audition? For the very special demands of the monologues? That's when you need to make sure that you're deeply connected through your conduits, first. If you allow other considerations to creep in too soon, you'd find yourself squelching impulses.

Victor has pulled out a monologue book and pages through, looking for an interesting monologue.

VICTOR: Okay, I've found a possible monologue. Lots of sensory stuff, and tons of memories, already, without having to work at it. Great. What next?

LESLIE: Free yourself to imagine those memories, with us watching. When they occur, put the book down and have a little think. You know what I mean?

VICTOR: You mean, go to that other place, in my mind?

LESLIE: Exactly. But don't withdraw 100% from us. That'd be contrived, for a Perception actor. For you guys, sensory awareness of the here and now and imagining/remembering transportation to another time and place co-exist easily.

VICTOR: Okay, I'll give it a shot.

Victor reads a line, stops, gazes off into the distance, then looks at us to see our reaction.

POLLY: Victor, are you just doing that because you think you're supposed to?

Victor laughs.

VICTOR: I guess you can't fake conduit stuff.

LESLIE: That's an important insight. Somehow, we can tell the difference between a good, theatrical impulse that comes from your careful consideration of how you might deliver this monologue, and an impulse from your conduits. Keep going. Just let whatever happens, happen.

Victor offers a bit more of the speech.

VICTOR: Okay, for some of that I was just going through the motions. Like a good student. But there were also a couple of times I submitted to the power of the language, like you suggested. I think that's going to work for me as a way of trying on monologues.

POLLY: Can I try?

Victor tosses Polly the monologue book.

LESLIE: I'm going to make you work fast on this, to learn to trust impulses. Just find something and start reading. Just focus on speaking as action. That's one of your conduits, as a Personal actor. The other is Relationship, so we'll give you someone to make contact with. Sally? Mike? How about you get closer and be there for her. Listening, watching, with physical contact as well. Don't worry if it doesn't fit the given circumstances. Polly, just let your conduits lead you.

Polly reads the monologue slowly, and there are moments of intense connection with Sally and Mike.

POLLY: I can't believe I got that far on a first reading.

VICTOR: I really liked how you read so slowly, took your time.

SALLY: It was like you felt your way into the speech. And it didn't bother me a bit that you keep your focus on the book. I knew we were connected.

IRIS: You should use that as an audition speech.

Auditions and Using the Real

MIKE: My auditions are always crap. I would never have been accepted here if they didn't do improvs in groups.

SALLY: You're not the only one who hates auditions, Mike. All of us Relationship people, we've got to perform without a partner, which is even worse for me because of how important sensory awareness of my partner is.

POLLY: Or you might have to read opposite the stage manager, who doesn't feed your relationship needs. For me, reaction is what I draw on, and what do I get from a stage manager?

VICTOR: Oh boo hoo hoo. What about us Power actors? Think of all the wacky games that get played at auditions – and someone like me picks up on every nuance.

IRIS: Why are you guys all looking at me? I hate auditioning too, you know.

LESLIE: A couple of comments and then some strategies.

First, I have strong feelings about auditions. One is that in the long run, it matters less whether you get any specific role than if you feel you consistently show your best work in auditions. There's nothing worse, in my opinion, than walking away from an opportunity knowing that you shot yourself in the foot, that you denied yourself a chance at career advancement. That's because I feel very strongly that your courage is your single most valued commodity, far more significant than your so-called talent. Anything that eats away at your courage is dangerous. A mismatch between what you can do, what you want to do in an audition, and what you actually do is as bad for your courage as a mismatch between your Creative Personality type and an acting teacher.

Another is that there is a limit to the amount of psychic energy you have available at any given time. If you eat up a portion of that energy not only feeling anxiety, but attempting to hide that anxiety through bluff, how much psychic energy is going to be left over for the acting you'll do for these individuals who are judging you under such anxiety-creating conditions?

Let me demonstrate what I mean. Put your hand together. Press with your left, and press back with your right. Push as hard as you can with both hands, involving your arms and your back. If you've dedicated equal energy to both hands, neither will move. Now, disguise that static non-movement with a superficial smile, and circulate among the group, chatting socially about the weather, being sure not to let the pressure in your hands drop for a second.

It doesn't take long for people to get the point.

LESLIE: That, for me, is the perfect metaphor of auditioning, if an actor attempts to hide her natural anxiety about the situation which is, we can all agree, legitimately filled with tension. My guess is that your training has already or will (and should!) include exercises for relaxation and concentration, techniques to refocus your awareness away from anything that interferes with your work as an actor. I'm going to add a very specific strategy that builds directly on your conduits.

I should mention, before we begin exploring, that you'll not be able to tell exactly how this might work for you until you can test it out in a real audition situation. I think you can lay the groundwork, even practice some techniques so that they're at your fingertips. The real test, as with so much of what we're doing in this workshop, will be in actual situations in your working life as an actor.

Okay, here's how the technique works. First, you have to buy into a fundamental concept: Using the Real. This means that you learn to use whatever you are really feeling as an element of the scene you are performing. By the way, this is the only time that I'm an advocate of making your work about the expression of what you're really feeling as an actor. And the only reason I do that is because the intense anxiety of an auditioning actor require equally intense amounts of psychic energy to suppress, and if you can express some of those emotions through the character, then you'll use up less psychic energy in suppressing.

Let's take an example. Can one of you recount an auditioning experience that is particularly memorable because of the level of anxiety you experienced?

SALLY: I was once at an audition where I was so nervous I threw up in the washroom, and when I came out of the stall the stage manager was right there, and she was the person I had to read opposite. The whole time I was reading, I kept thinking, this woman knows I was puking my guts out five minutes ago.

LESLIE: How was the audition?

SALLY: Terrible, I'm sure. The director kept on interrupting and giving me the same direction, about five times. I never did understand what he wanted.

LESLIE: You've just given us a very good symptom of insufficient psychic energy. A bit of good advice, in any job interview, is to listen. Hard to do, when you're struggling with intense anxiety that you're also attempting to hide! What was the scene you were reading?

SALLY: I don't remember. That's how out of it I was.

LESLIE: So you weren't able to give even the basic indications of your acting ability, or at least that's the way I'm sure it felt when you left the audition.

SALLY: I cried all the way home. You're right, it was much, much worse than when I did a good job at an audition and wasn't cast, or got a supporting role and not the lead.

POLLY: How would you have felt if you'd got the part, after that audition?

SALLY: I'd have been stunned. Thrilled. I'd have figured he'd talked to someone about what I was really capable of.

VICTOR: Or that the guy was a jerk, and cast you entirely on looks.

SALLY: Probably not looks. I was still puke green, the only time he saw me.

VICTOR: Who said he'd be looking at your face?

IRIS: Tacky. Tacky.

VICTOR: Hey, it's not me, but if we're honest, we know that's some of what goes on.

LESLIE: I think we could talk for hours about the questionable activities that plague our profession. But for now, let's focus on what is the responsibility of the actor auditioning – delivering the best possible demonstration of aptitude for the opportunity on offer. From what Sally's shared, we've a clear indication of the pitfalls of high anxiety coupled with intense efforts to hide the true feelings of the performer.

Now, I'm going to suggest an alternative approach, that Sally might have been able to use if she'd known her Creative Personality type at the time, and if she'd practice the technique of using the real. First, a reminder of your type, Sally?

SALLY: I'm Psychic: Relationship and Perception.

LESLIE: Let's hear from others: how was Sally's Creative Personality type particularly affected by the situation?

IRIS: Her hyper-sensitivity to sensations would kick in, making her super aware of things like the faint smell of vomit. Sorry, I hope that didn't offend anyone.

SALLY: Not me. You're absolutely right. I was terrified they could smell the puke on me.

MIKE: Also, since the stage manager knew, and Sally knew she knew, then any Relationship stuff that might have kicked in during the reading was cut off because of the real relationship.

POLLY: And Sally's Psychic awareness of the stage manager's attitude – she was probably picking up on all sorts of signals.

LESLIE: And perhaps interpreting them incorrectly, due to anxiety. What might have been concern and sympathy could be misread as disgust or disinterest.

SALLY: Actually, I thought she was concerned and sympathetic. That was part of the problem. Because she knew, I couldn't let it go and pretend it never happened. Every time I'd glance over at her, I'd see on her face that she was worried for me.

VICTOR: I get that so clearly. If she were neutral, it would be easier to endow her with the character's attributes. For the scene.

LESLIE: Good summary of the special sensitivities of the combination of Perception and Relationship. Now, here's the fundamental key to Using the Real. All you have to do is ADD to the given circumstances a specific correlation between your situation and the character's. It's that simple.

SALLY: You mean, I should have played that my character just threw up?

LESLIE: Why not? I'll tell you why it works, and maybe you'll see how easy it is. It works because the effort to suppress reality is too much. The reality exists. The person who is standing there reading the scene did indeed just threw up. That's part of the authenticity of the moment. You don't need to express that reality. You don't need to add a line to the scene. It simply exists, and you need do nothing to change it or erase it. The problem is your effort to disguise that reality! The second you decide to let even the slightest glimmer of that reality show, the second your creative self finds an outlet for that reality in the enacting of the scene, the pressure eases for the suppression mechanisms.

POLLY: You make it sound easy, and obvious, but the problem in auditions is you're not thinking straight.

LESLIE: Absolutely. I'm sure, in the normal run of things, anything Sally was really experiencing would naturally constitutes the raw material she could use (or not) in her acting. That's why the conduits are going to be needed to make Using the Real a viable strategy during situations of high anxiety.

Let's return to the beginning, where we started in our discussions of charismatic energy. It is, essentially, creative energy. It is associated with flow, with freedom from effort, with intuition and organic, inventive solutions to creative problems.

Remember, also, that you only want to and need to muck around with your conduits when things are NOT going well. If flow's happening, go with it! Who cares which conduit or what process unleashes that energy?

There are, indeed, audition experiences that are thrillingly creative, correct? Without any conscious effort at using conduits.

MIKE: More often when I'm given a chance to work with people a bit, that relaxes me and I can do some good work, take some risks.

IRIS: If I know exactly what I'm supposed to do, but that might be from dance, where auditioning is completely different. You're asked to execute combinations, you learn them and do them, and you know right away if you've got it right or not. As soon as you know you've mastered the step, you can just feel the music, and the movement flows into it, and you know you're showing your real capacities.

VICTOR: I like it when the director works with you. I hate it when they're out there in the dark, though that only ever happened in high school. I think my drama teacher watched too many old movies.

LESLIE: You may not be aware of it, but you're all talking about opportunities to release charismatic energy through your conduits. But you're focusing on things that are not in your control: what you can perceive of the director, whether sufficient time is spent so relationships form, whether there's clarity in the required actions, or opportunities for establishment of a director's authority – can you shift your experience of an audition so you habitually open yourself to authentic experiences through your conduits, that are under your control?

MIKE: I don't see how I can use Relationship if I'm given less than five minutes with complete strangers.

LESLIE: Good point, but perhaps that's more because you're accustomed to tapping the warm, opening side of the Relationship conduit for your charismatic, creative energy. How about using the other side? My guess it that, what you really feel in those situations is the closing, cool, even destructive side, but you don't want to let that show, so you're in Sally's situation of experiencing a sensation that you must use an equal amount of psychic energy to suppress.

MIKE: I don't think it would be a good idea to show how much I dislike that sort of audition.

LESLIE: I agree. I'm not saying you let the auditors know what you think of their poor choice of audition process. But it could become the obstacle that you fight, increasing the dramatic, energetic presence you bring onto the stage, even for a few minutes. Remember that relationships are all about fluidity, change. If you start with the closed sensation – well, that's a place from which the warm energy emerges.

Most important – if you know you can release even a bit of the closed, destructive energy in your monologue or scene, your psyche is relieved of the strain of unrelieved suppression.

IRIS: One of our teachers puts us through a number of exercises where we enter a room and inhabit the space that we're really in. I think that would work for auditions, helping to focus our awareness on what's really going on around us, including what people are saying to us.

LESLIE: That's an excellent suggestion for anyone with a Perception conduit, particularly as you blend the energy unleashed by sensory awareness into other creative possibilities. For example, sensory awareness of the audition space, the colour of the walls, the ambient sound, the smells, the sensations from your own body, could feed your imagination, as you evoke the physical reality of the monologue or scene, and of the character in the scene. If you're Psychic, which is Perception and Relationship, you can feed this sensory awareness by keying off of the other people in the space. If you're Visionary, which is Perception and Power, you can explore the sensations of authority and command that come from your senses, along with a wonderful humility and willingness to submit, which is very appealing to those auditioning you. If you're Innovative, which is Perception and Action, you can use your sensory awareness to provide yourself with spontaneous, authentic reactions so that you initiate appropriate activity, both in response to the auditioning team and also in the context of the monologue.

What all of these strategies have in common is a very specific type of using the real, so that the adrenalin of the high-stakes situation is blended naturally with the flowing, effortless, organic, and above all creative energy of the charismatic.

You won't be entirely relaxed. I don't think that's possible or even wise. You want to be in a state of heightened energy. But if you can release charismatic energy along with the adrenalin, you'll be more likely to come up with creative solutions to the challenge of using that energy, and the specifics of the reality of the audition, in a way that enhances your presentation.

POLLY: How can we practice? Or can we? Do we have to wait for a high-stress situation to develop this strategy?

LESLIE: Ultimately, yes, I think you do. However, the sort of thing I would recommend, in preparation, would be linking your preparatory rituals to your conduits, and practicing those so that they become customary. If you have any sort of a superstitious ritual, before auditions or performances, my guess is that you've put it together because it is particularly suited to your conduits. My suggestion: build on those rituals or favourite warm ups to fine tune them in accordance with your Creative Personality type.

IRIS: Like our personalized warm-ups?

LESLIE: I was thinking of something even more superstitious, but yes.

Auditioning is just one high-stress situation where some intentional manipulation of your conduits could reduce anxiety. One of the side-benefits of knowing your individual creative engine is knowing how to put the key in the engine and snap it into high gear to survive the least pleasant acting situations.

VICTOR: What about when your real feelings for your acting partner are the opposite of what the scene requires. A love scene with someone you despise or fear? A violent scene with someone you want to protect?

MIKE: Those don't bother me, because the relationship complexity gives you room to blend in a touch of the opposite feeling, right?

LESLIE: Victor, are you aware that the relationship words you used: despise, fear, violence and protection, are also linked to commanding and submitting?

VICTOR: About thirty seconds after they came out of my mouth.

POLLY: Okay, I'll say it. Wouldn't it be better to accept our individual strengths and weaknesses as actors, and plan our careers so we showcase the strengths? Isn't that what we do when we pick audition pieces?

LESLIE: Can't you do both? Are the two mutually exclusive? I think you need to set things up so that your conduits unleash maximum creative energy, as that is very attractive to other creative artists, as well as to audiences. At the same time, you can be alert to the pitfalls that offset the gifts, both of which are unique to your creative temperament, and put in place strategies to compensate appropriately.

So I guess the only place where we differ is that I would recommend acknowledging what you call weaknesses, and in fact using them somehow, to ensure that you're able to showcase your unique talent even in an audition.

IRIS: Can we talk more about those weaknesses? I get how we're supposed to acknowledge them, but I'm not clear how we could use them. I thought we were training to get rid of them. Things like inhibitions.

POLLY: I think we have to grow up, if we want to make it professionally. There's no place for prudes, or crippling shyness.

MIKE: But some stuff goes deeper than that. If you read about how society teaches us to deny ourselves, in order to conform to stereotypes.

LESLIE: Let's go back to the monologue Mike was working on. Who's he talking to? In the scene?

POLLY: All of us? Is it a direct-address speech?

LESLIE: Yes, like a soliloquy. Would you imagine he's addressing a group that is receptive or judgmental?

SALLY: I'd say receptive, or he'd never reveal what he does.

LESLIE: And in an audition? What's the real-life relationship at work there?

MIKE: Completely judgmental. Could you do the speech as if you're in that sort of a relationship?

LESLIE: You might start off open, friendly, and only slowly realize that they're not friendly, they're judging you, and then look for a moment when you could be more confrontational, challenging them on their judgement of you.

VICTOR: That'd be a real feeling.

IRIS: What about Action? There doesn't seem to be anything to do, like in so many monologues, though there's lots of possibilities to imagine doing things.

LESLIE: And that's doing something, isn't it?

IRIS: I didn't know that counted.

Everything Counts

LESLIE: Everything counts, for Action actors. Anything that you initiate, to have an effect on your environment, including yourself, is Action. The problem, in a monologue, is finding things to react to. And you can't plan a reaction, because that's going to be something you initiate, right? And probably a fake something, designed to demonstrate to the audience that your character is reacting.

IRIS: Wow. I just got something. About the way my Action and Perception conduits work together. I never, ever thought of all my awareness and imagination being actions as well. Not consciously. But I've used that, lots of times. Choosing to see. Deciding to allow myself to remember. Or, I guess I should say, showing the audience that the character is choosing to remember. And I react to memories and imaginary things, all the time. It's reaction even when it's invisible, right?

LESLIE: Oh, yes. What you've been saying has just given me an idea. It could be a very brave bit of work, for a Perception actor, to do the activity of imagining, and reveal it to the audience, particularly if the images were of the sort that society tries to squelch. And I'm also curious if that could happen without any obvious activity – no movement or facial expressions or dialogue. Just the action of remembering or imagining. And Iris, you're the perfect one to demonstrate, with your Perception and Action blend.

Would you be willing to stand in front of us, and explore a private imaginative event. Actually do the imagining, in front of us, and initiate that as an action, to have an effect on us and on yourself. Then, react to whatever is going on inside of you. But don't do anything. Don't initiate anything except the use of the perception conduit?

IRIS: Does it have to be about sex?

Laughter

IRIS: It's a serious question. Everything seems to be about sex, these days.

VICTOR: Well, Freud would say that it's either sex or death. Not a lot of other options, if you're looking for the biggies.

LESLIE: Modern writers seem to enjoy taking us to places that would have made us all blush not that long ago. So actors are often asked to go, publicly, where the rest of us hesitate to go even in fantasy. Iris, it's your choice of memory, and you don't have to disclose it. Sex is only one option. Are you okay with this?

IRIS: No, it's fine. I'm curious to see what will happen, so I'd like to try, and go to a very private, dangerous place.

Iris stands before the group. There is a definite physical manifestation of feeling, followed by a clear shift out of the envisioning, a realization and a reaction both to us watching and to whatever she's been thinking and feeling. The group applauds.

SALLY: If you could do that at will, you could do film work. It was so real, and so subtle. I loved it.

LESLIE: How did it feel?

IRIS: It was easier than I thought. There's something about the conduits, at least for me. It feels good, it flows, there's nothing mechanical, but it's also not me. It floats free. I just do it, and there's fewer strings attached than when I'm creating a whole character.

LESLIE: Interesting observation. I wonder if it's because the conduit energy is neutral. It's creative. It's charismatic. But it's not coloured in any way, by any social context, until you direct it somewhere. So it's not going to be part of the familiar emotional baggage unless you put it into a context that summons those associations.

IRIS: I like this approach a lot, for that reason. I like that it's effortless, and that it feels natural, and that it's unique to me without forcing me to be me up here in front of you all.

LESLIE: Isn't it ironic that you come to that conclusion, having just performed something that was incredible risky because it was so personal and so exposed.

POLLY: I just don't understand why she can't do that every time.

LESLIE: Remember when we explored how socialization can get in the way of accessing our conduits? Now, as we really push ourselves to dissect our acting processes, we're discovering some interference or crimping or encrustation or noise in our conduits that is the result of familiar strategies we've already developed in our acting. Earlier, someone mentioned working to eliminate habits and inhibitions that block you from playing a character unlike yourself.

MIKE: That was me.

LESLIE: And there's been reference a couple of times to individuals falling into a few of the 'same old, same old' acting habits. What I call encrustation.

SALLY: I think we've all done that, in this workshop, even if no one nailed us for it at the time.

LESLIE: So when we work on our creative conduits, striving for access of the richest, fullest, most profound creative energy, flowing freely into our explorations, our planning, our training, our rehearsals, our performances – we're going to have to combat our acting habits, which are just another form of rigidity.

VICTOR: And laziness.

SALLY: Specially if they work.

LESLIE: Here again, I'll say that self-knowledge is the goal, and any acting strategy that is based on mis-perception or wilful blindness is not only self-indulgent and crippling, but potentially dangerous, if we remember that actors deal with explosive and overwhelming energies that can permanently damage the fragile psyche – resulting in the equivalent of a dancer who destroys her feet or a singer who shreds her vocal chords. Do you folks know someone who withdrew from acting for that sort of a reason?

IRIS: I know quite a few dancers who had to quit because of injuries. Some were bad luck, but quite a few were from stupidity. Insufficient warm up. Ignoring fatigue or pain.

LESLIE: I know someone who insisted on lecturing through laryngitis, and he lost his voice, permanently. His vocal chords were damaged and never recovered. But what about actors?

MIKE: Well, we're a pretty neurotic bunch. I think we all know someone who's crashed and burned.

LESLIE: Some of that might be the result of self-selection. Theatre, specially in high school and other amateur settings, does attract people with certain unfortunate psychological disabilities. But let's talk about someone with talent, and training, and good luck, who paid a psychological price.

POLLY: What about the drug use, and alcoholism? Does acting cause the abuse, or do potential abusers drift into acting?

VICTOR: Or is that just the culture of theatre. Everyone goes out to the pub after rehearsal.

LESLIE: I know of a couple of actors, very successful, very skilled and talented, who quite abruptly developed crippling stage fright. And I'm talking life-threatening. Heart attack intensity.

SALLY: Didn't Laurence Olivier have that?

LESLIE: Yes, he writes about that with great honesty in *Confessions of an Actor*. Perhaps that's an example of the sort of psychological price that an actor might pay. I don't think we should kid ourselves. This work we do is potentially dangerous, and self-knowledge is an important ingredient of safety as well as of success in our careers. To say nothing of satisfaction.

IRIS: Some auditions are fine, for me, but others I'm just about crippled with stage fright.

Stage Fright

LESLIE: We really need two different terms, one for the sensations of heightened adrenalin, to which many of us become addicted but which enhance a performance, if channelled into the demands of the role, by heightening our sensory awareness, our tuning to fellow actors and the audience, our energy levels, so necessary for the intense and sustained activity of the play, and our experience of the humbling transcendent power of live theatre.

Let's call that stage fright, thinking of the intentional pleasure seeking we associate with Halloween, haunted houses, horror movies, etc.

For that other condition, let's use the term: stage terror, and save this for conditions of acute, physically debilitating, career-ending psychological trauma, such as suffered by Laurence Olivier.

I believe that an awareness of ones Creative Personality type can assist in the management of stage fright and decrease the possibilities of stage terror.

If we think of the fight/flight impulses of our species, and the fundamentally unnatural activity that is acting, and by that I mean self-exposure, in front of large numbers of strangers or, worse yet, a small number of people with power over our careers, then we can position stage fright correctly as the releasing of intense chemical changes required for flight or fight that are not used for the purpose intended, and therefore linger, potentially toxically, in our systems. We're all aware of the physiological sensations of excess adrenalin – I'm plagued by wobbly tummy, for example. I quickly learned what I could and could not eat before a performance.

The problem with the adrenalin is that it needs somewhere to go. Ideally, it flows naturally into the performance itself, providing an authentic core energy to all that ensues. Unfortunately, adrenalin-induced energy is not as malleable as the pure creative energy unleashed by the conduits, and in large doses it resists intentional manipulation.

If we consider auditions as a high-stress, maximum adrenalin-inducing situation, we can explore how an understanding of adrenalin coupled with an awareness of Creative Personality type can turn a problem into a strategy for excellence.

Memorizing and Knowing

IRIS: What about forgetting lines?

LESLIE: If you remember anything while under stress, it's probably because it moved past the stage of mechanical memorizing into that deeper level of learning that you need to perform text.

VICTOR: Can you explain what you just said?

LESLIE: It's the difference between learning your lines so you can say them perfectly in the shower, as opposed to knowing them well enough to act a scene. Pure memorization, via focussed repetition, occurs in one area of the brain, but quite a different area of the brain is used when you no longer need conscious intellectual effort to recall language. Think, for example, of musicians when their fingers practice a set of notes, first slowly, and then faster and faster until their fingers are moving more quickly than their conscious attention can monitor. In fact, if they try to control what their fingers are doing, they make mistakes.

When the complete package starts to emerge, in your work on the role, when your senses, your movement, and your intellect build up strong connections, then it's as if your body remembers as well as your mind, giving you the sensation of knowing the lines. You've moved beyond memorization to ownership.

IRIS: Why do we forget lines in a scene we know really well – in the body, like you say?

LESLIE: Yes, that happens. You know when you're exploring a scene in acting class or rehearsal, and stuff starts to cook, and suddenly the lines are gone? That can be a very good sign, can't it? Other areas of your brain are firing, and new connections are being formed between those firings and the area where your intellect has stored the words.

IRIS: But if it's in performance? What's going on then?

LESLIE: That's impossible to generalize. Sometimes I suspect it's the actor's equivalent of the musician thinking about what his fingers are doing. We need a very special type of monitoring, controlling awareness when we perform. Another metaphor I'd use is my driving. I can't tell you the number of times I've been heading for a relatively unfamiliar destination, and turned off at my regular exit instead. It's not that I'm not paying attention to the other cars on the road, you'll be glad to hear. It's that I'm not paying attention to this particular journey. I wonder if, when I suddenly forget what I'm supposed to say next in a scene I've performed thirty times without a problem, if I've let it get that little bit too repetitive, and at the moment I realize that I'm doing the scene right now, I'm blank. If I'd staying in that automatic delivery mode, I'd not lose the lines, though my acting wouldn't be the best. It's realizing I've drifted, which happens when I'm back, that wipes the slate clean.

MIKE: Do conduits make a difference, in how easy or hard you find learning lines?

LESLIE: The transition from rote memorization to knowing is a perfect example of conduit and consideration overlap. You must say those lines. That's the chameleon consideration. You must take ownership of those lines, for which you need your conduits. As you allow your conduit energy to flow into the shape created by those words, then your brain will build those connections and shift naturally from learning to knowing.

If you blank in performance, the panic snaps shut your conduits. If you could open your mind to their energy, the connections will reform and the known words will return to your conscious awareness. In theory, anyway. In practice, any of a number of things tend to rescue us, as various parts of our brains and those of our colleagues kick into high gear.

Camera Acting

SALLY: We've mentioned acting for the camera a couple of times, and

211

I was wondering if you could say a little more about how the various conduits fit in with that? I ask because, even though we're all training for a career in theatre, we've got to be pragmatic, right? We're going to be going after TV and film work sooner or later.

LESLIE: An excellent question. I've mostly considered theatre acting, in developing this approach, because of the very special demands that public performance puts on an actor's psyche. But acting for the camera makes equally challenging demands. Any thoughts on how the chameleon skills and the charismatic energy might serve you in the specific work conditions of a film shoot, for example?

POLLY: Well, the charismatic is the obvious thing that stars bring. The camera just drinks it up. The little experience I've had was mostly hurry up and wait, you know what I mean? Hours and hours, sitting around, then they want the climactic moment, out of sequence, full out. And they wonder why we're temperamental!

MIKE: Plus, what sort of a relationship are we supposed to have with a camera?

IRIS: Like we're supposed to ignore it, that huge thing right there? Plus the lights, and the cables, and the crew standing around drinking coffee. At least in the theatre the audience sit quietly in the dark, for the most part.

SALLY: I remember someone telling me, in theatre you deliver a performance to the audience, but for the camera, you're supposed to invite it in.

VICTOR: The best lesson I learned, in the acting on camera class, was the trick of scale. You need to find out, in advance, what the planned shot is, so you can deliver the right degree of subtlety or free, full enactment. Like, if I'm being filmed from a helicopter, and I'm on the top of a mountain, it's gotta be arms out, head back, full out energy. But if it's going to be my eyes two feet high on the screen, then it's got to be an almost invisible flicker. Just an eyelid, a hair on an eyelid.

LESLIE: What I'm hearing, and it matches up with my observations and experiences, is that the chameleon skills are in demand, not only to transform yourself into the character, but also to deliver the precision required, for things like hitting your mark and matching up for continuity. But the charismatic flow has to be on tap, ready to go, full out or subtle, and completely under your conscious control so that you can turn it on even after waiting, even when shooting out of sequence, even with the cinematic apparatus and personnel very much in your face. Sally, your comment makes me want to grab a group of actors, rent a TV studio, and experiment with controlling charismatic energy so it invites the camera in. Wouldn't it be fun to have a clear-cut technique, based on all we've been exploring with Creative Personality types, for changing from theatre to film and back again.

The group eagerly volunteers to be my guinea pigs but, sadly, time does not permit.

Charismatic Chameleons

MIKE: You can have all the talent in the world, but if you're not trained, there are limits to what you can do.

IRIS: And if you have all the training in the world, but you're cut off from your charisma, you're not going anywhere either.

VICTOR: Not true. A skilled technician can always get work. And what about stars – the camera loves them and they play the same role over and over.

SALLY: But if we think about our favourite actors, the ones we truly admire, is it because they're great technically, or because of the charisma?

Here followed a short debate about favourite actors, including rejection of others' choices, and a disagreement about whether charisma was all really that mattered.

LESLIE: Okay, we're straying into a familiar debate, aren't we? Technique versus inspiration. Acting as craft versus acting as talent. Discipline versus intuition. My take on this is pretty straightforward. I want them both. Everyone who you've described as a charismatic actor – well, that's getting complicated because of two possible definitions, or rather, manifestations, of charismatic energy. There's the high-energy, attractive, extroverted, star persona type of charisma, that we can spot in politicians, sales people, and famous personalities from all walks of life.

SALLY: Like Princess Diana.

LESLIE: Good example. That's one use of the word charisma. We might call it 'star power.' But there's also the unlocking of profound energy from the psyche, which fuels the creative process in creating character and energizes the performance of that creation.

I agree that star-power charisma can attract a great deal of attention for an actor. But for me, the greatest benefit of charismatic energy is in the authentication it brings to even a supporting or ensemble performance.

POLLY: Can you have one without the other? The different kinds of charisma, I mean. Seems like charismatic stars who play themselves over and over aren't all that creative.

LESLIE: I think it's the same energy, flowing into a different kind of

213

acting. The chameleon-like capacity for transformation, that I also value, is just one type of disciplined, sellable skill that a performer can offer. The ability to tap your individual charismatic energy over and over, as required, even just to be yourself vividly and richly in public, on call – that's not something to be sneered at. In Cameron Crowe's *Conversations with Wilder*, Billy Wilder tells a story about working with Marilyn Monroe. He was amazed at what happened when she 'turned on the juice' – as often for her fans as for the camera. He describes the complete transformation of her presence – the unleashing of that compelling charisma.

IRIS: She's not a good role model, though. In fact, all of those charismatic stars who lack discipline on the set and in their private lives – that's not a road I want to take, no matter how famous it might make me.

SALLY: One thing I've learned from this workshop is just how dangerous charisma can be. I mean, isn't that why we're socialized, why our pipes get crimped? I keep thinking of those shows about finding oil, and they're digging deeper and deeper, and suddenly they hit, and it's 'Look out, baby!'

VICTOR: What about the opposite, technique without charisma. Is that acting?

LESLIE: Well, maybe you can tell me. Technique would then consist of the chameleon-like transformation without the extra jolt of creative energy. In other words, blending in for its own sake, not as part of any sort of artistic expression. Isn't that what we do every day? Isn't that, in fact, what socialization is?

MIKE: But that doesn't take any effort. Not like when we have to move and speak like someone from a different age, say for Restoration Comedy. So isn't there a difference between normal socialization and the huge transformations we do?

LESLIE: Well, the style of speaking and moving that is unfamiliar would be normal, if everyone did it. I don't think sitting at a desk and raising your hand to visit the washroom feels normal to a little kid the first few weeks of school.

VICTOR: But surely we have to learn to do things on a bigger scale?

LESLIE: Well, yes. And I'd point to styles of performance like opera as a good example. I think there are performers who master the scale of vocal and physical presence that opera requires without necessarily unleashing a corresponding charismatic energy. Not the stars, who even if they're not particularly good chameleons still blend incredibly disciplined technique with huge amounts of charisma. But there's a mechanical type of singer who offers the look and sound of opera as an empty, mechanical performance.

IRIS: I think there are dancers like that. In fact, some choreographers want that from their dancers. They want a doll or a machine-like ensemble.

SALLY: But what do we want? I don't know of anyone who wants to be a mechanical actor, all technique and no heart, but I can see the pay off if you have tons of heart, if they really get up there and pour themselves into the role.

POLLY: Is it about what we want? I mean, really, the profession? Isn't it about grabbing any job we're offered, and figuring out how to survive?

LESLIE: Do you think knowing about your Creative Personality Types will help you survive?

MIKE: It's like you said. There's no one out there to take care of us, except ourselves. We have to keep the engine tuned, or it will end up destroyed by all the 'slings and arrows of outrageous fortune,' if you know what I mean.

LESLIE: I'm glad to hear that, because this has been a fun experience for me, meeting you and working with you in these sessions. I wish you all the best in your future careers, and I look forward to the day I can say, 'I knew them way back when!'

IRIS: Before you go, could you leave us with a summary of the conduits and types, for future reference?

Summation

THE CONDUIT OF ACTION

The Action conduit unlocks an easy and rich flow of energy simply by initiating activities and by responding to what others are doing. It is experienced through sensations of activity and of impulse.

When the Action conduit is combined with the Perception conduit (*Innovative CP Type*), the conduit is put to work in service of a plan, something envisioned in great detail. The reactions are connected with a highly-tuned awareness of every aspect of the environment. Reactions can also occur long after the actual event or in response to an imaged action, given the Perception conduit's capacity to remember and fantasize.

When the Action conduit is combined with the Relationship conduit (*Personal CP Type*), the conduit is put to work in service of relationships, which might be in the process of growing intimacy or withdrawal. The reactions become particularly focussed on the activity of others.

When the Action conduit is combined with the Power conduit (*Dynamic CP Type*), the conduit is put to work in order to assume or give up control and responsibility. Activity, whether initiated or reactive, can be strikingly powerful or humble.

THE CONDUIT OF PERCEPTION

The Perception conduit unlocks an easy and rich flow of energy by imagining and remembering, or by using all of the senses within the present environment.

When the Perception conduit is combined with the Relationship conduit (*Psychic CP Type*), the conduit is put to work in service of relationships, which might be current and real, or imagined or remembered. Because these combined sectors result in astute observers, relationship signals that are often missed by others are easily perceived; hence, they can easily shift back and forth from warming up and cooling down.

When the Perception conduit is combined with the Power conduit (*Visionary CP Type*), the conduit is put to work in service of potency and humility. The imaginative side creates scenarios or dwells on memories that fuel intense confidence or shame; the observing side identifies signals of inferiority and superiority on all sides.

When the Perception conduit is combined with the Action conduit (*Innovative CP Type*), the conduit is put to work doing things, either in direct reaction to events all around, or in response to past events that are recalled in vivid detail or in preparation for an imagined future.

THE CONDUIT OF RELATIONSHIP

The Relationship conduit unlocks an easy and rich flow of energy through interaction with another performer. This sector is tuned to the constant shift and change within relationships, which open up to increased intimacy and warmth, or close down to increased disdain and antipathy.

When the Relationship conduit is combined with the Power conduit (*Magnetic CP Type*), the conduit is put to work in service of empowerment, either for oneself or for the others involved in the relationship. The results can be quite overpowering for the recipient!

When the Relationship conduit is combined with the Action conduit (*Personal CP Type*), the conduit is put to work in service of activity within the relationship, regardless of the initiator. Reactions become strongly connected with opening up or closing down relationships.

When the Relationship conduit is combined with the Perception conduit (*Psychic CP Type*), the conduit is put to work in service of awareness and imagination; the constant shift of relationships provide fuel for intense observation as well as fantasies and memories.

THE CONDUIT OF POWER

The Power conduit unlocks an easy and rich flow of energy through an awareness those forces and individuals before which one bows in humility, and those above which one rises with authority.

When the Power conduit is combined with the Action conduit (*Dynamic CP Type*), the conduit is put to work in service of activity to establish and maintain control and status, whether commanding or in service of the more powerful. Reactions become strongly attuned to the demonstration of power and humility by others.

When the Power conduit is combined with the Perception conduit (*Visionary CP Type*), the conduit is put to work in service of awareness of relative status, imagined or real. Astute and sensitive observation of those above and below is offset by a capacity to remember and imagine subtle indicators of relative power.

When the Power conduit is combined with the Relationship conduit (*Magnetic CP Type*), the conduit is put to work in service of relationships. Sometimes the shifting temperature of a relationship needs to be controlled, other times accepted. The partners in such a relationship can be quite puzzled, because they are sometimes on the receiving end of commanding, other times of submitting (see page 224 for the chart of conduit energies).

Works Cited

Barton, Robert. *Acting.* Belmont, CA: Wadsworth/Thomson Learning, 2002.

Colvin, Geoff. *Talent is Overrated.* New York: Portfolio, 2008.

Conroy, Marianne. "Acting Out." *Criticism* XXXV, no. 2 (Spring 1993): 293–63.

Crowe, Cameron. *Conversations with Wilder.* New York: Knopf, 1999.

Hayes, Elliott. *Homeward Bound.* Toronto: Playwrights Canada Press, 1991.

Jesse, Anita. *The Playing is the Thing.* Burbank, CA: Wolf Creek Press, 1996.

Kempinski, Tom. *Duet for One.* New York: Samuel French, Inc., 1981.

McGaw, Charles. *Acting is Believing.* New York: Holt, Rinehart and Winston, 1975.

Olivier, Laurence. *Confessions of An Actor.* New York: Simon and Schuster, 1982.

Pinter, Harold. *Old Times.* London: Eyre Methuen Ltd, 1971.

Williams, Tennessee. *Suddenly Last Summer.* New York: New Directions, 1958.

Development of the Theory
An Annotated Bibliography

My journey as an actor and as a teacher of acting is described in the introduction. Now, in conclusion, I offer a more detailed description of the
evolution of the ideas that are presented in this book. Here, then, is the
more academic, scholarly section, filled with footnotes, written for those
actors and teachers of acting who, like me, also enjoy reading and theorizing.

Stanislavsky, the Method, and a Shelf-full
of Acting Textbooks

Stanislavsky and those who absorbed and adapted his theories were criticized almost from the beginning, but I wasn't aware of any scepticism
until several years after beginning my teaching career. The most influential books that contributed to my early understanding of Stanislavsky
include his autobiography, *My Life in Art*, and Charles McGraw's acting
textbook, *Acting is Believing*.[1] Books published in the 1970s by Robert
Benedetti, Robert Cohen, Uta Hagen and Michael Shurtleff reinforced
my assumptions about the fundamental validity of this approach. Any
scepticism I might feel was buried and evidence that professional actors
of great skill and verve didn't use his approach, I simply discounted. I knew
that Strasberg's approach was not Stanislavsky's, but North American
acting training seemed relatively homogeneous: everyone taught a variation of what had come to be called, generically, the Method. The time was
ripe for rebellion.

For me, it began with Jeremy Whelan's *New School Acting*, when he
described his repulsion at the emotional abuse that seemed to accompany
far too many coaching sessions. I then devoured Don Richardson's *Acting
Without Agony*, who railed against 'orgies of self-indulgence,' and several

books by Charles Marowitz, who could always be counted on to unleash his invective against any of 'the more bone-headed fallacies of the Method' (*Directing the Action*, 22). These diatribes were balanced by more scholarly researchers, such as Sharon Carnicke and Bella Merlin, who clarified the unfortunate effects of translation, publishing, and censorship on our misperceptions of Stanislavsky's theories.[2]

Until recently, I was content to turn my nose up at Method acting as a bastardized form of the great master. David Krasner's collection of essays, *Method Acting Reconsidered*, inspired me to reconsider my antipathy to Method teachers. When I returned to the source, I discovered that many of the myths about the Method are not, in fact, what the originators taught.[3] I have also realized that I was negotiating a transition from a mismatch (Strasberg's intense use of the Perception conduit; Meisner's intense focus on Relationship) to a more successful match between Stanislavsky's interest in action and my Dynamic CP type.[4]

Even discounting the Method in favour of Stanislavsky, I remain sceptical of the labour-intensive preparation for an activity with such clear ties to childhood play.[5] I had also observed, over and over, that there was no direct correlation between the reality of the actors' emotions and how deeply an audience was moved. I was horrified at the self-indulgence of emotion-centered acting and leery of the dangers of the sort of 'possession' which I had experienced first-hand and observed my students perversely seeking or avoiding assiduously, either of which interfered with their acting. As Robert Lewis noted in *Slings and Arrows*, 'It feels just great to experience that groundswell of emotion rising in you and the temptation to self-indulgence is almost irresistible.'[6]

I fell in love with theatrical masks in university, thanks to an introduction by Fred Euringer, in large part because the discipline of masks allowed me to draw upon my conduits of Action and Power. In later years, after decades of exploration in classrooms, rehearsal halls, and non-theatrical settings, I began to read scholarship that affirmed my experience: masks and Method were oil and water.[7]

Participation in social action theatre introduced me to another venue in which Method acting was not particularly useful and I was thrilled to discover books that explored theatre from a that perspective. Keith Johnstone's *Impro* was particularly inspiring, thanks to his highly theatrical explorations of status which matched so perfectly with my Dynamic CP Type.[8] With Elin Diamond, I preferred Brecht's alienation to an emotionally oppressive search for truthful action.

Another significant theatrical exploration that shaped my interest in the psychology of acting was my work in story telling and autobiographical performance. Just when you'd assume an actor would be most natural, when the self would be most clearly on view, that's when chameleon-like skills are required for disciplined performance. The sprawling and paradoxical must be shaped into narrative, and the self must be organized into character.[9]

My academic training at the graduate level was in theatre history and, through my reading about the crowd-pleasing actors of previous generations, I acquired a healthy respect for the type of acting that preceded Stanislavsky.[10] It has always irritated me to read generalized condemnations of melodramatic acting as hilariously exaggerated and manifestly unreal. The truth of the matter is that every actor who has held an audience enthralled has found a way to blend the charismatic with the chameleon.[11]

While training actors to perform Shakespeare, I found my scepticism about the Method approach affirmed as I explored Elizabethan psychology and characterization. I was happy to allow that the Method might serve the film and television industries, but I was quite sure that classical actors and opera singers needed something different. This attitude was reflected in the acting textbooks I read, and later wrote, that addressed pre-modern performance styles.[12] When I began to teach acting to students preparing for a career in opera, I quickly discovered that many of the givens of naturalistic acting were of limited benefit and perhaps even dangerous.[13]

In addition to the flood of challenges and re-workings of Stanislavsky, Strasberg, et. al, the theoretical considerations that have altered the face of the humanities and social sciences in the past 100 years are finally reaching theorists of acting. Like many practitioners, I avoided the jargon-filled musings of theorists like the plague. I eventually felt compelled to venture into the labyrinth of 'isms' and ploughed through representative texts in search of insights that could have some practical application.[14] Some of what I encountered offered additional support to my growing concerns about the ascendancy of Method acting training.

I have never entirely turned my back on the rich tradition of Stanislavsky-inspired acting training, and therefore must acknowledge the many teachers, authors, and colleagues who have enriched my understanding of the psychological realism approach to acting, as well as to the many professional colleagues and writers about acting who have challenged this approach in private conversation, in shared rehearsal experiences, and in the books and articles that fill up my bookshelves, for I am an inveterate collector of writings about acting.

Two scholars who challenged Stanislavsky inspired me to explore the psychology of acting, and therefore mark the location of overlap between this section and the next. Richard Hornby's *The End of Acting*, with its examination of the psychology and phenomenology of acting, was hugely influential, in large part because I resisted his application of Freudian psychology and the subsequent identification of acting as neurosis. Natalie Crohn Schmitt's description of Stanislavsky's debt to long-outdated psychological theory challenged claims about the 'laws of nature' that, sadly, still accompany descriptions of psycho-realist approaches to acting. It was time to broaden my horizons.

Psychological Gold and Dross

Concurrent with these explorations, I continue to pursue a long-standing interest in the psychology of acting that brought me into contact with some theories of perception, emotion and personality that encouraged me to build upon the purely practical applications of my discoveries, so useful in directing and in training actors, by crystalizing my observations and intuitions into written form.

Stephen Aaron's *Stage Fright, The Way of the Actor* by Brian Bates[15] and Glenn Wilson's books on the psychology of the performing arts were my preliminary demonstrations that the application of psychological theories to the work of an actor might bear significant fruit. I was also finding acting textbooks, such as Rob Cameron's, with entire chapters on Psychology and Acting. I was thrilled to discover the Fischers' *Pretend the World is Funny and Forever*, an psychoanalytical analysis of performing artists, as it refuted the mythology that actors are, by definition, a neurotic lot.[16]

Gordon Armstrong is another whose bridging of the gap between science and theatre launched me on an exploration of what insights about acting might be found on the floors of my university library I otherwise would never visit. He and others offered support for my thoughts about what I came to call the genetic components of an actor's craft, the 'species-specific ways in which we operate'.[17]

Many scientists have turned their attention to the theatre, and many theatre scholars have made use of the theories of science. I read every one of these interdisciplinary research papers I could locate.[18] I found myself on an eclectic tour of psychological theories, each of which shed some light on what hitherto I'd been happy to designate 'mysterious,' the psychology of the actor's process.

These readings gave me the confidence to venture into some of the more specialized areas of psychology, including perception and emotions,[19] motivation and memory, [20] nonverbal communication and neuropsychology.[21] This type of reading can be heavy going for people like me, who are after all just visitors to the discipline, but some, such as Paul Watzlawick's *The Invented Reality* and *Descartes' Error* by Antonio R. Damasio, proved accessible and fascinating.

Always, the trails I followed fed my work as an actor and with actors. Therese Hannah and her colleagues turned me on to a theories of how personalities are constructed and Rhonda Blair introduced me to Steven Pinker's computational theory of mind. An article by Harold Gardiner on Dramatic Intelligence led me to his theories on multiple intelligences; writings on emotional intelligence led me to James Averill's theories of emotional creativity. Popularized works on neuropsychology, specifically the divided brain, provided fascinating reading. I began with Ramon Delgado's *Acting With Both Sides of Your Brain,* then moved on to Rhawn Joseph's *The Right Brain and the Unconscious* and Daniel Pink's *A Whole New Mind.*

The other seminal influence from psychology was the various popularized books and scholarly articles I read about identity, temperament, and personality typing.[22] I'd encountered the Myers–Briggs test on more than one occasion, but now I read some of the theory behind that assessment instrument. Naomi L. Quenk's *Beside Ourselves* proved the most accessible introduction to Jungian typology.

It was in the on the library shelf dedicated to psychological studies of creativity where I discovered the writings of Mihaly Csikszentmihalyi, whose work on flow provided me with what became a central metaphor for the phenomenology of the charismatic in acting, though my application is somewhat different than his.[23]

Psychologists who study creativity do not often turn their eyes upon actors, preferring rather to focus on those who create significant works of art (writers, painters, sculptors, composers, choreographers) or whose names are associated with great innovation (Einstein, Darwin, Ford, Freud). Occasionally they do consider brilliant musicians, and in particular child prodigies, but the creativity of interpreters is less easily dissected and so less often the subject of intense research.[24] Despite their narrow focus, I have found that many of the theories of creativity illuminate the experiences reported by actors.[25]

Relationship Energy
- Activities that connect us with each other or cut off that connection
- The capacity to construct relationships or destroy them
- Sensations of warming up to someone or cooling off intimacy

Power Energy
- Activities through which we take control and so command, or that result from the giving up of control and submission
- Hierarchical relationships such as masters and servants
- Sensations of authority or humility

Perception Energy
- Activities of the senses and of the mind
- Observation and envisioning which can empower or humble
- Sensuality and fantasy within relationships

Action Energy
- Initiating interactions and reacting to others
- Leading or following
- Sensations of activity and of impulse

Laban's Drives	*Charismatic Conduits*
Spell	Power
Action	Action
Vision	Perception
Passion	Relationship
Laban's Incomplete Efforts	*Creative Temperaments*
Stable (Weight/Space)	Dynamic
Mobile (Time/Flow)	Psychic
Remote (Space/Flow)	Visionary
Near (Time/Weight)	Personal
Awake (Space/Time)	Innovative
Dream (Weight/Flow)	Magnetic

Pragmatic Research

Duncan Ross challenges all who teach and write about acting to consider whether their approaches are "organic" by which he does not mean ad hoc, letting it all just happen, but rather connected to the constant, spontaneous changes within the living organism, all such changes taking place for the continuation of the organism. By that definition, I would judge my approach organic.

I agree with Martin Welton: a theory about an actor's creativity is only worth disseminating if it results in better acting. I would take this one step further, and say that an approach to teaching acting is only worth disseminating if it results in better rehearsals and performances.[26]

In *Essays on Performance Theory*, Richard Schechner notes the gap between what performance is to those who do it and what it is to those who only observe it (260). Jill Dolan takes this one step further, and identifies within academia a pervasive tension between those who do theatre and those who discuss it: 'If you know some of the intricacies of theory, how can you possibly translate them into a clear, workable acting suggestion? Likewise, if you trade in the language of superobjectives, how can you possibly see past The Method to theorize resistant feminist practice?'[27]

I fear I have only acquired a tourist's familiarity with the jargon of postmodern theory and applied psychology. Like any tourist, I risk embarrassment in this attempt to absorb and use terminology that I do not, in truth, 'own.' And I'm not particularly comfortable in the strange new world of jargon and statistics; I share Arnold Wesker's scepticism about theories: "I am not a semiologist and have read very little on the subject. And what I've tried to read I've found to be mostly incomprehensible ... they've answered everything except one question: what makes one sentence into a line of poetry and makes another sentence dull, lifeless' (366).[28]

Although I have read everything I can find on the psychology of acting, much of what I read seems to have little direct application to the classroom, rehearsal hall, or performance space. In part, that is because so much of psychology is ruled by the standards of empirical research, and the sorts of things that can be measured and subjected to statistical analysis tend to be those things that are of least interest to practitioners.[29] For example, Tony and Helga Noice's hugely detailed scientific study of the cognitive processes involved in memorizing lines is in keeping with the frequent question actors hear from non-actors: 'How did you memorize all those lines?' Much of what they describe offers scientific support for a phenomenon I have long observed, in my own acting and in the classroom and rehearsal hall, what I have come to call the difference between learning your lines and knowing your lines. The first is pure rote memory, the second is the 'deep elaboration' that the actors interviewed by the Noices describe. The Noices are fascinated by the number of lines this allows an actor to remember. I'm far more interested in the nature of that deep elaboration.

Fortunately, an alternative approach to research, that of the participant-observer, has migrated from anthropology into social psychology and thence into explorations of the performing arts. As soon as I read Kenneth Aigen's application of to this style of research to music therapy, I realized I'd found a model within which I could function. Support for this approach is offered by researchers like Gay McAuley and Kristen Hastrup.

This book follows in a well-established tradition of experiential investigation. Like Barbara Sellers-Young, I've attempted 'to illustrate my own process of trial and error, success and failure, as I looked for a means to blend practice, theory, and method,' creating 'a kind of personal narrative of discovery.'[30] Clearly, my theory of the charismatic chameleon has emerged from the scientific and artistic explorations of a many others. I can only echo Samuel Taylor Coleridge: A dwarf sees farther than the giant when she has the giant's shoulders on which to mount.

Laban for Actors

It would be wrong to present this as a new approach to acting. It is, rather, a reconsideration of some familiar approaches and a new expansion and application of the work of many who have gone before. In particular, anyone familiar with the writings of Rudolf Laban will recognize a remarkable similarity between some of his theories of my description of the creative temperaments (see page 224).

Like many of my colleagues, I have long used Laban's concepts of quick and sustained time, direct and flexible space, and strong and light weight to provide acting students with a movement vocabulary. The evocative verbs of Laban's Movement Efforts: punch, dab, press, glide, slash, flick, wring, and float, have set my students moving in interesting ways and opened the door to some energetic improvising around comic stereotypes. All of this emerged from a rather vague understanding of Laban's theories and no direct contact with any of his writing.

Many years ago I participated in an acting workshop during which the instructor introduced us to the words Awake, Dream, Remote, Near, Stable, and Mobile. This provided me with the sensation that Laban's theories could be applied to some of the more complex challenges of acting. At the time of the workshop, I was more interested in being an actor than training actors, so I made use of what worked for me without any attempt to grasp the intellectual framework within which the techniques rested.

When I began to teach acting, I was able to read extensively about Stanislavsky's theories and found many sources for classroom explorations of his approach to psychological realism. But the only references I could find to Laban was a brief introduction to the movement efforts in Louis John Dezseran's *The Student Actor's Handbook*.[31] I poured over *The Mastery of Movement*, trying to locate any acting guidelines in Laban's description of Incomplete Actions, where the terms Awake, Dream, Remote, Near, Stable, and Mobile are introduced, but found no correlation between his writings and my memory of the workshop experience. Later, I tackled his other publications but found little of use in my quest.

Jean Newlove's *Laban for Actors and Dancers* increased my understanding of Laban's concept of Incomplete Actions, but the words on the page, though evocative, did not suggest any clear guidance for the training of actors. Though I knew of many teachers of Laban who, by reputation, were reconfiguring the teaching of acting, I could find no systematic description of their pedagogical methodology, save such elusive references as Simon Callow's description of his acting training in *Being an Actor.*

> The work itself was a synthesis of Laban's analysis of movement (splitting it into its component units in terms of their direction of energy) with Jung's theory of psychological types (sensing, thinking, intuiting, feeling). What it amounts to – the theory known as Movement Psychology – is a praxis of character in action, an account of the physical embodiment of character and impulse. The intellectual framework is complex and all-embracing; but its difficulty stems from its grounding in sensations. How can one talk about sensations? Feeling them, being aware of them, learning to identify and separate them, to crystalize and concertize them, to be able to summon them and use them: that's Yat's work, and the whole work of the school was dominated and unified by it.

Callow also refers to 'Emotional, intuitive, physical, and intellectual sensation; quick sensations and sustained ones; direct and flexible, bound and free, strong and light,' an evocative blending of Laban's efforts and the psychological experience of movement and character but woefully inadequate; Callow describes it as 'puzzlingly difficult,' something that 'can't be demonstrated and imitated.'[32] I found a few other references and discussions, direct and indirect, to support my interest in Laban's approach to the training of actors.[33]

The observations of Laban-inspired movement teachers like Peter Kellerman or Anna Cutler affirmed what I had learned about my own acting: that direct attention to movement effectively translated abstract feelings into physical expression and that initiating movement aroused something that a Method actor would call 'real feeling.' My intuitions crystalized into awareness as I encountered the writings of Lea Logie, Alice Rayner, and Barbara Sellers-Young.

At a much later date, after many of my ideas had been explored in this Laban-inspired but essentially ill-informed context, I had the privilege of working closely with several movement instructors who have studied what I would term 'traditional' Laban. My respect for Laban's intuitions was reaffirmed even as I realized the benefits of isolation from the highly regulated world of Certified Movement Analysts. I have since come across other acting books that demonstrate Laban's influence, such as Epstein and Harrop's *Basic Acting* and Brigid Panet's *Essential Acting* as well as several references to the use of Laban movement training within theatre programs.[34]

The ideas and exercises in this book can only be described as *inspired* by Rudolph Laban. I have no idea if my discoveries are legitimate applications of Laban's theories. Laban was not, after all, either an actor or a teacher of actors and, although I remain respectful of his insights and striking imagery, I am happy to be freed for the burdens of discipleship.

Great Minds Thinking Alike?

In preparing this book I've returned to some of my old favourites, acting textbooks that have influenced my teaching over the years. This is a particularly rewarding experience when I survey my detailed notes, made when I accepted without question the assumptions encoded by each author. I am reminded that, as a creative artist, I stand to learn as much or perhaps even more from those who do not share my conduits, but who are able to suggest ways of accessing the riches that their conduits reveal.[35]

I've discovered that many of those who inspired me in the past or challenge me in the present refer in their writings to something comparable to what I call charismatic energy. In *On the Technique of Acting* Michael Chekhov evoked an actor's 'higher ego' (15) and in *The Shifting Point* Peter Brook wrote of the actor's 'essential radiance.'[36] In *Towards a Poor Theatre* Grotowski also speaks of an actor's 'radiance' (259). Strasberg described

Pauline Lord's work as "complete, unified, effortless, and revealing" and later "electric" (15), a quality that could also be absent, leaving work that was seemingly natural but empty.[37]

In the years since my understanding of creative personality types has crystalized, I continue to read acting textbooks and books about acting, but from a new perspective. Now, I spot indicators of the CP type of the author.[38] However, I have learned to heed the warning of Marshall Duke and accept that, having developed a theory of personality types, I will inevitably see evidence for that theory everywhere around me.[39]

In my eclectic reading I regularly encounter statements that duplicate my own observations, albeit using a different vocabulary. Eugenio Barba has made an actor's energy the focus of much of his research. He writes: 'Faced with certain actors, a spectator is attracted by an elementary energy which seduces without mediation, even before he has deciphered the individual actions or questioned himself about their meaning and understood it,' and then observes: 'It is continuous mutation, growth, taking place before our very eyes. It is a body-in-life. The flow of energies which characterize our daily behaviour has been derailed. The tensions which secretly govern our normal way of being physically present come to the surface in the actor, become visible, unexpectedly.'[40]

Eric Morris is another who has sought what he calls acting from the ultimate consciousness. He writes, 'If we accept as the truth that the major portion of our talent lives in the unconscious, then we must find ways to contact it and draw the most from it! We must create a liaison with it so that every time we act we can 'plug into' that bottomless well of creativity' (40).

Declan Donnellan describing 'blockage' mirrors exactly what I mean when I talk about the sensation of effort, by which we know that charismatic flow is absent:

> Whenever actors feel blocked the symptoms are remarkably similar, whatever the country, whatever the context. They feel sluggish and lost; occasionally, the actor starts to feel exposed, with a sense of being judged emanating from outside and within. Two aspects of this state seem particularly deadly: the first is that the more the actor tries to force, squeeze, and push out of this cul-de-sac, the worse 'it' seems to get, like a face squashed against glass. Second is the accompanying sense of isolation. The problem can be projected out, and 'it' becomes the 'fault' of the script, or partner, or shoes. But two basic symptoms remain the same, namely paralysis and isolation – an inner locking and an outer locking. At worst this causes an immobility from eye to brain to heart to lung to lips to limbs, and an over-

whelming sense of being alone, a creeping sense of being both responsible and powerless, unworthy and angry, too small, too big, too cautious, too, too, too . . . me. When acting flows, it is alive.[41]

I also regular find evidence of an actor's experience of the flow of charismatic energy. Anne Jackson writes, "There is a vitality, a life force and energy, a quickening, which is translated through you into action, and because there is only one of you in all time, this expression is unique. And if you block it, it will never exist through any other medium and will be lost. The world will not have it."[42]

Over the years I have read a fair number of autobiographies by actors and interviews with actors, but an astute reader will already have noted that very few of them appear in the bibliography. I've come to agree with John Mitchell: 'Great artists often work intuitively, and an examination of the few who have attempted to explain their approach to art reveals that, in most cases, they fail to state clearly their methodology. At best they end up with a *description* of how they work. What is lacking is an *analysis* of how they work.'[43] I would add that stars, who talk about their acting in connection with the self-publicity required to maintain their position in the public eye, describe their processes in accordance with prevailing myths about acting. For that reason, I rely on first-hand observations in rehearsal halls rather than the reflections (in prose or sound bites) that editors have selected for public consumption. I remain indebted to every actor who has shared her process, publicly or privately, particularly those who do not share my conduits.[44]

The Actor as Chameleon

It was John Harrop's *Acting* that sparked the crystallization of my thoughts on the actor as chameleon:

> If, then, the apparent representation of reality, lifelikeness, is not a sufficient or necessary criterion for the judgement of acting, can we point to anything that gives us a basis for discriminating between acting we would call good and bad? What we come back to is the basic element of theatre, the actor's body as fundamental presence and sign. Although, as we have already suggested, there can be no absolutely precise vocabulary of signs, it is the sign the audience sees; the skill with which an actor creates that sign will have a significant effect upon the audience's experience of the theatrical event. The more skillfully the actor makes the sign, the more

likelihood is there that the audience will experience it as the actor intended. So it is not lifelikeness, it is not feeling or engendering of emotion per se, but skill (in creating the sign) that seems to be a basic way of approaching the actor's craft. (45)

Like Harrop, I have come to value the capacity of an actor to express emotions far above her capacity to feel, though if that's the means by which the most vivid and flexible expressions are achieved, I would hesitate to discount real emotional experiences in an actor's craft.

Creating a Character

There seem to be two prevailing metaphors for what happens when an actor creates a character: what might be called the mosaic approach (we are so complex that any character can be found within ourselves, even if well-buried, and therefore an actor draws upon different aspects of herself to build a character; see, for example, Ruth Quinn) and the wardrobe approach (we inhabit characters like putting on a suit of clothes, and therefore an actor puts on the character, walks in her shoes, sees the world through her eyes, and soon the clothing fits and the character lives; see, for example Ruth Zaporah). I have long found Schechner's phrase 'not not me' an invaluable trick of language for discussing the paradoxical relationship between an actor's experience of performing a character.[45] I find it fascinating to read how others negotiate the paradox, and the questions they asked about the fundamental phenomenon of the actor's experience, what might be called the psychology of the acting process.[46]

My culturally endorsed assumptions about 'performing oneself' received a death blow from Philip Auslander, whose scrutiny of acting theory through the lens of post-modern psychology.[47] If, as some theorize, there is no essential self to be revealed in our acting, what then is going on when an actor experiences sensations of authentic engagement with a fictional character?

The Limits of Empathy

I became increasing concerned about an assumption I had long held, that the combination of empathy and homework on the part of an actor could illuminate any human experience, as expressed, for example, by Uta

231

Hagen, who recommends reading biographies and histories 'until you *know* you've lived in those rooms with those people, eaten that particular food, slept in that strange bed behind those curtains; danced, jousted and tilted with the best of them,' and who writes with naïve confidence, 'Customs, architecture, fashion, social needs, politics – all change, all come and go, but throughout history people have breathed, slept, eaten, loved, hated and had similar feelings, emotions, needs' (30). My reading about the sociology of emotions[48] invited me to reconsider the danger of such assumptions, and I became leery of the deadly combination of arrogance and ignorance. Robert Brustein addresses this concern:

> Self-knowledge can't re-create a historical environment. It can tell you something about the psychological condition of classical characters, but not what motivated these people in relation to their political, social, and cultural surroundings. As long as Method actors are playing characters close to themselves, generally working-class Americans with explosive personalities, they can impress us with their power and believability. But the moment they step into the shoes of heroic characters from the past, they are likely to stumble and fall. (86)

As does Phillip Zarrilli: Young actors often confuse their own common-place personal/emotional life experiences with those of the characters they are asked to play. Since both one's personal emotional life and acting involve intense 'feelings,' and since characters are often analysed using a psychologically based set of assumptions about behaviour, this confusion is not surprising.'[49] Support for a more critical analysis of an actor's assumed capacities for empathy also comes from D.K. Collum's 1976 doctoral dissertation, 'The Empathic Ability of Actors: A Behavioural Study,' which found that 'actors have a higher empathic facility than non-actors' but that 'this facility *decreases* with an increase in training and experience' (7, emphasis mine).[50]

Believable Acting and the Audience's Experience of Meaning

After the intellectual challenges of post-modernism, I could never again read acting books that set the goal as truthful, real acting, or that instructed how best to draw upon the actor's self, with complacent absorption what I have come to believe is an insidious fallacy. I applaud Phillip Zarrilli's invitation to examine the language we use and the assumptions encoded therein, when we theorize about acting. His discussion, in his introduction to *Acting [Re]Considered*, of the tricky term 'truth' and concepts of 'believability' and 'honesty' is particularly inspiring. What is the poor actor to make of a teacher commenting, 'I don't think you believe what you are doing?' Zarrilli recommends the actor 'attempt to fill in the gaps between this particular language and what he needs to do as an actor, that is, he can translate the confusing language into terms that are more actable and thereby make choices which appear to the teacher/director as 'believable'.'[51]

At the same time, it is clear that actors experience something that very much feels like real emotions, and that there is a reality to the actions that they perform before the audience. In seeking further illumination of this paradox, I was struck by David Saltz's suggestion that what actors experience is very like playing a game with a complicated set of rules, or conventions.

The actor's actions abide by the rules (conventions) of the game, and are understood to endure for the length of the game. Therefore," actors perform real and sincere actions on stage by adopting game intentions that arise if they accept as part of the convention of performance a rule that actors work to achieve the conditions of satisfaction implied by the characters actions." ('How to Do Things on Stage,' 39). Richard Schechner puts this slightly differently, when he says actor are like the skilled liar: "This lying is a very complicated business in which the skilled liar – a person who can make a convincing face – *knows* he is lying but *feels* he is telling the truth" (*Essays on Performance Theory*, 274).

Andruis Jilinsky substitutes the term 'living' for 'true' or 'believable' or 'real,' a choice that I find particularly appealing. I also like the way Kurt Daw addresses this issue:

> A commonplace in theatre (I've often invoked it in this book) is, acting should be truthful. It should be organic .... Theatre is certainly *not* truthful, if by that we mean that the dialogue must come from life and record that which truly happened. Theatre is not documentary. When we use the terms *truthful* and *organic* about acting, we mean something about the *process*, not the product. We mean that the actions undertaken by the actor follow the natural patterns of thought and behaviour in life. (137).

Timothy Wiles comes at the question from a different perspective: 'The actor's closeness of feeling with the character he portrays does not represent the pinnacle of realism and 'truth to life' upon the stage. Far more 'true' is the fact that the actor *is* an actor and is performing in a theatre, not living in the character's quarters which he has re-created so slavishly by means of affective memory' (26).

Another fundamental shift in my thinking came from reading dense theoretical considerations of the experience of the audience[52] which challenged me to rethink exactly how meaning occurs in the theatre, although it was the timely reading of David Mamet's *True and False* that abruptly shifted my focus from believability to 'getting out of the way' of the audience's eagerness to meet the production more than halfway. It is apparent, also, that audiences don't want to forget that actors are not their characters, that the tension between the actor-as-actor and the actor-as-character is very much part of the appeal of what Donald Braid calls 'experiential meaning'.[53]

One of the most pervasive, and fallacious the assumptions promoted by Method acting books and teachers has to do with an audience's suspension of disbelief. Here is one example of the ubiquitous, and so persuasive, proclamations, this one from Edward Easty:

> We know the one element that never fails to excite an audience, never fails to completely absorb them in the play they are watching, is that which they see around them in life and know to be true. It is when the audience can feel what the actors are feeling, experience what they experience, recognize the love, anguish, desire, hatred, or jealousy of the actor's role, that they become aware of the actor's art. It is this art, the art of achieving reality, real tears, real laughter, real expression, movement and voice, that will comprise this book. (27)

Theorists like Umberto Eco and Eli Rozik have, quite simply, decimated Stanislavsky-inspired assumptions about the relationship between an actor's experience of performing and the complex communication system within which that performance is 'read.' Because semiotics makes for tough going for anyone unfamiliar with the jargon, I much prefer Ted Cohen's description of what he calls the miracle of imagination: "First is the miracle of the artist imagining himself to be an aged king, a forlorn and betrayed middle-aged woman, a wanton seducer. And then there is the presentation of this imagining — the presentation of the old King Lear, of the Countess Almaviva, of the insatiable Don Giovanni, of the worldly but vulnerable Marlow — so that an audience can use this presentation as the instrument of its own imagining" (406–7).

In 'Catharsis and the Actor,' Ian Watson also challenges the myth of the actor becoming the character, a form of transportation, by suggesting that the actor in fact adopts the external attributes of role in order to disappear into role so that the *audience* experiences transportation out of ordinary reality through temporary acceptance of stage fiction as reality. In other words, the actor isn't transported, except intermittently, and in fact experience transportation as much through conscious awareness of a relationship with the enthralled audience as through character's experiences.[54]

Elly Konijn's research challenges all Stanislavsky-based assumptions about an actor's experience of emotions in performance by demonstrating not only what actors actually experience, but also that "observers in general are not able to distinguish between posed and spontaneous emotional expressions. They even ascribe more credibility to posed emotional expressions than they do to spontaneous emotional expressions" ('Actors and Emotions,' 134).

Another impetus to a reconsideration of the prevailing myths about the need to truly become the character is offered by David E.R. George, who addresses the audience's role in the construction of a character's reality, and stated the obvious, "In our realist tradition, the actor must simultaneously appear to be the character but not actually become the character, if for no other reason than the fact that the character does not know how the play is going to end or what his next cue is." George also reinforced my analysis of realism as a set of conventions when he pointed out that actors learn to mimic sincerity, because the dominant convention in western theatre is 'stylized and skillful role-playing and dissemblance' (355–6). Shortly after reading George's article I encountered Ian Watson's application of semiotics to celebrity, in which he explores not only how the audience experiences character, but also that special energy that actors bring to their work. It is out of such observations that my understanding of an actor's charismatic energy was born.

Charisma

It was H. Wesley Balk who first introduced me to the idea that the charismatic could be unleashed in a performer. Once I'd latched onto the term, I searched for others who discussed this phenomenon directly or indirectly. I had a look at what the social scientists such as David Aberbach, Stuart J.M. Weierter, and Lionel Tiger had to say and was thrilled to find that psychologists also found a link, as I did, between flow, creativity, and charisma.[55]

The most striking articulation of what I wanted to explore I found in those seeking to describe the primal power of the actor, such as Richard Dyer.[56] Beckerman attributes the source of an actor's charisma his capacity to 'leap into the impossible' (20–1). Peter Hall is more pragmatic: "Stars are not essentially defined by acting talent. They are those with extraordinary physical presence, those whom the men and women in the audience are drawn to watch and find desirable" (394).

My conceptualization of the actor as charismatic chameleon solidified, ironically, while acting in and later while preparing actors to participate in simulations. This is a type of role playing in which the charismatic is so muted as to be imperceptive, a type of acting that is also undertaken in Boal's Invisible Theatre.[57] I came to the conclusion that it is the injection of the charismatic, as much if not more than the demonstration of skills, performative as well as chameleon, that separates actors from role players analysed in Erving Goffman's *The Presentation of Self in Everyday Life* and those who adopted his dramaturgical metaphor.[58]

Courage

I've come to believe that the single most irreplaceable quality required by an actor is not that elusive thing we call talent. Nor is it a set of physical and psychological attributes. It's courage.[59] Robert Benedetti describes this attribute strikingly:

> Your sense of purpose is what will give you courage and power as an actor. It grows from your respect for your own talent, your love for the specific material you are performing, and you desire to use both to serve your audience. It is this drive to be *at service* through your art that will finally overcome the self-consciousness of your ego and carry you beyond yourself, giving you a transcendent purpose from which comes dignity, fulfillment, and ongoing artistic vitality.[60]

And, I believe that the single most significant benefit of a rich understanding of Creative Personality types will be a decrease in the damage done to the courage of young actors by teachers and directors oblivious to the dangers of a myopic, rigid delivery of a single system of acting.

Leland Roloff's analysis of a performer's 'consent'[61] has become, for me, the alternative to 'talent' as the elusive attribute I believe our training of actors must nourish so that their courage can be sustained in the face of the horrific conditions of employment that permeate the only forums in which they can exercise their gifts. Roloff writes:

A performer's personal morality requires a continued openness, a capacity to consent, as well as a continued ability to be an observer, a spectator, of one's own creation. In this sense, morality is akin to the health and well-being of the performer's consciousness. If we think of ego as the sum of energy that is brought to consciousness, and that which drains or vitiates ego as those complexes which inhibit a rich and full participation in and to life, we can get some sense of the demands, personal and moral, placed upon the performer. (20)

And nothing eats away at the courage of a student actor as quickly and permanently as a mismatch in Creative Personality temperament.

Destructive Mismatches

In addition to clarifying the complexities of Stanislavsky's theories, in contrast to the narrow focus of American Method acting, Bella Merlin's article on Albert Filozov documents overt manifestations of a mismatch of Creative Personality Types. Merlin lays claim to an unbroken connection to Stanislavsky: she studied with Albert Filozov, who trained with Mikhail Kedrov, who took over the direction of Moliere's *Tartuffe* when Stanislavsky died in 1938. However, the legacy was not the self-selection by inspired acolytes, as we see in the legacy of master-teachers in North America, but state-mandated system (as of 1935) challenged from within by those who, despite a mismatch, rose to the prominence of master-teachers.

The first clue comes when Merlin notes Filozov's "equivocal attitude" to the Method of Physical Actions, dating from his encounter with Kedrov while a student, combined with 'the constant directive from his pedagogues — 'to find action, action, always action'" (229). Filozov remembers, "Students were criticized harshly if — from Kedrov's point of view — they were not executing a definite action in every moment on the stage." In other words, Filozov couldn't demonstrate the use of the conduit that inspired Stanislavsky and his disciples. The result for Filozov: 'going onto the stage wasn't interesting for me. And in effect — I didn't know *anything*.' Filozov came to feel that the Method of Physical Actions had 'in effect killed Russian theatre" (231).

There was, however, another teacher, Evgenia Maryes, who had acted with Stanislavsky. Filozov's assumed that the efficacy of her teaching was the result of her having been an actor, rather than a director, but his stories reveal she offered an invitation to the perception conduit through strategies from Stanislavsky designed to stimulate the actor's fantasy, including observations from real life.

One of the benefits of a mismatch of Creative Personality types is the realization that teachers must account for diversity in students. Merlin reports exactly such an epiphany for Filozov: "A theory won't work unless you put in the personality of the person you are going to teach and the personality of the person who is teaching."[62]

Sadly, most acting teachers and textbooks present their favoured acting strategies in the form of an absolute, along the lines of 'THIS is what makes a good actor,' or 'Your internal process must focus on THIS to achieve the necessary effect,' the advice being offered in keeping with each teacher's own conduits to the exclusion of all other temperaments.[63] Re-reading first-hand accounts of the explorations of Strasberg, Adler and Meisner proved particularly fascinating in this regard.[64] I was struck suddenly, in a way I never had been before, by absolute statements: 'this is the only way,' and 'good acting depends upon this and this alone.'[65] Often, I glimpsed what I took to be evidence of a mismatch between creative personality types, as when John Strasberg describes his father's teaching style:

> In class, when an actor didn't understand or couldn't do what he wanted, he occasionally reacted with an anger that was vicious and destructive, as though he felt that the actor was deliberately not understanding. I used to think this reaction was normal for a teacher, as I saw it in a lot of them. I did it too, until I realized that people's misunderstanding wasn't resistance to me, and that it was possible that the actor didn't understand or wasn't capable of doing what I wanted. (113)

Later, John Strasberg articulates the experience of the actor within a mismatch: 'It's no wonder I felt weird, alone, and confused, as though there were something very wrong somewhere. I had to get to the point where stopped thinking that the something wrong was me' (144).

I'm always looking for evidence of mismatching CP types, but since most textbooks are written by teachers who enjoyed a productive experience with a master-teacher and wish the same for their students, few write openly about, or even hint at, their failures.[66]

David Mamet is, as usual, brutally direct in his condemnation of acting teachers; in *Some Freaks* he writes:

> Most acting training is based on shame and guilt. If you have studied acting, you have been asked to do exercises you didn't understand, and when you did them, as your teacher adjudged, badly, you submitted guiltily

to the criticism . . . As you did these exercises it seemed that everyone around you understood their purpose but you – so, guiltily, you learned to pretend . . . You were loath to believe your teachers were frauds, so you began to believe that you *yourself* were a fraud. This contempt for yourself became contempt for all those who did not share the particular bent of your school of training. While keeping up an outward show of perpetual study, you began to believe that no actual, practicable technique of acting existed, and this was the only possible belief supported by the evidence. (31–2)

Even honourable and well-meaning teachers can scar students by misreading as resistance a mismatch of creative temperaments. Robert Barton's excellent textbook, *Acting: Onstage and Off*, contains Barton's credo: "I believe that most actors, if pressed, would say they prefer to work internally, if possible. It is more fun to dig inside and tap real emotions, to cry tears that are genuine, to summon laughter that isn't forced. It's more of a genuine rush to share the character's feelings" (180). In making this claim, Barton is purposefully blinding himself to countless reports from actors who do not, in fact, share this attitude. In other words, a charismatic actor-teacher experiences the natural myopia of our species: what I experience must be what every actor I admire experiences, and therefore must be presented to students as the only valid and viable approach to acting.

Eric Morris articulates why this is inevitably so. In an interview published by Eva Mekler in *The New Generation of Acting Teachers* he explains:

> I'm still an actor, and it still affects the way I teach. You see, I have an understanding of the actor's problems and the actor's obstacles, and what the actor has to deal with in the profession because I am an actor . . . . I give direction from an internal place and whenever the actor is having a problem I relate to it as 'our' problem. [67]

When explaining why he was drawn to the Method, he observes, 'That made sense to me.' In other words, Morris's sensitivity is also his blind spot, because he trusts his instincts about how to act but assumes that his process matches that of his students. He, like any great actor-teacher, has much to teach students who share his Creative Personality type, and it is very likely that his successful private classes are dominated by such students. Those for whom his approach doesn't make sense suffer the pains of insidious comparison between themselves and those who flourish within a well-matched student teacher relationship.

In the same volume, Joan Darling describes vividly what such students experience: 'I felt in those two years at Tech that there were some people who were just magical and I was afraid that I wasn't magical enough. I couldn't stand the idea that charisma, star quality, all of that stuff, couldn't be taught. If I didn't have it and it couldn't be taught, what was a young, ambitious person to do?' (265)

It's not just students who are discouraged by mismatches. Here's Jennifer Martin, a movement teacher: "Sometimes we beat up on ourselves a little bit: 'I just didn't get through to that student. I didn't give them something to help them solve that problem. I wish I were smarter, I wish I had more tools, I wish I were wiser with a capital W.'"[68]

I am not alone in seeking a better match between acting strategy and individual temperaments. In his excellent advice about choosing an acting teacher, Stephen Wangh writes: 'If the subject is artistic, a good teacher can make you feel safe, creative, and self-confident, while a poor teacher can leave you heartbroken. Of course, one of the things that will help you feel creative and self-confident is the technique itself. It must be a system that makes sense to you . . . It must also offer you tools that speak to the needs you have at this particular point in your training.' Later he speaks of the need for 'a match between the teacher's style of giving criticism and your way of hearing it' (319). He is describing a good match of Creative Personality Types. When he describes feeling safe and inspired, he elaborates with a description of what I would identify as a partial match of temperaments: 'There may be some exercises you do not like, and there may even be days when everyone else in the class seems to be having a good time while you feel like you're just not getting it. That's to be expected.'[69]

In sharing my approach with actors and teachers of acting, it has been the revelations about mismatched temperaments that have had the most immediate and significant positive impact. In particular, teachers have realized that students who appear reluctant and stubborn, might in fact be struggling with a painful mismatch between acting strategy and CP type.[70]

The result of an open and widespread acknowledgment of Creative Personality types would be twofold. First, finding a good fit between teacher and student would be more important, in program selection and entrance auditions, than prestige or talent. Second, training programs would undertake to offer a variety of approaches, either through a collection of faculty able to offer charismatic, inspiring mentorship to all temperaments, or through the rejection of myopic, legacy teaching in favour of the toolbox approach.

Toolbox or Legacy?

The spirit of a toolbox textbook is captured by Deb Margolin's wry observation, 'Acting is an emergency, and in an emergency you do whatever works' (128). Jerome Rockwood has this to say about the arbitrary divide between 'outside' and 'inside' actors:

> Accusations are hurled back and forth by both camps. The presentational actor is accused of being 'external,' 'shallow,' and 'empty inside" the representational actor is charged with boring his audience with an excess of realistic trivia. These are, of course, bad actors. When we put fine actors of both schools side by side, it isn't always easy to tell which actor is practicing which method. Moreover, there are probably very few purists in either camp. The able actor borrows this, alters that, rejects the other until, as we have noted previously, he comes up with his own unique system – a blend of anything and everything that works for him. For this reason it is wise for the actor to study and work with as many different kinds of teachers and directors as possible. (4)

As Liv Ullman noted, 'I don't think any method will ruin a good actor, because a good actor will always use what he needs' (161).

Speaking for the other point of view, in 'Zen and the Art of Actor Training' Robert Benedetti writes:

> The eclectic approach has much to recommend it, especially in a large program offering a variety of skills and approaches. But for the individual teacher, alone or within such a program, a focus is needed. We cannot be all things to all students, nor should we ignore our own theatrical values and tastes; we will not produce committed, powerful actors by choosing an evasive, diffuse training philosophy. By our teaching, we are creating a part of the theatre of the future, and it will be our testament; we should give careful thought to what it will say. (94)

Richard Brestoff mediates between these opposing views:

> With so many options, what should an actor do? Should he gather a representative sampling of many approaches, collecting various tools for his acting toolbox? Or should he study one method in depth in the hopes of acquiring a single and coherent acting method? Most acting teachers would say that acquiring a complete technique requires both approaches. A single training system has the advantage of giving the actor a way to

241

approach his craft step-by-step. But since no single system can possibly contain all that might be helpful to an actor, the student must also gather what tools he can from other sources. But even after an actor has chosen his path of study, he still faces more questions. Is this the best teacher for him? Are these exercises truly effective? Is he growing as an actor? The actor must continually evaluate his progress. (xiii)

However, this is expecting a great deal from the students who experience the seductive allure of psychological authoritarianism, to use Deborarh Greer's term. She observes, ' Once the young actor has accepted that his or her worth in the acting department will large part be judged by self-less conviction and ability to bare the soul in the name of the craft, the resistance to a charismatic hierarchy is nearly impossible' (149).

It will come as no surprise that I most admire the toolbox acting teachers who prefer to offer their students a toolbox of approaches, helping students to pick and choose from among the techniques explored, putting together a personalized compendium of problem-solving strategies and viable means of establishing a working environment within which they can flourish. In keeping with my personal rejection of the systemized teaching within a well-established legacy, I conclude, with Ned Manderino, that there is no one single theory that can describe the entire process of an actor's art. In *The Transpersonal Actor* he exhorts actors, and I would add, acting teachers:"Your duty to yourself is to capture the spirit of the time in which you live and that is accomplished by fully utilizing and breaking with established theories to create innovative approaches" (29).

Some acting teachers and their textbooks proclaim a commitment to diversity even as they reveal the bias that stems from their CP Type.[11] For example, although Linda C. Smith acknowledges that the personal creative process of individual actors mystifies and that sensitivity to difference is necessary, she is determined to find "the common ground of mutual creativity"(1) which, for her, is kinesthetic, so that she announces, "The concept behind any method of acting is the disciplined and orderly exploration of the human body and its environment" (2). A similar approach is taken by Claudia Sullivan, inspired by her mentor Paul Baker. She introduces her acting textbook by noting, 'Each system offers a unique approach to the process of acting. For some actors certain systems work well while other systems can seem ineffective' (18); later she promises, 'This book presents one approach which takes advantage of any and all other methods without limiting the individual actor to any particular one' (19). She then presents a series of exercises arising entirely from the Perception conduit.[72]

In his presentation of the acting approach known as Viewpoints, Steven Drukman makes some interesting observations about what he would designate as a postmodern approach to acting, which would, he suggests, be characterized 'in its blending of widely divergent techniques, in its refusal to privilege one aspect of its system over another, in its respect for the contingencies of various performance spaces and contexts and in its 'use what you will, discard the rest' spirit.'[73]

Drukman suggests a specific and persuasive reason for the resistance of the post-modern in acting training institutions. A music student can study theory intellectual and historically without any of the subtle nuances of theory undermining his musicianship, because the theory does not address the complex issues of the relationship between the performer and the music, but between the composer and the music. In acting theory, because the actor's instrument is her own psychological manifestations and physical presence, it is that very relationship that forms the subject of theories about acting. There is no instrument to master other than the expressive communication systems and persona of the self. Drukman captures the terror involved in that even that the theorists scrutinize when he quotes a favourite acting teacher justifying the preservation of a methodology that has been proven to work: 'When you're out there, and hundreds are watching, and your guts are hanging out, you need to believe in something' (31).

A postmodern intellectual community, however, simply will not allow such unexamined practices to remain unchallenged. Systems cannot be held to be valid simply because they have always worked, because the very criteria with which 'working' is now judged have shifted radically from those in place in the pre-postmodern world. Actors facing the challenge of preparing for a profession that required repeated gut-wrenching public displays might be forgiven for dodging the confusions and post-modern formulations, jargon, and layered significations, given the speed with which a post-modern tendency to debunking can undercut the profound courage required to do the work.

Teachers of acting, however, should not be let off so easily. The capacity for a sophisticated articulation of the teacher's own acting experiences, within the frameworks provided by a close encounter a variety of theories about acting, would raise the level of scrutiny not only of systems of acting but also of the ethics of teaching of this particular art form, a scrutiny which is, in the opinion of many, long overdue.

Master Teachers, Legacies, and the
Development of Systems of Acting

I have long sensed what Jean Alter observed, that actors are conservative in their approach to interpretation, to theatrical style, and to acting theory (261). Why else would an systematized approach to the teaching of acting, that dissatisfies as many as it assists, remain pre-eminent in theory, even as in practice each teacher, and each actor, adapts it subtly or strikingly to suit individual creative temperaments?

Even as they push against the rigidity of what they've inherited, followers of the various gurus insist on strict adherence to the master's name.[74] As Richard Brestoff observes, 'Most private acting teachers today are either students of those great master teachers, or were students of their students. And most teachers teach as they were taught. A student of Stella Adler's will teach her work, with minor variations. You teach what you know' (xii). One of the reasons is the ego-needs of the teachers promoting the legacy. In this, the students model themselves after their teachers, whose egos were equally well developed. As Richard Hornby, in 'Feeding the System,' reminds us, the personality cult of the master-teachers is reflected in their students who go on, in turn, to teach.[75]

Fervent disciples of Stanislavsky have transformed his open-ended, constantly-evolving, and entirely experimental strategies into a system that allows no challenges. Here is Sonia Moore on Stanislavsky: 'Many great men of letters . . . tried to formulate laws for dramatic creativity. But only Stanislavski succeeded in reconciling the contradictions between the actor as creator and the actor as character, and he alone developed the concrete technique by which an actor consciously transforms his psychological and physiological behaviour into those of the character and creates the unique life of a man in every role. Stanislavski alone discovered and systematized the laws that lead an actor to his ultimate goal: 'reincarnation' – the state in which he creates subconsciously.'[76]

As has probably already become clear, I have a particular distrust of all charismatic master teachers, but I save my most serious antipathy for Lee Strasberg. In large part, this is a reaction to his god-like status amongst his followers, which began early in his career[77] and, by the time of the emergence of his hegemonic legacy, made resistance almost impossible in the acting classrooms I inhabited as a young adult. I would always rejoice, therefore, to encounter a successful actor who add found a way to resist Strasberg's charismatic ascendancy in the hey-day of the Method. Here is Karl Malden:

I know that not everyone feels this way — I am definitely in the minority — but I did not come away from my experiences with Lee Strasberg as a fan of his. My personal opinion about criticizing actors is that the first element of that criticism must include recognition of how awfully hard the actor has worked, even if it's just for a five minute scene. My approach is always to being, "How would it work if . . . ?" Lee often started out with, "What are you doing?" As an opener, that question immediately puts you on the defensive. I suppose it could mean, "Explain to me what you were striving for." But when Lee said it, it always sounded like, "What did you think you were doing anyway? Why are you wasting my time?" Then Lee would often work his way all the way to, "How could you do that? It's all wrong." Time and again, I saw him leave actors stripped of their spirit and enthusiasm, totally demoralized. I never understood what good could come of that. How were they supposed to dredge up the energy to continue after a session like that? (212)

Another member of the resistance is Maureen Stapleton:

The simple fact is, I thought Lee talked too much and what he said was so convoluted, I didn't get it. It doesn't matter how fabulous a reputation a teacher may have: If someone's method doesn't work for you, then you're in the wrong place. My feeling was that if others could respond to him, okay, let them respond. All his talk drove me nuts. Moreover, Lee also exhibited a kind of rigidity that didn't appeal to me. I got along with him personally and kidded him, too. Still, I kept a working distance. I especially didn't like that "private moment and sense memory" stuff he pushed. It's okay up to a point, but that point too often was reached and then left in the dust. Who wants to see people get hysterical and start crying and moaning for real? To my way of thinking, unless you're a therapist or a doctor, you stay out of certain places in the human psyche. Frankly, I don't think Sigmund Freud was as nosey as Lee Strasberg. The whole business just didn't sit well with me; his classes could be disquieting at the very least and, in their most flagrant moments, downright intrusive. (65)

She also notes, 'For my taste things got too guru-ish and cultish at the Actors Studio. I wanted a teacher, not a god.'[78]

But these 'glitches' in the systematized approach are not reported in acting textbooks; rather, the name of the master-teacher becomes a touch-stone for excellence, and anyone who studies with someone who has studied with someone who in turn studied with one of the 'names' has an apparent validity as deliverer of the system, even though each subtly adapts the system in accordance with his or her CP type.[79] Sydney Pollack, in his introduction to Meisner's book, commenting on Strasberg, Adler, and Meisner, observed, 'Each one of these teachers has really made his own method, honing down and personalizing his approach over the years.' I see this as the natural evolution that results from individual creative temperaments. Pollack continues, 'Though they all were extraordinary teachers, Sandy's approach has always been for me the simplest, most direct, least pretentious and most effective' (xiv) I see this as evidence of a good match between Pollack the young acting student and Meisner the charismatic teacher.[80]

But the other reason for the ascendancy of systemized teaching is the demands of students for a system, any system. In fact, students of acting are particularly prone to the seductive allure of charismatic authority, as Deborah Greer reminds us.[81] As John Strasberg notes, 'it's safe for them to feel that they can go to someone and learn A, B, C, D' (99). Andrei Belgrader expands upon this observation, noting:

> I have a deep respect for the Stanislavsky method, but one of its traps is that it tells you that acting is fair. And it is not fair. The Method seems to say, 'If you do this and this and this, you will be a wonderful actor, just like Marlon Brando.' This is not true because even if you do steps four, five, six and seven you might still be a lousy actor and Marlon Brando would be a genius forever anyway.[82]

Larry Silverberg identifies the longing of students:

> Maybe you have studied acting, a little here and a little there and you have noticed that there have been moments in your acting when something has 'clicked' and afterwards you thought, 'That is exactly where I want to be in my acting!' But you're not really sure what happened, how it happened or how to have it happen again. It all seems to be hit or miss. And you wish you had something solid, in terms of technique, that you could count on. Something from which to build on and to grow with. (xv)

Allan Miller identifies the problem with any system, when applied to artistic activity: 'What I learned was that when you prepare yourself for the expected you do only the expected. How do you prepare yourself for the unexpected so that inspiration can strike?'[83]

The mastery of acting technique should not be undertaken as an end to uncertainty, as a means to make it rational and outcomes sure. Rather, increased skills allow for new challenges, and thus continued flow experiences. However, the drive to institutionalize and measure outcomes in the arts has resulted in training regimens in which demonstrate-able mastery is an end in itself, thus ensuring a decrease in flow experiences! Sadly, students as well as faculty at academic institutions and coaches working privately contribute to the dangerous ascendancy of system over creative uncertainty.[84]

Even those of us who have had an unpleasant encounter with a disciple of one or another variation, which bred a guarded respect, an active distrust or perhaps even a violent antipathy, must acknowledge that the endurance of the legacy and its undeniable usefulness for many actors suggests that there must be something to it.[85]

I suspect that there is much that is brilliantly insightful and strikingly pragmatic in the observations of any master teacher, applied on a case-by-case basis to an actor at any precise stage of technical development struggling with a specific cluster of acting challenges which have emerged in the context of working in that time and place, within that cultural context. What is immediately apparent, when reading accounts of master teachers at work, is the supreme subtlety and flexibility of their methodology, coupled with the clarity and consistency of their expression of artistic values. I now seek a balanced view, honouring the insights and contribution of acting teachers from both sides of the Method/non-Method divide. It's clear to me at last that the greatest impact on my acting and teaching of acting has come from those with whom I share at least one conduit.[86] This clarifies how hard I must struggle to expand my repertoire of innovative approaches, now that I know the price paid by my students and by actors I direct if I fail.

Hegemony and the Ascendancy of Method Acting

Despite the many actors, teachers, and theorist who have challenged the tenets and practices of Method acting, hyper-naturalism remains ubiquitous in theatres and theatre classrooms and the Method offers, in the minds of many, the only spiritual and psychological indicator of truth in acting.

Unpacking the noun reveals that 'truth' is in fact cultural normalcy, which can be a weapon of oppression, and credibility, whereby an individual measures up to cultural expectations.[87] The enactment of a personal memory can become a type of a lie, even though it is assumed to be true and feels real, unless the devices that we use to frame experiences are challenged. I believe that every actor has a responsibility to resist easy assumptions of what is 'normal' and therefore 'believable' for, as Jan Evan

Meshkoff suggests, actors are 'culture bearers, and agents of socialization and identification' in their ubiquitous portrayal of the 'myths of modern culture' (1).What each generation deems 'real' consists of a set of theatrical conventions;[88] I, like Charles Marowitz, concluded that the danger of using 'natural' as a standard for authenticity in acting, is that the word far too often means familiar: what comes too easily, all the old acting tricks, and what has been pre-programmed by society and by contemporary theatre practice, including training.[89]

Many of my concerns about Method acting emerged while reflecting upon the experiences of female theatre professionals. Lauren Love's blending of theory and pragmatic strategies for acting represents, for me, the perfect summation of this resistance:

> Truth was Stanislavsky's aim for art, and the approach he developed for the actor was significantly influenced by the growing but relatively new science of psychology. Stanislavsky often discussed theatre and acting as projects that would seek out, discover and celebrate so-called universal human attributes and values. Post-modern, materialist feminist and queer theory discourses (among others) problematize this essentialism, noting that it fantasizes an ontological space which is untouched by ideological operations and contestations. Psychological realism as a genre in theatre and the method acting approach which is designed to serve its principles, rehearse liberal humanist ideals that privilege dominant ideologies as 'natural.' the 'truths' to which Stanislavsky's acting students are passionately required to aspire, are embedded in mainstream values that help to stabilize hegemonic class privileges. (278)

When my commitment to social action theatre blended with my interest in theorizing about the performance of gender, the result was still another challenge to the myth of truth in acting. After reading Sue-Ellen Case, I could no longer be complacent about the dangers of an authoritative voice pronouncing that one actor's work was true and another's not, when the criteria for truthfulness were not separated from culturally-mandated values of appropriate, normative behaviours. Once I'd encountered Judith Butler I began to wonder how the 'correct' performance of masculinity and femininity affected judgements of 'real' emotions and 'true' behaviour in the creation of stage characters.[90] My own theatre productions became laboratories in which to test some questions: Was cross gender casting simply a matter of mimicry? What made such performances 'real'? Perhaps there was no significant difference between playing a different gender and playing a different class or occupation? And where did the performance of race fit into the mix? I joined the throng experimenting with feminist, anti-Method theatricality, a form of applied theory that, in my case, resulted in an inter-disciplinary research grant to document the psychology of the performance of gender.[91]

When I returned to writings of others involved in non-traditional theatre, such as Joseph Chaikin, I discovered a similar concern with hegemony.[92] A review of various recently published handbooks for actors reveals a disturbing lack of awareness of these issues, despite the significance of the insights offered by those who challenge the cultural hegemony of assumptions of truthful acting.[93]

Ethical Standards for the Classroom and Rehearsal Hall

I have long been concerned about the potential for abuse in acting class. Although I agree with Robert Barton that we must be careful not to remove all emotional intensity from our work, or risk 'acting curriculum as pabulum',[94] I applaud his and other's thoughtful exploration of the dangers of 'practicing psychotherapy without a license'[95] and agree with Richard Owen Geer's prediction: "As the ethics of training and directing are debated, a higher value will be placed on those training techniques which are not psychologically invasive' (156).

First, however, I believe we must acknowledge what Robert Barton in 'Therapy and Actor Training' calls the legacy of 'sadistic gurus who have toyed mercilessly with actors' psyches' (105). Deborarh Saivetz reports that JoAnne Akaliatis found her Stanislavsky-inspired teachers 'manipulative, Svengali-like and confusing' (3). Ellen Gainor describes Strasberg's "annual ingénue breakdown" when he would attack someone with an intense and detailed fault-finding assessment apparently intended to shatter the person through a complete rejection of her work, and notes, "As practitioners trained in these techniques and used to working in these kinds of creative environments began to teach in other studios and in the academy, they came to influence succeeding generations of artists.'[96] Doug Moston also blames the disciples rather than the masters:

> Some acting courses, classes, and workshops are terrifying, if not dangerous, because the director or teacher bores into the actor's psyche in the name of art. Such behaviour is a cheap imitation of Strasberg, Stella Adler, and Sanford Meisner, the consequences of a desire to imitate attributes of great teachers but without substance or originality. The results are the development of trusting actors or students, diligently trying to comply.

Along the way, their dignity is compromised as well as their creativity and art. This crime is often perpetuated in the name of the Method, and should be rejected out of hand.[97]

I would argue, however, that we should not let the originators of the Method, or Stanislavsky himself, off the hook. Walt Witcover's description of his experience with the Affective Memory exercise, under Strasberg's guidance, documents an experience of shame and guilt. Yes, something was learned, and yes, he still uses this technique, but he approaches the exercise with extreme caution (137–40). Sadly, not all Strasberg acolytes demonstrate Witcover's discretion. And they are not the only pedagogical disasters. Gordon Phillips offers seven major types of acting teachers to avoid: cruel critics, impatient spoon-feeders, disciple-seeking gurus, frustrated actors, impractical theorists, and text-focussed analysts (169–70). And what do we make of the sadistic glee with which aspiring actors are cut from competitive training programs at regular intervals?[98]

The fact that psychological manipulation often bears attractive fruit, as demonstrated by Allan Miller's story of encouraging Barbra Streisand to perform for her absent father, makes the practice a more, rather than less ethically suspect. What is most disturbing in Miller's account is the absence of reflection upon the ethics of his coaching practice.[99]

I don't want to suggest that my approach is devoid of danger. What is the energy that the conduits unleash? Freud, Jung, and their disciples have much to say about the energy released when an individual breaks through the false separation of consciousness and unconsciousness, or when the masks of role playing are set aside in favour of conscious interaction with the archetypes that inhabit the psyche.[100] I take a Jungian approach, inspired by Peter Brook's description in *The Open Door*, of the essence of theatre, which he calls 'the present moment:'

Like the fragment broken off a hologram, its transparency is deceptive. When this atom of time is split open, the whole of the universe is contained within its infinite smallness. Here, at this moment, on the surface, nothing in particular is happening, I am speaking, you are listening. But is this surface image a true reflection of our present reality? Of course not. None of us has suddenly shaken of his entire living fabric: even if they are momentarily dormant, our preoccupations, our relationships, our minor comedies, our deep tragedies are all present, like actors waiting in the wings. Not only are the casts of our personal dramas here, but like the chorus in an opera, crowds of minor characters are also lined up ready to enter, linking our private story with the outside world, like a giant musical instrument ready to be played, are strings whose tones and harmonies are our capacity to respond to vibrations from the invisible spiritual world which we often ignore, yet which we contact with every new breath. Were it possible suddenly to release into the open, into the arena of this hall, all our hidden imageries and motions, it would resemble a nuclear explosion, and the chaotic whirlpool of impressions would be too powerful for any of us to absorb. So we can see why an act of theatre in the present which releases the hidden collective potential of thought, image, feeling, myth and trauma is so powerful, and can be so dangerous.[101]

When the power of the director is blended with the vulnerability of an apprentice actor, the unhealthy relationships expands, as Ingmar Bergman explains through alter-ego, Vogler, in *After the Rehearsal*:

A director who doesn't believe in his actor can be very encouraging. He can also remain passive, which drives the actor into a nervous breakdown. He makes use of his advantage, which is that the actor has to expose himself under the lights while the director remains in the darkness of the auditorium. He makes a fool of the actor, exhorts him to think, not to think, to control himself, to let go, to be natural, to be stylized, and so on. A director can kill an actor. (18)

Sadly, I believe that we must conclude that our profession is plagued with a disregard for professionalism and ethics.[102]

Kazimierz Braun, who lists Karol Wojtyla (Pope John Paul II) as one of his mentors, addresses the question of ethics in *Theater Directing* and offers a list of principles for work with student actors on the human and on the artistic level (180). Sadly, I have not seen much evidence of reflection upon such ethical considerations in directing textbooks and manuals readily available in the North American market.[103] With Suzanne Burgoyne Dieckman, I'd like to see 'an explicitly-stated code of ethics guiding the training of actors' (1), but I fear such self-regulation is a distant possibility.[104]

Honouring Diversity

Honouring diversity is central to my teaching ethics. There is nothing new in this ideal. Every acting teacher that instructs students to draw upon the self as a source for characterization does the same. Morris Carnovsky used to ask his students:

> I could even say to you now, at this moment, 'are you acting?' and I daresay the answer would be yes, and it would be the right answer. Even as you sit there in your very interesting and different ways, listening to me, each one of you backed up by your own peculiarities, your lifelong individuality, I want you to realize how completely unique you are. (33)

However, this acknowledgment of the actor's interpretive artistry is quite different than allowing for the master-teacher's limitations, which is what this book proposes. Here I follow in the footsteps of H. Wesley Balk, whose description in *Performing Power* of the evolution of his own teaching, in response to a newfound understanding of perceptive mode dominance, sets the standard for honest self-reflection and commitment to artistic mentorship:

> How often I have attributed the inability of students to perceive what I did in a scene to a lack of training, sophistication, or perception on their part. It was indeed the last of these, but not in the way I had always thought; for though they may have been weak in a perceptual area in which I was strong, the reverse is true in other modes. We sometimes think of people as dull, obstinate, or imperceptive when they do not relate to the same thing we do in a performance. It has now become a fascinating exercise to try to understand the mode makeup and dominance that is responsible for a student's reaction (or for audience reactions in general) to a performance. Students and performers can become our teachers in the best sense of that word. Instead of bemoaning their lack of insight, teachers can search for the insight and perception in them that can help develop our own. If they do miss a significant point, it presents an opportunity to help them perceive what they missed by appropriate exercise of our own projective channels. It is also instructive to sort out and improve the projective and perceptual matches between directors and performers. (42)

My hope is that this book will help others to adapt their teaching practice in accordance with this ideal.

Sadly, the status quo for acting teachers, whether they ascribe to Strasberg, Stanislavsky, or any alternative approach, is described by John Strasberg:

> There is no art form that will tell you that in this situation or in that situa-

tion this is what you should do. You won't find a karate master, you won't find a singing teacher or anybody who will tell you that. But you will find acting teachers – too many – who will and you can imagine the effect on you if you are a young talented person and vulnerable and somebody is telling you that there is a very specific way, an exact way, to do it. You could become terrified that you aren't good enough because you couldn't do an exercise in class – which is criminal. So you have to be very careful about choosing a teacher.[105]

Hélène Beauchamp has articulated what is, for me, the ideal teacher of acting:

At first, it is the teacher who will make the student aware of what it is to be engaged in a creative moment. For this to happen, it is essential that the teacher be able to recognize those moments when the other is alive with creativity, to know what it is, what it looks, sounds, and feels like. When the teacher recognizes creativity in what the student does or proposes, it is her or his obligation to say so, in order for the student, in turn, to know. It is essential for the theatre student to be accompanied by a teacher/spectator who is constantly aware of what the actor is in the process of inventing and giving.

She then describes an ideal match between teacher and student, the latter

in a state of confidence about the self and about the context of experimentation s/he is immersed in, and in a relationship of confidence with his/her teacher, who is then involved both as pedagogue and as theatre artist. As pedagogue, the teacher knows which experimentation to propose, which context to build in order to provide this specific student with the space needed to create. As artist, the teacher recognizes when creation occurs, when the student is 'seized by creation' and, recognizing it, says so" 'that's it', 'yes', 'continue'. This enables the student to recognize what is happening in his/her own 'space within' because s/he is then reading the outer signs of this creative activity. Thus, the teacher guides the student in his/her own capacities and provides that student with genuine autonomy as a creator'. (21)

It is time to set aside the authoritative, arrogant certainty that there is *one* way to train actors, in favour of classrooms and rehearsal halls that are equally supportive of all six Creative Personality Types.

Notes

1   Patti Gillespie, in 'The Teaching of Acting in American Colleges and Universities, 1920–1960,' suggests that I am representative of the norm in this regard (367).

2   A common theme in contemporary acting texts that remain faithful to Stanislavsky, is a challenge to the near-universal conflation of American Method with Stanislavsky under which I and others laboured for so long. See, for example, Bruce J. Miller, *The Actor as Storyteller* and Robert Barton, *Acting*.

3   Here, for example, is Strasberg's refutation, in *A Dream of Passion*, of one of the myths of Method acting, 'the assumption that the actor is not aware of the imaginary nature of the performance. In other words, the actor forgets that he is acting. Obviously, this is impossible. If the actor really forgot that he was acting, he would naturally drop his cues, his dialogue, and all of the scene directions' (52). And here's what he has to say about emotional self-indulgence, another trait associated with Method actors: 'When the actor arrives at the moment of high intensity, he must be able to stay with the sensory concentration; otherwise, the actor's will is out of control and he may be carried away by the emotional experience' (115). Lorrie Hull reports, via Susan Strasberg, her father's admonition to young actors, 'You're being natural, but that's not enough. Natural I can see on a street corner. What we ask is that you be real. Art is both more beautiful and terrible than life' (xv).

4   I suspect that Stella Adler had a similar experience, as reported in *The Technique of Acting*: 'I resented acting with some of the principles that were used at the Group Theatre. Because of this, I became a stranger. I excluded myself from the way in which they rehearsed, and the way the plays were directed.' When she met Stanislavsky in Paris, she blurted out, 'Mr. Stanislavski, I loved the theatre until you came along, and now I hate it!' They discuss a certain role: 'I told him that I was very unhappy about a play that I was in at that time called *The Gentle Woman* by Don Powell. I told him that I failed in certain moments of the play when I could neither continue the character nor understand how to continue the character.' But when they worked together, 'I was able to be completely at ease, completely at home. I felt as if I had worked with him for a lifetime' (119–21).

5   In this I was greatly influenced by the work of Richard Courtney and Donald Winnicott. See also Robert Leach, who reports that Meyerhold saw an actor as 'akin to the child when he or she is playing: for the child, the play is 'real'' (40).

6   Page 42. I particularly enjoy Lewis' resistance to self-indulgence, such as that offered in *Advice to the Players*: 'I remember an admonition from my early training: 'Characterization is the overcoat you put on after you have all the under-dressing.' Nonsense. What actually happens is that once you've got all that lovely underwear of thought and emotion going, you're so hot you never get around to the overcoat' (162).

7   See, for example, Donald Pollock, Aldo Tassi, David Griffiths, Peter Lamarque, and John Rudlin on Copeau's use of masks. Jerzy Grotowski's appeal to Action and Power was also, for me, a welcome alternative to Strasberg's focus on Perception and Relationship.

8   Other favourite authors include Robert Pasolli, Dario Fo, Augusto Boal, Jeff Wirth, Jo Salas, and of course Bertolt Brecht, though I learned more by reading books about him by Martin Esslin, James McTeague and Fredric Jameson; as Peter Thompson reminds us, Brecht was a 'compulsive articulator' with a 'taste for contradiction' (102) so he did not leave a comprehensive guidebook. Dennis C. Beck addressed many of the issues that concerned me, even inspired, as he is, by Stanislavsky. I also found Gerry Large's research fascinating as I worked through my thoughts on acting in social action theatre.

9   I was not alone in wrestling with these issues, as I discovered when I encountered du Rand, Malpede, Joni Jones, and Marvin Carlson's 'Performing the Self.'

10 An attitude affirmed by the scholarship of Joseph R. Roach, E.T. Kirby, Jarmila Veltrusky, Howard Skiles, to name but a few.

11 I wish all teachers of psychological realism shared Kurt Daw's insight: 'Upon seeing a performance by the one genuinely 'Del Sarte'-trained actor I've ever met, I found much less to ridicule than I had been led to expect' (74). Most, however, are like Richard Brestoff, who categorically dismisses the acting styles against which Stanislavsky rebelled as inherently false. See Pat Rogers for a study of David Garrick that captures this 18th century actor's charisma.

12 Gordon Craig summarized my attitude: 'The hundred most excellent plays of the world are supernatural in form and in content . . . . It is therefore better that the actor should avoid *as far as possible* the attempt to interpret these plays in a 'natural' way' (89). Other authors in this section of my bookshelf include Jerry Crawford, Hardie Albright, John Harrop & Sabin Epstein, and Malcolm Morrison along with Robert Cohen's *Advanced Acting* and Robert Barton's *Style for Actors*.

13 In *The Complete Singer-Actor* H. Wesley Balk asserts that strategies borrowed directly from Method acting can, in fact, damage a singer's vocal instrument: 'I am convinced that it is the attempt to duplicate physically this chemically induced state of emotion that causes vocal and physical tension when young actors try to be emotionally 'real' or 'honest.' To 'feel it,' they tense their bodies and voices, hoping to produce the intense feeling of the emotional state. In so doing they effectively block the flow of real feeling. In a physical sense it is simply bad acting, but it can cause great damage to the voice if practised over a period of time' (57). Earlier, Balk commented, 'Unfortunately, striving for a naturalistic result places singers in a very strange situation. There they are in the midst of one of the most highly stylized dramatic forms known, and they are asked to be *natural*?' (30) For an even

stronger condemnation of the Method, see his *Performing Power*. Reading Burgess & Silbeck, June Goldner, Ben Spatz, Ethan Mordden, Pearl Wormhoudt, Barry Green, Eloise Ristad and Shirlee Emmons & Alma Thomas in connection with teaching and directing singers further broadened my reflections upon the nature of the performance experience. Tracey Moore and Joe Deer & Rocco Dal Vera, in contrast, created textbooks for singer-actors that work entirely within the legacy of Method.

14 I will always be grateful to Marvin Carlson for his clear, succinct, and practical writing on theory and performance; I found Keir Elam and Bert O. States much heavier going. I also appreciate the overview offered by Mark Fortier and Janelle Reinelt.

15 *The Way of the Actor* blends psychology with philosophy and mysticism, a mix prompted me to consider the very special energy that the conduits unlock. Richard Schechner has also explored this intersection, as have Stratos E. Constantinidis, Rachel Karafistan, Mark Olsen, and Kathryn Wylie-Marques.

16 Many are the psychologists who contributed to the myth of the neurotic actor (Hammond & Edelmann, DeCosta, Buse & Amdursky, Fenichel, Field, Lane, and Taft, to name but a few). Philip Weissman is representative: 'Acting will attract those who have excessive inner needs for, and urgent insatiable gratifications from, exhibiting themselves. Psychoanalytic investigation reveals that these are individuals who have failed to develop a normal sense of identity and body image during the early maturational phases of infancy. This is the actor's plight' (11). For a contemporary approach to neurotic actors, see Linda H. Hamilton's *The Person Behind the Mask* and for a popular version see Ann Brebner's *Setting Free the Actor*. Jan Evan Meshkoff refers to a study by H.L. Barr and others that described actors as 'intellectually bright with excellent conceptual communicative abilities, using creative thinking but with poorly integrated personalities' (7). Wayne Smith explains the impetus for this sort of consideration when he notes, 'If the portrayal is sufficiently skilled to convince us, the audience, of the 'truth of the characterization,' then it is only natural for us to wonder what affects the portrayal must have on the actor's self or psyche. And for that reason, people often speculate regarding the schizophrenia of the actor of many parts' (29). That which some psychologists describe in negative terms can be reconfigured as a positive attribute directly linked to creativity. For example, Jan Even Meshkoff suggests that actors and actresses, like other strikingly creative individuals, have a high degree of 'ambiguity tolerance' (15) when it comes to sex-role stereotyping. We might extend that description to suggest that actors have ambiguity tolerance towards all manner of self-definition, and it is that capacity to avoid simplistic categorization that allows them to excel in their chosen profession.

17 Rhonda Blair, 'Reconsidering Stanislavsky,' 177. See also Derrick De Kerckhove, James R. Hamilton, and Thomas R. Whitaker.

18 See, for example, Eric J. Nuetzel, John Emigh, Malgorzata Sugiera, R. Keith
    Sawyer, N.P. Alekseev et al., Antje Diedrich, Charles Neuringer & Ronald
    Willis, Stephen B. Fried, Harald G. Wallbott, Bruce G. Shapiro, Jonathan
    Pitches, Henry Gleitman, Jonathan Levy, Stratos E. Constantinidis, Jean-
    Marie Pradier, P.V. Simonov, L.S. Vysotsky, David Orzechowicz, Thalia R.
    Goldstein, Virginia Koste, and Dennis P. Wolf. Along the way I encountered
    Freud everywhere, but also Carl Jung, via Katharine Hitchcock & Brian
    Bates, Lacan via Georges Baal, and Pavlov via Vladimir J. Kone ni.

19 Claire Armon-Jones, James R. Averill, Errol Bedford, Dacher Keltner &
    Jonathan Haidt, Joseph E. LeDoux, Kevin N. Ochsner & Lisa Feldman
    Barrett, C. Terry Warner, Philip J. Koch, Donald L. Nathanson, Louis H.
    Stewart, and Alan Allport.

20 Michael J. Apter, Jonathan Miller, Pierre Philippot and Alexander Schaefer,
    Jerome Bruner & Carol Fleisher Feldman, and Henri Zukier.

21 Howard S. Friedman, Louise M. Prince, & Ronald E. Riggio, Ross W. Buck,
    Virginia J. Savin, & Robert E. Miller, Ralph Exline, Joel R. Davitz & Lois
    Jean Davitz, Ray L. Birdwhistell, Edward T. Hall, Paul Ekman & Wallace V.
    Friesen, Adam Kendon, Marianne LaFrance, and Stanley Feldstein.

22 See, for example, Lewis R. Aiken, John C. Houtz, Michael Daniels, Jan
    Strelau, Don Riso & Russ Hudson, Steven Reiss, Susan D. Calkins & Nathan
    A. Fox, Marvin Zuckerman, Alan W. Brownsword, Jane Hardy & Ruth G.
    Sherman Jones, David Keirsey & Marilyn Bates and Dawna Markova.

23 For others making use of Csikszentmahalyi's theories of flow, see Michael
    Apter, Melvin P. Shaw, Jason Brown, David Schuldberg, Barnaby Nelson &
    David Rawlings, Jeffrey Martin & Keir Cutler, Fausto Massimini and
    Richard G. Mitchell. See Colin Wilson for a popularization of
    Csikszentmahalyi's concept of peak experiences. I am also indebted to
    Csikszentmahalyi for the precision with which he identified the function of
    status in human social systems: 'Every human group, no matter how small
    and simple, has a set of goals aimed at ensuring its own continuity. These are
    the norms or rules without which the social system would lose its identity
    and decay into a crowd engaged in a 'war of all against all.' A central feature
    of every social organization is a hierarchy that differentiates power relation-
    ships among people of different statuses. Social differentiation is itself
    genetically based.' He then explains that the internalization of social goals
    results, when those goals are met, with a sense of *communitas*: the self might
    lose autonomy, but it gains through identification with a larger, more
    powerful entity. See 'The Flow Experience and Its Significance for Human
    Psychology,' 25–7.

24 See Scott G. Isaksen, Mark A. Runcio, Guttorm Floistad, Robert Weisberg,
    Larisa V. Shavinina & Michel Ferrari, and Gudmund J.W. Smith. Jill Nemiro's
    interest in interpretive artists is a notable exception. See also Policastro &
    Gardner and Paula Thomson et al.

25 The theory of creativity I found most directly applicable to acting was
    Guilford's SOI Model, with its emphasis on the interpersonal, the social, and

the practical in human creativity, which I encountered in an article by Usha Khire. I also found Richard Brower's *The Monk and the Warrior in the Garden of Renewal* fascinating and inspirational. For a popularized introduction to creativity, see Ken Robinson's *Out of Our Minds*. For a comprehensive study of charismatic flow, see Stephen Rupsch's 'Sublime Union.'

26 I'm reminded of the hilarious portrait of Stanislavsky in rehearsal that appears in Mikhail Bulgakov's *Black Snow*. Vasily Toporkov confirms that Stanislavsky spent endless hours working on aspects of the actors' work that were never seen by an audience (48).

27 *Essays on Gender, Sexuality, Performance*, 31. Julian Meyrick is particularly insightful about the huge divide between the concerns of practitioners and the fascinations of academics, the pragmatic necessity of performance v. the publication record resulting from hair splitting, teasing out ambiguities, etc. and subsequent 'obscuratism' (236). Katy Ryan identifies the myopia that afflicts 'those of us who *think* about theatre more than *do* theatre and confesses: 'It is now clear to me that my ease with the notion of performativity was easy precisely because I had not crossed over into its referent: performance' (206). Kristen Hastrup observes, 'All theoretical work is different from a practical engagement in the unique performed act, of which Bakhtin has reminded us that the event as a whole cannot be transcribed in theoretical terms without losing its event-ness, so to speak. Whatever else they are, theories are also sentences, and this leaves us with the necessity of fixing the unique and non-repeatable act in repeatable words that defy the essence of the act described but which may nevertheless contain it' (22). I also appreciate Michael Bogdanov's perspective: 'Once upon a time theatre practitioners outnumbered the theorists by a thousand to one. Now it is the other way round. ... How do we stop the plays being swamped by the gelatinous blancmange of academia?' (241).

28 The danger of much post-modern theorizing, Johannes Birringer argues, is that we arrive at a place where it becomes impossible to theorize, because a critique of the 'power structure that provides the grammar of thinking through acting about acting' results in a rejection of any type of guide to theatre, much less 'a clearly definable method of acting based on a theory' (83). Anna Furse echoes this critique: 'Theatre artists who enter academia today can discover a critical literature that has in more recent years come to be a parallel industry alongside our own: a theoretical institution that is sometimes sparklingly illuminating and liberating and at others bogged down in deadly dull discourse.' She also suggests why practitioners have not developed an alternative, noting that the work is messy and complicated and, in many cases, artists are 'deliberately seeking to deregulate the senses, knock the rational stuffing out of us, drive towards a poetry of dreams and unutterable truths' (72). Or, as Fausto Massimini so succinctly puts it, 'most people are not used to putting the contents of their consciousness into words' (71). Whatever the reason, questions of vocabulary haunt anyone

writing about such an elusive creative and psychological process as acting.

29   I'm still undecided about Alba Emoting. It is geared towards the summoning of real emotion, a goal that I have concluded is entirely misplaced, and it discounts the social construction of emotion. It is difficult to tell whether it will prove a fruitful amalgamation of science and acting. See Susana Bloch et al, Roxane Rix, Pamela D. Charbora, and Richard Owen Geer as well as Manfred Clynes, whose *Sentics* offers support for Bloch's theories.

30   'Somatic Processes,' 173, 185.

31   For a more recent, and thorough, introduction to Laban's movement system, including drives, see Barbara Adrian.

32   Page 39. I am still looking for a detailed description of Yat Malmgren's approach, and remain puzzled why this has yet to emerge, for students of the Drama Centre are now acting teachers making an invaluable contributions in England and North America. The Laban/Barteneiff Institute of Movement Studies, in contrast, enjoys a high profile, but my cursory examination of associated publications and activities suggested that the application of Laban's theories to the training of actors has no place in this reverential and dance-oriented institute.

33   See, for example, Irmgard Bartenieff, Stanton B. Garner, Vera Maletic, Valerie Preston-Dunlop, Samuel Thornton, David Petersen, and Jeffrey Scott Longstaff. Many of the references I found to Laban emerged from the therapeutic community; for example see Marion North, Stephen K. Levine, Ilene A. Serlin, Petra Kuppers, Joan W. Lishman and Clive Barker on Joan Littlewood. I was fascinated by descriptions of Laban's movement analysis in use by anthropologists, particularly the reference to 'kinesthetic sympathy,' the result of the LMA observer retaining the data through body memory; for descriptions see Allison & Elizabeth Kagan Jablonko or Sally Ann Ness. I also delved into the field of Movement Psychology; for example see Peter E. Bull, James J. Conley, Sverker Runeson, and Eckart Scheerer. Not all studies of Laban are hagiography: see, for example, Patricia Vertinsky.

34   As reported, for example, by Lea Logie, Paul Kassel, and Thomas Casciero.

35   For example, *Irreverent Acting* by Eric Morris was a great inspiration, for its title alone. My notes reveal that I have integrated his advice about using the real into my own teaching, and his idea of 'obligations' evolved into what I call 'considerations.' But years ago I was horrified at his recommendations about using the real relationship between acting partners as fuel for summoning real emotions in a scene. I now realize that this insight is offered by and for Relationship actors. And who but a Perception actor could articulate, so clearly, the yin and yang of that conduit, as does Peter Lobdell: 'The imaginative and the real are not fighting for the actors' attention; rather they create and allow both to exist simultaneously' (186).

36   Page 231. Lorna Marshall and David William write of Brook's seeking performers who manifest 'transparency,' a state of openness, immediacy, along with a state of connectedness and responsiveness he calls 'the invisible network' (174).

37 Stanislavsky referred to 'creative mood,' a concept that Jean Giebel develops in light of contemporary theories of emotion. Joanna Rotté quotes Stella Adler:

> I'm really not interested in helping an actor become a good actor, unless he becomes the best self that he can become. That is missing for me in the actor in performance. There has to be a level of grandeur about him, grandeur is the wrong word, of size in the instrument, in the soul of the actor. That's the most important thing to me. That he doesn't remain small, that he can take his place as an artist and collaborate with any artist. When he has that, then I feel that's actually what acting is about. Acting with size forces open all the channels which life closes off. It opens them up and allows you to achieve yourself. (201)

When Viola Spolin describes the goal of her theatrical games, she uses 'spontaneity' and 'personal freedom' and speaks of awakening 'the total person, physically, intellectually, and intuitively' (5). I believe she is describing charismatic energy released in 'an explosion–or spontaneity–and as is the nature of explosions, everything is torn apart, rearranged, unblocked' (6). Michael Kirby suggests that it is the charismatic that distinguish acting from non-acting: 'Acting involves a basic psychic or emotional component . . . . He lacks the psychic energy that would turn the abstraction into a personification' (7).

38 For example, here is Ian Watson, in 'Catharsis and the Actor,' describing Grotowski's appeal to Innovative actors through a blending of action with perception: 'Through various exercises, involving physical and vocal reactions to their immediate surroundings, the performers examined the relational give-and-take flow between the external environment and their inner being' (311). Another teacher with a similar approach is Mabel Todd, here described by Jack Clay: 'Mabel Todd's teaching method uses creative images, and was based on her deep knowledge of body mechanics . . . . convinced that [her students] must, through accurate anatomical knowledge and dynamic imagery, come to their own personal self-use' (19). Clive Barker invents an approach he calls 'kinescenics,' which, as it involves 'the articulation of character relationships through movements in space' ('In Search of the Lost Mode,' 14), suggests a Personal CP Type.

39 Duke writes, 'Gombrich's known stories effect also provides a possible explanation for why there are so many and varied theories of personality and why it is typically possible to find at least some evidence for all of them if we search hard enough. If each personality type is a 'story,' then once we have the stories, we can and do find them. Thus, if we propose four different personality types, and if all we have is four narratives, then we will see only these four, thereby confirming – sometimes speciously – our theory' (40).

40 Eugenio Barba, 'The Dilated Body,' 369–70. I also appreciate the way Barba

addresses the question of gender and how he links his concept of energy to Jungian archetypes. In 'The Actor's Energy' he announces, 'Typical male energy and typical female energy do not exist. Or at least, they do not exist in the theatre. There exists only an energy specific to a given individual. The actor's or actress's task is to discover the individual propensities of his or her own energy and to protect their potentialities, their uniqueness' and warns, 'Some choices, apparently 'natural', become a prison' (238). In *A Guide to Theatre Anthropology* he writes, 'Anima-energy (soft) and Animus-energy (vigorous) are terms which have nothing to do with the distinction between masculine and feminine, nor with Jungian archetypes. They refer to a polarity, pertinent to the anatomy of the theatre' (62). See also Barba's *The Paper Canoe* for further explorations of an actor's energy.

41 Pages 6–7. Donnellan's experience of isolation and paralysis suggests that the blockage sensation he describes from first-hand experience are those of the Relationship and Action conduits. Power and Perception conduits offer other symptoms, not just the powerlessness he mentions, but sensations of huge capacities building up behind the blockage as well as sensory overload.

42 Page 191. I love Daphne Du Maurier's evocative description of creative flow: 'Vanity, vanity, all is vanity, said the preacher, except during that moment when the writer felt the flash and wrote ... what did he write? The flash has gone. It's as swift as that, as ephemeral, as fierce, but, like the song that ended, the memory lingers on' (98). Du Maurier's warnings of the dangers of mistaking pleasure for creative flow are as valid for actors as for writers: 'The moment of the inner glow, and the purr of pleasure, are two very opposite things. The inner glow can bring despair in its train, or a high temperature, or such fever of intensity that nothing but a ten-mile walk or an icy swim will break the spell and release the writer to the world of day-by-day. The purr of pleasure is an indication that the writer has never left the world at all. He has been watching himself at work, hearing his own voice; and the fret with which he waits for public opinion-the criticism of friend, publisher, reader-points to the doubt within. He must be praised, he must be flattered, he must be boosted by some means other than his own life spark: otherwise there is no momentum, all is sound and fury, signifying nothing' (95). See also Eberhard Scheiffele and Lesa Lockford & Ronald J. Pelias.

43 'Applied Psycho-Analysis in the Director-Actor Relationship,' 223.

44 Here, for example, is Harriet Walker articulating how her Relationship conduit functions: 'After thrashing away on my own, I may well find the key to my character in another actor's eyes, in the way he or she looks at me/her' (47). And here is Roberta Carreri sharing her creative process: 'The body's movements create internal pictures ... I hold my breath and balance a moment, just long enough to experience the picture created through the dynamic quiet' (138).

45 Richard Schechner, *Between Theater and Anthropology*, 113. In 'The Creators' Patterns' and ''The Fruits of Asynochrony,' Howard Gardner and his colleagues have undertaken studies of creative people that reveal a signifi-

cant portion of them as having some sort of tension (asynchrony) in one or more areas that form the foundation of personality. In fact, it might be argued that creative people seek out asynchrony, perhaps as a correlation to the transformational imperative, tension and instability being preferred to coherent stability. I find a powerful parallel between this theory and the concept of 'not not me.'

46   See, for example, Brian Bates, 'Performance and Possession,' Katharine Hitchcock & Brian Bates, and Marla Carlson.

47   Jan Meshkoff reports that contemporary psychologists have decided that typology records the persona that has been constructed as a means of communicating the idea of individuality, a compromise between the psyche and society as to what a person should appear to be, in other words a series of choices in societal roles to play and personal styles of communication (26). See also Louise M. Stinespring and Einor Fuchs. Colin Counsell explains the fundamental misperception: 'Stanislavskian actors model and judge their character's psyches on their own—or rather, on what they *deem* their own to be. This is a crucial distinction.' But our experience of selfhood, our 'subjectivity' is fragmented, made up of a variety of interactions with the culture around each of us, Counsell suggests. 'We rarely experience this fragmentation because, in order to operate as a competent social individual, it is necessary to adopt the posture of a coherent, unified subjectivity, albeit that this is illusory. Actors too are social subjects, and view themselves as such a coherency. By definition, then, they base their characters' psyches on an inaccurate model' (31).

48   Claire Armon-Jones, J. Coulter, Palmer & Jankowiak, and Rom Harré. Cultural Anthropologists also talk about the cultural models of emotions; see, for example, Palmer & Jankowiak and Just.

49   'Action, Structure, Task, Emotion,' 145. Zarelli concludes with a broader indictment: 'Given their practical concern with performance, most commonplace theories of acting and the emotions do not reflect metatheoretically on the nature, process, practice, or phenomenon of acting/performance and of emotion within that process.' The limits of empathy were articulated powerfully as far back as William James and echoed by many contemporary thinkers such as Karl Scheibe, Nathan Stucky, and Ian Watson in 'Culture, Memory, and American Performer Training.' Ronald J. Pelias also offers a persuasive challenge to traditional approaches such as the magic if; he suggests that empathy in this context can too easily become exploitation, a means of gaining control, mastering, and silencing the marginalized. The assumption of an actor's ability to transcend cultural difference is regularly challenged by those who position all naturalistic acting within a larger sociological context. See Marianne Conroy, Bruce A. McConachie's 'Metaphors We Act By,' William B. Worthen, and Phillip B. Zarrilli's 'Thinking and Talking About Acting.'

50   There are certain problems of identification that should not be minimized, but rather acknowledged as a natural component of the difference between

the world the actor is privileged to inhabit and the quite different world evoked by the playwright. A case in point is Stephanie Fayerman, who played the role of Ilona in Howard Baker's *The Power of the Dog*. Fayerman frames her reflective and revealing comments with a more general discussion of the 'creatures who inhabit the outer edges of what is considered acceptable human behaviour,' noting that these women are essentially unknowable because so seldom encountered on stage or acknowledged as anything other than aberrations in real life.

Having acknowledged the significance of difference, Fayerman then confesses, 'Given the fact that virtually all Ilona's extremeness stems from a wartime situation, something I have never known, the force with which I 'recognized' her, on first reading the play, was nonetheless staggering.' Fayerman proceeds to suggest a correspondence between her own experiences of marching in demonstrations, shop lifting, and walking alone at night with the fictional character's participation in the horrific events in 1944–5 Poland. Although Fayerman offers 'the capacity to be or do whatever is appropriate to the moment' as both an expediency and a component of an actor's craft, she remains oblivious to how her assumption of easy identification diminishes the political and humanitarian significance of Ilona's experiences and choices (54).

Fayerman's subsequent comments on her experiences rehearsing and performing the role suggest that she did not linger in the bland and comfortable assumptions of easy identification and obvious correlation, but discovered a myriad of ways in which the fictional Ilona might challenge Fayerman's assumptions and illuminated the experiences of a separate individual in another, quite different time and place. For this maturation of perspective we can credit, in part, the ruthless anti-sentimentality of Baker's script and the political ideological orientation of the Joint Stock company which produced the piece. Fayerman's short diary reveals, above all else, the raw courage and disciplined determination required to move beyond the familiar in search of the complete chameleon-like transformation in service of the story of another.

51 Pages 8–10. David Jones, in *Great Directors at Work*, observes that, for Stanislavsky, 'truth' means 'Stanislavsky believes It' (35).

52 Susan Bennet, Susanne Langer, Bruce Wilshire, Richard Knowles, Kendall Walton, Victor Turner, Maria Shevtsova, Franco Ruffini, Marco De Marinis, Anne Ubersfled, J.L. Syan, Martin Esslin in *Field of Drama*, and Erving Goffman in *Frame Analysis*.

53 Others writers who have challenged my assumptions about how meaning occurs in the theatre include Ian Watson, Steve Tillis, John Drummond, Susan Bassnett, and Mária Minich Brewer.

54 Bill Bruehl offers an explanation for this and other myths about acting: 'Until Stanislavski, critical theories about the actor's inner workings almost always proceeded from an audience point of view that focuses on how well actors express feelings' (6). I would argue that little has changed, and that the

prevailing fallacies of the Method are fuelled as much by the naïve admiration of audience members as by myth-making apparatus of the Actors' Studio. For an example of someone writing about acting and speculating on process entirely based on observations of performances, in this case on film, see Steve Vineberg who, even as he celebrates the achievement of Method actors, dissects the dangerous legacy of the charismatic actor-teachers, writing for example of Strasberg's 'air of omniscience, his ecclesiastical style and patriarchal obstinacy, his presentation of himself as the chief nurturer of that most delicate plant, talent, and his fits of chastising fury' (101).

55 See, for example, Gregory J. Feist, James M. Donovan, Raymond Nickerson, Reed Larson, Jeanne Nakamura, and Mary Ann Collins & Teresa M. Amabile. There is a striking connection between an actor's experience of creative flow and religious experiences; see, for Stephen Rupsch and Thomas Csordas.

56 The paradoxical tension between performance and performer that I have tried to evoke with my metaphor of the charismatic chameleon, Fairfil Caudle describes physiologically:

> It is the minute gradations, textures, rhythms and patterns of the voice, eye movements and facial expression, posture and movement, and breathing, that are most readily detected by the audience as emotion, belief, conviction or doubt, attitude, mood, age, or any of hundreds of subtle variations in demeanour. These are in fact the author's 'bodyscape.' It is the information from these subtle cues that the audience detects and it is these that together can mean the difference between a performance of great impact and a lack-lustre one. (48)

Beckerman describes the same phenomenon as follows: 'It is the interpenetration of the sequence by the performer's spontaneous energy that gives artistic performance its tremendous fascination;'

As part of his semiotic analysis of the communication systems associated with the performer, Jon Whitmore addresses personal qualities, which he labels 'a personal style, charisma, or élan.' This quality is heightened when individual transforms herself into a performer before an audience. In fact, as Jon Whitmore suggests, performers can't divorce themselves from this quality. The audience senses this quality as part of the performance experience; they might be charmed, entertained, engaged, or put off by this quality, regardless of production or role. Directors can cast by identifying this quality and the potential effect it might have on audience. Other names Whitmore uses for this attribute: radiant energy, aura, sexiness, moodiness, magnetism, evilness. He asks, 'What are the elements that constitute a person's charisma? What special features endow certain individuals with a unique charm or power that can mesmerize an audience? Personal energy? A relaxed physical presence? An unusually attractive physical appearance? A warm and engaging voice? Penetrating eyes? A magical smile? Impenetrable concentration? The best answer is probably none and all of these things – and more.' In response to charisma, 'the audience's concentration was instantly heightened, their sensors became fine-tuned.' For that reason alone, directors need to recognize 'the special sign system that exists, independent of the play and its characters, in the communicative powers of the performer's personality' (67–9).

57   For vivid descriptions of Invisible Theatre events, see Martin Maria Kohtes, Jonathan Gray, and Bonnie Burstow.

58   For a particularly vivid and exciting application of the theatrical metaphor, see Bernard J. Baars and the collection edited by Dennis Brissett & Charles Edgley; others making use of the theatrical metaphor include Theodore R. Sarbin, Karl E. Scheibe, and Linda Albright et al. Although I believe, with Jane Marla Robbins, that some of the strategies actors use can be of help in everyday life, such applications confirm the fundamental difference between the charismatic chameleon and social role playing.

59   In this I have been inspired by the writings of David Mamet, in particular *Truth and Lies*. See also Barbara Shulgasser. For a popularized approach to courage, see Susan Jeffers; for a dense theoretical study, see Nicholas Ridout. In *The Element*, Ken Robinson identifies fear as the most common obstacle to finding your element.

60   *The Actor and You*, 109. From the perspective of a psychologist, here is Gudmund Smith: 'The degree of tolerance towards the threat of uncertainty, ambiguity, even chaos, must be a critical factor for creative functioning' (387).

61   Roloff defines consent as 'a grace, a capacity of mind, a largeness, if you will, by which something can enter, can infuse, can ignite a quality of spirit that will lead humans out of ignorance into another revelation,' led him to observe: 'All consents are not conscious ones at all, but are rather actions upon psyche because the matching of symbolic material has bypassed ego's judgments' (15). Lionel Tiger describes the necessity of optimism as a survival strategy for our species and in particular for those called upon to exhibit charismatic potency in the forum of politics. He concludes, 'it remains a critical factor in leadership and social achievement in general that members of operating groups sustain at least some moderate belief that they will succeed and even do well in what they are undertaking' (14). Tiger suggests that there is in fact a 'the biochemistry of status' as revealed by heightened levels of whole blood serotonin in dominant primates. Given our understanding of the connection between serotonin levels and experiences of clinical depression, this insight into the experience of charismatic power suggests the source of the pleasure we feel in performing, and the profoundly damaging impact of any blow to the courage required to perform (12).

62   Merlin continues, 'Therefore Filozov attempted – when he himself became involved in the training of young actors in the 1990s – to accommodate each individual's needs, personality, and sensitivity when he worked on particular roles' (230). Filozov also talked to Merlin of the need to 'wake up the soul' – 'first you have to wake up the spirit and then mould it and then rearrange

DEVELOPMENT OF THE THEORY – ANNOTATED BIBLIOGRAPHY

it. . . . If an actor is fully 'awakened' to his or her inner life, each scene will provoke a spectrum of emotions and sensations – in effect, the development of a state of constant inner improvisation' (232)

63 Some contemporary examples: Eugenio Barba in 'The Dilated Body,' pronounces, 'One often forgets the theatre's elementary, which is always that of relationship' (376). Lorna Marshall offers 'a rich inner landscape coupled with physical ease and readiness' (105) as the secret for that mysterious and highly desirable quality she calls stage presence. David Downs, whose entire book draws on the Perception conduit, announces, 'A good actor must become a person alive to the world, evaluating and discovering the mystery of human response; whose 'thinking body' stores up such awareness with deep understanding; and whose totality responds artfully, on cue, to the many levels of stimuli creating any dramatic situation' (67). This tendency towards a blinkered perspective is not limited to acting teachers; Douglas Hedley's chapter on 'The Creative Imagination' offers a study of the phenomenology of imagination heavily weighted towards the perception conduit; I'd argue that there is no direct connection between the any single conduit and the capacity for creative insight and artistry.

64 It's important, I believe, to read not only the eulogizing biographies and worshipful reports of acolytes, but also the clear-eyed assessment of eye-witnesses and collaborators; see, for example, Harold Clurman's *The Fervent Years* and Robert Lewis's *Slings and Arrows*. See also Cindy Adams, Foster Hirsch, Cheryl Crawford.

65 Lee Strasberg announces, 'It is important to stress that every good actor, whether he knows it or not, follows precisely the same intuitive procedure' (163). What remains unsaid is the intuitive process is that used by the master teacher. So Stella Adler taught her students that seeing was the key to acting, according to Joanna Rotté, and that 'the source of acting is the imagination, and the value of the actor's contribution depends upon use of imagination' (59).

66 Often, it's a less engaged observer who is able to reflect thoughtfully on personal bias. Peter Elsass documents his experience as an observer who does not 'get' a conduit, in this case of Power, even while seeing it in action, in his description of Keith Johnstone: 'I myself have seen him working with actors, and been forced to realize how adding a status difference between two actors gave life and presence to their acting' (337).

67 Page 190. Later in the same interview Morris presents his commitment to his students' autonomy as working professionals: 'The way I prepare my actors to work with a director is to train them solidly to learn how to push their own buttons. I train them to know their instruments and to know their craft so well that a director can make any kind of demand on them, and they will know how to accommodate him' (191). He remains oblivious to the contradiction inherent in his pedagogy.

68 Her colleague, Richard Nichols speaks of the seductive allure of legacy

teaching: 'There's always a danger with some of the self-use techniques of getting so caught up in our own gratitude for what we've gotten from a given technique , that all of a sudden–'bam!'–we begin to apply it to everyone else.' He also notes the short stretch from healing to abuse. See Bruce Lecure, 'A Forum of Senior Movement Educators,' 83, 84.

69 Page 320. Sande Shurin writes of the need for harmony between temperament and working method (9).

70 Robert Barton & Janet Gupton describe the use of teaching assistants in an acting program, facilitating the process whereby a student who has had an excellent experience with a teacher prepares to become, in turn, a teacher of acting. Time is spent 'learning to say what needs to be said in a way that it can be heard' (174), suggesting a sensitivity to diversity in creative temperaments, but the assistants are also given help 'finding methods to get reluctant or stubborn actors to try new approaches' (176) instead of recognizing that a mismatch has likely occurred.

71 I've come to realize that one of the explanations for Stanislavsky's longevity as an inspiration for actors and teachers of acting is the containment, within his complex and evolving theories, of techniques that offer a direct invitation to each of the four conduits. Yoshi Oida's *The Invisible Actor* also offers something for all four conduits. He begins with perception, and movement with awareness is fundamental to his approach, but he also writes at length about relationships with other actors as a source of inspiration, and his meditation on the actor's relationship with the great energy sources of nature speaks directly to an awareness of the transcendent, guaranteed to move an actor with a power conduit. From quite a different perspective, Charles Waxberg affirms diversity in *The Actor's Script*, not only when he reminds actors that they must select objectives that inspire them artistically, and then describes a variety of ways that such inspiration can occur (45), but also when he describes the audience using the metaphor of the four elements to depict doorways to individual personality: 'Fire signs are governed by their *spirit*; earth signs are governed by the *physical world*; air signs are governed by their *intellect*; and water signs are governed by their *emotions*' (92).

72 Baker's legacy of student-centred teaching should be the model for us all; he writes, 'As a teacher you do not begin to teach, thinking of your own ego and what you know. You begin with the student and where he is. This kind of action takes lots of self-denial. You will have to give up much of the built-in pleasure of showing how smart you are and how well you know the subject . . . This kind of teaching takes a great deal of discipline. The work usually appears extremely tentative, and it does not have recognizable forms . . . It takes a lot of confidence for a teacher to make this the student's course . . . It takes a willingness to look inept and confused when the student is trying to find his way. It takes a determination to back off and let the student experiment in a flexible environment. *If you as a teacher have an idea of what you want out of the student and force that on him, you have already failed him and*

wrecked the course' (i-iii). He is also capable of absolutes, emerging from his Perception conduit, such as 'I do not believe that any kind of fine creative work can emerge without visualization' (52).

73 Page 33. Drukman's article suggests a completely different relationship between theory and practice for the theatre artist. Drukman's search for a viable contemporary approach to acting is understandable given his description of his generation's university curricula, in which the debunking of Freud, Marx, Mendel, Darwin, and Einstein requires a familiarity with 'this century's governing ideas, *and* the problems with them' (31). He points to the discrepancy between the theoretical training of musicians, who are considered ill-prepared without some immersion in the theories of their teachers, and their teachers' teachers' halcyon days, and that of actors, observing, 'the lessons young theatre students usually learn are fundamentally the same as those their teachers and their teachers' teachers learned' (31). Elsewhere in his presentation of Viewpoints as a quintessentially postmodern acting theory, he identifies, less self-consciously, other aspects of the postmodern when he refers to the belief of one of the founders of the system that 'there are no systems of art-making' (31) and then goes on to describe the dividing and labeling of actors' perceptions which appear to constitute the sum total of the Viewpoints theory.

74 Although Lawrence Parke encourages individual tailoring in keeping with actors' differing psychologies, he sets out a system, in which all the various elements fit together as Stanislavsky intended (257, xii). Alison Hodge feels that contemporary practitioners tend to replace 'the notion of a comprehensive system in favour of identifying first principles within the context in which their training operates' (8); I wish this trend was closer to the universal.

75 Page 68. In contrast, Lisa Wolford reminds us of the pitfalls of legacies in her description of the rapid dissemination and subsequent misrepresentation of Grotowski's theories.

76 *Training an Actor*, 14–5. Lorinne Vozoff announces the 'natural correctness of Stanislavsky's System' (5). Irina and Igor Levin, equally respectful to the Stanislavsky legacy, acknowledge the transmission via Russian students of the great master; as a result, their approach is notably different from that transmitted via American master-teachers and directors.

77 Here is Cheryl Crawford on the early days: 'As rehearsals progressed and the actors discovered they were being trained and extended in a way they had never known before, Lee became their father figure-to some of them, their God figure. He relished this, naturally; his frustrations in the past had been acute' (54).

78 Page 45. Deborah Ann Greer explores the cult-like operations of the Group Theatre under Strasberg as well as the inherent dangers of the formation of charismatic groups in acting classrooms under a dynamic and dogmatic teacher. She asks, 'How can the teacher recognize and avoid the destructive attraction of a charismatic hierarchy and negative aspects of surrender and

control in his or her courses? How can theatre practitioners continue to invest in a proven and useful technique, such as the Method, and circumvent the dependency of charismatic group behaviours?' (147). Her response: learn the tell-tale signs, taken from Robert Lifton's eight psychological themes necessary and central to totalistic environments (35): milieu control, loading of the language, demand for purity, confession, mystical manipulation, doctrine over person, sacred science and dispensing of existence and the four components of charismatic groups: shared beliefs, behavioural norms, group cohesiveness & altered states of consciousness. See pp. 117–124 for her analysis of how these themes manifest themselves in a theatrical context such as Strasberg's studio. Also pp. 151–16 on how to avoid the trappings of guruism in the classroom. Cheryl McFarren's comparison of affective memory with trauma is equally damning of the unquestioned acceptance of Strasberg's method in acting classrooms.

79 For example, Brant Pope, in describing the 'Meisner program' at Florida State University, claims that the curriculum in that institution is based in a refining of Method through a return to Stanislavsky and the explorations of Manuel Duque, a student of Meisner and later mentor to Pope and others (147, 154, 157). When I was training as an actor, Michael Chekhov was a name heard only in passing; today he has achieved legacy status, with his own Institute that certifies instructors in his methods. I responded immediately to his evocation of the physical and his sensitivity to issues of power, as expressed in the books published under his name, but I'm appalled at the codification of his subtle and intuitive teachings into a system. See also Franc Chamberlain and James Luse. In 'Masking Chekhov and Revealing Action' John Harrop describes how Chekhov dies under the weight of Method's hegemony. Other less well known but equally significant master teachers include Richard Boleslavsky (via J.W. Roberts) and Michel Saint-Denis.

80 In contrast, Ned Manderino, whose *All About Method Acting* celebrates the Strasberg legacy, emphasizes finding which aspects of the Method suit your personality (vii); evidently Strasberg didn't emphasize action but didn't object when Manderino added that emphasis to his teaching of Strasberg's approach (ix). This suggests to me a partial mismatch between student and master teacher.

81 At the same time, we must not forget that some are drawn to acting classrooms in search of psychodrama, or what Freud would call neurotic exhibitionism. Freud's analysis of the emotional transference that takes place between a patient and a therapist during psychoanalysis suggests the neurotic potential of acting as John Mitchell explores in *The Director-Actor Relationship* (15). Freddie Roken, whose presentation of the similarities is offered in praise of acting rather than in condemnation, offers this summary: 'In terms of acting theory, transference thus parallels the actor's oscillation between emotional and ideological involvement on the one hand, applying psychological experiences of the past 'to the person of the physician at the present

moment,' and various modes of *Verfremdung* on the other, i.e., the resolution of this identification. Transference is thus a method for processing different kinds of memories, what Freud called *Nachträglichkeit,* through which the past gets meaning or is understood in terms of the present. Freud's use of the term *agieren* is also relevant in this context, because 'acting out,' as it is termed in English, is actually an extreme form of Stanislavski's dramatic acting through which in the psychoanalytic process past events are repeated 'with a sensation of immediacy which is heightened by [the patient's] refusal to recognize their source and their repetitive character.' 'Acting out' is the impulsive and sometimes even aggressive form of remembering and reporting the traumas of the past' (183). Roken's quotations from *The Language of Psychoanalysis* by J. Laplache and J.B. Pontalis are particularly interesting, in that they suggest the intense neurotic need that fuels the conflation of past experiences with present role playing. The fundamental difference seems to lie in the patient's refusal to perceive the connection, in contrast with the actor's purposeful seeking of past experiences to fuel current enactments. However, it is possible that the actor has merely substituted one sort of willful blindness with another. The patient has sufficient self-awareness to have entered into a course of psychoanalysis, seeking an end to the 'impulsive a sometimes aggressive form of remembering,' while the actor is invited to avoid acknowledging the inevitable connection between the methods of psychological realism and her own private burden of unresolved psychological experiences.

82 Mekler, *The New Generation of Acting Teachers*, 300.
83 Quoted in Mekler, *The New Generation of Acting Teachers*, 217. Richard Mitchell's discussion of anomie further illuminates the dangers of systems of acting training. Anomie results in a powerful drive towards stability, security, certainty, escape from uncertainty, integration into an understandable and predictable social order, and an end to uncertainty about outcomes. Yes, it is comforting to think that, if you do X, you can count on Y occurring, but this is not really possible in creative arts, where the true state of affairs is the absence of norms, when the 'rules' are inapplicable or ineffective, perhaps even meaningless. Actors need to actively seek out instability, the absence of clear and pre-set outcomes based on pre-planned behaviours. That's the only way to acquire a sense of competence, which is a pre-requisite to flow. 'Flow is found in using a full measure of commitment, innovation, and individual investment to perform real and meaningful tasks that are self-chosen, limited in scope, and rewarding in their own right' (42) In other words, flow is a 'balanced, dynamic tension' between our longing for stability and clarity and our resistance to externally imposed rules. Mitchell continues, 'Creative acts of whatever order, in play or art or scientific inquiry, call for a willingness to follow the flight of hazardous processes, to surrender the self to forces beyond one's control. Creative life, which is to say a vitally experienced and satisfying life, cannot be led easily or safely. It is demanding, challenging, stressful'

(44). He then defines stress as 'a social-psychological condition of perceived urgency, importance, or significance associated with some set of persons or events. A stressful situation is one that matters, one that is real, meaningful, and commanding. Stress is simply and essentially stimulation' (57) His point— flow is not possible without it!

84 David Henry Feldman has developed a theory of human development that suggests a specific mental function or capacity, a powerful tendency to change reality, which he has labelled the transformational imperative. He suggests that the focus of this imperative is to move from the stable, rational experience of the world, in direct opposition to equilibration mechanism proposed by Jean Piaget, whose theory of development suggests that the maturation process exists to move the individual towards mature stability and mastery. I find that this has a direct correspondence with the description of so many actors of the need to find some way of being 'off balance' in order to unlock the most interesting explorations in rehearsal and the most highly charged performances. It also affirms the validity of the advice I so often give in acting class: learn to take risks, don't play it safe, you can't do that sort of scene without allowing yourself to be pushed off balance by your partner, etc. Studies of creative people have revealed that a significant portion of them have some sort of tension (asynchrony) in one or more areas that form the foundation of personality. In fact, it might be argued that creative people seek out asynchrony, perhaps as a correlation to the transformational imperative, tension and instability being preferred to coherent stability.

85 This range of responses plays itself out in each new wave of acting textbooks. William Esper is lauded as Meisner's most authentic protégé while Anne Johnstone-Brown positions Stanislavsky as the Moses of acting theorists even as she acknowledges that accomplished actors use a wide variety of techniques, as does Melissa Bruder. And then there's Harold Guskin, who writes about his training: 'Rather than freeing my inspiration, the conscious intellectual choices I made about my characters obligated me, closing down my instinct as well as my feelings. I worked hard at Stanislavski's technique to find the emotions I needed to fill the character, but it didn't truly work for me. It pulled me away from my true, free response to the script and the moment. By forcing me to favour memory over imagination, it shut down my connection to my unconscious thoughts, images, and fantasies. Using the technique always left me outside the intimate connection to the moment on stage or film. It took me out of the scene. I could always feel the gears turning. I felt as if I was in my own separate world, apart from the play going on around me. And the emotion never felt free. I was Acting' (39).

86 For example, I've always been fond of Peter Barkworth's approach. I now realize it's in part because of his approach to action which suggests that he and I share that conduit. Here's one eminently practical insight: 'It is good to go through your part to find which of the things you say can be things

which just occur to you. Comb through your part for new thoughts, and moves may well spring out of them, for new thoughts come with energy, and it is that energy which converts itself into a move' (30). Recently published acting textbooks that prove most inspirational are, predictably, those that speak most directly to my Dynamic CP type, such as *The Expressive Body*, by David Alberts, David Zinder's *Body–Voice–Imagination*, which feed into my Action conduit, and Sheila Kerrigan's *The Performer's Guide to the Collaborative Process*, with its marvellous section on power games in rehearsals.

87   Theories of cultural hegemony proved invaluable in sorting out my thoughts on these issues. See, for example, T. Jackson Lears, Bruce A. McConachie, Leslie T. Good, and Tobin Nellhaus. Sally Sommer reminded me of how culture determines aesthetics. David Haberman points out the danger of mistaking habitualized actions shared by a group, which he calls institutions, for instinctual nature. He warns that an institution 'renders behaviour typical and predictable. Institutions guide and control behaviour by setting up predefined patterns that funnel activity in one direction, thereby delivering the human being from the chaotic realm of boundless choice' (5). Nina Bandelj's study of Method actors at work confirms a reliance on cultural stereotypes. It seems that the ascendancy of Strasberg's approach, in partic-ular, is as much the result of the fame of film actors as of its effectiveness in live theatre performance, which is ironic if you consider the differences between theatre and film acting. See also Pamela Wojcik, Richard A. Blum, and Thomas W. Babson.

88   Peter Holland, in discussing Shakespeare's actors, notes, 'As soon as we accept that acting can be understood by its audience and that it is a technique that can be repeated and passed on we accept that it involves a system of some sort. All acting is formalized to the extent that it observes and uses what it sees as constituting reality, formalizing it into patterns that imitate and repre-sent that reality. Those formalized patterns are the only means by which the audience can understand the acting within the terms of the shared culture. Equally well, the audience may, and usually does, agree to accept this formal-ized pattern as a representation of reality for the purposes of the drama that is being performed' (43–4) See also Elizabeth Burns.

89   'Otherness,' 4.8. Marla Carlson acknowledges that Method acting perpetu-ates the status quo, but suggests that, if filtered through Bakhtin's theories of dialogism, the use of emotional memory can serve to transform individuals and societies. David Murray points out that, in improvisations, inexperi-enced actors reinforce the cultural oppression they want to escape (90). See also Elizabeth Burns, David Wiles and Gus Edwards. I was fascinated to learn that Anne Bogart developed Viewpoints as a challenge to 'the school of American realism that attempts to codify realistic effects,' according to Joan Herrington (155). See also Anne Bogart & Tina Landau, Joan Herrington, Tina Landau and Eelka Lampe's 'From the Battle to the Gift.'

90 Another seminal reading at this time was Eelka Lampe's description of Rachel Rosenthal's performance art which invited a radical reassessment not only of the performing of gender but also the nature of performance as a separate, though overlapping, consideration. Other thought-provoking scholars include Lesley Ferris, Jeanie Forte, Marie-Claire Pasquier, Barbara Freedman, Reid Gilbert, Susan McClary, Helene Keyssar, Dorothy E. Smith, Ellen Donkin & Susan Clement, Linda Walsh Jenkings & Susan Ogden-Malouf, Laurence Senelick, Jill Dolan, and Ida Prosky. I was also deeply affected by the experience of dancers such as Judith Hanna and Gelsey Kirkland. For writers who addressed the practical implications of gender performance for actors and teachers of acting, see Dennis Noe, Deanna Jent, Pamela R. Hendrick, Rhonda Blair, Elaine Aston, Elizabeth C. Stroppel, and Cláudia Tatinge Nascimento. Some of the most powerful challenges to naturalistic assumptions about performing gender come from scholars studying non-Western acting traditions. See, for example, Jennifer Robertson.

91 'Theatrical Images of Gender,' paper presented at the Annual Conference of the Canadian Psychology Association, Penticton, B.C, July 1995. I remain indebted to my colleague, the actor-psychologist Richard Walsh-Bowers, for this joint research.

92 'The conventional actor's inquiry tends to yield whatever it was designed to discover. Little remains to be discovered either about another person or about oneself. Instead, it sustains the stereotyping of people, the stereotyping of ourselves' (19).

93 For example, the useful handbook, *The Actor's Checklist* contains no references to status, hierarchy, or anything else that might inspire a Power actor. Rosary O'Neill appears oblivious both to power issues and to the insidious hegemony of discerning 'truthful' actions. She also assumes that intellectual discernment will uncover the psychological traits of a fictional character, that these mysterious impulses are somehow knowable to the character and to the actor. Given the challenge offered by postmodern theorists, it's strange to find these words as the definition of The Method: 'An acting process, based in nature, used to make an actor's performance truthful and believable' (62) in Doug Moston's *Coming to Terms with Acting*. See also Larry Moss or Hugh O'Gorman. Fortunately, a new generation of acting teachers and textbooks offer an infusion of non-Western practices within which to frame our naturalistic approaches, a welcome counterbalance to the hegemony of The Method. See, for example Adrian Cairns, Jade McCutcheon, Paul Kassel, F. Emmanuelle Chaulet, and Phillip Zarrelli's *Psychophysical Acting*.

94 'Therapy and Actor Training,' 105.

95 Janet Rule, 72. See also Suzanne Burgoyne et al. Sarah Benolken remembers one theatre professor who provided her with free amateur psychoanalysis several times a week (56). A strikingly insidious example is presented by Muriel Gold, who freely acknowledges her use of drama therapy and group therapy in her pedagogy. Marc Gordon says it best: 'To

be sure, many actors, directors, and teachers of acting believe they know much more about psychology than they actually do–certainly enough to be accused of practising psychotherapy without a license. Today practitioners often fear this tendency in themselves, and so the Method is linked to excesses and self-indulgence' (58). The exception would have to be Michael Schulman, whose PhD in psychology allows him unique insights as a student of Strasberg and subsequent teacher of acting. Janet Sonenberg's strategy, when developing her invasive pursuit of intense emotion in her student actors, was to partner with a psychotherapist. She also pays particular attention to the safety of the participants even as she acknowledges the frightening nature of their explorations.

96 Pages 166–7. Gainor concludes that it's not Stanislavsky whose approach is at odds with feminism, but certain types of directorial environments, acting instruction, and play writing associated with the Method. Alaina Lemon's study of Russian theatre schools might challenge that assumption.

97 'Standards and Practices,' 136.

98 Michael Kearns, *Acting = Life*, 4. Josette Féral documents one selection process, whereby as many as 1000 candidates are culled that is based on little more than a 'sensitivity' which is surely, in part, an alignment of CP Types. See also Julius Novick. Shannon Jackson compares the audition process, with its 'systems of protocol, ritualized behaviour, and boundary enforcement,' (22) to Foucault's disciplinary writing (24).

99 As Stephen Rupsch notes, 'The act of 'trying to feel' is often fruitless and manipulative. In fact, the teacher who insists that his/her students 'feel' a particular emotion can create an environment detrimental to inspiration, which potentially also leads to a student's psychological duress or confusion? (70).

100 In *Art and the Creative Unconscious* Erich Neumann writes of the artistic process: 'The vital energy leaves the human form that was hitherto its highest embodiment and awakens extra-human and prehuman forms. The human figure that corresponds in a psychological sense to the personality centred in the ego and the system of consciousness is replaced by the anonymous vitality of the flowing unconscious, of the creative force in nature and the psyche' (119).

101 Pages 97–9. See also Jan Evan Meshkoff, 28.

102 This tendency is not limited to teachers working within psychological naturalism. Paul Allain, in his discussion of Suzuki training, documents 'how the work starts to transgress taboos of pain, authority, aggression, and manipulation in training and performance.' Suzuki training 'tests mental endurance and aggression. Masochistic tendencies can be encouraged by the demands of the exercises.' Actors also report that group feeling is achieved by 'the sense of victory and achievement you feel at the end of a class by having survived it' (79). For confirmation of Allain's critique, see Terry Donovan Smith and Tadashi Suzuki's *The Way of Acting*.

103 One notable exception is Terry Schreiber, whose *Acting* not only endorses a toolbox approach, but addresses ethical considerations regularly.

104 With my colleague, Richard Walsh Bowers, I addressed the legacy of abusive directors that can be traced directly to Stanislavsky; this article offers a model for ethics based on that endorsed by accredited psychologists.

105 Mekler, *The New Generation of Acting Teachers*, 96.

Bibliography

Aaron, Stephen. *Stage Fright.* Chicago: University of Chicago Press, 1986.
Aberbach, David. *Charisma in Politics, Religion, and the Media.* New York: New York University Press, 1996.
Adams, Cindy (Heller). *Lee Strasberg.* Garden City, N.Y.: Doubleday, 1980.
Adler, Stella. *The Technique of Acting.* New York: Bantam Books, 1988.
Aigen, Kenneth. "The Music Therapist as Qualitative Researcher." *Music Therapy* 12, no. 1 (1993): 16–39.
Aiken, Lewis R. *Assessment of Adult Personality.* New York: Springer Publishing Company, 1997.
——. *Personality.* Springfield: Charles C. Thomas, 2000.
Alberts, David. *The Expressive Body.* Portsmouth, HN: Heinemann, 1997.
Albright, Hardie. *Acting.* Edited by Arnita Albright. Third. Belmont, CA: Wadsworth Publishing Company, 1980.
Albright, Linda, Christine Forest, and Kristina Reiseter. "Acting, Behaving, and the Selfless Basis of Metaperception." *Journal of Personality and Social Psychotherapy* 81, no. 5 (2001): 910–21.
Alekseev, N.P. et al. "An Experimental Study of the Emotionality of Theater College Students." *Soviet Psychology* 23, no. 3 (Spring 1985): 59–72.
Allain, Paul. "Suzuki Training." *The Drama Review* 42, no. 1 (T157) (Spring 1998): 66–89.
Allport, Alan. "Selection for Action." In *Perspectives on Perception and Action,* edited by Herbert and Andries F. Sanders Heuer, 395–419. Hillsdale: Lawrence Erlbaum Associates, 1987.
Alter, Jean. *A Sociosemiotic Theory of Theatre.* Philadelphia: University of Pennsylvania Press, 1990.
Amabile, Teresa M. *Creativity in Context.* Boulder: Westview Press, 1996.
Apter, Michael J. *Reversal Theory.* London: Routledge, 1989.
——. *Reversal Theory.* London: Routledge, 1989.
Armon-Jones, Claire. "The Social Functions of Emotion." In *The Social Construction of Meaning,* edited by Rom Harré, 57–82. Oxford: Basil Blackwell, 1986.
——. "The Thesis of Constructionism." In *The Social Construction of Meaning,* edited by Rom Harré, 32–56. Oxford: Basil Blackwell, 1986.
Armstrong, Gordon. *Theatre and Consciousness.* New York: Peter Lang, 2003.
——. "Theatre as a Complex Adaptive System." *New Theatre Quarterly* 13, no. 5 (1997): 277–88.

Aston, Elaine. *Feminist Theatre Practice*. London: Routledge, 1999.

Auslander, Philip. "Just Be Your Self." In *Acting (Re) Considered*, edited by Phillip B. Zarrilli, 59–67. London: Routledge, 2002.

Averill, James R. "Acquisition of Emotions in Adulthood." In *The Social Construction of Meaning*, edited by Rom Harré, 98–118. Oxford: Basil Blackwell, 1986.

——. "Individual Differences in Emotional Creativity." *Journal of Personality* 67, no. 2 (April 1999): 331–71.

Baal, Georges. "Toward a Freudian and Lacanian Psychoanalytical Theory for Theatre, Centred on the Actor's Role." *Assaph* 7 (1991): 35–59.

Baars, Bernard J. *In the Theater of Consciousness*. Oxford: Oxford University Press, 1997.

Babson, Thomas W. *The Actor's Choice*. Portsmouth, NH: Heinemann, 1996.

Baker, Paul. *Integration of Abilities*. San Antonio: Trinity University Press, 1972.

Balk, H. Wesley. *The Complete Singer-Actor*. 2d ed. Minneapolis: University of Minnesota Press, 1985.

——. *Performing Power*. Minneapolis: University of Minnesota Press, 1986.

——. *The Radiant Performer*. Minneapolis: University of Minnesota, 1991.

Bandelj, Nina. "How Method Actors Create Character Roles." *Sociological Forum* 18, no. 3 (September 2003): 387–416.

——. "How Method Actors Create Character Roles." *Sociological Forum* 18, no. 3 (September 2003): 387–416.

Barba, Eugenio. "The Actor's Energy." *New Theatre Quarterly* III, no. 11 (August 1987): 237–40.

——. "The Dilated Body." *New Theatre Quarterly* 1, no. 4 (November 1985): 369–82.

——. *The Paper Canoe*. Translated by Richard Fowler. London: Routledge, 1995.

Barker, Clive. "In Search of the Lost Mode." *New Theatre Quarterly* 18, no. 1 (February 2002): 10–16.

——. "Joan Littlewood." In *Twentieth Century Actor Training*, edited by Alison Hodge, 113–28. London: Routledge, 2000.

Barkworth, Peter. *About Acting*. London: Methuen Drama, 1991.

Bartenieff, Irmgard, and Martha Davis. "Effort-Shape Analysis of Movement." 1965. In *Research Approaches to Movement and Personality*. Body Movement: Perspectives in Research. New York: Arno Press, 1972.

Bartenieff, Irmgard, and Dori Lewis. *Body Movement :*. New York : Gordon and Breach, 1980, 1980.

Barton, Robert. *Acting*. Belmont, CA: Wadsworth/Thomson Learning, 2002.

——. *Style for Actors*. Mountain View, CA: Mayfield Publishing Company, 1993.

——. "Therapy and Actor Training." *Theatre Topics* 3–4 (1993–4): 105–18.

Barton, Robert, and Janet Gupton. ""Gogging"." *Theatre Topics* 10, no. 2 (September 2000): 169–83.

Bassnett, Susan. "Structuralism and After." *New Theatre Quarterly* I, no. 1 (February 1985): 79–82.

Bates, Brian. "Performance and Possession." In *Psychology and Performing Arts*, edited by Glenn D. Wilson, 11–18. Amsterdam: Swets & Zeitlinger, 1991.

———. *The Way of the Actor*. Boston: Shambhala Publications, 1987.

Beauchamp, Hélène. "Training to Survive, I." *Canadian Theatre Review* 88 (Fall 1996): 18–22.

Beck, Dennis C. "The Paradox of the Method Actor." In *Method Acting Reconsidered: Theory, Practice, Future*, edited by David Krasner, 261–82. New York: St. Martin's Press, 2000.

Beckerman, Bernard. *Theatrical Presentation*. New York: Routledge, 1990.

Bedford, Errol. "Emotions and Statements About Them." In *The Social Construction of Meaning*, edited by Rom Harré, 15–31. Oxford: Basil Blackwell, 1986.

Benedetti, Robert. *The Actor at Work*. Englewood Cliffs: Prentice-Hall, Inc., 1976.

———. *The Actor in You*. Needham Heights, MA: Allyn & Bacon, 1999.

———. "Zen in the Art of Actor Training." In *Master Teachers of Theatre: Observations on Teaching Theatre by Nine American Masters*, edited by Burnet M. Hobgood, 87–105. Carbondale: Southern Illinois University Press, 1988.

Bennett, Susan. *Theatre Audiences*. London: Routledge, 1990.

Benolken, Sarah. "My So-Called Life in Art." *Psychology of Aesthetics, Creativity, and the Arts* 5, no. 1 (2006): 55–8.

———. "My So-Called Life in Art." *Psychology of Aesthetics, Creativity, and the Arts* 5, no. 1 (2006): 55–8.

Bergman, Ingmar. *The Fifth Act*. Translated by Linda Haverty and Joan Tate Rugg. New York: The New Press, 2001.

Birdwhistell, Ray L. "Masculinity and Feminininity as Display." In *Nonverbal Communication: Readings with Commentary*, edited by Shirley Weitz, 144–48. New York: Oxford University Press, 1974.

Birringer, Johannes H. *Theatre, Theory, Postmodernism*. Bloomington: Indiana University Press, 1991.

Blair, Rhonda. "The Method and the Computational Theory of the Mind." In *Method Acting Reconsidered: Theory, Practice, Future*, edited by David Krasner, 201–18. New York: St. Martin's Press, 2000.

———. "Reconsidering Stanislavsky." *Theatre Topics* 12, no. 2 (Sept. 2002): 177–90.

———. ""Not...But"/"Not-Not-Me"." In *Upstaging Big Daddy : Directing Theater as If Gender and Race Matter*, edited by Ellen Donkin, and Susan Clement, 291–307. Ann Arbor: University of Michigan Press, 1993.

Bloch, Susana, Pedro Orthous, and Guy Santibañez H. "Effector Patterns of Basic Emotions." In *Acting (Re)Considered*, edited by Phillip B. Zarilli, 219–38. London: Routledge, 2002.

Blum, Richard A. *American Film Acting*. Ann Arbor: UMI Research Press, 1984.

———. *American Film Acting*. Studies in Cinema; No. 28. Ann Arbor, Mich.: UMI Research Press, 1984.

———. "The Stanislavski System from New York to Hollywood." *Central States Speech Journal* 30 (Winter 1979): 352–59.

Boal, Augusto. *Games for Actors and Non-Actors*. London: Routledge, 1992.

———. "Invisible Theater." In *Radical Street Performance: An International Anthology*, edited by Jan Cohen-Cruz, 121–4. London: Routledge, 1998.

———. *The Rainbow of Desire*. London: Routledge, 1995.

———. *Theatre of the Oppressed*. New York: Theatre Communications Group, 1985.

Bogart, Anne, and Tina Landau. *The Viewpoints Book*. New York: Theatre Communication Group, 2005.

Bogdanov, Michael, and Michael Pennington. *The English Shakespeare Company*. New York: Nick Hern Books, 1996.

Braid, Donald. "Personal Narrative and Experiential Meaning." *The Journal of American Folklore* 109, no. 431 (Winter 1996): 5–30.

Braun, Kazimierz. *Theatre Directing*. Lewiston: Edwin Mellon Press, 2000.

Brebner, Ann. *Setting Free the Actor*. San Francisco: Mercury House, 1990.

Brecht, Bertolt. *Brecht on Theatre*. 1964. Translated by John Willett. New York: Hill and Wang, 1976.

Brestoff, Richard. *The Great Acting Teachers and Their Methods*. Lyme, NH: Smith and Kraus, Inc., 1995.

Brewer, Mária Minich. "Performing Theory." *Theatre Journal* 37, no. 1 (1985): 13–30.

Brissett, Dennis, et al. *Life as Theatre*. Edited by Dennis Brissett and Charles Edgley. Chicago: Aldine Publishing Company, 1975.

Brook, Peter. *The Open Door*. New York: Parthenon Books, 1993.

———. *The Shifting Point*. New York: Harper & Row, 1987.

Brower, Richard. *The Monk and the Warrior in the Garden of Renewal*. Lanham, MA: University Press of America, 2001.

Brown, Jason. "The Inward Path." *Creativity Research Journal* 20, no. 4 (2008): 365–75.

Brownsword, Alan W. *Psychological Type*. San Anselmo, CA: Baytree Publishing Company, 1988.

Bruder, Melissa. *A Practical Handbook for the Actor*. New York: Vintage Books, 1986.

Bruehl, Bill. *The Technique of Inner Action*. Portsmouth NH: Heinemann, 1996.

Bruner, Jerome, and Carol Fleisher Feldman. "Group Narrative as a Cultural Context of Autobiography." In *Remembering Our Past: Studies in Autobiographical Memory*, edited by David C. Rubin, 291–317. Cambridge: Cambridge University Press, 1996.

Brustein, Robert. *Letters to a Young Actor*. New York, NY: Basic Books, 2005.

Buck, Ross W., et al. "Communication of Affect Through Facial Expressions in Humans." In *Nonverbal Communication: Readings with Commentary*, edited by Shirley Weitz, 51–64. New York: Oxford University Press, 1974.

Bulgakov, Mikhail. *Black Snow*. 1965. Translated by Michael Glenny. Harmondsworth: Penguin Books, 1971.

Bull, Peter E. "Individual Differences in Non-Verbal Communication." In *Individual Differences in Movement*, edited by Bruce D. Kirkcaldy, 231–45. Lancaster: MTP Press Limited, 1985.

Burgoyne, Suzanne, Karen Poulin, and Ashley with Rearden. "The Impact of Acting on Student Actors." *Theatre Topics* 9, no. 2 (1999): 157–79.

Burns, Elizabeth. *Theatricality*. London: Longman, 1972.

Burstow, Bonnie. "Invisible Theatre, Ethics, and the Adult Educator." *International Journal of Lifelong Education* 27, no. 3 (May/June 2008): 273 - 288.

Buse, William, and Audrey Amdursky. "Personal Myths." *Dynamic Psychotherapy* 4, no. 2 (Fall/Winter 1986): 131–9.

Butler, Judith. "Performative Acts and Gender Constitution." *Theatre Journal* 40, no. 4 (1988): 519–31.

Cairns, Adrian. "Zen and the Art of Acting." *New Theatre Quarterly* II, no. 5 (February 1986): 26–28.

Calkins, Susan D., and Nathan A. Fox. "Individual Differences in the Biological Aspects of Temperament." In *Temperament: Individual Differences at the Interface of Biology and Behavior*, edited by John E. & Theodore D. Wachs Bates, 199–217. Washington D.C.: American Psychological Association, 1994.

Callow, Simon. *Being an Actor*. Harmondsworth, Middlesex: Penguin, 1984.

Cameron, Ron. *Acting Skills for Life*. Toronto: Simon & Pierre, 1989.

Carlson, Marla. "Acting and Answerability." In *Method Acting Reconsidered: Theory, Practice, Future*, edited by David Krasner, 81–95. New York: St. Martin's Press, 2000.

Carlson, Marvin. *The Haunted Stage*. Ann Arbor: The University of Michigan Press, 2001.

———. "Invisible Presences." *Theatre Research International* 19, no. 2 (1994): 111–17.

———. *Performance*. London: Routledge, 1996.

———. "Performing the Self." *Modern Drama* 39 (1996): 599–608.

———. "Theater and Dialogism." In *Critical Theory and Performance*, edited by Janelle G. and Joseph R. Roach Reinelt, 313–23. Ann Arbor: University of Michigan Press, 1992.

———. "Theatre Audiences & the Reading of Performance." In *Interpreting the Theatrical Past: Essays in the Historiography of Performance*, edited by Thomas and Bruce A. McConachie Postlewait, 82–98. Iowa City: University of Iowa Press, 1989.

———. *Theatre Semiotics*. Advances in Semiotics. Bloomington: Indiana University Press, 1990.

———. *Theories of the Theatre*. Ithaca: Cornell University Press, 1984.

Carnicke, Sharon. "An Actor Prepares/Rabota Aktera Nad Soboi, Chast'I." *Theatre Journal* 36, no. 4 (December 1984): 481–94.

———. "Lee Strasberg's Paradox of the Actor." In *Screen Acting*, edited by Alan and Peter Krämer Lovell, 75–87. London: Routledge, 1999.

———. "Stanislavsky." *The Drama Review* 37 (Spring 1993): 22–37.

———. "Stanislavsky's System." In *Twentieth Century Actor Training*, edited by Alison Hodge, 11–36. London: Routledge, 2000.

Carnovsky, Morris. *The Actor's Eye*. Edited by Peter Sander. New York: Performing Arts Journal Publications, 1984.

Carreri, Roberta. "The Actor's Journey." *New Theatre Quarterly* VII, no. 26 (May 1991): 137–46.

Casciero, Thomas. "Laban Movement Studies and Actor Training." Ph. D. diss., The Union Institute, 1998.

Case, Sue-Ellen. *Feminism and Theatre*. New York: Methuen, Inc., 1988.

Caudle, Fairfil M. "An Ecological View of Social Perception." In *Psychology and Performing Arts*, edited by Glenn D. Wilson, 45–58. Amsterdam: Swets & Zeitlinger, 1991.

Chaikin, Joseph. *The Presence of the Actor*. New York: Atheneum, 1977.

Chamberlain, Franc. "Michael Chekhov on the Technique of Acting." In *Twentieth Century Actor Training*, edited by Alison Hodge, 79–97. London: Routledge, 2000.

Charbora, Pamela D. "Emotion Training and the Mind/Body Connection." In *Method Acting Reconsidered: Theory, Practice, Future*, edited by David Krasner, 229–43. New York: St. Martin's Press, 2000.

Chaulet, F. Emmanuelle. *A Balancing Act*. Gorham, ME: Starlight Acting Books, 2008.

Chekhov, Michael. *Lessons for the Professional Actor*. Edited by Dierdre Hurst Du Prey. New York: Performing Arts Journal Publications, 1985.

———. *On the Technique of Acting*. New York: Harper Collins, 1991.

Clay, Jack. "Self-Use in Actor Training." *Drama Review* 16, no. 1 (T-53) (March 1972): 16–22.

Clurman, Harold. *The Fervent Years*. New York: Da Capo Press, Inc., 1983.

Clynes, Manfred. *Sentics*. Garden City: Doubleday, 1977.

Cohen, Robert. *Acting One*. Mountain View, CA: Mayfield Publishing Company, 1992.

———. *Acting Power*. Palo Alto: Mayfield Publishing Company, 1978.

———. *Advanced Acting*. Boston: McGraw Hill, 2002.

Cohen, Ted. "Identifying Metaphor." *The Journal of Aesthetics and Art Criticism* 57 (Fall 1999): 4399–409.

Cole, Toby. *Acting*. Rev. ed. New York: Crown Trade Paperbacks, 1995.

Collins, Mary Ann, and Teresa M. Amabile. "Motivation and Creativity." In *Handbook of Creativity*, edited by Robert J. Sternberg, 297–312. Cambridge: Cambridge University Press, 1999.

Collum, D.K. "The Empathic Ability of Actors." Ph. D. diss., Florida State University, 1976. *DAI* (1977) 38, no. 4–A: 1741.

Colvin, Geoffrey. *Talent is Overrated*. New York: Portfolio, 2008.

Conley, James J. "Movement and the Personal Style." In *Individual Differences in Movement*, edited by Bruce D. Kirkcaldy, 247–56. Lancaster: MTP Press Limited, 1985.

Conroy, Marianne. "Acting Out." *Criticism* 35, no. 2 (Spring 1993): 293–63.

Constantinidis, Stratos E. "Rehearsal as a Subsystem." *New Theatre Quarterly* IV, no. 13 (February 1988): 64–76.

Coulter, J. "Affect and Social Context." In *The Social Construction of Meaning*, edited by Rom Harré, 120–34. Oxford: Basil Blackwell, 1986.

Counsell, Colin. *Signs of Performance*. London: Routledge, 1996.

Courtney, Richard. *Play, Drama & Thought.* Toronto: Simon & Pierre, 1989.

Craig, David. *A Performer Prepares*. The Applause Acting Series. New York: Applause, 1993.

Craig, Gordon. *Craig on Theatre*. Edited by J. Michael Walton. London: Methuen, 1983.

Crawford, Cheryl. *One Naked Individual*. New York: Boobs-Merrill Company, Inc., 1997.

Crawford, Jerry. *Acting In Person and In Style*. Dubuque, Iowa: Wm. C. Brown Company, 1983.

Crowe, Cameron. *Conversations with Wilder*. New York: Knopf, 1999.

Csikszentmihalyi, Mihaly. *Creativity*. New York: Harper Collins, 1996.

——. "The Domain of Creativity." In *Changing the World: A Framework for the Study of Creativity*, edited by David Henry Feldman, Mihaly Csikszentmihalyi, and Howard Gardner, 135–58. Westport, CT: Praeger, 1994.

——. *Flow*. New York: Harper & Row, 1990.

——. "The Flow Experience and Its Significance for Human Psychology." In *Optimal Experience: Studies of Flow in Consciousness*, edited by Mihaly Csikszentmihalyi, 15–35. Cambridge: Cambridge University Press, 1988.

——. "Introduction." In *Optimal Experience: Studies of Flow in Consciousness*, edited by Mihaly Csikszentmihalyi, 3–14. Cambridge: Cambridge University Press, 1988.

——. "Memes Versus Genes." In *Changing the World: A Framework for the Study of Creativity*, edited by David Henry Feldman, Mihaly Csikszentmihalyi, and Howard Gardner, 159 - 172. Westport, CT: Praeger, 1994.

Csordas, Thomas J. *Language, Charisma, and Creativity*. Berkeley: University of California Press, 1997.

Cutler, Anna. "Abstract Body Language." *New Theatre Quarterly* XIV, no. 54 (1998): 111–18.

Damasio, Antonio R. *Descartes' Error*. New York: G.P. Putnam's Sons, 1994.

Daniels, Michael. *Self-Discovery the Jungian Way*. London: Routledge, 1992.

Davitz, Joel R., and Lois Jean Davitz. "The Communication of Feelings by Content-Free Speech." In *Nonverbal Communication: Readings with Commentary*, edited by Shirley Weitz, 99–111. New York: Oxford University Press, 1974.

Daw, Kurt. *Acting Thought Into Action*. Rev. ed. Portsmouth, N.H.: Heinemann, 2004.

De Kerckhove, Derrick. "Theatre as Information-Processing in Western Culture." *Modern Drama* 25, no. 1 (March 1982): 143–53.

De Mallet Burgess, and Thomas and Nicholas Skilbeck. *The Singing and Acting Handbook*. London New York: Routledge, 2000.

De Marinis, Marco. "Dramaturgy of the Spectator." *The Drama Review* 31, no. 2 (1987): 100–14.

DeCosta, Louise, William Buse, and Audrey Amdursky. "Personal Myths." *Dynamic Psychotherapy* 4, no. 2 (Fall/Winter 1986): 131–9.

Deer, Joe, and Rocco DalVera. *Acting in Musical Theatre*. London: Routledge, 2008.

Delgado, Ramon. *Acting With Both Sides of Your Brain*. New York: Holt, Rinehart and Winston, 1986.

Dezseran, Louis John. *The Student Actor's Handbook*. Palo Alto: Mayfield Publishing Company, 1975.

Diamond, Elin. "Brechtian Theory/Feminist Theory." *The Drama Review* 32, no. 1 (Spring 1988): 82–94.

———. "Mimesis, Mimicry, and the "True-Real"." *Modern Drama* 32, no. 1 (1989): 58–72.

Dieckman, Suzanne Burgoyne. "A Crucible for Actors." *Theatre Topics* 1 (1991): 1–12.

Diedrich, Antje. "Talent Is the Ability to Be in the Present." *New Theatre Quarterly* 18, no. 4 (November 2002): 375–91.

Dolan, Jill. *The Feminist Spectator as Critic*. Ann Arbor: University of Michigan Press, 1988.

———. "Gender Impersonation Onstage." In *Gender in Performance: The Presentation of Difference in the Performing Arts*, edited by Laurence Senelick, 3–13. Hanover NH: University Press of New England, 1992.

———. *Presence and Desire*. Ann Arbor: University of Michigan Press, 1993.

Donkin, Ellen, and Susan Clement. *Upstaging Big Daddy*. Ann Arbor: University of Michigan Press, 1993.

Donnellan, Declan. *The Actor and the Target*. St. Paul, MN: Theatre Communications Group, 2002.

Donovan, James M. "Reinterpreting Telepathy as Unusual Experiences of Empathy and Charisma." *Perceptual and Motor Skills* 87 (1998): 131–46.

Downs, David. *The Actor's Eye: Seeing and Being Seen*. New York: Applause Theatre Books, Inc., 1995.

Drukman, Steven. "Entering the Postmodern Studio." *American Theatre*, January 1998, 30–4.

Drummond, John. "The Theatergoer as Imager." *Journal of Mental Imagery* 8, no. 1 (Spring 1984): 99–104.

Du Maurier, Daphine. *The Rebecca Notebook and Other Memories*. London: Victor Gollancz Ltd., 1981.

du Rand, Le Clanché. "Aesthetic and Therapeutic Inter-Play in the Creation of Autobiographical Theatre." *The Arts in Psychotherapy* 19 (1992): 209–18.

Duke, Marshall P. "Theories of Personality and Theories of Art." *Journal of Research in Personality* 36 (2002): 32–58.

Dyer, Richard. "Charisma." In *Stardom : Industry of Desire*, edited by Christine Gledhill, 57–59. London: Routledge, 1991.

Easty, Edward Dwight. *On Method Acting*. New York: House of Collectibles, 1966.

Eco, Umberto. "Semiotics of Theatrical Performance." *Drama Review* 21, no. 1 (1977): 107–17.

Edwards, Gus. *Advice to a Young Black Actor*. Portsmouth NH: Heinemann, 2004.

Ekman, Paul, and Wallace V. Friesen. "Nonverbal Leakage and Clues to

Deception." In *Nonverbal Communication: Readings with Commentary*, edited by Shirley Weitz, 269–90. New York: Oxford University Press, 1974.

Elam, Keir. *The Semiotics of Theatre and Drama*. London New York: Methuen, 1980.

Elsass, Peter. "The Healing Space in Psychotherapy and Theatre." *New Theatre Quarterly* 8, no. 32 (November 1992): 333–42.

Emigh, John. *Masked Performance*. Philadelphia: University of Pennsylvania Press, 1996.

———. "Performance Studies, Neuroscience, and the Limits of Culture." In *Teaching Performance Studies*, edited by Nathan and Cynthia Wimmer Stucky, 261–76. Carbondale: Southern Illinois University Press, 2002.

Emmons, Shirlee, and Alma Thomas. *Power Performance for Singers*. New York: Oxford University Press, 1998.

Epstein, Sabin R., and John D. Harrop. *Basic Acting*. Needham Heights: Allyn and Bacon, 1996.

Esper, William, and Damon DiMarco. *The Actor's Art and Craft*. New York: Anchor Books, 2008.

Esslin, Martin. *Bertolt Brecht*. New York: Columbia University Press, 1969.

———. *Brecht: A Choice of Evils*. London: Heinemann, 1965.

———. *The Field of Drama*. London New York: Methuen, 1987.

Evreinoff, Nicolas. *The Theatre in Life*. Translated by Alexander I. Nazaroff. New York: Brentano's, 1927.

Exline, Ralph. "Visual Interaction." In *Nonverbal Communication: Readings with Commentary*, edited by Shirley Weitz, 65–92. New York: Oxford University Press, 1974.

Fayerman, Stephanie. "An Actor's Diary." *Drama* 1985, 54.

Feist, Gregory J. "The Influence of Personality on Artistic and Scientific Creativity." In *Handbook of Creativity*, edited by Robert J. Sternberg, 273–96. Cambridge: Cambridge University Press, 1999.

Feldman, David Henry. "Creativity: Proof that Development Occurs." In *Changing the World: A Framework for the Study of Creativity*, edited by David Henry Feldman, Mihaly Csikszentmihalyi, and Howard Gardner, 85 - 101. Westport, CT: Praeger, 1994.

———. "Creativity: Dreams, Insights, and Transformations." In *Changing the World: A Framework for the Study of Creativity*, edited by David Henry Feldman, Mihaly Csikszentmihalyi, and Howard Gardner, 103 - 134. Westport, CT: Praeger, 1994.

Feldman, David Henry, Mihaly Csikszentmihalyi, and Howard Gardner. "A Framework for the Study of Creativity." In *Changing the World: A Framework for the Study of Creativity*, edited by David Henry Feldman, Mihaly Csikszentmihalyi, and Howard Gardner, 1 - 45. Westport, CT: Praeger, 1994.

Feldstein, Stanley. "Impression Formation in Dyads." In *Interactive Rhythms: Periodicity in Communicative Behavior*, edited by Martha Davis, 207–24. New York: Human Sciences Press, 1982.

Fenichel, Otto. "On Acting." *Psychoanalytic Quarterly* 15 (1946): 144–60.

Ferris, Lesley. *Acting Women*. Basingstoke: Macmillan Education, 1989.

Féral, Josette. "Mnouchkine's Workshop at the Soleil." *TDR* 33, no. 4 (T124) (Winter 1989): 77–87.

Field, Carole H. "Love Addiction in Performers." In *Psychology and Performing Arts*, edited by Glenn D. Wilson, 143–49. Amsterdam: Swets & Zeitlinger, 1991.

Fisher, Seymour, and Rhoda Lee Fisher. *Pretend the World is Funny and Forever*. Hillsdale, N.J.: L. Erlbaum Associates, 1981.

Floistad, Guttorm. "Creativity, Past, Present, and Future." In *Understanding and Recognizing Creativity: The Emergence of a Discipline*, edited by Scott G. et al. Isaksen, 202–46. Norwood, NJ: Ablex Publishing Corporation, 1993.

Fo, Dario. *The Tricks of the Trade*. 1987. Translated by Joe Farrell. Edited by Stuart Hood. London: Methuen Drama, 1991.

Forte, Jeanie. "Realism, Narrative, and the Feminist Playwright." *Modern Drama* 32, no. 1 (March 1989): 115–27.

Fortier, Mark. *Theory/Theatre*. London: Routledge, 1997.

Freedman, Barbara. "Frame-Up." *Theatre Journal* 40, no. 3 (October 1988): 375–97.

Fried, Stephen B. "Receptive Styles of Implicit Communication." *Perceptual and Motor Skills* 40 (1975): 230.

Friedman, Howard S., et al. "Understanding and Assessing Nonverbal Expressiveness." *Journal of Personality and Social Psychology* 39, no. 2 (1980): 333–51.

Fuchs, Elinor. *The Death of Character*. Bloomington: Indiana University Press, 1996.

Furse, Anna. "Those Who Can Do Teach." In *Theatre in Crisis? Performance Manifestos for a New Century*, edited by Maria M. and Caridad Svich Delgado, 64–73. Manchester: Manchester University Press, 2002.

Gainor, J. Ellen. "Rethinking Feminism, Stanislavsky, and Performance." *Theatre Topics* 12, no. 2 (Sept. 2002): 163–76.

Gardner, Howard. *Art, Mind, and Brain*. New York: Basic Books, 1982.

———. *The Arts and Human Development*. New York: Wiley, 1973.

———. "The Creators' Patterns." In *Changing the World: A Framework for the Study of Creativity*, edited by David Henry Feldman, Mihaly Csikszentmihalyi, and Howard Gardner, 69 - 84. Westport, CT: Praeger, 1994.

———. *Frames of Mind*. New York: Basic Books, 1983.

———. *Intelligence Reframed*. New York: Basic Books, 1999.

———. "Towards a Theory of Dramatic Intelligence." In *Creative Drama in a Developmental Context*, edited by Judith Kase-Polisini, 295–312. Lanham: University Press of America, 1985.

Gardner, Howard, and Constance Wolf. "The Fruits of Asynchrony." In *Changing the World: A Framework for the Study of Creativity*, edited by David Henry Feldman, Mihaly Csikszentmihalyi, and Howard Gardner, 47 - 68. Westport, CT: Praeger, 1994.

Garner, Stanton B. *Bodied Spaces*. Ithaca: Cornell University Press, 1994.

Geer, Richard Owen. "Dealing with Emotional Hangover." *Theatre Topics* 3–4 (1993): 147–58.

George, David E.R. "Letter to a Poor Actor." *New Theatre Quarterly* 8 (November 1986): 352–63.

Giebel, Jean Dobie. "Significant Action." In *Method Acting Reconsidered: Theory, Practice, Future*, edited by David Krasner, 159–67. New York: St. Martin's Press, 2000.

Gilbert, Reid. "'My Mother Wants Me to Play Romeo Before It's Too Late'." *Theatre Research in Canada* 14, no. 2 (Fall 1993): 123–43.

Gillespie, Patti P., and Kenneth M. Cameron. "The Teaching of Acting in American Colleges and Universities, 1920 - 1960." *Communication Education* 35 (October 1986): 362–71.

Gleitman, Henry. "Some Reflections on Drama and the Dramatic Experience." In *The Legacy of Solomon Asch: Essays in Cognition and Social Psychology*, edited by Irvin Rock, 127–41. Hillsdale, NJ: Lawrence Erlbaum Associates, Inc., 1990.

Goffman, Erving. *Frame Analysis*. Cambridge, Mass: Harvard University Press, 1974.

———. *The Presentation of Self in Everyday Life*. 1959. Woodstock: Overlook Press, 1973.

Gold, Muriel. *The Fictional Family*. Springfield: Charles C. Thomas, 1991.

Goldner, June Riess. "The Early History of the Solo Vocalist." In *Performers and Perfomances: The Social Organization of Artistic Work*, edited by Jack B. and Rosanne Martorella Kamerman, Social Stress in Singing, 1983.

Goldstein, Thalia R. "Psychological Perspectives on Acting." *Psychology of Aesthetics, Creativity, and the Arts* 3, no. 1 (2009): 6–9.

Goldstein, Thalia R., and Ellen Winner. "Living in Alternative and Inner Worlds." *Creativity Research Journal* 21, no. 1 (Jan 2009): 117–24.

Good, Leslie T. "Power, Hegemony, and Communication Theory." In *Cultural Politics in Contemporary America*, edited by Ian H. and Sut Jhally Angus, 51–64. New York: Routledge, 1989.

Gordon, Marc. "Salvaging Strasberg at the Fin de Siècle." In *Method Acting Reconsidered: Theory, Practice, Future*, edited by David Krasner, 43–60. New York: St. Martin's Press, 2000.

Gray, Jonathan. "Operation Mallfinger." *The Drama Review* 37, no. 4 (Winter 1993): 128–42.

Green, Barry, and Timothy W. Gallwey. *The Inner Game of Music*. Garden City, N.Y.: Anchor Press/Doubleday, 1986.

Greer, Deborah Ann. "Actor Training and Charismatic Group Structure." Ph. D. diss., Department of Theater Arts, University of Oregon, 2002.

Griffiths, David. *Acting Through Mask*. Mask: A Release of Acting, vol. 1, 2. Amsterdam: Harwood Academic Publishers, 1998.

Grotowski, Jerzy. *Towards a Poor Theatre*. New York: Simon and Schuster, 1968.

Guskin, Harold. *How to Stop Acting*. New York: Faber and Faber, Inc., 2003.

Haberman, David L. *Acting as a Way of Salvation*. Oxford: Oxford University Press, 1988.

Hagen, Uta. *Respect for Acting*. New York: Macmillan, 1973.

Hall, Edward T. "Proxemics." In *Nonverbal Communication: Readings with Commentary*, edited by Shirley Weitz, 205–29. New York: Oxford University Press, 1974.

Hall, Peter. *Making an Exhibition of Myself*. London: Sinclair-Stevenson, 1993.

Hamilton, James R. "Theatrical Enactment." *The Journal of Aesthetics and Art Criticism* 58, no. 1 (Winter 2000): 23–35.

Hamilton, Linda H. *The Person Behind the Mask*. Greenwich, CT: Ablex Publishing Corporation, 1997.

Hammond, Jacqueline, and Robert J. Edelmann. "The Act of Being." In *Psychology and Performing Arts*, edited by Glenn D. Wilson, 123–31. Amsterdam: Swets & Zeitlinger, 1991.

Hanna, Judith Lynne. *Dance, Sex and Gender*, 1988.

Hannah, Therese, et al. "Acting and Personality Change." *Journal of Research in Personality* 28, no. 3 (September 1994): 277–86.

Harré, Rom. "An Outline of the Social Constuctionist Viewpoint." In *The Social Construction of Meaning*, edited by Rom Harré, 2–14. Oxford: Basil Blackwell, 1986.

———. "Preface." In *The Social Construction of Meaning*, edited by Rom Harré, vii–viii. Oxford: Basil Blackwell, 1986.

Harrop, John. *Acting*. London: Routledge, 1992.

Harrop, John, and Sabin R. Epstein. *Acting With Style*. Englewood Cliffs, NJ: Prentice-Hall, Inc., 1982.

Hastrup, Kristen. *Action*. Copenhagen: Museum Tusculanum Press, 2004.

Hayes, Elliott. *Homeward Bound*. Toronto: Playwrights Canada Press, 1991.

Hedley, Douglas. *Living Forms of the Imagination*. London: T&T Clark International, 2008.

Hendrick, Pamela R. "Two Opposite Animals?" *Theatre Topics* 8, no. 2 (1998): 113–25.

Herrington, Joan. "Directing with Viewpoints." *Theatre Topics* 10, no. 2 (September 2000): 155–68.

Hirsch, Foster. *Method to Their Madness*. 1St Ed. New York :: W.W. Norton, 1984.

Hitchcock, Katharine, and Brian Bates. "Actor and Mask as Metaphors for Psychological Experiences." In *Psychology and Performing Arts*, edited by Glenn D. Wilson, 19–24. Amsterdam: Swets & Zeitlinger, 1991.

Hodge, Alison. "Introduction." In *Twentieth Century Actor Training*, edited by Alison Hodge, 1–10. London: Routledge, 2000.

Holland, Peter. "Hamlet and the Art of Acting." In *Drama and the Actor*, edited by James Redmond, 39–61. Cambridge: Cambridge University Press, 1984.

Hornby, Richard. *The End of Acting*. New York: Applause Books, 1992.

———. "Feeding the System." *New Theatre Quarterly* 23, no. 1 (February 2007): 67–72.

Houtz, John C., et al. "Creativity Styles and Personal Type." *Creativity Research Journal* 15, no. 4 (2003): 321–30.

Hughes, R.I.G. "Tolstoy, Stanislavski, and the Art of Acting." *The Journal of Aesthetic and Art Criticism* 51, no. 1 (Winter 1993): 39–48.

Hull, S. Loraine. *Strasberg's Method as Taught by Lorrie Hull.* Woodbridge: Ox Bow Publishing, Inc., 1985.

Hulton, Dorinda. "Joseph Chaikin and Aspects of Actor Training." In *Twentieth Century Actor Training*, edited by Alison Hodge, 151–73. London: Routledge, 2000.

Isaksen, Scott G., and K. Brian Dorval. "Toward an Improved Understanding of Creativity Within People." In *Understanding and Recognizing Creativity: The Emergence of a Discipline*, edited by Scott G. et al. Isaksen, 299–330. Norwood, NJ: Ablex Publishing Corporation, 1993.

Isaksen, Scott G., and Mary C. Murdock. "The Emergence of a Discipline." In *Understanding and Recognizing Creativity: The Emergence of a Discipline*, edited by Scott G. et al. Isaksen, 13–47. Norwood, NJ: Ablex Publishing Corporation, 1993.

Jablonko, Allison, and Elizabeth Kagan. "An Experiment in Looking." *The Drama Review* 32, no. 4 (1988): 148–63.

Jackson, Anne. *Early Stages.* Boston: Little, Brown, 1979.

Jackson, Shannon. "Ethnography and the Audition." *Text and Performance Quarterly* 13, no. 1 (Jan 1993): 21–43.

James, William. "On a Certain Blindness in Human Beings." In *Talks to Teachers on Psychology.* 1962, 113–29. New York: Dover Publications, Inc., 1899.

Jameson, Fredric. *Brecht and Method.* London: Verso, 1998.

Jeffers, Susan. *Feel the Fear.* New York: Ballantine Books, 1988.

Jenkings, Linda Walsh, and Susan Ogden-Malouf. "The (Female) Actor Prepares." *Theatre* 17, no. 1 (Winter 1985): 66–69.

Jent, Deanna. "Sex Roles in Acting Class." *Theatre Studies* 35 (1990): 18–27.

Jesse, Anita. *The Playing is the Thing.* Burbank, CA: Wolf Creek Press, 1996.

Jilinsky, Andrius. *The Joy of Acting.* Translated by Helen C. Bragdon. New York: P. Lang, 1990.

Johnston-Brown, Anne. *The 10 Commandments of Theatre.* Manchester, NH: Smith and Draus Publishers, 2007.

Johnstone, Keith. *Impro.* London: Methuen Drama, 1981.

Jones, David Richard. *Great Directors at Work.* Berkeley: University of California Press, 1986.

Jones, Jane Hardy, and Ruth G. Sherman. *Intimacy and Type.* Gainesville, FL: Center for Applications of Psychological Type, Inc., 1997.

Jones, Joni L. "Teaching in the Borderlands." In *Teaching Performance Studies*, edited by Nathan and Cynthia Wimmer Stucky. Carbondale: Southern Illinois University Press, 2002.

Joseph, Rhawn. *The Right Brain and the Unconscious.* New York: Plenum, 1992.

Just, Peter. "Going Through the Emotions." *Ethos* 19, no. 3 (September 1991): 288–312.

Kane, Leslie. *David Mamet in Conversation*. Ann Arbor: University of Michigan Press, 2001.

Karafistan, Rachel. "'The Spirits Wouldn't Let Me Be Anything Else'." *New Theatre Quarterly* 19, no. 2 (May 2003): 150–68.

Kassel, Paul. *Acting*. Boston: Allyn and Bacon, 2007.

———. "The Four Fundamental Verbs." *Theatre Topics* 9, no. 2 (1999): 181–95.

———. "Random Acts." In *Method Acting Reconsidered: Theory, Practice, Future*, edited by David Krasner, 219–28. New York: St. Martin's Press, 2000.

Kearns, Michael. *Acting = Life*. Portsmouth, NH: Heinemann, 1996.

Keirsey, David, Bates. *Please Understand Me*. Del Mar, CA: Prometheus Nemesis Book Company, 1984.

Kellermann, Peter Felix. "Concretization in Psychodrama with Somatization Disorder." *The Arts in Psychotherapy* 23, no. 2 (1996): 149–52.

Keltner, Dacher, and Jonathan Haidt. "Social Functions of Emotions." In *Emotions: Current Issues and Future Directions*, edited by Tracy J. and George A. Bonanno Mayne, 192–213. New York: The Guilford Press, 2001.

Kempinski, Tom. *Duet for One*. New York: Samuel French, Inc., 1981.

Kendon, Adam. "Coordination of Action and Framing in Face-to-Face Interaction." In *Interactive Rhythms: Periodicity in Communicative Behavior*, edited by Martha Davis, 351–63. New York: Human Sciences Press, 1982.

Kerrigan, Sheila. *The Performer's Guide to the Collaborative Process*. Portsmouth, NH: Heniemann, 2001.

Keyssar, Helene. *Feminist Theatre*. New York: St. Martin's Press, 1984.

Khire, Usha. "Guilford's SOI Model and Behavioral Intelligence with Special Reference to Creative Behavioral Abilities." In *Understanding and Recognizing Creativity: The Emergence of a Discipline*, edited by Scott G. et al. Isaksen, 369–99. Norwood, NJ: Ablex Publishing Corporation, 1993.

Kirby, E. T. "The Delsarte Method." *Drama Review* 16, no. 1 (T-53) (March 1972): 55–69.

Kirby, Michael. "On Acting and Not-Acting." *Drama Review* 16, no. 1 (T-53) (March 1972): 3–15.

Kirkland, Gelsey. *Dancing on My Grave*. New York: Doubleday, 1986.

Knowles, Richard Paul. *Reading the Material Theatre*. Theatre and Performance Theory. Cambridge: Cambridge University Press, 2004.

Koch, Philip J. "Emotional Ambivalence." *Philosophy and Phenomenological Research* 48, no. 2 (December 1987): 257–79.

Kohtes, Martin Maria. "Invisible Theatre." *New Theatre Quarterly* 9, no. 33 (February 1993): 85–9.

Konecni, Vladimir J. "Psychological Aspects of the Expression of Anger and Violence on the Stage." *Comparative Drama* 25, no. 3 (Fall 1991): 215–41.

Konijn, Elly. *Acting Emotions*. Amsterdam: Amsterdam University Press, 2000.

———. "Actors and Emotions." *Theatre Research International* 20, no. 2 (Summer 1995): 132–40.

———. "What's on Between the Actor and His Audience?" In *Psychology and*

Performing Arts, edited by G.D. Wilson, 59–74. Amsterdam: Swets & Zeitlinger, 1991.

Koste, Virginia. "Meta-Thinking." In *Creative Drama in a Developmental Context*, edited by Judith Kase-Polisini, 333–42. Lanham: University Press of America, 1985.

Krasner, David. "I Hate Strasberg." In *Method Acting Reconsidered: Theory, Practice, Future*, edited by David Krasner, 3–39. New York: St. Martin's Press, 2000.

———. "Strasberg, Adler and Meisner." In *Twentieth Century Actor Training*, edited by Alison Hodge, 129–50. London: Routledge, 2000.

Krasner, David, et al. *Method Acting Reconsidered: Theory, Practice, Future*. Edited by David Krasner. New York: St. Martin's Press, 2000.

Kuppers, Petra. "Toward the Unknown Body." *Theatre Topics* 10, no. 2 (2000): 129 - 143.

Laban, Rudolf. *Choreutics*. Translated by Lisa Ullmann. London: Macdonald & Evans, 1966.

———. *Effort*. Edited by F.C. Lawrence. London: Macdonald & Evans, 1974.

———. *A Life for Dance*. New York: Theatre Arts Books, 1975.

———. *The Mastery of Movement*. 1967. Edited by Lisa Ullmann. 4th ed. Plymouth: Northcote House, 1988.

LaFrance, Marianne. "Posture Mirroring and Rapport." In *Interactive Rhythms: Periodicity in Communicative Behavior*, edited by Martha Davis, 279–97. New York: Human Sciences Press, 1982.

Lamarque, Peter. "Expression and the Mask." *The Journal of Aesthetics and Art Criticism* 47, no. 2 (Spring 1989): 157–68.

———. "Expression and the Mask." *The Journal of Aesthetics and Art Criticism* 47, no. 2 (Spring 1989): 157–68.

Lampe, Eelka. "From the Battle to the Gift." *The Drama Review* 36, no. 1 (Spring 1992): 14–47.

———. "Rachel Rosenthal Creating Her Selves." *The Drama Review* 32, no. 1 (Spring 1988): 170–90.

Landau, Tina. "Theories in Practice." In *Anne Bogart: Viewpoints*, edited by Michael and Joel A. Smith Dixon, 15–30. Lyme, NH: Smith and Kraus, 1995.

Lane, Yoti. *The Psychology of the Actor*. Westport: Greenwood Press, 1960.

Langer, Susanne K. *Feeling and Form*. London: Routledge and Kegan Paul Limited, 1953.

Large, Gerry. "Lev Kuleshov and the Metrical-Spatial Web." *Theatre Topics* 10, no. 1 (March 2000): 65–75.

Larson, Reed. "Flow and Writing." In *Optimal Experience: Studies of Flow in Consciousness*, edited by Mihaly Csikszentmihalyi, 150–71. Cambridge: Cambridge University Press, 1988.

Leach, Robert. "Meyerhold and Biomechanics." In *Twentieth Century Actor Training*, edited by Alison Hodge, 37–54. London: Routledge, 2000.

Lears, T. Jackson. J. "The Concept of Cultural Hegemony." *American Historical Review* 90, no. 3 (February 1985): 567–93.

Lecure, Bruce. "A Forum of Senior Movement Educators." *Theatre Topics* 10, no. 1 (March 2000): 77–89.

LeDoux, Joseph E. *The Emotional Brain.* New York: Simon & Schuster, 1998.

Lemon, Alaina. "'Dealing Emotional Blows'." *Language & Communication* 24, no. 2004 (2004): 313 - 337.

——. "'Dealing Emotional Blows'." *Language & Communication* 24, no. 2004 (2004): 313 - 337.

Levin, Irina, and Igor Levin. *Working on the Play and the Role.* Chicago: Ivan R. Dee, 1992.

Levine, Stephen K. "The Expressive Body." *The Arts in Psychotherapy* 23, no. 2 (1996): 131–36.

Levy, Jonathan. "A Few Reflections on "Dramatic Intelligence"." In *Creative Drama in a Developmental Context*, edited by Judith Kase-Polisini, 343–51. Lanham: University Press of America, 1985.

Lewis, Robert. *Advice to the Players.* New York: Harper & Row, 1980.

——. *Slings and Arrows.* New York: Stein and Day, 1984.

Lishman, Joan W. "An Investigation Into the Effects of Training Programmes Upon Movement Leading to Dance with E.S.N.(S) Children." *Early Child Development and Care* 23 (1986): 139–68.

Lobdell, Peter. "Practicing the Paradox." In *Method Acting Reconsidered: Theory, Practice, Future*, edited by David Krasner, 179–87. New York: St. Martin's Press, 2000.

Lockford, Lesa, and Ronald J. Pelias. "Bodily Poeticizing in Theatrical Improvisation." *Theatre Topics* 14, no. 2 (September 2004): 431–43.

Logie, Lea. "Developing a Physical Vocabulary for the Contemporary Actor." *New Theatre Quarterly* XI, no. 43 (August 1995): 230–40.

——. "Theatrical Movement and the Mind-Body Question." *Theatre Research International* 20, no. 3 (1995): 255–65.

Longstaff, Jeffrey Scott. "Re-Evaluating Rudolf Laban's Choreutics." *Perceptual and Motor Skills* 91 (2000): 191–210.

Love, Lauren. "Resisting the Organic." In *Acting (Re)Considered: A Theoretical and Practical Guide*, edited by Phillip B. Zarrilli, 277–90. London: Routledge, 1995.

Lundrigan, Paul J. "Reality Therapy and "Method Acting"." *Journal of Reality Therapy* 11, no. 1 (Fall 1991): 72–75.

Luse, James. "The Heart as Center." In *Method Acting Reconsidered: Theory, Practice, Future*, edited by David Krasner, 189–97. New York: St. Martin's Press, 2000.

Malden, Karl. "When Do I Start?: A Memoir." New York, NY: Simon and Schuster, 1997.

Maletic, Vera. *Body, Space, Expression.* New York: Mouton de Gruyter, 1928 (1987).

Malpede, Karen. "Theatre of Witness." *New Theatre Quarterly* XII, no. 47 (August 1996): 266–78.

Mamet, David. *Some Freaks.* New York: Penguin Books, 1989.

——. *True and False.* New York: Pantheon Books, 1997.

Manderino, Ned. *All About Method Acting.* Los Angeles: Manderino Books, 1985.

——. *The Transpersonal Actor.* Los Angeles: Manderino Books, 1989.

Margolin, Deb. "Mining My Own Business." In *Method Acting Reconsidered: Theory, Practice, Future*, edited by David Krasner, 127 - 134. New York: St. Martin's Press, 2000.

Markova, Dawna. *The Open Mind*. Berkeley, CA: Conari Press, 1996.

Marowitz, Charles. *The Act of Being*. London: Secker & Warburg, 1978.

———. *Directing the Action*. New York: Applause Theatre Books, 1986.

———. *The Method as Means*. London: Herbert Jenkins, 1961.

———. *The Other Way*. New York: Applause Books, 1999.

———. "Otherness." *New Theatre Quarterly* XIV, no. 53 (1998): 3–8.

Marshall, Lorna. *The Body Speaks*. London: Methuen, 2001.

Marshall, Lorna, and David Williams. "Peter Brook." In *Twentieth Century Actor Training*, edited by Alison Hodge, 174–90. London: Routledge, 2000.

Martin, Jeffrey J., and Keir Cutler. "An Exploratory Study of Flow and Motivation in Theater Actors." *Journal of Applied Sport Psychology* 14 (2002): 344–52.

Massimini, Fausto, Mihaly Csikszentmihalyi, and Antonella Delle Fave. "Flow and Bicultural Evolution." In *Optimal Experience: Studies of Flow in Consciousness*, edited by Mihaly Csikszentmihalyi, 60–81. Cambridge: Cambridge University Press, 1988.

McAuley, Gay. "Towards an Ethnography of Rehearsal." *New Theatre Quarterly* 14, no. 53 (1998): 75–85.

McClary, Susan. *Feminine Endings*, 1991.

McConachie, Bruce A. "Approaching the "Structure of Feeling" in Grassroots Theatre." *Theatre Topics* 8, no. 1 (1998): 33–53.

———. "Metaphors We Act By." *Journal of Dramatic Theory and Criticism* Spring 1993: 25–43.

———. "Reading Context Into Performance." *Journal of Dramatic Theory and Criticism* Spring 1989: 229–37.

———. "Using the Concept of Cultural Hegemony." In *Interpreting the Theatrical Past: Essays in the Historiography of Performance*, edited by Thomas and Bruce A. McConachie Postlewait. Iowa City: University of Iowa Press, 1989.

McCutcheon, Jade Rosina. *Awakening the Performing Body*. Amsterdam: Rodopi, 2008.

McFarren, Cheryl Kennedy. "Acknowledging Trauma/Rethinking Affective Memory." Ph. D. diss., University of Colorado, 2003, 266.

McGaw, Charles. *Acting is Believing*. New York: Holt, Rinehart and Winston, 1975.

McTeague, James. *Playwrights and Acting*. Westport, Conn: Greenwood Press, 1994.

Meisner, Sanford. *Sanford Meisner on Acting*. Edited by Dennis Longwell. New York: Vintage, 1987.

Mekler, Eva. *Masters of the Stage*. New York: Grove Weidenfeld, 1989.

———. *The New Generation of Acting Teachers*. Harmondsworth: Penguin, 1988.

Merlin, Bella. *Beyond Stanislavsky*. New York: Routledge, 2001.

———. *Konstantin Stanislavsky*. London: Routledge, 2003.

———. "MaAlbert Filozov and the Method of Physical Actions." *New Theatre Quarterly* 15, no. 3 (1999): 28–235.

Meshkoff, Jan Evan. "Psychological Androgyny and Jungian Typology in Professional Actors and Actresses." Ph. D. diss., School of Human Behavior, United States International University, 1984.

Meyrick, Julian. "The Limits of Theory." *New Theatre Quarterly* 19, no. 3 (August 2003): 230–42.

Miller, Allan. *A Passion for Acting*. New York: Backstage Books, 1992.

Miller, Bruce J. *The Actor as Storyteller*. Mountain View, CA: Mayfield Publishing Company, 2000.

Miller, Jonathan. "Non-Verbal Communication," edited by R.A. Hinde, 359–72. Cambridge: Cambridge University Press, 1972.

Mitchell, John D. "Applied Psycho-Analysis in the Director-Actor Relationship." *American Imago* 13 (1956): 223–39.

———. *The Director-Actor Relationship*. New York: Institute for Advanced Studies in the Theatre Arts, 1998.

Mitchell, Richard G., Jr. "Sociological Implications of the Flow Experience." In *Optimal Experience: Studies of Flow in Consciousness*, edited by Mihaly Csikszentmihalyi, 36–59. Cambridge, UK: Cambridge University Press, 1988.

Moore, Sonia. *Stanislavski Revealed*. The Applause Acting Series. New York: Applause Theatre Books, 1991.

———. *Stanislavski Today*. New York: American Center for Stansilavski Theatre Art, 1973.

———. *Training an Actor*. Harmondsworth: Penguin, 1979.

Moore, Tracey, and Allison Bergman. *Acting the Song*. New York: Allworth Press, 2008.

Mordden, Ethan. *Demented*. New York: Simon & Schuster, 1984.

Morris, Eric. *Acting from the Ultimate Consciousness*. New York: Perigg Books, 1988.

———. *Irreverent Acting*. Los Angeles: Emor Enterprises, 1992.

Morrison, Malcolm. *Classical Acting*. London: A & C Black, 1995.

Moss, Larry. *The Intent to Live*. New York: Bantam Books, 2005.

Moston, Doug. *Coming to Terms with Acting*. New York: Drama Book Publishers, 1993.

———. "Standards and Practices." In *Method Acting Reconsidered: Theory, Practice, Future*, edited by David Krasner, 135–46. New York: St. Martin's Press, 2000.

Murray, David A.B. "Cultural Scripts of Language and Sexuality in Martinican Theater." *Cultural Anthropology* 14, no. 1 (1999): 88–110.

Nakamura, Jeanne. "Optimal Experience and the Uses of Talent." In *Optimal Experience: Studies of Flow in Consciousness*, edited by Mihaly Csikszentmihalyi, 319–26. Cambridge: Cambridge University Press, 1988.

Nascimento, Cláudia Tatinge. "Burning the (Monologue) Book." *Theatre Topics* 11, no. 2 (September 2001): 145–58.

Nathanson, Donald L. "About Emotion." In *Knowing Feeling: Affect, Script, and Psychotheraphy*, edited by Donald L. Nathanson, 1–21. New York: W.W. Norton Company, 1996.

Nellhaus, Tobin. "Performance, Hegemony, and Communication Practicies." *Theatre Annual* 49 (Fall 1996): 3–14.

Nelson, Barnaby, and David Rawlings. "Its Own Reward." *Journal of Phenomenological Psychology* 38 (2007): 217–55.

Nemiro, Jill. "Interpretive Artists." *Creativity Research Journal* 10, no. 2&3 (1997): 229–39.

Ness, Sally Ann. "Understanding Cultural Performance." *The Drama Review* 32, no. 4 (1988): 135–47.

Neumann, Erich. *Art and the Creative Unconscious.* New York: Harper & Row, 1966.

Neuringer, Charles, and Ronald A. Willis. "The Cognitive Psychodynamics of Acting." *Empirical Studies of the Arts* 13, no. 1 (1995): 47–53.

Newlove, Jean. *Laban for Actors and Dancers.* New York: Routledge, 1993.

Nickerson, Raymond S. "Enhancing Creativity." In *Handbook of Creativity*, edited by Robert J. Sternberg, 392–430. Cambridge: Cambridge University Press, 1999.

Nilan, Pam. "Making Up Men." *Gender and Education* 7, no. 2 (1995): 175–87.

Noe, Dennis. "Can a Woman Be a Man On-Screen." *Gay and Lesbian Review Worldwide* 8, no. 2 (March-April 2001): 21–2.

Noice, Helga, and Tony Noice. "An Example of Role Preparation by a Professional Actor." *Discourse Processes* 18 (1994): 345–69.

Noice, Tony, and Helga Noice. *The Nature of Expertise in Professional Acting.* Mahwah, NJ: Lawrence Erlbaum Associates, 1997.

North, Marion. "Catch the Pattern." *American Journal of Dance Therapy* 17, no. 1 (Spring/Summer 1995): 5–14.

———. *Personality Assessment Through Movement.* London: MacDonald & Evans Ltd., 1972.

Novick, Julius. "The Actor's Insecurity." *American Theatre*, April 1998, 20–1.

Nuetzel, Eric J. "Psychoanalysis and Dramatic Art." *Journal of Applied Psychoanalytic Studies* 2, no. 1 (January 2000): 41–63.

———. "Unconscious Phenomena in the Process of Theatre." *Psychoanalytic Quarterly* 64, no. 2 (April 1995): 345–52.

Ochsner, Kevin N., and Lisa Feldman Barrett. "A Multiprocess Perspective on the Neuroscience of Emotion." In *Emotions: Current Issues and Future Directions*, edited by Tracy J. and George A. Bonanno Mayne, 38–81. New York: The Guilford Press, 2001.

Oida, Yoshi. *The Invisible Actor.* Translated by Lorna Marshall. London: Routledge, 1997.

Olivier, Laurence. *Confessions of an Actor.* New York: Simon and Schuster, 1982.

Olsen, Mark. *The Golden Buddha Changing Casks.* Nevada City, CA: Gateways/IDHHB Pub., 1989.

Orzechowicz, David. "Privileged Emotion Managers." *Social Psychology Quarterly* 71, no. 2 (2008): 143–56.

O'Dell, Leslie. *Shakespearean Characterization.* Westport, Conn. London: Greenwood Press, 2002.

——. *Shakespearean Language.* Westport, Conn. London: Greenwood Press, 2002.

——. *Shakespearean Scholarship.* Westport, Conn.: Greenwood Press, 2002.

——. "Theatrical Images of Gender." Presented at the Annual Conference of the Canadian Psychology Association. Penticton, B.C, July 1995.

O'Dell, Leslie, and Richard Walsh Bowers. "Stanislavsky's Problematic Legacy and the Ethics of Theatre Practice." In *Stanislavsky and Directing: Theory, Practice and Influence*, edited by Anna Migliarisi, 129–50. Brooklyn: Legas, 2008.

O'Gorman, Hugh. *The 113 Keys to Acting.* Dubuque, IA: Kendall/Hunt Publishing Company, 2007.

O'Neill, Rosary. *The Actor's Checklist.* Belmont, CA: Wadsworth/Thomson Learning, 2002.

Palmer, Gary B., and William R. Jankowiak. "Performance and Imagination." *Cultural Anthropology* 11, no. 2 (May 1996): 225–58.

Panet, Brigid. *Essential Acting.* London: Routledge, 2009.

Parke, Lawrence. *Since Stanislavski and Vakhtangov.* Hollywood: Acting World Books, 1985.

Pasolli, Robert. *A Book on the Open Theatre.* Indianapolis: Bobbs-Merrill, 1970.

Pasquier, Marie-Claire. "Women in the Theatre of Men." In *Women in Culture and Politics: A Century of Change*, edited by Judith and Blanche Wiesen Cook Friedlander, Alice Kessler-Harris, 194–206. Indiana University Press, 1986.

Pelias, Ronald J. "Empathy and the Ethics of Entitlement." *Theatre Research International* 16, no. 2 (Summer 1991): 142–52.

Petersen, David. "Space, Time, Weight, and Flow." *Physical Education & Sport Pedagogy* 13, no. 2 (November 2007): 191–198.

Philippot, Pierre, and Alexander Schaefer. "Emotion and Memory." In *Emotions: Current Issues and Future Directions*, edited by Tracy J. and George A. Bonanno Mayne, 82–122. New York: The Guilford Press, 2001.

Phillips, Gordon. *Take It Personally.* New York: Applause Books, 2000.

Pink, Daniel H. *A Whole New Mind.* New York: Penguin, 2006.

Pinker, Steven. *How the Mind Works.* New York: W.W. Norton & Company, 1997.

Pinter, Harold. *Old Times.* London: Eyre Methuen Ltd, 1971.

Pitches, Jonathan. *Science and the Stanislavsky Tradition of Acting.* New York: Routledge, 2006.

Policastro, Emma, and Howard Gardner. "From Case Studies to Robust Generalizations." In *Handbook of Creativity*, edited by Robert J. Sternberg, 213–25. Cambridge: Cambridge University Press, 1999.

Pollock, Donald. "Masks and the Semiotics of Identity." *The Journal of the Royal Anthropological Institute* 1, no. 3 (September 1995): 581–97.

Pope, Brant L. "Redefining Acting." In *Method Acting Reconsidered: Theory, Practice, Future*, edited by David Krasner, 147–57. New York: St. Martin's Press, 2000.

Pradier, Jean-Marie. "Towards a Biological Theory of the Body in Performance." *New Theatre Quarterly* 6, no. 21 (February 1990): 86–98.

Preston-Dunlop, Valerie. *Rudolf Laban.* Plymouth: Northcote House Publishers Ltd, 1990.

Prosky, Ida. *You Don't Need Four Women to Play Shakespeare.* Jefferson, N.C.: McFarland, 1992.

Quenk, Naomi L. *Beside Ourselves.* Palo Alto, CA: Consulting Psychologists Press, Inc., 1993.

Quinn, Ruth. "The Performative Self." *New Theatre Quarterly* 19, no. 1 (February 2003): 18–22.

Rayner, Alice. "Soul in the System." *New Theatre Quarterly* I, no. 4 (November 1985): 338–45.

———. *To Act, To Do, To Perform.* Ann Arbor: University of Michigan Press, 1994.

Reinelt, Janelle G. "Introduction." In *Critical Theory and Performance*, edited by Janelle G and Joseph R. Roach Reinelt, 109–16. Ann Arbor: University of Michigan Press, 1992.

Reiss, Steven. *Who Am I?* New York: Jeremy P. Tarcher/Putnam, 2000.

Richardson, Don. *Acting Without Agony.* Needham Heights: Allyn and Bacon, 1988.

Ridout, Nicholas. *Stage Fright, Animals, and Other Theatrical Problems.* Cambridge: University of Cambridge Press, 2006.

Riso, Don Richard, and Russ Hudson. *The Wisdom of the Enneagram.* New York: Bantam Books, 1999.

Ristad, Eloise. *A Soprano on Her Head.* Moab, Utah: Real People Press, 1982.

Rix, Roxane. "Learning Alba Emoting." *Theatre Topics* 8, no. 1 (1998): 55–71.

Roach, Joseph R. "G.H. Lewes and Performance Theory." *Theatre Journal* 32 (1980): 312–28.

———. *The Player's Passion.* Theater—Theory, Text, Performance. Ann Arbor: University of Michigan Press, 1993.

Robbins, Jane Marla. *Acting Techniques for Everyday Life.* New York: Marlowe, 2002.

Roberts, J. W. *Richard Boleslavsky.* Theater and Dramatic Studies. Ann Arbor, Mich.: UMI Research Press, 1981.

Robertson, Jennifer. "The Politics of Androgyny in Japan." *American Ethnologist* 19, no. 3 (August 1992): 419–42.

Robinson, Ken. *The Element.* New York: Penguin, 2009.

———. *Out of Our Minds.* Oxford: Capstone Publishing Limited, 2001.

Rockwood, Jerome. *The Craftsmen of Dionysus.* New York: Applause Books, 1992.

Rogers, Pat. "David Garrick." In *Drama and the Actor*, edited by James Redmond, 63–83. Cambridge: Cambridge University Press, 1984.

Roken, Freddie. "Acting and Psychoanalysis." *Theatre Journal* May 1987: 175–84.

Roloff, Leland H. "Performer, Performing, Performance." *Literature in Performance* 3, no. 2 (April 1983): 13–24.

Ross, Duncan. "Notes on Organic Training." In *Actor Training 3*, edited by Richard P. Brown, 31–3. New York: Drama Book Specialists, 1976.

Rotté, Joanna. *Acting with Adler.* New York: Limelight Editions, 2000.

———. "An Interview with Stella Adler." *Theatre Topics* 12, no. 2 (Sept. 2002): 191–202.

Rozik, Eli. "Acting." *SubStance* 98/99, no. 2 & 3 (2002): 110–24.

Rudlin, John. "Jacques Copeau." In *Twentieth Century Actor Training*, edited by Alison Hodge, 55–78. London: Routledge, 2000.

Ruffini, Franco. "Horizontal and Vertical Montage in the Theatre." *New Theatre Quarterly* II, no. 5 (February 1986): 29–37.

Rule, Janice. "The Actor's Identity Crises." *International Journal of Psychoanalytic Psychotherapy* 2 (1973): 51–76.

Runcio, Mark A. "Cognitive and Psychometric Issues in Creativity Research." In *Understanding and Recognizing Creativity: The Emergence of a Discipline*, edited by Scott G. et al. Isaksen, 331–68. Norwood, NJ: Ablex Publishing Corporation, 1993.

———. "Creativity as an Extracognitive Phenomenon." In *Beyond Knowledge: Extracognitive Aspects of Developing High Ability*, edited by Larisa V. Shavinina and Michel Ferrari, 17–25. Mahwah, NJ: Lawrence Erlbaum Associates, 2004.

Runeson, Sverker. "Perceiving People Through Their Movements." In *Individual Differences in Movement*, edited by Bruce D. Kirkcaldy, 43–66. Lancaster: MTP Press Limited, 1985.

Rupsch Jr., Stephen Joseph. "Sublime Union." Ph. D. diss., Department of Theater Arts and Graduate School, University of Oregon, 2005.

Ryan, Katy. "A Body's Mind Experience in Tim Miller's Workshop." *Theatre Topics* 7, no. 2 (1997): 205–07.

Saint-Denis, Michel. *Training for the Theatre*. New York London: Theatre Arts Books Heinemann, 1982.

Saivetz, Deborah. *An Event in Space*. Hanover, NH: Smith and Kraus, 2000.

Salas, Jo. *Improvising Real Life*. Dubuque: Kendall/Hunt Publishing Co., 1996.

Saltz, David. "How to Do Things on Stage." *The Journal of Aesthetics and Art Criticism* 49, no. 1 (Winter 1991): 31–45.

———. "Texts in Action/Action in Texts." *Journal of Dramatic Theory and Criticism* 6, no. 1 (Fall 1991): 29–44.

Saltz, David Z. "The Reality of Doing." In *Method Acting Reconsidered: Theory, Practice, Future*, edited by David Krasner, 61–79. New York: St. Martin's Press, 2000.

Sarbin, Theodore R. "Emotion and Act." In *The Social Construction of Meaning*, edited by Rom Harré, 83–97. Oxford: Basil Blackwell, 1986.

Sawyer, R. Keith. "The Interdisciplinary Study of Creativity in Performance." *Creativity Research Journal* 11, no. 1 (1998): 11–19.

Schechner, Richard. *Between Theater and Anthropology*. Philadelphia: University of Pennsylvania Press, 1985.

———. *Essays on Performance Theory*. London: Routledge, 1988.

———. *Performance Theory*. New York: Routledge, 1994.

Scheerer, Eckart. "Muscle Sense and Innervation Feelings." In *Perspectives on Perception and Action*, edited by Herbert and Andries F. Sanders Heuer, 171–94. Hillsdale: Lawrence Erlbaum Associates, 1987.

Scheibe, Karl E. *The Drama of Everyday Life*. Cambridge, Massachusetts: Harvard University Press, 2000.

———. *Self Studies.* Westport: Praeger, 1995.

Scheiffele, Eberhard. "Acting." *Research in Drama Education* 6, no. 2 (2001): 179–91.

Schmitt, Natalie Crohn. *Actors and Onlookers.* Evanston, Ill.: Northwestern University Press, 1990.

———. "Stanislavski, Creativity, and the Unconscious." *New Theatre Quarterly* II, no. 8 (November 1986): 345–51.

———. "Theorizing About Performance." *New Theatre Quarterly* VI, no. 23 (Spring 1986): 231–34.

Scholarly articles for various. *Nurturing and Developing Creativity: The Emergence of a Discipline.* Norwood, NJ: Ablex Publishing Corporation, 1993.

Schreiber, Terry, and Mary Beth Barber. *Acting.* New York: Allworth Press, 2005.

Schuldberg, David. "Giddiness and Horror in the Creative Process." In *Creativity and Affect*, edited by Melvin P. Shaw and Mark A. Runco, 87 - 101. Norwood, NJ: Ablex Publishing Corporation, 1994.

Schulman, Michael. "Backstage Behaviorism." *Pyschology Today*, June 1973, 51–54, 88.

Sellers-Young, Barbara. "Somatic Processes." *Theatre Topics* 8, no. 2 (1998): 173–87.

———. "Technique and the Embodied Actor." *Theatre Research International* 24, no. 1 (1999): 89–97.

Senelick, Laurence. "Introduction." In *Gender in Performance: The Presentation of Difference in the Performing Arts*, edited by Laurence Senelick, ix-xx. Hanover NH: University Press of New England, 1992.

Serlin, Ilene A. "Body as Text." *The Arts in Psychotherapy* 23, no. 2 (1996): 141–48.

Shapiro, Bruce G. "Emotion and the Psychology of Performance." In *Knowing Feeling: Affect, Script, and Psychotheraphy*, edited by Donald L. Nathanson, 327–45. New York: W. W. Norton Company, 1996.

Shavinina, Larisa V., and Michel Ferrari. "Extracognitive Facets of Developing High Ability." In *Beyond Knowledge: Extracognitive Aspects of Developing High Ability*, edited by Larisa V. and Michel Ferrari Shavinina, 3–13. Mahwah, NJ: Lawrence Erlbaum Associates, 2004.

Shaw, Melvin P. "Affective Components of Scientific Creativity." In *Creativity and Affect*, edited by Melvin P. Shaw and Mark A. Runco, 3 - 45. Norwood, NJ: Ablex Publishing Corporation, 1994.

Shevtsova, Maria. "The Sociology of the Theatre, Part One:." *New Theatre Quarterly* V, no. 17 (February 1989): 23–35.

———. "The Sociology of the Theatre, Part Two." *New Theatre Quarterly* V, no. 18 (May 1989): 180–94.

———. "The Sociology of the Theatre, Part Three." *New Theatre Quarterly* V, no. 19 (August 1989): 282–300.

Shulgasser, Barbara. "Mountebanks and Misfits." In *David Mamet in Conversation*, edited by Leslie Kane, 192 - 210. Ann Arbor: University of Michigan Press, 2001.

Shurin, Sande. *Transformational Acting*. New York: Limelight Editions, 2002.

Shurtleff, Michael. *Audition*. New York: Bantam, 1978.

Silverberg, Larry. *The Sanford Meisner Approach*. Lyme, HN: Smith and Kraus, 1994.

Simonov, P.V. "The Method of K.S. Stanislavski and the Physiology of Emotions." In *Stanislavski Today*, edited by Sonia Moore, 34–43. New York: American Center for Stanislavski Theatre Art, 1973.

Skiles, Howard. "A Re-Examination of Baldwin's Theory of Acting Lines." *Theatre Survey* 26, no. 1 (1985): 1–20.

Smith, Dorothy E. "Femininity as Discourse." In *Becoming Feminine: The Politics of Popular Culture*, edited by Leslie G. Roman, Linda K. Christianshmith, and Elizabeth Ellsworth. New York: Falmer, 1988.

Smith, Gudmund J.W. "The Creative Personality in Search of a Theory." *Creativity Research Journal* 20, no. 4 (2008): 383–90.

———. "The Role of Unconscious Processes in the Evolvement of Creativity." In *Beyond Knowledge: Extracognitive Aspects of Developing High Ability*, edited by Larisa V. and Michel Ferrari Shavinina, 27–37. Mahwah, NJ: Lawrence Erlbaum Associates, 2004.

Smith, Linda C. "Voice, Movement and the Iris Warren Method." In *Actor Training 3*, edited by Richard P. Brown, 1–30. New York: Drama Book Specialists, 1976.

Smith, R. Wayne. "Actor-Character Personality Identification in a Theatre Production." *Empirical Research in Theatre* 1, no. 1 (1971): 29–38.

Smith, Terry Donovan. "Method(Ical) Hybridity." In *Method Acting Reconsidered: Theory, Practice, Future*, edited by David Krasner, 245–59. New York: St. Martin's Press, 2000.

Sommer, Sally R. "Patterns of Life." In *Actor Training 3*, edited by Richard P. Brown, 35–46. New York: Drama Book Specialists, 1972.

Sonenberg, Janet. *Dreamwork for Actors*. New York: Routledge, 2003.

Spatz, Ben. "To Open a Person." *Theatre Topics* 18, no. 2 (September 2008): 205 - 222.

Spolin, Viola. *Improvisation for the Theatre*. Evanston: Northwestern University Press, 1983.

Stanislavsky, Konstantin. *An Actor Prepares*. New York: Theatre Arts Books., 1984.

———. *My Life in Art*. Soviet Arts. Moscow: Foreign Languages Pub. House, 1950.

Stapleton, Maureen, and Jane Scovell. *A Hell of a Life*. Simon and Schuster, 1995.

States, Bert O. "The Actor's Presence." In *Acting (Re) Considered*.

———. "The Anatomy of a Dramatic Character." *Theatre Journal* 37, no. 1 (1985): 87–101.

———. *Great Reckonings in Little Rooms*. Berkeley: University of California Press, 1985.

———. "The Phenomenological Attitude." In *Critical Theory and Performance*, edited by Janelle G and Joseph R. Roach Reinelt, 369–79. Ann Arbor: University of Michigan Press, 1992.

Stewart, Louis H. "The Archetypal Affects." In *Knowing Feeling: Affect, Script, and Psychotheraphy*, edited by Donald L. Nathanson, 271–87. New York: W.W. Norton Company, 1996.

Stinespring, Louise M. "Just Be Yourself." In *Method Acting Reconsidered: Theory, Practice, Future,* edited by David Krasner, 97–109. New York: St. Martin's Press, 2000.

Strasberg, John. *Accidentally on Purpose.* New York: Applause Books, 1996.

Strasberg, Lee. *A Dream of Passion.* Boston: Little, Brown, 1987.

Strelau, Jan. *Temperament.* New York: Plenum Press, 1998.

———. *Temperament, Personality, Activity.* London: Academic Press, 1983.

Stroppel, Elizabeth C. "Reconcilling the Past and the Present." In *Method Acting Reconsidered: Theory, Practice, Future,* edited by David Krasner, 111–23. New York: St. Martin's Press, 2000.

Stucky, Nathan. "Deep Embodiment." In *Teaching Performance Studies,* edited by Nathan and Cynthia Wimmer Stucky, 131–44. Carbondale: Southern Illinois University Press, 2002.

Styan, J.L. *Drama, Stage and Audience.* Cambridge: Cambridge University Press, 1975.

———. "The Mystery of the Play Experience." In *Performing Texts,* edited by Michael and Robin F. Jones Issacharoff. Philadelphia: University of Pennsylvania Press, 1988.

Sugiera, Malgorzata. "Theatricality and Cognitive Science." *SubStance* 31, no. 2&3 (98/99 2002): 225–35.

Sullivan, Claudia N. *The Actor Alone.* Jefferson, NC: McFarland & Company, Inc, 1993.

Suzuki, Tadashi. *The Way of Acting.* Translated by J. Thomas Rimer. New York: Theatre Communications Group, 1986.

Taft, Ronald. "A Psychological Assessment of Professional Actors and Related Professions." *Genetic Psychology Monographs* 64 (1961): 309–83.

Tassi, Aldo. "Person as the Mask of Being." *Philosophy Today* 37 (Summer 1993): 201– 210.

Thomson, Paula, E.B. Keelin, and Thomas P. Gumpel. "Generators and Interpretors in a Performing Arts Population." *Creativity Research Journal* 21, no. 1 (2009): 72–91.

Thomson, Peter. "Brecht and Actor Training." In *Twentieth Century Actor Training,* edited by Alison Hodge, 98–112. London: Routledge, 2000.

Thornton, Samuel. "Laban and the Language of Movement." In *Discovering the Self Through Drama and Movement: The Sesame Approach,* edited by Jenny Pearson, 78–83. London: Jessica Kingsley Publishers Ltd, 1996.

———. *Laban's Theory of Movement.* Boston: Plays, Inc., 1971.

Tiger, Lionel. "Power is a Liquid, Not a Solid." *Social Science Information* 39, no. 1 (2000): 5–16.

Tillis, Steve. "The Actor Occluded." *Theatre Topics* 6, no. 2 (Sept 1996): 109 - 119.

Toporkov, Vasily Osipovich. *Stanislavski in Rehearsal.* New York: Theatre Arts Books, 1979.

Turner, Victor. "Liminality and the Performative Genres." In *Rite, Drama, Festival, Spectacle: Rehearsals Toward a Theory of Cultural Performance,* edited by John J. MacAloon, 19–41. Philadelphia: Institute for the Study of Human Issues, 1984.

Ubersfeld, Anne. "The Pleasure of the Spectator." *Modern Drama* 25, no. 1 (March 1982): 127–39.

Ubersfeld, Anne., et al. *Reading Theatre*. Toronto Studies in Semiotics. Toronto: University of Toronto Press, 1999.

Ullman, Liv. "Conversation with the Actress." In *Playing to the Camera*, edited by Bert Cardullo, Harry Geduld, 157–65. New Haven: Yale University Press, 1998.

Veltrusky, Jarmila. "Engel's Ideas for a Theory of Acting." *The Drama Review* 24, no. 4 (1980): 71–80.

Vertinsky, Patricia. "Movement Practices and Fascist Infections." In *Physical Culture, Power, and the Body*, edited by Jennifer Hargreaves and Patricia Vertinsky, 25 - 51. New York: Routledge, 2007.

Vilga, Edward. *Acting Now*. New Brunswick, N.J. London: Rutgers University Press, 1997.

Vineberg, Steve. *Method Actors*. New York: Schirmer Books, 1991.

Vozoff, Lorinne. *Changing Circumstances*. Portsmouth, NH: Heinemann, 2000.

Vysotsky, L.S. "On the Problem of the Psychology of the Actor's Creative Work." In *The Collected Works of L.S. Vygotsky*, edited by R.W. Rieber and Aaron S. Carton, Volume 6. New York: Plenum Press, 1987.

Wallbott, Harald G. "Big Girls Don't Frown, Big Boys Don't Cry." *Journal of Nonverbal Behavior* 12, no. 2 (Summer 1988): 98–106.

Walter, Harriet. *Other People's Shoes*. London: Penguin, 2000.

Walton, Kendall L. *Mimesis as Make-Believe*. Cambridge, MA: Harvard University Press, 1990.

Wangh, Stephen. *An Acrobat of the Heart*. New York: Vintage Books, 2000.

Warner, C. Terry. "Anger and Similar Delusions." In *The Social Construction of Meaning*, edited by Rom Harré, 135–66. Oxford: Basil Blackwell, 1986.

Watson, Ian. "Catharsis and the Actor." *New Theatre Quarterly* 4, no. 16 (November 1988): 306–14.

———. "Culture, Memory, and American Performer Training." *New Theatre Quarterly* 19, no. 1 (February 2003): 33–40.

———. "Naming the Frame." *New Theatre Quarterly* 50 (1997): 161–70.

———. "Training with Eugenio Barba." In *Twentieth Century Actor Training*, edited by Alison Hodge, 209–23. London: Routledge, 2000.

———. "'Reading' the Actor." *New Theatre Quarterly* 11, no. 42 (May 1995): 135–46.

Watzlawick et al. *The Invented Reality*. New York: W.W. Norton & Company, 1984.

Waxberg, Charles S. *The Actor's Script*. Portsmouth, NH: Heinemann, 1998.

Weierter, Stuart J.M. "The Organization of Charisma." *Organizational Studies* 22, no. 1 (2001): 91–117.

Weisberg, Robert W. "Creativity and Knowledge." In *Handbook of Creativity*, edited by Robert J. Sternberg, 226–50. Cambridge: Cambridge University Press, 1999.

Weissman, Philip. *Creativity in the Theatre*. New York: Basic Books, Inc., 1965.

——. "Development and Creativity in the Actor and Playwright." *Psychoanalytic Quarterly* 30 (1961): 549–67.

Welton, Martin. "Against Inclusivity." *New Theatre Quarterly* 19, no. 4 (November 2003): 347–51.

Wesker, Arnold. "The Nature of Theatre Dialogue." *New Theatre Quarterly* II, no. 8 (November 1986): 364–68.

Whelan, Jeremy. *New School Acting.* West Collingswood, NJ: Whelan International Publications, 1994.

Whitaker, Thomas R. "Holding Up the Mirror." *Social Research* 63, no. 3 (Fall 1996): 701–30.

Whitmore, Jon. *Directing Postmodern Theater.* Ann Arbor: University of Michigan Press, 1994.

Wiles, David. "Burdens of Representation." In *Method Acting Reconsidered: Theory, Practice, Future,* edited by David Krasner, 169–78. New York: St. Martin's Press, 2000.

Wiles, Timothy J. *The Theater Event.* Chicago: The University of Chicago Press, 1980.

Williams, Tennessee. *Suddenly Last Summer.* New York: New Directions, 1958.

Wilshire, Bruce W. *Role Playing and Identity.* Bloomington: Indiana University Press, 1982.

Wilson, Colin. *Access to Inner Worlds.* Rider & Co, 1983.

——. *Super Consciousness.* Watkins, 2009.

Wilson, Glenn D. *Psychology for Performing Artists.* London: Whurr Publishers, 2002.

——. *The Psychology of the Performing Arts.* London: Croom Helm, 1985.

Winnicott, Donald. *Playing and Reality.* London: Tavistock, 1971.

Wirth, Jeff. *Interactive Acting.* Fall Creek, OR: Fall Creek Press, 1994.

Witcover, Walt. *Living on Stage.* New York: Back Stage Book, 2004.

Wojcik, Pamela Robertson. "Typecasting." *Criticism* 45, no. 2 (Spring 2003): 223–49.

Wolf, Dennis P. "Dramatic Imaginations." In *Creative Drama in a Developmental Context,* edited by Judith Kase-Polisini, 313–31. Lanham: University Press of America, 1985.

Wolford, Lisa. "Grotowski's Vision of the Actor." In *Twentieth Century Actor Training,* edited by Alison Hodge, 191–208. London: Routledge, 2000.

Wormhoudt, Pearl Shinn. *With a Song in My Psyche.* Philadelphia: Xlibris, 2001.

Worthen, William B. "Stanislavsky and the Ethos of Acting." *Theatre Journal* 35 (March 1983): 32–40.

Wylie-Marques, Kathryn. "Opening the Actor's Spiritual Heart." *Journal of Dramatic Theory and Criticism* 18, no. 1 (Fall 2003): 131–60.

Zaporah, Ruth. *Action Theatre.* Berkely, CA: North Atlantic Books, 1995.

Zarrilli, Phillip B. "Action, Structure, Task, Emotion." In *Teaching Performance Studies,* edited by Nathan and Cynthia Wimmer Stucky, 145–59. Carbondale: Southern Illinois University Press, 2002.

——. "Introduction." In *Acting [Re]Considered,* edited by Phillip B. Zarrilli, 7–22. London: Routledge, 2002.

——. *Psychophysical Acting*. New York: Routledge, 2008.

——. "Thinking and Talking About Acting." *Journal of Dramatic Theory and Criticism* Spring 1989.

Zinder, David. *Body - Voice - Imagination*. London: Routledge, 2002.

Zuckerman, Marvin. "Impulsive Unsocialized Sensation Seeking." In *Temperament: Individual Differences at the Interface of Biology and Behavior*, edited by John E. & Theodore D. Wachs Bates, 219–55. Washington, D.C.: American Psychological Association, 1994.

Zukier, Henri. "Aspects of Narrative Thinking." In *The Legacy of Solomon Asch: Essays in Cognition and Social Psychology*, edited by Irvin Rock, 195–209. Hillsdale, NJ: Lawrence Erlbaum Associates, Inc., 1990.

Index

The Charismatic Chameleon

THE FOUR CONDUITS

ACTION initiating/reacting	PERCEPTION sensory awareness/imagination & memory
POWER commanding/submitting	RELATIONSHIP opening to warmth & constructing/closing, cooling, destroying

THE SIX CREATIVE PERSONALITY TYPES

Dynamic	Action & Power
Innovative	Action & Perception
Personal	Action & Relationship
Visionary	Perception & Power
Magnetic	Relationship & Power
Psychic	Relationship & Perception